Estonia

THE BRADT TRAVEL GU

PUBLISHER'S FOREWORD
Hilary Bradt

The first Bradt travel guide was written in 1974 by George and Hilary Bradt on a river barge floating down a tributary of the Amazon. In the 1980s and '90s the focus shifted away from hiking to broader-based guides to new destinations – usually the first to be published on these places. In the 21st century Bradt continues to publish these ground-breaking guides, along with others to established holiday destinations, incorporating in-depth information on culture and natural history alongside the nuts and bolts of where to stay and what to see.

Bradt authors support responsible travel, with advice not only on minimum impact but also on how to give something back through local charities. Thus a true synergy is achieved between the traveller and local communities.

*

After years of travelling to familiar places as a tour leader, I jumped at Neil Taylor's offer to spend a few days in Estonia. What a wonderful country! I loved the way the grim Soviet-style architecture near the Tallinn airport gave way to this lovely medieval city; the vibrancy of the emerging Estonian culture, long suppressed; and the otherness of a place that was only a couple of hours away by air. That was nearly eight years ago. Tourism is now established, but the beauty and vibrancy remains: I can't wait to make a return trip with this new edition of *Estonia* in my pocket.

Hilary Bradt

19 High Street, Chalfont St Peter, Bucks SL9 9QE, England
Tel: 01753 893444; fax: 01753 892333
Email: info@bradtguides.com
www.bradtguides.com

Estonia

THE BRADT TRAVEL GUIDE
Fourth Edition

Neil Taylor

Bradt Travel Guides Ltd, UK
The Globe Pequot Press Inc, USA

Fourth edition 2005
First published 1995

Bradt Travel Guides Ltd,
19 High Street, Chalfont St Peter, Bucks SL9 9QE, England
Published in the USA by The Globe Pequot Press Inc,
246 Goose Lane, PO Box 480, Guilford, Connecticut 06437-0480

British Library Cataloguing in Publication Data
A catalogue record for this book is available from the British Library

ISBN-10: 1 84162 095 5
ISBN-13: 978 1 84162 095 4

Photographs
Front cover Stolting Tower and Oleviste Church, Tallinn
(Mark Wadlow/Russia and Eastern Images)
Text Hilary Bradt (HB), Tricia Hayne (TH), Jonathan Smith (JS),
Mark Wadlow (MW)

Illustrations Carole Vincer
Maps Alan Whitaker, Matt Honour

Typeset from the author's disc by Wakewing, High Wycombe
Printed and bound in Italy by Legoprint SpA, Trento

Author/Contributors

AUTHOR

Neil Taylor is Director of Regent Holidays, a British tour company that has specialised in travel to the Baltic states since they regained their independence in 1991. He visits Estonia about four times a year. He writes and broadcasts on travel trade topics and is on the boards of ABTA (Association of British Travel Agents) and AITO (Association of Independent Tour Operators).

In 2000 Neil was awarded the Lifetime Achievement Award by the British Guild of Travel Writers.

CONTRIBUTORS

Michael Bourdeaux is an Honorary Canon of Rochester Cathedral and has made a lifelong study of religion in the Soviet Union and in other countries of the former communist bloc. In 1969 he founded Keston College, a study centre on his subject. His most recent book was *Gorbachev, Glasnost and the Gospel*, which also contains a study of the freedom movement in the Churches in the Baltic states. Contact: www.keston.org.

Wiltraud Engländer has written a German guidebook on the nature of the Canary Islands. She has travelled in Estonia extensively whilst working on a television series on the natural history of the Baltic countries. In 2004 she filmed singing birds all over Europe for a DVD on bird songs.

David Mardiste was born in Australia and has lived in Estonia since 1993. He is the former Reuters correspondent in Tallinn and now works there as a freelance journalist. He aims to develop a bed and breakfast at his great-grandfather's farm in southern Estonia.

James Oates is an investment banker who has specialised in central and eastern Europe for over 15 years. He takes an active interest in the Baltic financial markets.

Carol Pearson is the granddaughter of August Maramaa, mayor of Viljandi. Her mother fled Estonia in 1944 when Soviet troops swept across the country; in 1947 she arrived in the UK as a refugee and met and married an Englishman. Carol Pearson is a writer and journalist and lives in Norwich.

Tiia Raudma was born in Australia and has lived in Estonia since 1990. She took great delight in being in Tallinn when the Soviet Union imploded and Estonia regained its independence. When not busy in her government job, she dabbles in writing, translating and editing.

Linda Reiss left Saaremaa for Sweden with her parents in 1944 when she was ten years old. Since 1965 she has worked as an artist in Bristol, England.

Maila Saar works for Estonian Holidays in Tallinn, specialising in tours for English-speaking groups. She has contributed to several English–Estonian dictionaries and written a guidebook to London for Estonian tourists.

Tina Tamman has worked since 1986 as an analyst of the Estonian media at BBC Monitoring. She has written two Estonian novels, not yet translated into English.

Clare Thomson Clare's mother is an Estonian who left in 1944. Her first book, *The Singing Revolution*, was about Clare's first visit to Estonia, her mother's homeland, in 1989, and is the best-known record of events at that time. She has since divided her time between London, Belgium and the Baltics and is currently writing a book about Ghent.

DEDICATION

To my godchildren, Christopher, Francesca and Duncan

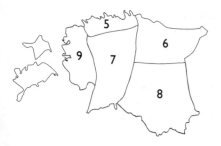

Contents

LIST OF MAPS

Introduction

Readers of the British press in May 2004 had their fill of speculation on what difference it would make to the accession countries now that 'they were a part of Europe'. In the case of Estonia, it made no difference at all to day-to-day life, as visitors there as early as 1994 were seeing this process well underway. By then visas had gone for most tourists, whilst credit cards, a hard currency, and the market economy had come in. A few years later Estonia would be ahead of western Europe in many fields of technology. Estonian visitors to London today are amazed to see locals writing cheques, putting coins into parking meters and paying bus fares in cash. Why, they wonder, are mobile phones not being used instead?

Each edition of this book has needed less and less practical information as so much more can be taken for granted. Twenty-four-hour shops (including Sundays) mean that what might have been forgotten can always be replaced. Tallinn can satisfy gastronomic cravings of ever greater obscurity. In the early 1990s the opening of a French or Italian restaurant was a major news item. Now it seems normal to expect not only Argentinian restaurants, but Japanese and Turkish ones as well. In the summer of 2003, I was very surprised to find a Korean restaurant in Valga, the small town on the Latvian border. I probably should not have been. I had after all on the same trip visited a steak-house in Narva, on the Russian border, and drunk Guinness on several Estonian islands.

I am glad to say that this fourth edition of the guide continues the pattern of being larger than its predecessors. Some hotels and restaurants of course close or decline in standard so have to be removed. Many more, however, open to take their place. About ten of the hotels listed for Tallinn were not even on the drawing board when I prepared the previous edition of this book in 2001. I can now start to include manor houses around the country, as former ruins become deluxe hideaways. I am glad to note that both private and public money is coming into the cultural field. The year 2003 saw the reopening of Rakvere Castle and the establishment of the Viinistu Art Gallery in the unlikely location of a small coastal village. Viljandi has been able to honour its most famous artist, Paul Kondas, who sadly died, officially unrecognised, in 1985.

I think I can finally claim that the book is complete in the sense that everywhere in Estonia likely to be of interest to foreign tourists is now covered. I feel ashamed that I did not reach Põlva County until 2003 and those beginning to find Tallinn too conventional should certainly go for the day to Naissaar Island to see what happens to an area where normal life stopped in 1940. Saaremaa, Estonia's largest island, has taken a very different route and this section has been the most difficult to update. Rumours circulate for years there, but once action is decided, it takes place very quickly, so a new hotel, air service or attraction will suddenly be a regular part of the landscape. Let us hope that plans to join it to the mainland with a tunnel are not realised. It needs its distance to keep its charm and its empty roads.

Emptiness is not an expression that springs to mind to anyone who limits their time in Estonia to a weekend in Tallinn. However it is a joy that can be experienced through much of the country for most of the year. As new hotels open along the northern coast and in the forests near to the Latvian border, and will surely do so soon along Lake Peipsi, a tour of Estonia need no longer be largely an urban experience. Estonians seem to think their country can be enjoyed only during the short summer season from June to August. It is a pity that still too few tourists break from this pattern, since if they do so, they can enjoy 16 hours of daylight in May and the gently changing colours of the trees during autumn. Even winter presents a drama of its own and, with the roads being so well maintained then, driving is not difficult.

I have now made about 40 visits to Estonia and each time discover more people and events that deserve a mention. In this fourth edition of the guide I have written about the most successful collective owner in Soviet Estonia; a Saaremaa family of ten, not one of whom died of natural causes; and the first cricket match to be played in the country. I can speculate on whether a light-bulb or another head will replace Lenin outside the former Communist Party headquarters in Pärnu (though I could not delay publication for this dispute to be resolved). And as Estonians begin to feel easier about discussing the past, more can be said about the German and Russian occupations, which were understandably ignored in the early 1990s.

FEEDBACK REQUEST
I am always pleased to hear from readers, whether they send bouquets, brickbats or suggested changes. All that matters is that they leave Estonia with a positive impression. Please write or phone to Bradt Travel Guides Ltd, 19 High Street, Chalfont St Peter, Bucks SL9 9QE, England; tel: 01753 893444; fax: 01753 892333; email: estonia@bradtguides.com.

Part One

General Information

ESTONIA AT A GLANCE

Location Northern Europe, borders with Russia and Latvia. Tallinn, the capital, is 85km from Helsinki, 320km from St Petersburg, 1,800km from London

Area 45,227km²

Population 1,360,000 of whom 65% are ethnic Estonian, 28% ethnic Russian and 7% from other racial backgrounds

Capital Tallinn (400,000 inhabitants)

Major towns Tartu (105,000 inhabitants), Narva (82,000 inhabitants), Kohtla-Järve (76,000 inhabitants), Pärnu (52,000 inhabitants)

Government Parliamentary democracy

Administrative division 15 counties (maakond), 193 townships (vald)

Currency Kroon divided into 100 sents. The kroon is tied to the euro at an exchange rate of €1 = 15.65EEK.

Language Estonian, a member of the Finno-Ugric group

Alphabet Latin

Religion Predominantly Lutheran, though all major faiths are represented in the population

Weights and measures Metric

Electricity 220 volts, 50Hz

National flag Horizontal blue-black-white

National anthem *Mu isamaa, mu onn ja room* ('My fatherland, my joy and happiness')

National flower Cornflower

National bird Barn swallow

Public holidays January 1 (New Year), February 24 (Independence Day), Good Friday, May 1 (May Day), June 23 (Victory Day), June 24 (Midsummer), December 25 and 26 (Christmas)

Background Information

HISTORY
Ancient history

Evidence of settlements on the current territory of Estonia goes back about 7,000 years. From 5000BC until the late Bronze Age around 1000BC there was clearly extensive farming, fishing and hunting. Much archaeological work remains to be done throughout the country but excavations at Kunda on the north coast, halfway between Tallinn and the Russian border, have produced several thousand artefacts made from bone and stone. Similar, smaller discoveries have been made in the valley of the Emajögi River near Tartu – and also beside the river Pärnu – indicating the importance of fishing at that time and the lack of urban development. The first signs of artistic development – designs on axe-heads and on pottery – date from around 2000BC, while hill forts, cattle rearing and simple agricultural settlements also date from this time.

As Estonia has no sources of metal, the few bronze tools dating from this period came from what is now Poland. Although the Roman Empire never reached Estonia, the trading links it established brought iron tools and jewellery, although the poverty of Estonia is clearly shown by the small number of such objects found in tombs and by the fact that so few were robbed. The Roman author Tacitus refers to the 'Aestii' tribes in his writings but this term refers to the whole Baltic area beyond Germany. It was another thousand years before the term became limited to its current usage.

From around AD800, Estonia enjoyed a relatively peaceful Viking invasion. The Vikings were mainly interested in trading routes to Kiev and Istanbul and needed to avoid the Mediterranean in view of the Saracen pirates. Novgorod in Russia was also expanding rapidly as an entrepôt between east and west and Estonia was to benefit from this transit traffic; the Estonians exported furs, timber and honey whilst importing metal. Minimal written material remains from this period but the thousands of Arabic, German and Byzantine coins which can be seen in museums all over Estonia show the extent of the trade. Skirmishes with Russia were frequent in the 12th century, but Estonian historians proudly point out that 13 Russian attacks were repelled between 1030 and 1192. In the 12th century, for the first and last time in the country's history, Estonian pirates frequently raided Denmark and Sweden. It would be 700 years before Estonia again controlled its coastline.

Centuries of occupation

From around AD1200, Estonian history was to be one of constant struggle against a succession of invaders, forcing the country to look east, south or west according to the occupying power. For the next 500 years, the country's fate depended on the Danes, Germans and Swedes. From 1721 until 1991, the Germans and the Russians sometimes shared control, sometimes fought over it, but never, except between 1920 and 1939, relinquished it. Different enemies would even repeat the same battles. In 1227 the German crusaders finally defeated the Danes on Saaremaa Island. Seven hundred years later, in 1944, Saaremaa saw the last and most bitter battle between the Nazi German and Soviet forces.

In 1201, the German Bishop Albert, having established a diocese in Riga, subdued the Latvian countryside in the following few years and then turned his attention to Estonia. After three years of bitter fighting between 1208 and 1211, the Teutonic Knights subdued Estonia. The Germans were sufficiently concerned about possible renewed Estonian resistance and attacks from Russia that they formed an alliance with the Danes. In 1219, a small Danish force landed on the Estonian coast and built a fortress to secure their new base. The Estonians called this settlement Tallinn – meaning Danish Castle (or City) – and the name was never changed. Half-hearted attempts were made by the Danes to broaden the territory under their control, but none succeeded.

Bishop Albert died in 1229 and the initial crusading fervour of the Teutonic Knights was soon to fade, together with their three traditional vows of poverty, chastity and obedience. They ran the country as autonomous feudal barons, with no central authority. Religious domination gave way to economic domination. Estonians in the countryside were reduced to vassal status working the estates, although in the towns they had greater freedom to operate small businesses. One major revolt took place during the two centuries of German occupation. It began on St George's Day (April 23) 1343, when in a single evening 1,200 Germans were massacred, and finished two years later, by which time a tenth of the Estonian population had been killed, reducing it from 150,000 to 135,000. Fighting took place throughout the country and when it was finally over, the Danish King Valdemar IV was more than happy to sell Tallinn and the surrounding countryside to the Teutonic Knights. They could keep control relatively easily; the Estonians lacked size and national leadership, the Swedes had to struggle to maintain control of Finland, the Russians were defending their eastern borders against the Mongolians and the Lithuanians were conquering the Ukraine. Therefore, until the middle of the 16th century, Estonia was to remain a German colony. No major rebellion ever took place again.

If the aim of Estonia's invaders was usually economic, a religious excuse could always be found. Ivan the Terrible, coveting the port of Narva to support his foreign trade, justified his invasion in 1558 on the grounds that the Germans had abandoned Christianity and were burning Russian icons. Viljandi and Tartu fell soon afterwards. Three years later, the Swedes seized Tallinn to prevent further Russian expansion.

The 1570s saw constant warfare in Estonia between the Swedes and the Russians which came to an end in 1582 with a final Swedish victory following their seizure of Narva. The population by then had fallen to 100,000. Although the Germans had lost formal sovereignty, and were not to regain it until 1941, they maintained their economic grip on the country. The nominal justice system stayed in their hands, as did the local police forces. Ironically, the Swedes allowed the Baltic Germans, as they came to be known, to impose a far harsher regime on the local Estonian peasants than was ever allowed in Sweden itself. However, as it was distanced from this day-to-day control, the Swedish occupation is still regarded as the most tolerable in Estonian history. During the recent Soviet period, it was often surreptitiously described as a 'golden era'.

The rise of the Estonian language

Tartu University was established in 1632 by King Gustav II who had appointed his former tutor, Johan Skytte, as provincial governor in Estonia three years before. Skytte had previously been Chancellor of Uppsala University. In his opening speech at the university, he expressed the hope that not only the nobility but also some poor peasants should be able to benefit from education there. However, as he was never able to confront the Germans on serfdom, his ideal could not be put into practice. During the Swedish period, the Estonian language was studied seriously for the first time and the inauguration of printing presses in Tartu and Tallinn in the 1630s led to the production of grammars, hymns and biblical stories in Estonian. Because so few Estonians were granted an education by their German masters, these books were all produced by Swedes.

End of Swedish rule

Swedish rule came to an end for a variety of reasons. First, severe famine struck Estonia three years in succession from 1695 to 1697, killing 70,000 people or about 20% of the population. Second, the Swedish crown had repeatedly tried to curtail the power of the Baltic-German landlords and third, Peter the Great, like many previous and subsequent Russian leaders, envied the ice-free Baltic ports. His first attack on the Swedish empire, at Narva in northeast Estonia, ended in humiliating defeat at the hands of the 18-year-old Swedish king, Charles XII. However, with the founding of St Petersburg in 1703 as a secure base for a further attack, he then formed an alliance with Poland and could successfully pursue the Great Northern War which was in due course to lead to the total conquest of the Baltics. This war would devastate Estonia to an extent it would never witness again. The general in charge of this scorched earth campaign for Peter the Great was proudly able to report to him that: 'There is nothing left to destroy; not a cock crows from Lake Peipsi to the Gulf of Riga'. Only Tallinn was spared, primarily because Peter the Great enjoyed being there, but also because he realised its value as a military and naval base. Tartu, and all other major Estonian towns, were not. Even Tallinn survived only in an architectural sense. In 1710, plague struck, killing 70% of Tallinn's population of 10,000.

Peter the Great soon realised how best to use the Baltic Germans; being eager to learn from abroad, he had no inhibitions about using foreigners to help his administration. The Germans kept order amongst the Estonian peasantry and collected taxes, whilst the Russian army and navy provided national security. This modus vivendi was to suit both sides for the next hundred years. In the words of one traveller at the end of the 18th century, 'Estonian men go cheaper than niggers in the American colonies, a manservant can be bought for 30 roubles, a maidservant for ten roubles and a child for four roubles'.

Napoleon's invasion of Russia in 1812 finally ended the close relationship between the Russian Tsars and the Baltic Germans. The latter found the increasing taxes needed for the war, together with the abolition of serfdom in 1816, an unwarranted intrusion into their traditional lifestyle and both were resisted strongly. By keeping control of land totally in their own hands, they were able to forestall the economic and political aspirations of the Estonian population for a few more decades, quite a feat considering that there were only about 200 Baltic-German families and 800,000 Estonian peasants. Catherine the Great had toured the Baltics in 1764 and had been struck by the mistreatment of the local peasantry. However, no serious action was taken until the accession of Alexander I in 1801. The Russians, unlike the Baltic Germans, were afraid that some of the ideas spread across western Europe by the French Revolution might reach Estonia and that concessions in advance would be the best tactic to resist them. The Baltic Germans turned out to be correct for another 40 years. The development on their estates of a textile industry and of distilleries greatly increased their incomes. Their complacency became apparent from their lifestyle; their manor houses became more opulent and their sojourns to the spring Tallinn season stretched from February ever further into March. Whatever was fashionable in London, Paris or St Petersburg quickly reached Tallinn. One British visitor in 1844 complained that 'only the Germans could have formed such a state of society. It is a machine, with everything for show and nothing for reality'.

Peasant uprisings

Reality had in fact already intruded into the countryside three years earlier when the first serious peasant uprising occurred in 1841; rumours had circulated that the Tsarist government was willing to allocate land in central Asia to peasants from the Baltics, who then went in increasing numbers to the governor-general's office in Riga to make their claims. The news that these rumours were false led to disturbances in many parts of Estonia; the uprisings were ruthlessly suppressed and resulted in the first in all too many series of banishments to Siberia that were to tarnish Estonian history for the next 110 years. Yet lessons were drawn from this, together with the shortage of labour brought about by the Crimean War, forcing the introduction of legislation allowing peasants to buy land and curtailing the still excessive powers that landlords had over them. For the next 80 years, developments for Estonia were positive. By 1900, for instance, 40% of privately owned land was in Estonian hands and, in 1890, Russian civil servants took over the administration of justice from the German landlords.

Hope for Estonia was not now restricted to the countryside. The increasing industrialisation led to an Estonian middle class in the towns not willing to be docile appendages to the German factory owners. The population in the towns was still very small in the mid 19th century – Tallinn had 20,000 inhabitants and Tartu 14,000 – but what was significant was that by then Estonians had become the majority and Germans the minority. The arrival of the railway in 1870 would greatly increase urban activity and hence the population as well. By 1897 Tallinn had 64,000 inhabitants of whom only 10,000 were Baltic Germans. Its port had started to compete with Riga and it exported grain and vodka, both relatively new products from the Estonian countryside. From 1877 anyone who paid taxes was entitled to be placed on the electoral register, so for the first time Estonians were able to take part in local administration.

The National Awakening

The second half of the 19th century is normally described in Estonia as the period of 'National Awakening'. No specific event brought it about, and no specific organisation would ever lead it, but trends in both town and country radicalised the Estonian population into demanding what would eventually lead to full-scale independence. The intellectual ferment came from Tartu University, the practical and financial support from Tallinn, but the individual activists from all over the country. Their reputations are as strong now as during their lifetimes and, as they could be presented as anti-Tsarist and anti-capitalist, their works could be openly published and studied during the Soviet period. They quarrelled and competed bitterly but this did not matter in the long term as they succeeded in propagating the concept of an Estonian culture with a long and serious tradition. One of the first Estonians to receive a university education was Friedrich Robert Faehlmann who then became a lecturer in the Medical Faculty at Tartu University and in 1838 founded a 'Learned Estonian Society'. Yet it used a German name, *Gelehrte Estnische Gesellschaft*, rather than an Estonian one, and all its written and oral proceedings were in German.

Johan Voldemar Jannsen founded the first Estonian newspaper in Pärnu before moving to Tartu, where in 1864 he established what is still the best-known paper in Estonia, *Eesti Postimees*. He covered rural issues extensively and so produced a paper that could be both popular and populist. Ironically, his name had been Germanised as it was felt that an Estonian name was inappropriate for his first job as a sexton. He took the middle name Voldemar as this was the name of his Baltic-German landlord. His daughter Lydia Koidula was to become equally famous as a poet and playwright. One of the regular contributors to *Postimees*, Carl Robert Jakobson, left in 1878 to found his own paper, *Sakala*. Jakobson had spent many years in St Petersburg and felt that Estonians should collaborate with Russian radicals to overthrow German economic dominance. Having made a lot of money from writing school textbooks, he bought a farm in Vandra, central Estonia, and started to write extensively on agriculture.

Increasing literacy helped to spread the ideas of these authors. As Lutheranism was the primary religion, the clergy taught reading to spread knowledge of the Bible whereas the Catholic and Orthodox tradition had been to limit access of the Bible to the clergy. By the mid 1880s, 85% of the population could read, and by the turn of the century the circulation of *Postimees* had increased from an initial 3,000 to 10,000. About 35 books were published each year in Estonian in the 1850s, reaching 250 by the 1890s. The first Song Festival was held in Tartu in 1869, with 800 singers and an audience of 15,000.

Russification of the Baltics

The founding of the German Empire in 1871, following the Prussian defeat of the French, caused considerable panic in St Petersburg in view of German power in the Baltics and their many officials at the Tsarist court. The subsequent 'Russification' of the Baltic provinces was as much a religious campaign as a linguistic one. Lutheranism was seen as a threat to the Orthodox Church and hence to the power of the Russian state. Tartu University went through this process of 'Russification' in 1889, resulting in the dismissal of most of its German-speaking staff and the reintroduction of the Russian name for the town, Yuriev. As Russian also became compulsory in schools and in the civil service, this helped to marginalise the role of the Baltic Germans, few of whom could speak Russian. Ironically, a move which in St Petersburg had the aim of increasing central control had the opposite effect in Estonia. To most Estonians, the Germans had been their masters and any reduction in their powers was to be welcomed. Estonians were hardly independent in the late 19th century, but at least they saw their culture respected and ever greater scope for using their own language. The Tsarist Russians would never interfere in day-to-day life whereas such interference had been the hallmark of the Germans for hundreds of years.

The Bloody Sunday massacre in St Petersburg on January 9 1905 led to dissent throughout the Russian Empire including Estonia. A powerful communist underground movement had been operating in Tallinn for two to three years under Mikhail Kalinin, who was later to be a member of both Lenin's and Stalin's Politburo. Knowledge of the military ineptitude which had led to Russia's defeat at the hands of the Japanese later in 1905, spread quickly and gave confidence to demonstrators both in town and country. Many of the manor houses that belonged to Baltic Germans were attacked and burnt down. Yet these demonstrations and attacks lacked real focus; in Latvia they were clearly social rather than nationalistic. Various groups in Estonia would have liked to monopolise them but none succeeded. The nationalist groupings that did form at this time were to be as divided as their successors in the late 1980s, and over the same gradualist/putschist issues. Tallinn saw a cruel imitation of Bloody Sunday on October 16 1905 when 60 demonstrators were killed in Market Square. Further cruelty was to follow as the Tsarist army re-established control throughout the country; 500 alleged conspirators were executed and several thousand banished to Siberia.

Konstantin Päts, the future president, fled abroad and was sentenced to death in his absence. He was, however, allowed to return in 1910 when he re-established his newspaper, *Teataja*.

The start of World War I strained but did not break the relationship between the Baltic Germans and the Russians. The former still enjoyed greater autonomy than they would have done as part of the German Empire and a lifestyle that could not be re-established elsewhere. Taxes increased and many trading routes were blocked, but at the start of the war Estonia suffered little in comparison with most of Europe. No Estonian army units equivalent to the Latvian Riflemen (who became fervent supporters of the Bolsheviks) were formed at this stage. This move only came about in February 1917 as a reaction to the Russian Revolution, a time when such a unit could be genuinely autonomous. It was also a time when the issue of independence could again be raised. A unique event in Estonian history took place on March 26 when a demonstration of 40,000 flag-waving Estonians marched through the streets of St Petersburg. It had an immediate effect with the granting of autonomy to Estonia and the appointment as governor of an Estonian, Jaan Poska, who was at the time mayor of Tallinn. A full government was quickly established and, in October, Konstantin Päts became its provisional head. It was fortunately in place just before the October Revolution broke out in St Petersburg since, whilst considerable autonomy, if not full independence, might well have been acceptable to a Kerenski regime in Russia, it was certainly not to the Bolsheviks. Within a few days of coming to power, the Bolsheviks dissolved the Estonian National Assembly but an underground Committee of Elders was able to continue its work and, crucially, could send delegations abroad to present Estonia's case to Western governments.

Independence 1918–40

Independence was to come very suddenly to Estonia, as it would do again in 1991; on this first occasion, however, it was initially to last just one day, February 24 1918, which is still celebrated as Estonian National Day. It is easy to forget the continuing strength of the German army in early 1918. It had advanced through the Baltic area in 1917 and, taking advantage of the weakness of the new Soviet state, was able to seize much of Estonia early in 1918. Under the Treaty of Brest-Litovsk, which the Soviet government had been forced to sign with the Germans on March 3 1918, the island of Saaremaa was ceded to the Germans and they were granted the right to maintain police forces throughout the country. In all but name, the Germans occupied the whole country, imposed their language on it and arrested many Estonians linked with the independence movement. Konstantin Päts was imprisoned in Lithuania. So during the course of 1918, the Estonian independence movement had three powerful opponents, the Germans, the White Russians and the Bolsheviks. Yet it found immediate support amongst the Western allies and the delegations sent abroad were able to secure de facto recognition from the British, the French and the Italians. Despite the armistice of November 1918, the German army was not initially disarmed in the Baltics and it took British intervention to lead, if not directly, to a lasting Estonian independence. On November 19, the German government gave de facto recognition to the Estonian government, several of whose members they had just released from prison.

November and December 1918 were critical months for Estonia; the Soviet army nearly reached Tallinn and 75% of the country fell into their hands. With the appointment of General Laidoner, however, a counter-attack began in the New Year and by the first anniversary of the Declaration of Independence on February 24, the whole country was back in Estonian hands. General Laidoner was to remain chief of staff until his arrest by the Soviet authorities in 1940.

A British fleet of three cruisers and nine destroyers had finally reached Tallinn on December 12 1918. A larger fleet was originally envisaged, but the mission was almost called off when a mine off Hiiumaa Island sank one of the cruisers on December 4. The Estonians hoped that British land forces would follow but this was not to be, although extensive and immediate supplies of arms and ammunition were given. The British navy fought and defeated the Soviet Russians in Tallinn harbour over Christmas 1918. Regular military supplies, plus coal, wheat and oil were all delivered to Estonia from Britain in early 1919 and appeals from the White Russian armies that Estonian forces should be brought under their control were ignored. Many naval battles were fought between the British and Soviet forces during 1919 and British losses amounted to a cruiser, two destroyers, a submarine and eight torpedo boats. According to a Soviet history of Estonia produced in 1953, 'British and American imperialists had assigned ten million pounds for the purpose of suppressing the revolution in Estonia'. Christmas 1919 brought reports in the British press about possible warfare between Latvia and Estonia over their mutual border and these were taken sufficiently seriously that even the Prime Minister, Lloyd George, became involved in discussions. He personally ordered a mission to be sent under Sir Stephen Tallents to attempt to resolve the issue. The dispute was in fact comparatively minor and centred largely on one small town, called Valga in Estonian and Valka in Latvian. After six months of bitter negotiations, Tallents was able to obtain agreement from both sides for a border running through the town.

The Tartu Treaty

Long negotiations were also needed with the new Soviet authorities before the Tartu Treaty was finally signed on February 2 1920. These negotiations took place against a background of constant fighting, which ended only with the signing of an armistice on January 3 1920. The fighting still involved White Russian forces, as hostile to potential Estonian independence as were the Bolsheviks. The most crucial provisions of the treaty were the recognition of the Estonian State by Soviet Russia and a clearly designated frontier. It was because of this diplomatic recognition that in 1940 the USSR was forced to claim that Estonia had voluntarily joined the union. The frontier is now a source of dispute between Russia and Estonia as the Russian Federation maintains control of about 5% of what had been Estonian territory between

1920 and 1940. Most current maps of Estonia printed there indicate the border as agreed by the Tartu Treaty. Although in the late 1990s the Estonians publically agreed to the border imposed by Russia, the Russian government by mid 2004 had still not signed a border treaty with Estonia.

The 1920 constitution granted universal suffrage, a secret ballot and elections based on proportional representation. The parliament 'Riigikogu' had one hundred members but no single political party, or even a stable coalition, was ever able to maintain power for more than a few months. Between 1919 and 1933, Estonia had 20 governments, mostly of a centre-right disposition with the agrarian parties being the strongest. Nonetheless, a state pension scheme and compulsory education were immediately introduced and the estates of the Baltic Germans were expropriated.

Estonia was finally recognised by Britain and France on January 26 1921, but recognition by the United States did not follow until July 1922, although membership of the League of Nations had been granted in September 1921. An early foreign policy objective was the founding of a Baltic League, to link the three new republics with Poland and the Scandinavian countries in a defence union against the USSR, but this foundered on apathy in Scandinavia and hostility in Lithuania, whose capital Vilnius had been seized by the Poles in 1920. The need for it seemed less important when the USSR started to sign individual non-aggression pacts with the three Baltic states in the late 1920s. Estonia was the last to sign, in May 1932. Ironically, these agreements were supposed to last until December 1945. The three did finally form a 'Little Baltic Entente' in 1934 but it was totally ineffective in formulating a common foreign policy towards Nazi Germany or Soviet Russia.

On December 1 1924 a Communist Party-attempted putsch was quickly suppressed, as it did not lead to a mass uprising. Soviet writers had to admit that tactics which had been very effective in Tsarist times, were no longer appropriate and if insurrection were to succeed at all in Estonia, far greater work amongst the industrial population would be needed. That one of the first economic measures of the new government in 1920 had been the seizure of the estates owned by the Baltic Germans and the distribution of the land to the local peasants, ensured that rural support for any communist movement was likely to be minimal.

League of Freedom Fighters

Estonia was to suffer, as did all European countries, from the aftermath of the 1929 Wall Street crash. Imports and exports in 1932 were less than half of the 1929 figure. This provided fertile ground for the establishment of the fascist 'League of Freedom Fighters', known as VAPS. Based initially amongst ex-servicemen, this organisation soon extended its support amongst the civilian population. It had fertile ground on which to grow. Anyone with unrealistic expectations of an independent Estonia and unrealised ambitions was drawn into this seemingly patriotic movement. Its first aim was to strengthen the hand of the presidency at the expense of the Riigikogu (parliament). Following a successful referendum, which the VAPS organised in October 1933, a new constitution was inaugurated in January 1934 giving the president largely dictatorial powers. VAPS hoped that the leader of the Estonian army in the war against the Bolsheviks, General Laidoner, would stand for them as president in the subsequent elections but he wished to distance himself from an organisation so clearly imitating the German Nazis. These elections never took place, since on March 12 1934 one of the four candidates, acting Prime Minister Konstantin Päts, staged a *coup d'état* and proclaimed a state of emergency as a pretext for cancelling the elections. He dissolved VAPS, arrested 500 of their members and banned all other political organisations. He therefore beat VAPS at their own game and granted himself all the powers they would have given General Laidoner. Päts shrewdly appointed Laidoner as Commander-in-Chief and, with his loyalty assured, was then able in October 1934 to dissolve the Riigikogu. Päts replaced it with a tame two-chamber National Assembly, one to be elected in the traditional way on the basis of personal majorities and one to be filled with his own appointees and those of the chambers of commerce. The first chamber had 80 seats as against the 100 in the former Riigikogu and, as 50 of the candidates were returned unopposed, the success of the government was not in doubt.

The economic success that Päts was to bring about assured him of political stability. He guaranteed minimum prices for butter and eggs and offered subsidies to farmers who brought virgin lands under cultivation. Estonia became self-sufficient in barley, hay, wheat and rye. Subsidies were also offered to industries using Estonian raw materials, such as the oil-shale along the north coast. Tariffs on imports protected these fledgling factories. Unemployment fell to such a low level in 1937 that Polish labourers were brought in during the summer to help with the harvest. Päts was lucky too; economic conditions improved throughout Europe from 1934 and the policy of subsidies had begun under the previous government. He nonetheless did claim personal credit for this turnaround in Estonia's fortunes.

By 1938 Päts felt able to promote the idea of a new constitution which would curtail many of his powers. It claimed to strike a middle road between the 1920 constitution that had given minimal powers to the president and the authoritarian 1934 one that did the same towards the legislature. The president still had far more powers than his opposite numbers in say France or the United States, but more political debate was still possible in Estonia at that time than in most other countries of eastern or central Europe. The British newspaper, the *Manchester Guardian*, was able to write that these constitutional changes 'came quietly, amid general rejoicing; all will wish that other dictatorial interludes will end as happily'. Päts's local opponents saw them as window-dressing to enable him to maintain his arbitrary rule. The first election under this constitution was held in February 1938. Political parties were still banned, but many individuals totally opposed to Konstantin Päts stood and won seats. These included Jaan Tonisson, a former prime minister, and Neeme Ruus, who would become secretary of the Communist Party two years later following the incorporation of Estonia into the USSR. Dissident voices were, however, much in the minority and during these final two years there was little co-ordinated opposition to Päts. He continued to rely on the support of the farmers and the Tallinn business elite. With 70% of the population living in the countryside, this was a logical move, but by forbidding active trade unions, he antagonised industrial workers and exposed them to the approaches of the underground communist movement.

Few could have predicted in February 1938 that independent Estonia was only to exist for a further two years. Diplomatically it rode a skilful tightrope between Nazi Germany and Soviet Russia and confidence exudes from all the books and brochures published at the time. Despite the outbreak of World War II, the Estonian Tourist Board still promoted holidays in Tallinn as an adjunct to the Olympic Games due to take place in Helsinki in June 1940. Yet the signing of the Ribbentrop–Molotov Pact in August 1939 sealed its fate, together with that of Latvia and Lithuania. The published section of the pact largely concerned trade. Germany would buy more coal and oil from the USSR (anticipating wartime difficulties from other sources) and the Soviets would buy German machinery. Under the secret protocols, Estonia, Finland and Latvia were to come under the Soviet field of influence, and most of Poland and Lithuania under Germany's. In September 1939, the USSR quickly took advantage of these secret protocols, knowing that with western Europe at war there would be little reaction. A mutual assistance pact was imposed on Estonia under which Soviet army, navy and air-force bases were set up around the country. These were used as springboards for the Soviet invasion of Finland. In the spring of 1940, the Baltic Germans were summoned 'home', even though most had not lived in Germany for generations. A possible countervailing force to the USSR was therefore removed and increased Estonia's vulnerability.

Soviet domination

On June 18 1940, the same day France fell to Germany, Estonia fell to the USSR. This date was chosen deliberately to minimise the chance of British or American protests. The standard Soviet history of Estonia admits as much in writing that 'the switch-over was facilitated by the international situation, with the imperialist powers involved in a war and consequently unable to render military aid to the Estonian bourgeoisie'. Andrei Zhdanov from the Soviet Politburo arrived in Tallinn the following day to finalise the takeover. Demonstrations were organised to 'welcome' him although trainloads of Russian speakers from outside the city had to be brought in to ensure satisfactory numbers. By August 6, Estonia had become a Soviet republic. On July 30, all the leading members of the former government had been arrested and taken to Russia. Konstantin Päts and General Laidoner would both die there, still in captivity, during the 1950s.

The Soviet system was rapidly imposed on all fields of life. By the end of August, 90% of private companies had been nationalised and any private property of more than 130m^2 was expropriated. The kroon was withdrawn from circulation in September and replaced, at a very disadvantageous exchange rate, by the Soviet rouble. From September, religious education in schools was forbidden and the Faculty of Theology at Tartu University was closed. Christmas was made a working day. The dismissal of senior Estonians culminated on June 14 1941 with a purge in which around 10,000 were dragged from their homes without warning on this one single day and deported to Siberia. At most, a few hundred would ever see their homeland again, and then only after the death of Stalin in 1953. All contact with the outside world suddenly stopped; in theory, Estonians could now travel freely to Vladivostok but they could not send a letter or take a boat to Helsinki or Stockholm. Only in agriculture was change handled with more subtlety and less speed. Large estates were seized and the land distributed to peasants. Most independent farmers were able to keep their holdings, although much of the produce had to be sold at fixed prices to the co-operatives. English was replaced as the first foreign language taught in schools by either Russian or German. Newspapers were obliged to take a very pro-German line in covering the war, so joyfully reported the bombing of Britain, and German advances into the Balkans.

World War II

Despite constant warnings from their agents all over the world and from the British government, the USSR was totally unprepared for the German invasion on June 22 1941. Lithuania and Latvia fell within days as there was minimal resistance from either the Soviet army or the local population. Following the June 14 purge, which had been as ruthlessly carried out there as in Estonia, it is not surprising that the Germans, coming so soon afterwards, were seen as liberators in the three Baltic states.

They occupied Estonia more slowly, as their aim was to concentrate on reaching Leningrad and only in Tartu was there serious fighting. The mainland was entirely in German hands by the end of August; as Soviet forces on the islands were totally cut off from their supplies, they were no further threat and the Germans waited until October before occupying them.

Alfred Rosenberg, the commissioner for the 'Ostland', had been born in Tallinn and it is perhaps for this reason that he classified Estonians as Aryans rather than as Slavs; yet the Germans made no effort to win serious support amongst the local population. The nationalisation that had been introduced by the Soviets was simply taken over and run by Germans. Higher quantities of grain than the Soviets ever demanded were requisitioned from the farmers and rations for Estonians were about half those granted to Germans. The Gestapo was less active than the NKVD had been, probably because all likely dissenters had already been deported or killed and the Jewish population of Estonia was minute compared to that in Latvia or Lithuania. Estonians who under other circumstances might have volunteered for service to fight the Russians, were only conscripted at the last minute as a desperate measure when the Germans were in defeat. Only in 1944 was the national anthem again played and could the Estonian flag be raised, but by then it was far too late. The Russians started their re-invasion with bombing raids on Tallinn, Tartu and Narva; as so often in Estonian history, Narva became a battleground. In July and August there

GERMAN OCCUPATION

Charles Bourgeois

The German occupation came as a liberation for the Estonian people. The regime was far less despotic and there was no comparison between it and the horrible terror which, under the Soviet regime, held everyone in its grasp the whole time and controlled the smallest details of life.

Among the German soldiers and officers there were cultivated people with whom one could talk, whose attitude was friendly, and who knew how to evade the more severe orders; they were human, whereas the representatives of the Soviets all seemed to be barbarians. One will never forget those round heads, with a line of hair at the back cut in a straight line by the regimental razor. A form of haircut which they all had, and which showed in this small detail, the rule of iron under which they were living.

They were good children, these Russians, and they had good hearts, but real conversation was impossible with them and they had no general ideas. Their judgements were falsified by the perfect flowering of Soviet technique and its coarse-grained materialism, so that everything they said had a colossal a priori basis, as stupid as it was narrow. Any form of controversy was thus discouraged from the start. What purpose could it have served?

One can never sufficiently stress the width of the gulf made by the Eastern schism. These Russian Christians, having been separated from us for so many centuries, no longer have the same reactions as ourselves in anything, not even in religion. For centuries they have looked on us as enemies and as the worst type of heretics, and they take no interest in what we may have in common. Instead they merely notice that our customs are different, and see in this a mark of a different faith. Even those who practised their religion were far away from us.

The Russians automatically carried out the orders of their leaders, no matter how savage, and this absolute obedience made these good children terribly dangerous, given the calibre of the Politburo leadership. They were without conscience, personality or human dignity, being just slaves.

The Estonians could now breathe again. They did not care greatly for the Germans. They had known the yoke of the Baltic barons and their arrogance; indeed their grandparents still remembered the beatings they had received from them. Nevertheless the contrast was great, and furthermore the German soldiers were not the barons; one could live alongside them and the peasant was allowed to keep his land.

From 'A Priest in Russia and the Baltic', published in 1953. Despite writing in a positive manner about the German occupation, Bourgeois was in fact imprisoned by them for two years from 1942 to 1944.

was fighting in much of eastern Estonia. On the western coast over 70,000 Estonians took the chance to flee to Sweden; 30,000 others were later to withdraw to Germany as the German army continued its retreat. By the end of the war, 10% of the Estonian population of one million had fled abroad.

On September 17 1944 the German forces received orders from Berlin to retreat from Estonia within the next ten days. On this very same day a new Estonian government was formed in Tallinn under Otto Tief who had been a minister in several governments during the 1920s but was untarnished by close links to Konstantin Päts or to either occupying power. Tragically, this government was to last for only five days. On reoccupying Tallinn on September 22, the Soviet authorities immediately dissolved it and the leaders were arrested.

Soviet occupation

The 45 years from 1944 until 1989, although recent, are the hardest period of Estonian history to describe. The Soviet authorities invited some British journalists to Tallinn in October 1944 but then felt it necessary to censor their reports. No Westerners were subsequently permitted entry into Estonia until 1960. From then until the early 1980s they usually had to stay in Tallinn and were not allowed a stay longer than four nights. (Longer stays could have led to undue close contacts with the local population.) Much was written within the exile community both in Sweden and in the USSR but neither source could be trusted. Whilst Estonians are quite willing to discuss their experiences during the Soviet era, little has been written about it and museums rarely want to include items from this period in their collections. Estonians who had successful careers under Soviet tutelage understandably do not wish to remind others of this. Those who suffered are usually too modest to launch into print. Equally understandably, Russian historians are not yet ready to take a dispassionate look at how their empire was run and then lost.

Whatever regime came to power in Estonia at the end of the war, they had a desperate situation to remedy. The tenth of the population who had fled or been killed represented a crucial cross-section of Estonian society. All the major factories had been destroyed, as had half the livestock in the countryside.

It was little consolation that the situation in the surrounding republics of Russia and Latvia, indeed throughout eastern Europe, was even worse. It was in agriculture that the new Soviet regime was first to make its mark. The lessons of over-rapid collectivisation had been learnt from the experiences of the early 1930s and farmers could initially keep their smallholdings. Larger farms that had not been seized either during the first occupation in 1940 or by the Germans were divided or given to the new Russian settlers brought into Estonia. However, as the farmers had no independent outlets for their produce, the introduction of the *kolkhoz*, the collective farms, did not in practice greatly affect their day-to-day lives. The first was set up on Saaremaa Island in 1947 and inevitably was named after Viktor Kingissepp, the revolutionary activist who had lived on the island and who was executed for terrorist activities in 1924. By March 1949 over 500 collectives had been established, rising to nearly

3,000 by June of that year. The process was complete in a macabre sense too. March 1949 saw as brutal a deportation as had taken place in June 1941 when many farmers were sent to Siberia on the flimsiest of pretexts, usually a failure to devote sufficient energy to the *kolkhoz*. The aim of these deportations was to accelerate the collectivisation of agriculture. Purges, however, were just as rampant within the Communist Party; they hit the higher ranks of the Estonian Communist Party throughout the eight years from reoccupation in 1945 until the death of Stalin in 1953. This was despite the fact that ethnic Estonians never formed more than 40% of its membership, so nervous was the Kremlin of possible divided loyalties. Mirroring similar purges throughout eastern Europe at the time, Party secretary Nicholas Karotamm was one of many senior members of the still small Estonian Communist Party to be dismissed for such colourful crimes as 'rightist opportunism' and 'promoting peaceful co-existence with class-hostile elements'. Those who survived the purges were often referred to as 'Yestonians' since the long periods they had spent in Russia marked their accents and lifestyles.

The development of heavy industry along the northeastern coast by the Soviet Union was to lead to environmental and ethnic disputes still unresolved today. The modest, pre-war, oil-shale exploitation at Kohtla-Järve was rapidly expanded so that the gas produced from it could by 1948 meet all the needs of Leningrad. (Only in 1953 was Tallinn partially supplied.) Phosphate and uranium mines, chemical plants and papermills were all also developed and expanded in this area. The extra workforce required was mostly brought in from Russia so the area became, and still is, largely Russian speaking. Over 200,000 Russians were moved into Estonia between 1945 and 1953, with the result that the number of ethnic Estonians, who had represented about 95% of the national population before the war, fell to 70%.

Forest Brothers

The Soviet authorities could impose their will with relative ease on the open countryside and in the towns. This did, however, leave the forests, which they were unable to control until well into the 1950s. These forests provided a relatively safe haven for an extensive underground guerrilla movement that could move swiftly and safely to attack vulnerable targets. The movement became known as the 'Forest Brothers' and, although neither organisation would ever be aware of the other, the techniques they used in Estonia came to be used with equal effect by the Viet Cong in Indo-China. The Forest Brothers were a Baltic-wide phenomenon but it was impossible for co-operation to be established between the three countries. Russians might control villages by day, but rarely by night. Intelligence was so good that successful attacks could be launched on arms depots, on convoys and on isolated individuals with minimal chances of a successful reprisal. Over-ambitiousness and the very occasional betrayal were the main problems the movement initially faced. Once the Western powers made clear their lack of interest in the former Baltic states, it was futile to hope for the imminent overthrow of the Soviet regime, but the Forest Brothers could maintain morale and a commitment to Estonian culture at a time when the future looked particularly bleak. Eventually the Soviet authorities were able to curtail the activities of the Brothers.

The March 1949 deportations, when 22,000 Estonians were taken to Siberia, created a climate in which only the most courageous could continue resistance. By 1950, the Baltic Sea was too well patrolled for boats to have any chance of reaching Finland or Sweden. Internal passports, ration books and job allocation made a partisan existence ever more precarious. The development of the timber industry led to forest patrols and the collectivisation of agriculture reduced the possible hiding places in barns and outhouses. Anger and bitterness drove those who did remain in the movement to acts of ever greater daring. Banks were robbed and senior officials who had been implicated in the deportations were murdered. Isolated acts of resistance would continue throughout the occupation but from the mid 1950s it would be hard to justify the term 'movement' any more. One of the most famous Brothers, Kalev Arro, disguised himself as a vagrant for 20 years before being killed in a shoot-out in 1974. Another, August Sabe, lived as a fisherman and drowned in September 1978 whilst trying to escape from security forces. The Estonian community abroad marked his death as that of the last Forest Brother when the news reached them the following year. The Soviet authorities had planned to celebrate the arrest of 'this dangerous criminal' but realised just in time that such publicity could only be counter-productive. The greatest tribute to the Forest Brothers comes ironically in Soviet histories of Estonia: that frequent mention has to be made about 'bandit' activity in the late 1940s shows how powerful they were.

By the 1970s, 'banditry' had given way to dissidence, and resistance moved from countryside to town. The increasing range of consumer goods and higher real wages for minimal work led to an apathetic acceptance of the Soviet regime on the farms. In the towns, the intellectual thaw introduced by Khrushchev and the minimal contacts that again became possible with foreigners and the Estonian Diaspora gave cause for hope in the 1960s. The Soviet invasion of Czechoslovakia in August 1968 caused great concern in Estonia but fortunately stagnation rather than further repression followed. It was well known that the Estonian SSR enjoyed a higher standard of living than any other of the republics and, if the local population detested the 'import' of Russian workers and pensioners, it was at least comforting to know that they were abandoning home in Russia for the hint of Western life that Estonia could still offer. This differential in living standards would remain until the demise of the USSR. Estonia always had better goods in the shops, better housing and a more dependable social infrastructure than any of the other republics, including its Baltic neighbours. Yet, as access to Finnish television increased in the 1970s and 1980s, cynicism towards the USSR was bound to strengthen as the local population took the lifestyle portrayed in American soap operas as the standard to which they should aspire.

Opening up to the West

Although only a minute percentage of the population was allowed to use it, the re-establishment of the ferry service to Helsinki in 1965 also gave cause for hope. In that first year, 9,000 Finns came over, rising to 95,000 by 1977. (In 2000 the comparable figure was 2.5 million.) For many tourists, this trip was just a 'booze cruise', and for the Soviet regime it was an easy foreign currency earner. But it enabled some exiled Estonians to return home for brief visits and to show the country that it was not completely forgotten abroad. Some of the foreign currency would illegally 'trickle down' to the local population to enable them to enjoy Western goods not seen since 1939. Latvia and Lithuania would have to wait another 20 years for a similar international link.

Courageous public attacks on the most vulnerable aspects of Soviet policy took place regularly in the 1970s and early 1980s. Estonians suffered long prison sentences for writing to Kurt Waldheim, the UN Secretary-General, to complain about Soviet rule, for protesting against the expulsion of Alexander Solzhenitsyn from the USSR in 1974, for demanding Soviet implementation of the 1975 Helsinki Agreement and for publicising the dangers of pollution from industry along the northeast coast. In 1979 Estonian dissidents combined with Latvian and Lithuanian groups to demand the publication in full of the Ribbentrop–Molotov Pact and also that the three Baltic republics should be declared nuclear-free zones. Yet prison sentences were lower than they had been in the 1950s and 1960s. 'Only' five to six years was now the norm rather than 25 under Stalin and ten under Khrushchev. Arrests would always ensure publicity in the West and increasing protests from abroad towards any Soviet institution.

The holding of some of the events of the 1980 Olympic Games in Tallinn gave the city its first exposure to the outside world since 1940. For thousands of residents drafted in to work in the tourism and service industries, it was also their first contact with foreigners. For three weeks, English suddenly became a living language and Tallinn a cosmopolitan city. If direct dialling abroad, foreign newspapers and wide menus in cafés disappeared as quickly as they had been introduced, at least the yachting harbour at Pirita and a restored Old Town remained. The Soviet Union was, however, entering a period of deep stagnation. Leonid Brezhnev finally died in November 1982 after two years of critical illness, and his successor Yuri Andropov was to live for little more than a year. Konstantin Chernenko was in similar ill health and he died in March 1985. Only then did Mikhail Gorbachev become general secretary and the policies he launched were to lead to the dissolution of the USSR, although this was hardly his aim. In 1983, probably unbeknown outside Estonia itself, Arnold Rüütel was elected as chairman of the Estonian Supreme Soviet. At the time, this body was powerless and irrelevant but he was to turn it into the main body co-ordinating the drive to independence. Eighteen years later, in 2001, he would be elected president of Estonia, which by then had been independent for ten years.

Two even more crucial issues had first to be tackled: the proposed new port at Muuga to the east of Tallinn and the proposed new phosphate mine at Rakvere, further east towards Narva. Both would require the immigration of at least 10,000 Russians, and both were ecologically unsound. The phosphate mine would have been lethal, polluting both Lake Peipsi and the Pärnu River.

The Chernobyl nuclear disaster, which took place in April 1986, further strengthened Estonian concerns about large-scale Soviet industrial development. In 1987 there were major clashes, fortunately all peaceful, between the Soviet authorities and many different groups of protesters. That year was also to see many 'firsts' – protest banners in English, public argument with Gorbachev during his visit to Tallinn, references in the press to public opinion, and finally the complete abandonment of both projects. The environment was a perfect issue to choose since it could not be branded as 'capitalistic' or 'nationalistic' and the reaction to Chernobyl in the West forced Moscow to face it. Yet as progress on this environmental issue moved so quickly, 1987 also brought out into the open the Ribbentrop–Molotov Pact, which could not avoid the sovereignty issue. On August 23, the anniversary of its signing in 1939, about 2,000 people gathered in Hirve Park to demand the publication of the 'secret' protocols which had allowed the USSR to absorb the three Baltic states.

The year 1988 was to be a year of autonomy, a word that frightened the Kremlin but that could not justify a military reaction. As with most radical Estonian movements, it began in Tartu University, where a dozen well-known academics published an economics discussion paper in September 1987. (Tactically it was still unwise to attempt publication in the capital.) Its main points were that the republics should be largely self-regulating in the economics field and should be able to trade independently with each other and with the outside world. A convertible rouble would have to be the mainstay of such an economic policy. A greater role was foreseen for the private sector although this was not yet specified, again for tactical reasons. The initial public debate could therefore centre on the obsessive over-centralisation of the Soviet system whilst the real agenda of nationalism and a capitalist economy could remain hidden until it was safe to bring it out completely into the open. Limited economic autonomy was formally granted in 1988 but implementation was difficult, given the threat it posed to the jobs of those supposed to publicise and carry out these policies. Many previous taboos were broken in 1988. The 1941 and 1949 deportations could be condemned in the press, February 24 (the former national day) discreetly celebrated and, more important than anything else, the Estonian flag could be publicly displayed. Karl Vaino who had been the inert general secretary of the Estonian Communist Party for the previous ten years, was finally dismissed by Moscow in June. In the same year, by subtle, gradual and often obtuse manoeuvres, Estonia was to achieve independence without a single violent death and without the trade blockades that Lithuania had to endure. (Latvia was to follow a similar gradualist course.) The last militant outburst took place on February 2 1988 when a demonstration in Tartu was brutally dispersed by the Soviet police. Fortunately, this was the last police outburst too. The most famous, and the happiest, demonstration in Estonia's history took place in September 1988 when 250,000 people, a quarter of the adult population of the country, packed the Song Festival ground in Tallinn and for the first time the word 'independence' came into the public domain.

The gradualist vein continued in 1989 and 1990 but it was a lonely task for Estonia. Whilst most Western countries had never given diplomatic recognition to the Soviet takeover of the Baltic states, they were not yet willing to provoke Moscow by re-establishing embassies in any of the three capitals. Many Western newspapers warned the Baltic states of the dangers of 'secession'. A stable Soviet Union under Mikhail Gorbachev, a leader to whom the West immediately warmed, was a far more crucial goal but this was a leader who could not, and still does not, understand the background to Baltic demands for independence. To him, it simply reflected 'narrow-mindedness'. On February 15 1991 Gorbachev wrote in a letter to several Western leaders: 'The speeches of a few unbalanced individuals who manage to climb onto high rostrums do not provide any clue to their deeply held opinions. I hope that reason will prevail, although irrational and extreme nationalist fervour, with fascist overtones, can be very vociferous, especially in Lithuania.' A few months later, these 'unbalanced individuals' would be presidents and prime ministers in their newly independent countries.

Gorbachev was perhaps right in projecting a future for a USSR with greater political and economic autonomy for the republics and this might have suited many of the non-Baltic ones quite well. They could not look back to a relatively prosperous period of 20 years between 1920 and 1940, the renewal of which was bound to be the aspiration of all three Baltic republics. They could also observe many positive aspects of Soviet rule which did not apply in the Baltics.

In 1989, Estonian was again recognised as the official language, there were further moves towards economic autonomy, and the Ribbentrop–Molotov Pact was published in full by *Pravda* in Moscow. It therefore became impossible for the Soviet government to maintain its claim that Estonia had 'voluntarily' joined the USSR in 1940. The 50th anniversary of the pact on August 23 was marked by a rare and very effective symbol of Baltic co-operation – a human chain of two million people that stretched from Vilnius to Tallinn. The following year saw contested elections and the increasing marginalisation of the Russian-speaking community, but it did not see Estonian support for the Lithuanian declaration of independence on March 11. Continuing the gradualist approach, Estonians now talked about a 'period of transition' and of practical measures that could accompany it rather than full independence, which could still not realistically be implemented. Certain issues, such as conscription into the Soviet army, were deliberately fudged to avoid possible clashes. Joint ventures with Western companies began and were tactfully presented as being in the spirit of *perestroika*. Closer links were established with the nascent regime of Boris Yeltsin in the Russian Federation, who was just as eager to see the end of Gorbachev's Soviet Union.

The year 1991 began ominously. The outbreak of the Gulf War in January gave Moscow scope for increased military activity in the Baltics which it was hoped would not be noticed in the West. Thirteen civilians were killed in Vilnius defending the television tower and four in Riga defending the radio station. A visit by Boris Yeltsin to Tallinn, in which he proposed mutual

SINGING FOR FREEDOM – THE 1990 SONG FESTIVAL

In 1990, up to half a million people, one-third of the population of Estonia, gathered together in Tallinn to sing the first Estonian programme since the war. The streets and trams were filled with men and women in regional national dress. Crowds reserved places on the pavements in advance to watch the choral procession as it passed through the centre of town and along the coastal road to 'Song Square' Stadium. It took at least three hours for the dizzying display of 28,000 singers to pass, a seemingly endless stream of men balancing shining brass instruments and women wearing colourful striped skirts, tartan bodices and white blouses fastened with large silver brooches. The ancient conductor, Gustav Ernesaks, came by in a horse-drawn carriage acknowledging the cheers with a wave and a nod of his head. (He died in 1994 and in 2004 a statue of him was unveiled in the Song Festival Grounds.) 'Viva Latvia!' was the cry welcoming a group of Estonians from the southern neighbour and a roar of applause greeted a group of dark, long-nosed Georgian men in crimson suits; but it was the Lithuanians, still suffering from the Russian blockade, who won the loudest cheer.

School groups bore banners displaying, not the post-war number system, but their old, historical names. A choir from a Russian-language school expressed its loyalty to Estonia by wearing costumes of blue, black and white. There was no applause for the choir from the 'Friendship Society', the Soviet organisation which had monopolised foreign cultural relations for years and which was to be liquidated a few months later.

recognition of the Russian Federation and the three Baltic states, helped to prevent similar violence in Estonia, as did a smoother relationship between the fledgling Estonian government and the local Soviet commanders. A referendum held on March 3 gave substantial support for the independence movement, with 64% voting in favour and 17% voting against. As the Russian-speaking minority in Estonia is about 30% of the population, this showed considerable support amongst them for a break from the USSR. The early summer brought increased tension in all three countries. Negotiations were deliberately stalled by Moscow on the pretext that the proposed Union Treaty should take priority; shop prices rose and supplies dwindled. The Estonian government was divided on the Narva issue – whether or not to grant special status to this border town which had a tiny Estonian population. The only positive development was increasing Western interest in the Baltics, which reduced the likelihood of further military action. There was no doubt that independence would be re-established, but it would probably take longer and be a more painful process than was at first foreseen.

Independence

August 20 1991 could easily have repeated the pattern of February 24 1918 when Estonia enjoyed just one day of independence. With hindsight, we know

'Horrible,' said one almost sympathetic onlooker, 'to be singing in that choir today.'

In 1990, for the first time since the war, there were no communist portraits or slogans, and previously banned religious and patriotic songs were sung instead of the 'red' ones which had always been added to the programme. These included 'Eesti Vabaks', a one-way ticket to Siberia in previous years for anyone who dared to sing it. Looking down from the sunlit hilltop, over the flood of people towards the giant but remote half-moon-shaped stadium, I heard the song chanted over and over again. It was the only moment resembling anything like a protest in an otherwise relaxed and rather unemotional gathering.

Small shacks set up around the perimeters of the grounds sold ice-cream, chocolate, sausages and tomatoes, while hard-currency stalls supplied Czechoslovakian beer to Estonian émigrés and the tiny minority of local Estonians who had any valuta. It was not very fair on the majority. People wandered aimlessly about the grounds during the concert. Others sat on plastic bags and made boat-shaped sun-hats out of newspapers. Small Estonian children collecting beer cans urged Western consumers to drink up fast. An elderly woman went up and kicked two young Estonian men as they lay sprawled out on the grass reading newspapers as the Estonian national anthem was being sung. Later an Estonian friend said: 'Surely in a democratic society they should be allowed to do what they want?'

From 'The Singing Revolution', by Clare Thomson

that the attempted coup in Moscow against Gorbachev could not have succeeded but, given the willingness of the Soviet military to fight in the Baltics earlier in 1991, further similarly frenzied activity was quite possible. August 20 was the second day of the coup when its outcome remained uncertain. Yet the Estonian Supreme Council bravely met in the parliament building in Toompea and issued a declaration which proclaimed independence and sought diplomatic recognition. The building was at that time surrounded by Soviet troops rushed in from Pskov, the nearest Russian town to the Estonian border. Diplomatic recognition was granted within days by over 40 countries and only a week later, on August 29, the first embassy was reopened in Tallinn by the Swedes. In the meantime, on August 24, Lenin had been removed from his pedestal and the Russian government under Boris Yeltsin made clear its support for the new Estonian government. On September 14, US Secretary of State James Baker visited Tallinn. Continued independence was now assured.

Looking back now on 13 years of independence, it is only the first year that can really be described as dramatic. The handover of Soviet assets, the withdrawal of the Soviet military, the status of ethnic Russians and the designation of the border with the new Russian Federation caused much friction, but fortunately no violence. By late 1992 a pattern was set which has

A LIMINAL STATE
Estonia, September 1994

Five Aeroflot sky-tubs by the lumpy runway
sport blue and white paint now: ESTONIAN AIR
Like gulls with a storm in the offing
they face the same way as the wind.

There are trains cut in half at the border
like worms; an independent engine
pulls out from the platform while its rolling stock
stays Russian. lines have to be drawn

like today: PAKA (*bye for now*
not quite like *adieu*) flyposts most walls
with a Red Army helipad cap, a walrus neck
that seems an easy target from behind.

Like kids with their parents' cameras
there are families posed edgily outside
the place people tried not to mention,
with a name plate saying anything but KGB.

The barracks is a film set waiting
for a new producer and a cast of thousands.
The windows are kicked out from the inside,
bunk rooms trashed. Here's half a skip of uniforms.

Round the base, there's been a fly-buzz of types
in leather jackets all this last year,
men in a small way of business but expanding
and with foreign friends. Out there in the bay

ochre hulks have faced home up the Gulf of Finland
for months as if waiting the word
(the Moscow–Tallinn post goes quicker
these days via London.)

Beneath the stained ziggurat
of the Olympic pride yachting complex
a sharp Finnish hydrofoil suns its wings.
A car ferry trots out in the team's new colours

and is not yet anybody's news.

From 'The Wasting Game' by Philip Gross, published by Bloodaxe Books continued uninterrupted since then. Estonia had turned immediately westwards, and both small and large private companies were established, some 100% Estonian, others joint ventures. Air and sea transport links to Scandinavia and Germany were rapidly expanded, Western consumer goods poured in, followed by a similar flood of Western tourists and the Estonian Diaspora. June 20 1992 marked the country's transition from a Soviet republic to a completely independent economic structure with the reintroduction of the kroon as the national currency. It was tied to the German Mark at the rate of 1DM = 8EEK, a rate that has held ever since. The rate is now €1 = 15.65EEK. With each passing currency crisis across the border in Russia, the Estonians are perhaps entitled to feel ever more detached from their Soviet past. The annual rate of inflation in 1993 and 1994 was around 25%, but is now down to 3–4%.

The sinking of the ferry *Estonia* in September 1994 showed how in tragedy as much as in success Estonia had joined the West. A press conference was held at which Prime Minister Mart Laar both spoke, and then answered questions, in fluent English. Given the transformation already in place, the world's press could descend on Tallinn within hours, book into a hotel, plug in their computers, transmit their films and file their copy with almost the same ease as they would from within their home countries. The possible causes of the tragedy were immediately subject to extensive public analysis and formal enquiries were established.

Even the early tourists in 1993 found it hard to believe what a 'normal' country they were visiting. Many did not need visas, and those who did bought them on arrival in a few minutes. Gone were currency and customs forms, hour-long airport check-ins, police registration, and black-market exchange rates; in were credit cards, telephone cards, piped music, Chinese restaurants, Irish bars, and British newspapers available on the day of publication.

Preparing for the EU

For many Estonians, there was a euphoric unreality about independence. It came so unexpectedly, and after such a seemingly entrenched Soviet occupation, that its instant success had sometimes to give rise to concern. A collapse on the Tallinn Stock Market in 1997 was a useful warning about the uncertainties of the business world, and unemployment, resulting from bankruptcies and business failures, served a similar function. Whilst few Estonians regret the demise of the USSR emotionally, there are many older people who have suffered economically and some now regret the loss of former cultural links. Pensioners need the financial support of the next generation and miss the collective facilities that the old regime provided. Members of the ethnic Russian community, concentrated along the northern coast from Tallinn to Narva, feel cut off from their relatives across the border. The middle-aged and young amongst them must retrain and learn Estonian, otherwise there is little future for them.

For most Estonian young people, however, the Soviet Union and even Russia is now a very abstract concept. They are unlikely to go there and they are certainly not learning the language any more, given that English offers so many more opportunities. They travel, but always westwards and usually just for a short period of time. Estonian salaries are now sufficiently high, given the low cost of living, to keep young people at home. Unemployment has not been a serious issue since independence and those in their twenties and thirties are very career-orientated so will often change jobs. Yet salaries are still not high enough to persuade enough couples to start families early and the population fell by about 10,000 a year from 1991 until 2003. As in many western European countries, women feel obliged to put a career before a family and social pressures to 'settle down' are absent. The appointment in 2003 of a Minister for Population (a poet with four daughters) shows the government's concern about this falling population and there is now increasing financial support for those willing to start a family. If salaries continue to rise ahead of inflation, so do the consumer pressures to spend, spend, spend. It used to be a derelict factory that greeted tourists on the way into Tallinn from the airport. In 2004 it was two competing shopping centres.

Estonia winning the Eurovision Song Contest in 2001 was as unexpected as independence had been in 1991 and was probably greeted with equal acclaim. Larger and jealous competitors doubted Estonia's ability to host the event in the following year, but it was a great success and several million fewer people would confuse the Baltics and the Balkans as a result. Full use of the programme was made to promote Estonia as a serious tourism destination.

Membership of the European Union and NATO became early goals of Estonian foreign policy and these were both achieved without difficulty in spring 2004. No attempt was made by Estonia to work with its Baltic neighbours in this endeavour. In fact, the reverse was the case, as Estonia rarely hid its contempt for what it saw as economic backwardness in Latvia and Lithuania. The country's most famous foreign minister during the 1990s, Toomas Hendrik Ilves, liked to point out that the only link between the three Baltic countries had been the Soviet and German occupations. He also described Estonia as a Nordic rather than as a Baltic country.

EU standards were imposed years before 2004, probably at a more rigorous level than in many countries which were already members. If a café or a factory closed, this would rarely be as a result of bankruptcy but usually because the owners did not think it worthwhile to meet these standards. As working hours' directives came to be observed, tourists no longer ran the risk of a coach-driver trying to fit two shifts into one day, but equally they could not drink milk straight from the farm. Estonian diplomats abroad lobbied hard in all EU capitals and proved that they could understand and implement all the legislation pouring out of Brussels.

If on occasion Estonians or others feel frustrated at the lack of resources available in certain fields, they can always be comforted by looking across the Russian border for confirmation of the progress made since 1991. In the last edition of this book, I suggested that the election of Arnold Rüütel, a graduate of an agricultural college rather than of Tartu University, as president in 2001 was a reaction of the 'have-nots' in contemporary Estonia, many of whom live in the countryside. It was perhaps a warning that not every Estonian can afford a car and a Mediterranean holiday. Probably the 'have-lesses' would have been a fairer description given the affluence found in so many villages now.

Autumn 2003 saw a 67% 'yes' vote for joining the EU, which can be interpreted as a greater pro-business vote than the 2001 election displayed. Autumn 2005 sees the next presidential election. If Arnold Rüütel stands again and wins, the result will reflect some scepticism of the very pro-European agenda being pushed in Tallinn and Tartu. If he loses, Estonia will have made the final break with its Soviet and Tsarist past.

Major dates in Estonian history

1219	June: King Valdemar II of Denmark occupies Estonia
1248	Lubeck law adopted for Tallinn as it joins the Hanseatic League
1343–45	St George's Rebellion against Danish rule
1346	Denmark sells Estonia to the Teutonic Knights
1525	First book printed in Estonian
1632	Opening of Tartu University
1710	Treaty of Nystadt brings Estonia into Tsarist Empire
1739	Earliest publication of the Bible in Estonian
1816	Abolition of serfdom in the Tsarist Baltic provinces (this occurred in Russia in 1861)
1864	First publication of an Estonian daily newspaper, *Postimees*
1869	First Estonian Song Festival held at Tartu
1872	Strike at Kreenholm factory
1905	Uprisings in Tallinn follow those in St Petersburg
1918	February 24: Proclamation of independence. The very next day German troops seize Tallinn. They withdraw on November 11 December 12: British fleet arrives in Tallinn
1920	February 2: Signing of the Tartu Peace Treaty between Estonia and the USSR
1921	January 1: Estonia joins Eastern European time, one hour behind St Petersburg and Moscow time July 1: Wearing of Soviet military uniforms is banned July 19: Flights from Tallinn to Stockholm begin
1924	December 1: A communist putsch attempt is crushed
1928	January 1: Kroon is introduced as the national currency July 3: First steamer service to the UK starts
1933	August 11: Proclamation of state of emergency
1934	March 12: Ban on all political parties November 27: Study of English made compulsory in all secondary schools
1937	June 1: The first British-built submarine is delivered to the Estonian navy
1936	February: Import of all Soviet printed matter forbidden
1939	August 23: Signing of Ribbentrop–Molotov Pact which places Estonia in the Soviet field of influence

	September 28: Estonia forced to sign a Mutual Assistance Pact with the USSR which allows 25,000 Soviet troops to be stationed in Estonia
1940	June 16: Soviet occupation begins
1941	June 14: Deportations to Siberia August 28: German troops occupy Tallinn
1944	September 17: German troops retreat from Tallinn. Formation of Estonian provisional government, dissolved five days later with arrival of Soviet troops
1949	March: Further deportations to Siberia
1950	Population of Tallinn reaches 200,000
1964	March 12: President Urho Kekkonen of Finland spends three days in Estonia, the first foreign leader to visit the then Soviet republic since the war
1965	Twice-weekly ferry service to Helsinki opens: to be Estonia's only direct link outside the USSR until 1989
1980	July 19: Opening of Olympic Games sailing and yachting events at Pirita outside Tallinn
1989	February 24: Estonian flag is raised on Tall Hermann Tower August 23: Human chain of two million people linking Vilnius with Tallinn to commemorate 50th anniversary of Ribbentrop–Molotov Pact
1991	August 20: Following failed coup in Moscow, Estonia declares re-establishment of independence. Recognised by Moscow on August 24
1992	June 20: Reintroduction of kroon as Estonian national currency October 5: Election of Lennart Meri as president of Estonia
1994	August 31: Withdrawal of last Russian troops from Estonia September 28: Sinking of the *Estonia* en route from Tallinn to Stockholm with the loss of 850 lives
1996	September 20: Re-election of Lennart Meri as president of Estonia
1998	March: Accession talks with EU begin
2000	Erki Nool wins a gold medal in the decathlon at the Sydney Olympics
2001	May 12: Dave Benton and Tanel Padar win the Eurovision Song Contest with *Everybody* October 8: Arnold Rüütel inaugurated as president of Estonia
2003	September 14: With 67% of participants in favour, Estonia votes in a referendum to join the EU
2004	April 2: Estonia joins NATO May 1: Estonia joins the EU

ECONOMY

James Oates

Estonia stands out. It has come from being part of one of the least open economies in the world to being one of the most open. Starting as one of the most bureaucratic regulatory regimes, it has become one of the most flexible. From one of the most backward industrial economies it has become a pioneer in the use of technology. In this transformation it has been able to achieve high rates of economic growth, low inflation and a transformation in the living standards of most Estonians.

This is not to say that there have not been losers. Pensioners, especially, but also those in the middle of their careers under the Soviet system have found it very difficult to adapt to the radical and wrenching changes that the country has been through. Yet it is fair to say that for the large majority of Estonians prospects have never been brighter. Increasingly Estonia resembles its Nordic neighbours, and the gap between Russia and Estonia, who so recently shared the same state, grows wider every year.

Even before the restoration of Estonian freedom and independence in 1991, key economists and political leaders were considering how the hidebound and desperately impoverished economy of Soviet Estonia might best be transformed. The key element was to establish a stable currency. The Soviet rouble, by the advent of de facto Estonian independence in 1991, was already essentially worthless. Thus it was that the newly re-formed Bank of Estonia, under its dynamic new governor, Siim Kallas, put into place the conditions for monetary reform and a new currency. The decision was taken to tie the currency to the German mark and to fully back each note or coin issued with reserves. In this the Bank of Estonia was undoubtedly helped by the recovery of the pre-war gold reserves that had been sent to the Bank of England and other central banks in 1939. So it was that on June 20 1992 the new currency, the Estonian kroon (EEK), was introduced. Unlike in Latvia or Lithuania, there was no transition period to the new currency, and the first of the elements of 'shock therapy' was in place.

Perhaps the key to Estonian economic success has been clarity. Through all of the various governments since the restoration of independence, there has been a consistency of economic policy. In tax, for example, the first government under Prime Minister Mart Laar established a single, flat tax rate of 26% for everybody. There were no exceptions and it made for a very simple tax code and very little tax avoidance. In fact Estonians can fill out their tax return on a single sheet of A4 paper, although these days they tend to fill out the form over the internet. The commercial code was simplified, and all aspects of doing business were speeded up. In recent years corporation tax in Estonia has been set at 0%, which has made Estonia an increasingly attractive base for operations throughout the Nordic area. Simple business procedures and generally low taxes have attracted large flows of foreign direct investment.

Meanwhile successive governments have maintained a disciplined approach to government expenditure. In the constitution of the republic, the government is forbidden from running a deficit budget. In the mid 1990s, the government therefore hardly borrowed any money. Although some local governments, such as the City of Tallinn, did tap the financial markets from time to time, the Republic of Estonia only raised a credit to create a benchmark for the country. Unsurprisingly that benchmark was quite high for such a small country; from the first rating in 1997 Estonia has been rated as investment grade by the relevant agencies.

It has not just been the policies of the government and the Bank of Estonia that have driven Estonian economic growth. One of the major strengths of the Estonian economy is the quality of its labour force. Estonia has a generally highly skilled workforce. Indeed it is estimated that over half the population is involved at any one time with further education at graduate or post-graduate level. Rates of literacy, numeracy and language skills are generally substantially above the European Union average. In addition to a general commitment to education, the country has embraced new technology to a degree almost unmatched anywhere else. The use of email and mobile technology is amongst the highest in the world, and second only to Estonia's Nordic neighbours. The government has implemented a radical agenda for e-government, an area in which the country is now a global pioneer. Investors have taken note, and there are now several companies that specialise in information technology that are listed on the Tallinn Stock Exchange. The general use of technology in such areas as banking has created a hugely techno-literate society and substantially reduced costs.

From the days of decaying Soviet heavy industry, Estonia has been transformed into a largely service-driven economy. However, one area has not changed since Soviet times – indeed it has not changed for centuries – the importance of the harbours. The Port of Tallinn, despite ongoing political tension between Estonia and the Russian Federation, has increased its shipments almost every year. Russian grain, coal, oil and metals are exported, while a variety of international products are imported for onward shipment to Russia. Increasingly these 'cargoes' may be human beings, for Tallinn has become an increasingly attractive destination for cruise ships. Tourism is another part of the economy that has boomed, and many Swedish or Finnish visitors come to the spas on Estonia's west coast, or to their own holiday homes across the country. High-tech businesses continue to grow, and Elcoteq's plants in Tallinn manufacture a significant number of mobile phones for export on behalf of Nokia and other companies. In financial businesses, Hansabank, based in Tallinn, has established operations across the Baltic region and is now beginning to move into new markets in Russia.

From a very unpromising start, Estonia has become one of the most open and liberal economies in the world. Indeed it is increasingly held as a model for the whole process of transition. Estonia stands out; as former Prime Minister Mart Laar said, Estonia has become 'the little country that could'.

GEOGRAPHY
Wiltraud Engländer

Estonia has the most varied nature of all the Baltic countries. The most northwestern part of the extensive east-European plain, it protrudes into the Baltic Sea as a kind of peninsula. The Baltic Sea, in turn, has left its traces on Estonia in the formation of the landscape. Numerous bays, straits and islets enrich the coast. Its coastal terraces, sand dunes and beaches are still natural in many places and invite endless walks. Estonia's larger and smaller islands with their old windmills and fishermen's houses exhibit their own kind of rugged charm.

The northern and western regions were shaped by the glaciers of the Continental Ice Belt. Intensive erosion during several Ice Ages and the denuding effect of the sea left behind a rather flat landscape, with a mean height of only 50m. Estonians are nevertheless proud of their highest peak, Suur Munamägi, reaching 318m. Minerals embedded in northern Estonia's bedrock – oil-shale, phosphorite, limestone and the Cambrian blue clay – are now extracted for use in industry. Erratic rocks of different size are scattered all over Estonia, especially in the north. These rocks were transported from the Swedish coasts by great movements of ice.

Vast marshes and wild forest areas on the mainland form a wilderness which, although common all over Europe hundreds of years ago, now remains only in the Baltic countries. Many otherwise rare species have been preserved here in considerable numbers. Due to its location, Estonia is a melting pot for species diversity: eastern Russian, northern Scandinavian and even Arctic species as well as southern and western European species occur here together. For some of these species the Baltic Sea marks the border of their distribution.

The other side of the coin is less positive, however. Estonia's environment suffered considerably from 45 years of Soviet occupation. According to the European Commission, there are three major environmental problems in Estonia, the first being air pollution due to CO_2 emissions from the oil-shale power plants, which are among the worst polluters in Europe and the source of almost all the air pollution in Estonia. The two other major problems are waste management and water quality. In order to live up to EU standards, Estonia is now accelerating the building of new landfills and the construction of new treatment plants. It has committed itself to fulfil the European demands on oil-shale pollution by the summer of 2009. Financial support is being provided by the EU. Before its admission to the EU, Estonia joined international environmental conventions for the protection of the Baltic Sea and assistance from Western countries is beginning to ensure that this valuable ecosystem has a future. Following accession to the EU, the country is expected to experience increased consumption of energy and natural resources and greater waste production. It is hoped that it will be possible to avoid a repetition of the failures of Western countries made in the face of increasing environmental pressure under similar circumstances.

The remains of the Soviet regime are still obvious. The Baltic countries served as food suppliers during the Soviet era, and more land came under the plough than is needed at present. Now these areas are abandoned and the land is overgrown by herbs, wild flowers, junipers and bushes, and will soon turn into secondary forest. As a new member of the EU its agriculture is moving forward to a more effective but also more intensive form. The future will show how this will influence the landscape.

Luckily, as a side effect of the ineffective economy, large areas of biological importance remained more or less intact, and many species that are rare in western Europe have been preserved in relatively good condition. The occupation of border areas, especially along the coast, was an important factor in environmental preservation, since military areas were completely out of bounds and the landscape was preserved in its natural state. After the liberation many of these areas were turned into nature reserves and are now some of the most valuable wild areas.

NATURAL HISTORY
Wiltraud Engländer
The Baltic Sea

The Baltic Sea has played a key role in the history of Estonia. As a main travel route it was important not only for trading, but also for its wealth in fish, an important resource for the people living on its shores. The fish are a mixture of species of freshwater and marine origin. The salinity of the Baltic surface water is only 5–7 per thousand. Due to decreasing salinity from south to north, the number of species varies from 40 in the south to 20 in the Gulf of Finland and the Gulf of Bothnia.

In the open sea there are three main marine species: herring, sprat and cod. Herring and sprat are the most important commercial fish species for Estonia. Smelt, sea-trout, eel, vimba and salmon migrate between fresh water and the sea. There is also a tradition of catching lampreys during their migration upriver. Freshwater fish are found in the coastal areas, but rarely penetrate into the open sea. Perch, roach, pike, pike-perch, ide, bream, silver bream and ruff are also common in inland water bodies.

The Baltic Sea is a sanctuary for the grey seal. Their breeding numbers in Estonia are greater than in Finland or Sweden. The most important nursing colonies for the whole Baltic are the coasts of the western islands. By the end of winter the pups are born at the edge of the ice or on the rocky shores of the islands west of Saaremaa. Pup mortality is high due to pollution, lack of food and injuries. The worst enemies of grey seals are fishermen, who hold them responsible for depleting the fish stocks. In fact, industrial overfishing has been taking a serious toll on the fish stocks for many years, with a consequent effect on the availability of fish for both seals and man.

The ringed seal has declined to one-tenth of its historical population during the last century, mainly due to overhunting. Heavy pollution in Riga Bay, leading to sterility in females has, together with other factors, kept the reproduction rate low so that the population is not able to recover. The nursing areas are on the edge of the ice. Mothers give birth in early spring. They maintain breathing holes sheltered by ice floes, where the pups are hidden during their first weeks. In May ringed seals become more social: they gather in groups to change their fur and bask in the sun.

Coasts and islands

Estonia is a land of islands. About 1,500 small and large islands are scattered along the shore of the mainland to the west and north of the country, taking up one-tenth of its area. The largest and most attractive islands are Saaremaa,

Hiiumaa, Muhu and Vormsi. The rocky, stony or sandy coasts allow a great variety of natural habitats. Together with the relatively undisturbed coasts in the northwest they are an important stronghold for breeding and migrating birds.

In the north of Estonia the rocky shelf of the continent shows on the surface. Steep and brittle limestone clint cliffs developed in the Ordovician period, 500 million years ago. These limestone formations are so special to Estonians that limestone has been declared the 'national rock'. The most outstanding clint cliffs are found near Ontika and are 56m high. Between Ontika and Toila, the Valaste Juga waterfall with its 20m height might not be the world's most impressive cataract, but it is Estonia's highest and worth seeing. Some smaller Silurian clint cliffs can be visited on the northern shore of Saaremaa near Panga and Muhu.

A special type of habitat is the stony alvars on the shores of western Estonia and the islands of Saaremaa and Hiiumaa. The limestone bedrock with its thin topsoil and fragile plant communities is unique. Between the grey pebbles small plants struggle to find a hold. When the soil turns a bit richer junipers start to grow. In the past grazing kept the juniper bushes down; nowadays they are threatening the fragile vegetation by simply overgrowing it.

When the glaciers retreated from Estonia after the Ice Age, the land started rising when relieved of the pressure. This process is still continuing; today the coast is rising at an average of 2mm per year and new coastal meadows are permanently developing. The new land, used by man from the start, has evolved into a new type of landscape: wooded meadows, a habitat that holds the highest number of plant species per square metre in the whole of Europe. Carpets of flowers change their colours successively and in early summer several species of orchids grow among hundred-year-old oaks. The re-introduction of grazing is now being encouraged, since vegetation that is not grazed or mowed will be quickly overgrown by reeds or bushes and the diversity and richness of species would be lost for ever.

Lakes and rivers

In the central and southern parts of Estonia the Continental Ice Belt carved valleys and deposited large amounts of gravel. The result is the lovely landscape of the Haanja, Otepää and Karula Heights with their hills, valleys and lakes. There are some 1,450 natural and manmade lakes in Estonia, the largest being Lake Peipsi (Europe's fifth-largest lake) and Võrtsjärv.

Of the more than 7,000 rivers, streams and drainage ditches, nine are over 100km in length. The north Estonian rivers flowing into the Gulf of Finland form scenic waterfalls as they spill over the edge of the clint cliffs. The rivers of south Estonia, such as the Võhandu, Ahja and Piusa have carved picturesque valleys with high outcrops of red sandstone.

Many rivers in Estonia are still unregulated or their courses have been modified only to a moderate extent, and thus a remarkable amount of flood plain has been preserved in more or less natural condition. Inland waterways are, however, sometimes badly overgrown due to too many fertilisers being swept into the water.

Ancient peat bogs

One-fifth of the country's territory is covered by marshes. The majority of these began as lakes that were gradually turned into quagmires by the spreading shoreline vegetation, although about a third were formed by the paludification of mineral land. Starting from nutrient-rich fens and evolving through the transitional marshes, the development of a swamp finds its final form in a raised marsh, or bog – an amazingly autonomous and resilient ecosystem. A bog consists mainly of peat mosses that get all the minerals they need from precipitation and dust particles. Peat mosses grow annually at a rate of 1–1.5mm. It has taken thousands of years for the bogs in Estonia to develop peat deposits with an average thickness of 5–7m. The thickest peat layer – 17m – is recorded in Vällämäe bog in the southeast. The oldest marshes are about 10,000 years old. In several parts of Estonia peat bogs are heavily exploited, but the country still has the most extensive living peat bogs in Europe.

Wild forests

Almost half of Estonia's territory is covered by forest and woodland. Estonia is located on the border where the coniferous Euro-Siberian taiga meets the northern part of Europe's deciduous forests. Scots pine is the most common tree, followed by silver birch and downy birch, Norway spruce, grey and common alder and aspen. Botanists distinguish 23 different forest types. On sandy soils dry pine forest is most common, whilst other forest types include temperate spruce forests, hardwood–spruce mixed forests and dry heath pine forests. Where the soil is moist there can be found transitional swampy forests, bog pine forests, fen birch forests or swampy black alder forests. A speciality on the poor soils of the seaside is alvar forest.

The largest patch of forest can be found in northeast and mid Estonia, from the northern coast to the Latvian border. On Hiiumaa and in the northeast, large tracts of primeval forests have been preserved. Estonia's forests are managed less intensely than those in western Europe and their drainage has been less efficient. Biological diversity in the forests is therefore often higher than elsewhere.

In autumn, thousands of people go to the woods to gather berries and mushrooms; mushrooms are even exported. Usually there are two peaks of mushroom growth: late summer and mid autumn, depending on the weather, especially on rainfall.

Due to their inaccessibility, peat bogs and forests are an important stronghold for many species. Most of Estonia's mammals and many bird species live in these habitats.

Wildlife
Mammals

Many European species extinct in other countries can still be found in Estonia. There are around 100–200 wolves, 1,000 lynx and 600 bears living in Estonia.

When hunting dropped off in the mid 1990s, wolf numbers rose to about 500. Recently, however, the government has offered a cash reward for every wolf killed. Protection versus control of the large predators is a very sensitive political issue, leading to serious conflict about their management. In a recent poll to establish the number of wolves the public would accept as appropriate, it was found that the currently maintained number of between 100 and 200 wolves was generally accepted as the best. Unlike in other countries, Estonians are willing to live together with wolves, as long as there are not too many, so the country might play an important role in the survival of wolves within Europe.

Brown bears are an attraction to hunters from the west, having been hunted to extinction in most other European countries. The government regulates the 'sport' by issuing licences. In autumn the shy bears come to feed in the oat fields, and with luck can be observed at several places in the evening.

Roe deer are the most abundant mammal species and they can often be seen in fields and along forest borders in the early mornings. Wild boar are very common, too, and their traces can be seen in many forested areas. Conversely, elk are elusive and shy, although signs of their feeding activities can be seen at transitional zones of forest and wetlands. They browse branches of shrubs and small trees and thus cut them back quite severely. Foxes can sometimes be seen crossing the road or fields. Raccoon dogs and badgers, although rather common, will hardly be seen. They are nocturnal animals and spend most of the day in their dens, which the two species occasionally share and also use for hibernation. The raccoon dog is a new species in the Baltics. It has immigrated from the east and is now spreading further to western countries.

European beavers leave their traces everywhere in the forests and wetlands. Their lodges and dams can reach an impressive size. Nevertheless they are shy and difficult to see. The last evening light may offer possibilities for a sighting. Spring is also a good time, for after the ice melts the beavers are busy felling trees for fresh food. The region's otters and pine martens are more elusive creatures, and far more difficult to spot.

Estonia was one of the last strongholds of the very rare and extremely threatened European mink. In other parts of Europe this species has been largely replaced by the introduced American mink, which is bigger and more aggressive and thus has an advantage in competition. The situation is alarming, since in just a few years the remaining populations have shrunk drastically in numbers, and only a few hundred individuals are left in the wild. In an attempt to save the species, the islands of Saaremaa and Hiiumaa were cleared of the competing American mink. Initiated by Tallinn Zoo, an ambitious re-introduction project was started in 2000. Several dozen European mink were released on both islands each year with the aim that a self-supporting population would establish itself. With a back up of 200 animals breeding in captivity, a species that would otherwise have disappeared is now likely to survive for ever. European mink in captivity can be visited in Tallinn Zoo.

Several species of dormouse live in the forests, but they are almost impossible to encounter. The most secretive animal of Estonia's forests is the extremely rare and elusive flying squirrel. It is a symbol for large and natural virgin forest, yet only about 200 of them live in the east of Estonia. Even the scientists who study them see one only about once a year.

Amphibians and reptiles

The wealth of wetlands and ditches in Estonia favours a rich amphibian life. During the Soviet time, due to intensified agriculture, amphibians had a rather hard time. Now, with the Baltic's economy still down on a low level and only few fertilisers used in subsistence farming, amphibians are recovering fast. The night concerts of frogs and toads sometimes sound like a scene from the tropical rainforest. They spawn in shallow ditches and beaver ponds which are warmed by the sun and create the best conditions for the developing tadpoles. Brown frogs spawn at the water, but then move away to the surroundings in summer, whereas several species of green frogs stay close to the water all summer. The common toad and the common newt are quite widespread, while others – the crested newt, the green toad, the natterjack or the pool frog – are rather rare and are consequently under protection. Amphibians hibernate underwater, but only when there is a thick layer of ice are they safe from predators such as otter and mink.

Three species of lizards and two species of snakes make up Estonia's reptiles. The common lizard and the common viper prefer moist environments. The grass snake is most abundant in more open habitats, although it is often preyed upon by white storks. All Estonian reptiles have been included in the list of protected species.

Birds

A total of 333 bird species have been found in Estonia, two-thirds of them breeding on the coast or in the forest and wetlands. Birdlife is at its peak from the end of April to the beginning of July. In spring, vast areas of coastal meadows in the west are flooded by the melting snow in the rivers. These wet areas offer plentiful food to breeding greylag geese and a new colony of barnacle geese which has established itself here. These areas are also favoured for breeding and feeding by wader species such as dunlin, avocet, lapwing and black-tailed godwit and by the rare great snipes for their splendid displays. The coasts are scattered with boulders of various sizes. Many small stones are turned by turnstones in search of food. In spring the black-and-white oystercatchers perform their noisy territorial ceremonies and search for mussels and worms to feed their chicks. Between gravel and stranded material sandwich and Caspian terns hide their nests. Eider ducks rely on their camouflaged plumage for protection when they sit motionless on the nest. The coast is also home to the white-tailed eagle, Europe's biggest and rarest eagle species. About 40 pairs now breed in Estonia, ten pairs alone on Saaremaa. On the coast of Estonia's islands even birds from Sweden and Finland find a refuge during winter.

Old forests with trees more than 200 years old are a necessity for the shy black stork to build their nests. The many dead trees are still home for the white-backed woodpecker, a species extremely rare in the rest of Europe. Black woodpeckers and three-toed woodpeckers are the more exceptional of the six woodpecker species in Estonia. Another European rarity, the capercaillie, still exhibits its scenic early-morning displays in Estonian forests. Rather inconspicuous, on the other hand, are half a dozen owl species. The Ural owl, long-eared owl and Tengmalms owl are more abundant, the huge eagle owl is rather rare. The lesser spotted eagle can be called a true 'Baltic eagle'. It can often be seen sitting on posts, whereas the golden eagle will rarely be encountered.

Wetlands and peat bogs are the breeding grounds for the common crane. In spring the pairs fly over the plains calling loudly and searching for a secret spot for their nests; they are very shy and should not be disturbed. Wetlands are perfect breeding habitats for many wader species, such as golden plover, wood sandpiper, lapwing, curlew and whimbrel.

The symbolic bird of rural areas, the white stork, is a new species here. It bred in Estonia for the first time in 1841. During the decades the numbers rose and there are now about 2,000 pairs breeding on trees and artificial platforms.

Estonia is not only important for many breeding birds, it is also a vital stepping stone along the East Atlantic flyway. Like a funnel, the shape of the Baltic coast determines birds' migration routes. Millions of birds of 39 different species pass through Estonia in spring and autumn along the northern coast, along the coasts of Lake Peipsi and over the mainland of west Estonia. In winter and early spring thousands of long-tailed ducks, scaups, common scoters, velvet scoters and black-throated divers congregate in Riga Bay and Väinameri. They winter in the ice-free areas before they leave in an impressive mass migration. Large flocks of Bewick's swans and up to 100,000 barnacle geese come from Britain and the Netherlands in early spring to stop near Matsalu and Saaremaa island. After a few weeks they fly off again to their Siberian and Scandinavian breeding grounds. During their moult migration in July and August up to 200,000 common scoters pass through Estonia. By August the first breeding birds start their autumn migration to the south: 30,000 common cranes use Estonia as a resting ground. They feed on the coastal meadows together with large flocks of greylag geese. During mild winters the autumn migration for some species can last up to December.

Good birdwatching localities along the coast are Vilsandi Island west of Saaremaa, Saareküla on the southeast coast of Saaremaa, Käina Bay on Hiiumaa and the Hiiumaa Islets, and Matsalu Bay. All these areas are recognised as Important Bird Areas of European or global importance. In the last century bird-ringing stations were founded along the Baltic coasts. The bird station in Puhtu co-ordinates the work of ornithologists monitoring millions of migrating birds every year.

NATURE CONSERVATION AREAS

During the last 15 years Estonia has enlarged its percentage of protected areas from 3% to almost 10% of its territory. The most important areas are the islands Saaremaa and Hiiumaa, and the nature reserves of Matsalu, Nigula and

Endla. Estonia also has an impressive percentage of areas with the highest protection status within Europe, only Finland having slightly more. There are 210 plant and 300 animal species in Estonia that are endangered or rare and need special protection.

Lahemaa National Park

The beautiful and varied Lahemaa National Park is situated in the very north of Estonia. The northern part of the park is formed by a rugged coastline with four promontories, some marvellous bays and a couple of islands, the biggest of which is Mohni. The southern part is made up by karstland and mires. Within the park 200 bird species nest, whilst elk and brown bear live there but are rarely observed. The decreasing population of the pearl oyster finds a last stronghold in the rivers of the park. There are many places of architectural and historical value worth visiting; some of them operate as museums or offer visitor services. There are 12 nature trails introducing different landscapes of the park. Guided tours are available by pre-arrangement. The visitor centre is located at Palmse.

Vilsandi National Park

The northwestern coast of Saaremaa Island, from Atla up to the Harilaid peninsula, the bigger island of Vilsandi and the adjacent smaller 160 islands and islets are included in Vilsandi National Park. One-third of the country's protected plant species can be found here and are safeguarded in the botanical–zoological reserve. The region is also designated an Important Bird Area, hosting 247 breeding bird species, of which the most numerous is the eider duck with over 8,000 breeding pairs. The national park is an important stopover area for migratory birds like barnacle geese and Steller's eider. Vilsandi is open to the public daily, but visitors are advised to pre-arrange their visit with the headquarters in Loona, south of Kihelkonna.

The islands of Saaremaa and Hiiumaa and several islets around them form part of the Biosphere Reserve of the West-Estonian Archipelago. This relatively large area has a special conservation objective as a representative example of a natural or only minimally disturbed ecosystem.

Karula National Park

East of Valga, in the southeast of Estonia, the picturesque landscape is protected as a national park. The rounded moraine hills have been left by glaciers and are interspersed with more than 30 lakes.

Soomaa National Park

Soomaa National Park protects the largest area of central-Estonian mires. Four large bogs, Kuresoo, Valgeraba, Ördi and Kikepera, are located in the catchment of the longest river in the country – the river Pärnu. Its tributaries separate several bog areas. The wooded meadows of the river Halliste, formerly a botanical reserve, are now also included in the national park. This area is subject to extensive flooding in spring especially in the lower reaches of the river. Several plant and bird species that are rare in the rest of Estonia can be found here.

Above Overview of
Tallinn Old Town (MW)

Left Alexander
Nevsky Cathedral,
Tallinn (HB)

Left Town Hall Square, Tallinn (JS)

Below left Clock on the Holy Ghost Church, Tallinn (HB)

Below right Traditional dancing (TH)

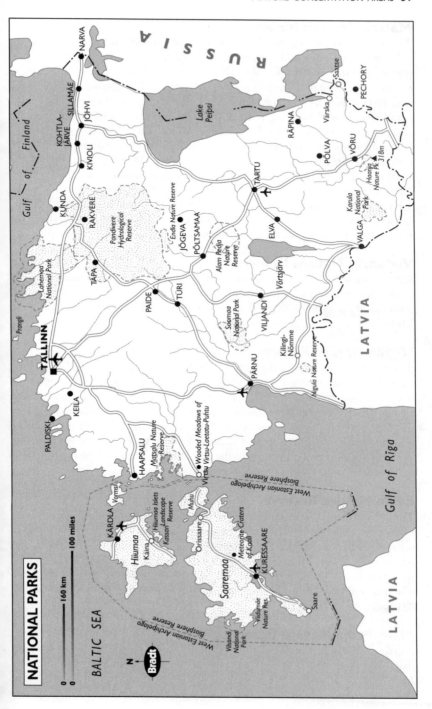

NATIONAL PARKS

Matsalu Nature Reserve

The reserve is located on the west coast of the country and includes the shallow Matsalu Bay and its surrounding coastal areas. The spectacular flood plains on the mouth of the rivers are important for specific plant communities and many wader species. Matsalu is also famous for its wooded meadows which are managed landscapes of great botanical value. The coastal meadows, as well as being used as pastures, are excellent feeding areas for waders and barnacle geese. Fifty islands along the shore are important for many plant species and breeding birds. Around the bay extensive reed beds grow. The bird-ringing centre in Penijõe near Matsalu co-ordinates the marking of more than 100,000 birds each year throughout the country. Guided tours as well as boat trips to the reed bed area are available by arrangement with the headquarters in Lihula. Around Matsalu and on the coast of Haeska there are several towers for birdwatching, and visitors are encouraged to report on their sightings.

Viidumäe Nature Reserve

On the western part of the island of Saaremaa an area is designated for the protection of rare plants and communities of spring mires and pine stands with oak undergrowth. Guided tours can be arranged at the headquarters in Viidu.

Nigula Nature Reserve

The reserve is located in the very southwest of Estonia. Attempts are being made to create a bigger reserve that also includes the Latvian region of northern Vidzeme. On the Estonian side of the border the reserve embraces a vast peat-bog area with over 370 large pools and five forested islands. It is rich in plant and bird species, especially birds of tundra and peat-bog habitats which breed here. On the coast at Kabli there is a trapping site for bird ringing. There is a 3.2km trail on boards in the bog. The headquarters of the reserve is in Vanajärve, where visits may be pre-arranged.

Endla Nature Reserve

The area of Endla Raba consists of a sophisticated peat-bog ecosystem with many pools. The rivers that form the water resources of the Pandivere region separate different bogs. The peat layer is on average 3–4m thick and occasionally even 7m. All bird species of wet and wooded areas can be observed here. There is a 1.4km board trail through the bog passing two watchtowers. Pre-arranged guided tours are available on request at the headquarters in Tooma.

Alam-Pedja Nature Reserve

North of the large Emajõgi River, in the Võrtsjärv Basin, lies a vast lowland that collects all the flowing waters from the surrounding elevations. The Alam-Pedja Nature Reserve is situated in the northeastern part of this basin. Rain water from a huge catchment area is carried down by numerous rivers and brooks. The only outflow by the Suur-Emajõgi River is very slow due to the extremely small gradient. The rivers of Alam-Pedja and the area north of it are part of the Pandivere Hydrological Reserve.

The nature reserve is among the biggest in Estonia. The density of the human population is especially low here, almost comparable to the density of wolf, bear and lynx in the area. Otters are abundant although it is almost impossible to see them. More likely you could come across one of the hundred or so beavers. Alam-Pedja is known as the largest and most densely populated nesting site of the great snipe in the Baltic countries.

A nature trail starts at Selli and leads over 4km of trail and boardwalk to Sillaotsa. To reach the semi-arch trail, turn off southwest towards Palupõhja at the Laeva cross along the road from Tartu to Tallinn. From Sillaotsa it is 1km along the road back to Selli. For a boat trip on the waterways of the Alam-Pedja Nature Reserve you should bring your own boat. A starting point could be in Põltsamaa. Mind the dams!

Haanja Nature Park

The park is located in the highest part of Estonia, the upland of Haanja. You can admire the highest peak in Estonia and the whole Baltic, the Suur Munamägi (318m), and the deepest lake in Estonia, the Rõuge Suurjärv (38m). At the top of the mountain peak there is a watchtower. Haanja Nature Park has a number of picturesque valleys and lakes as well as places of historical and archaeological interest.

Other reserves

Numerous reserves are designated for nature conservation as well as recreation. There are 13 landscape reserves, mainly in the northeast and southeast; 25 mire reserves, mainly in the north and east but also south of Matsalu; two ornithological reserves on Saaremaa and Hiiumaa; two botanical reserves protecting the wooded meadows around Vilsandi National Park and south of Karula National Park; six botanical–zoological reserves, mainly south of Matsalu; and one geological reserve at the meteorite craters of Kaali on Saaremaa. One of the prettiest reserves is the landscape reserve of the Hiiumaa islets. The islets are of different geological origin and maintain various plant and animal communities. Visits to the islets should be pre-arranged with the headquarters in Salinõmme.

Brown bear

You are in safe hands!

Estravel AS American Express Travel is the leading travel agency and destination management operator in the Baltic states, and a member of Finland Travel Bureau Group. We have more experience in handling meetings, conferences, group and individual tours than any other travel agency in Estonia. We have our own full-service offices in Tallinn, Tartu, Pärnu, Jõhvi, Kuressaare, Riga and Vilnius. Due to our large purchase volumes we negotiate the best rates in the market. So whatever your needs may be in Tallinn or any other Baltic destination, please contact us, and consider it done.

People and Culture

THE PEOPLE

In the first independence period, ethnic Estonians made up over 90% of the population of 1,100,000. Estonia lost nearly 20% of its population between 1941 and 1945. Many of those deported to Siberia died there or en route. Military and civilian casualties were high during the fighting and then many fled as refugees to Sweden before the return of the Soviet army in 1944. By 1945 the population had dropped to 900,000 and although it would increase again to 1,400,000 by 1989, only 60% were then ethnic Estonians. Most of the remainder were Russian immigrants allocated as workers to the new factories along the northeast coast. The census carried out in 2000 reported a worrying drop in the population to 1,370,000, caused by later marriage and a very high divorce rate. (Primary schools around the country are closing because of this lower birth rate.) Ethnic Estonians represent 65% of this figure and Russians 28%. Ukrainians and Belarussians make up most of the remainder.

LANGUAGE

Estonian is a Finno-Ugric language so has little in common with most other European languages. Anyone over 25 or so will have had to learn Russian at school so it must still be regarded as the second language, although Estonians are reluctant to speak it. English will soon replace Russian in this role since it is the common language for most tourists and business visitors, and is widely spoken in hotels and shops. Younger people in the towns always speak some English but for travellers in the countryside, where foreigners are few and far between, a knowledge of even a few Estonian words can be invaluable. In the northeast of the country, Russian is extensively spoken. For basic Estonian words and phrases, see *Appendix 1, Language*, page 257.

RELIGION

Michael Bourdeaux

All too often visitors take the Alexander Nevsky Cathedral in Tallinn, its onion domes dominating the city on the Toompea Hill, as a symbol of the city. In reality it symbolises two-and-a-half centuries of Russian domination, now fading into the past. Yet as the main Church of the Russian people, or nearly 30% of the population, the Russian Orthodox Church is by a large margin the most significant presence in Estonia after the Lutheran Church.

ESTONIAN CULTURE

Ronald Seth

There must have been a natural culture lying dormant in these people. The two cultures, which have forced themselves on Estonia, are bad ones. The Russian culture, exact in the niceties of greeting ladies, kissing hands and flashing looks under eye-lashes, had coarse, brutal and unpleasant foundations. The Baltic Germans, clicking their heels with military precision, and bowing stiffly from the hips, have for the last decades deteriorated so swiftly into a decadence which can still be read in the lines under their eyes. It is inevitable that both should have made an impression on the Estonians. Hands are still occasionally kissed but not very often now. Hats are lifted effusively and hands are shaken at every possible opportunity. One hears less, however, the clicking of heels. There seems to be in the Estonian an undercurrent of sensitiveness which very rarely errs. Graciousness, a facile politeness, blended with the simple directness of their peasant ancestry, are the formidable points of the modern Estonian character.

Yet they are nevertheless a pleasure-loving people. They work hard for six hours a day, enjoy themselves fourteen hours and sleep four. They drink hard, but who blames them when they produce such excellent vodka. They have definite ideas on food and the majority of it is good. They like to be well-dressed, and the young women will sacrifice nourishment for it. They have homes, but these appear to be chiefly *pied-à-terre*, in which to eat dinner and to sleep. Perhaps it is because they do not know the joys of open fires.

From 'Baltic Corner', 1938

Estonia became Christian far later than the heartland of Europe and more than two centuries after the Slavic lands around Kiev and Novgorod. Although the Swedish Bishop Eskil of Lund consecrated Fulco as the first bishop of Estonia in 1165, the main period of Christianisation, enforced by German overlords, was the 13th century. German domination remained complete, which brought Estonia into the Reformation, accomplished between 1523 and 1525 without conflict, leaving Lutheranism as the State Church.

There were Christian schools in the villages as well as in the towns. Christian literacy was far more advanced than in Russia, with the first translation of the New Testament appearing in 1686, as compared with 1825 in Russia. However the years 1710–1918 saw two centuries of Russian domination during which the Protestant Church, by its very nature alien to the Russian tradition, could not freely develop and it became more conservative than its German counterpart. A Russian law of 1832 reduced the evangelical faith to that of a 'tolerated religion', while the 20% of Russian immigrants considered the Orthodox Church to be the state religion. German influence had, however, been so strong that even as late as 1939, with 200 years of Russian colonisation now in the past, 49 of the 227 clergy were German.

As part of the Tsarist empire, Estonia benefited from the 1905 reforms which allowed freedom of conscience to a limited degree and there was an awakening of the Lutheran Church fostered by the clergy. Independence from Russia in 1919, following the upheaval of the revolution, guaranteed religious liberty and permitted the Lutheran Church to establish a new framework for Church government, with a synod being responsible for the election of bishops.

A decree of 1925 proclaimed the separation of Church and State, but Christian teaching continued in schools and the Faculty of Theology at Tartu University was responsible for the training of the clergy. There is an interesting statistic for 1934: 78% of the population declared themselves Lutheran, and 19% Orthodox, even though the Russian population had been reduced to below 10% during these years of independence. Apart from the obvious fact that many of the Lutherans must have had nominal adherence only, the Orthodox Church had clearly made significant gains amongst Estonian people. (No 'wavering' believer of non-Russian nationality would be likely to claim to be Orthodox.)

The Soviet occupation of 1940 and annexation at the end of World War II was a disaster for believers, just as for Estonia as a whole. Communist atheism would now devastate the Church, as it had already done in Russia and Ukraine. Approximately two-thirds of all clergy were murdered, deported to Siberia or banned from office. No sure statistics are available, but the Orthodox Church now became a political tool and was given significant privileges, with the obvious aim of imposing Moscow's influence on a recalcitrant but cowed population. This probably led to a decline of allegiance to Orthodoxy among Estonians, but the Orthodox hierarchy gained notably in influence.

The most significant religious figure in Estonia in the communist period was the Bishop of Tallinn, Alexi. He was appointed in 1961 at the astonishingly young age of 32. With the surname Ridiger, his father was of the old German aristocracy, but his mother was pure Russian and he grew up bilingual. His appointment can only have meant that the Soviets saw him as a man who would help render the Russian overlordship in Estonia as acceptable to the people. He did, however, protect his own churches and the Pühtitsa Convent at Kuremäe remained one of the few female monastic institutions in the Soviet Union which never seemed seriously threatened. After his translation to the diocese of Leningrad, he eventually became Patriarch Alexi II of Moscow. In the 1980s he was a leading figure in the Conference of European Churches.

In broader outline however, Estonia was subjected to the same Stalinist 1929 Law on Religious Associations which controlled and brutalised Church–State relations throughout Soviet territory. Protestants could preach (with censorship) in a limited number of open churches, the Orthodox could celebrate the liturgy, but beyond that virtually no feature of normal Christian life was possible. Illegal were the teaching of children, parish activities and charitable work. The training of the Lutheran clergy was virtually impossible, though when circumstances improved, there was a correspondence course, while Orthodox candidates could attend a seminary in Russia. The ban on religious literature was virtually complete. Every school and university held its compulsory classes in atheism, though students often did not take them very seriously. The Soviets attempted to replace Christian rituals of baptism and confirmation by 'new Soviet traditions' as the press called them, but these efforts collapsed long before the end of communism.

By the 1970s, less than 10% of the population professed any belief in God, but this statistic is almost certainly warped by intimidation; admitting to such a belief could, and often did, lead to dismissal. Long before the lifting of communist oppression and the abolition of the old law under Gorbachev in 1990, the Lutheran Church was beginning to become more engaged with society again. There was the remarkable example of Pastor Harri Mõtsnik. He committed an unforgiveable sin against communism in 1970 when, at the age of 42, he gave up a legal career to become a Lutheran pastor. His sermons became manifestos of religious and even national liberation. In one he said:

> Freedom is not an illusion, but an experience of reality. It is a vital need. It is not out of place to remember the valiant men and women who have chosen the noble path of self-sacrifice rather than self-interest and furthering their own careers; they have chosen the struggle for freedom as the only way of hope for the Estonian people, setting on one side the fear which they surely experience within and in face of the totalitarian regime which confronts them. Truth is their guide along the way.

Needless to say, the KGB mercilessly harassed Pastor Mõtsnik, so much so that his health eventually gave way. Overall Estonian Lutherans played nothing like the role in throwing off the yoke of communism which Catholics did in Lithuania, but neither should their influence be discounted.

In the Soviet period the Orthodox Church was an instrument of Russification – one might almost say Sovietisation. Linguistically and culturally the dominance was complete, despite the original tradition that the Orthodox liturgy would use the language of the people. However, at the same time Russian Orthodoxy provided a haven for genuine religious belief, perhaps more readily available than in many parts of Russia itself, and enjoyed by perhaps some 30,000 people or more, including many Estonians as well as Russians.

After 1991 a split was inevitable between the Russian Orthodox Church as such and a revival of genuine Estonian Orthodoxy. As early as the mid-19th century, significant numbers of Estonian peasants came to see the Orthodox Church as closer to their spiritual needs than the Lutheranism of their landlords. The inter-war years saw the establishment (partly for political reasons in the climate of the time) of an independent ('autocephalous') Estonian Apostolic Orthodox Church, as it was called, which was of course summarily abolished by the Soviets in 1945. Renewed independence brought about a revived conflict between the Russian and Estonian elements in the local

Orthodox Church and the split was formalised in 1997, when the Estonian Orthodox Church reconstituted itself under the Archbishop of Helsinki.

Any visitor to Tallinn can experience the splendour of Russian Orthodox worship at the Alexander Nevsky Cathedral and can go on to witness the Estonian variant in the other Orthodox church in the Old City. Of course, there are many places in the countryside where there is only one Orthodox Church and it is likely to cater for both Russians and Estonians. Some 54 of the 85 parishes have declared independence from Russia, but divisions are not neat.

CULTURE
Tiia Raudma and David Mardiste
Art

Art in Estonia is often understated and, like Estonians themselves, quite a mix of environment and history. Not surprisingly, there is very little early indigenous art or art which predates the various occupying forces, whether German, Danish, Swedish, Polish or Russian.

Estonian museums have small collections of pottery from the early peoples of this region, who used a comb or string to impress designs on their pottery, but not much else survives from early Estonian Finno-Ugric art. Some decorative circular clasps have been found in burial sites, which indicates the idea that metalwork was reasonably well-developed, but no substantial treasures have been unearthed to clearly define early art and craft styles.

Most of the documented and surviving art therefore dates from the arrival of the Danes and Germans in the 12th century, and is predominantly religious in form. The best examples are in church graveyards and in some Tallinn churches, where Renaissance paintings and altarpieces that survived the Reformation can be found. On the altar of the Niguliste Church, for example, are four figures of saints, said to be the work of Tallinn-born master Michel Sittow (1469–1525), who studied under Hans Memling in Bruges. The designs of the tombstones for Tallinn doctor Johannes Balliv (1520) in Niguliste are also thought to be by Sittow. The other important Renaissance work in Estonia is from the workshops of Arent Passer (from The Hague), which included the portals of the house of the Blackheads. Passer, who was Tallinn's master builder, was inspired by the mannerism of the Netherlands and executed the sarcophagus of Swedish army commander Pontus de la Gardie and his wife Sophia Gyllenhielma in Toomkirik, the Lutheran Cathedral.

It was not until the late realism period that Estonian art started to define and portray something of Estonia. This coincided with the 'National Awakening' of the Estonian population. Early Estonian artists studied and often worked abroad. The best place to view their works is in the main hall of the Estonian Art Museum in Tallinn. Here you can see the wonderful creations of painter Johann Köler (1826–99) and sculptor Amandus Adamson (1855–1929). The twin portraits of Köler's elderly peasant parents are particularly striking. This museum is due to move in 2005 from its current location opposite the Dome Church to a new building in Kadriorg Park.

A visitor to Tallinn, walking along the bay or in Kadriorg Park, is bound to notice Adamson's imposingly large angel monument dedicated to those who died in the sinking of the Russian warship *Russalka* in 1902. The cross held aloft by the angel is both an old and a new phenomenon – having been removed during the Soviet occupation, it was restored when independence was restored.

Estonian artists produced some distinctive work in the national romanticism style. Kristjan Raud (see box page 51) is remembered particularly for the illustrations accompanying the folk epic *Kalevipoeg*, and Oskar Kallis (1892–1917) died young but left his mark with vivid designs and colour. Portrait artists, such as Ants Laikmaa (1866–1942) and Nikolai Triik (1884–1940), painted well-known figures. Impressionists and post-impressionists, such as Konrad Mägi (1878–1925) and Peet Aren (1899–1970), still surprise with their depictions of Estonian landscapes and city scenes.

Being an artist during the Soviet occupation was in one way a pampered existence. There was no uncertainty about selling your work, or having to hold down a job and painting on the side, which is the lot of artists everywhere. On the other hand, artistic freedom wasn't an option, and artists became fed up of the mandatory busts of Lenin and Stalin (he went out of fashion after his death), or murals depicting grateful Estonian maidens in folk costumes welcoming the 'liberating' Red Army and happy Estonian collective farm workers gathered around mighty combine-harvesters. Scenes such as this are still to be found: just visit the Estonia Opera Theatre and look up. There has been much heartache about this ceiling painting. Unlike the wall mural in the White Room at the Estonia Theatre, now covered with a strategically placed mirror, it can't just be hidden, while painting over it would destroy an artistic work in its own right.

For more Soviet-Stalinist realism, try to fit in a visit to Sillamäe, on the northeast coast. It was built after the war as a secret nuclear installation and the town is an amazingly complete ensemble of Stalinist architecture, with a splendidly decorated House of Culture.

Graphic art was honed to a fine edge by many Estonian artists during the post-war period. Amongst Estonians, the work of graphic artist Eduard Wiiralt (1898–1954), whose themes ranged from rural Estonia to the camels of north Africa and the absinthe addicts of Paris, is highly esteemed. A visitor to the many galleries selling art in Estonia will see works by Vive Tolli (including her distinctive scenes of Tallinn) and Kaljo Põllu (look out for his atmospheric series depicting ancient Finno-Ugric themes), amongst others.

Modern Estonian art is flourishing, with many new directions explored. For a very Estonian yet universal feel, look out for the work of Jüri Arrak. He has a very un-Estonian choice of colours – lots of red, and other bright tones – but is one of the few artists to have commented through his pictures, which have religious or mythical themes, on the political turmoil of the recent years. Look, too, for works by Raul Meel, who started with patterns of letters from a hard-to-find private typewriter, and recently branched into a provocative use of national symbols and repetition of geometrical form and text, in order to raise questions about Estonian society.

During the Soviet era, art was kept in palaces and was clearly defined as art – approved art, that is. Many artists kept works aside, unexhibited, and it is only in the last few years, with a series of retrospectives at the impressive functionalist Tallinn Art Hall of artists like Meel and Põllu, that the public has had the opportunity to glimpse this long-suppressed development.

In general Estonian art is moving out of state galleries into private ones, and from there into banks, hotels and embassies. Estonian art is also finding its way into everyday life such as pubs. For a good example, check out neo-conceptional artist Jaan Toomik's post-nuclear landscapes on the walls in the Pub With No Name in Tallinn.

Estonians are moving on from the weighty experience of the Soviet occupation. Sculptures that form part of Soviet war memorials have been preserved because of their artistic value, despite the temptation to move or remove them to help blot out the horrors of the last 50 years. A visitor to Tallinn needs several days to visit all the private art galleries showing off today's successful and aspiring artists. The wealth of museums also ensures that no aspect of the long history of art in Estonia remains undiscovered. Sadly, the small exhibition space at the National Art Museum means that rotation is the order of the day, so there is no guarantee that any particular painting will be on display when you wish to visit. However, when the new building opens in Kadriorg in 2005, this will no longer be a problem.

As a final note, when wandering around Tallinn and checking out the galleries and museums, don't forget to look up at the façade on the Draakon ('dragon') Gallery at the start of Pikk Street. The stone dragons, pharaohs and other Egyptian details are a tribute to the art nouveau period at the start of the 20th century. The building itself is one of the many art treasures of Tallinn.

Literature

Estonians have always taken literature very seriously, and over the last two centuries the flow of writing has reflected the main traditions found in other European countries. However, few of the important character-defining novels from the last hundred years have been translated into English. This is unfortunate because Estonia's literature reveals a great deal about Estonians' preoccupations and *Weltanschauung* ('view of life'). However, the situation is improving, with recent good translations of the novels of Jaan Kross.

Estonia's lively tradition of writing and reading goes back a long way: the Estonian word for book (*raamat*) has its roots in an Old Slavonic word, which suggests that Estonians' first contacts with books occurred due to Orthodox missionaries. Nevertheless, despite the early arrival of Danish and German culture in the 12th and 13th centuries, it took a while for the first book to be published in the Estonian language. The Lutheran catechism was published in 1525, to be followed by the first full translation of the Bible in 1739. In the meantime, the first Estonian-language primer arrived in peasant schools in the 17th century.

ESTONIAN BANKNOTES

David Mardiste and Tiia Raudma

Estonia's banknotes depict a number of historic figures, giving an interesting overview of the country's cultural background.

The largest denomination, the 500EEK note (8EEK = 1DM, fixed by law) depicts a sturdy man with an impressive beard and small spectacles: **Carl Robert Jakobson** (1841–82). Although a major figure in Estonian culture – writer, teacher, publisher, agricultural reformer – he was also a politician. When the new currency was first unveiled in 1992, the wags immediately drew the conclusion that the predominance of politics over culture was exemplified by putting a politician on the most valuable note.

The 100EEK note, the one most commonly used, is graced by the portrait of Estonia's best-known literary figure – poet and playwright **Lydia Koidula** (1843–86). The 100EEK note is often called a 'Koidula', as in 'Can you lend me a Koidula?'. Lydia Koidula, like C R Jakobson, was a major player in the Estonian National Awakening in the second half of the 19th century. She was the daughter of J V Jannsen who founded the first Estonian-language newspaper, on which she worked as co-editor. They helped destroy the myth that you couldn't be educated and cultured in Estonia unless you expressed yourself in German, the language of the landed gentry.

The 50EEK note depicts the composer **Rudolf Tobias** (1873–1918), who wrote the first Estonian symphonic work. Tobias was almost forgotten during the Soviet occupation, since his most enduring compositions, such as the spectacular oratorio *Jonah's Mission,* had religious themes. Tobias has experienced a re-birth since the restoration of independence with *Jonah's Mission* being performed across the world. The reverse of the note features the Estonia Opera and Concert Hall in Tallinn.

The 25EEK note introduces **Anton Hansen Tammsaare** (1878–1940), the foremost novelist in Estonian literary history and an active social commentator. He is the author of *Truth and Justice,* a family saga that covers three generations on the farm and in the city, from the 1870s to the 1930s. (The reverse of the note shows Tammsaare's own farm at Varagamae.) The story mirrors the fate of the Estonian people from the National Awakening period to the time of inter-war independence. An important part of any intellectual debate on the topic of Estonian literature is the dispute over the merits of the various volumes of *Truth and Justice,*

The flowering of Estonian literature had to wait until the time of the National Awakening in the mid-1800s. Suddenly there were poetry, plays, novels, short stories, recorded folklore and journalism in Estonian – in addition to the existing literature in German. The major players included F R Kreutzwald (1803–82), who recorded Estonian folklore and produced the national epic *Kalevipoeg,* the story of the mythical founder of the Estonian and whether the Estonian character was actually the way Tammsaare depicted it. Although the work has not been translated into English, an idea of Tammsaare's writing skills can be judged by reading the English translation of his humorous novel, *The New Devil of Porgupohja*. Not surprisingly, Tammsaare's essays were selectively censored during the 50-year Soviet occupation.

The 10EEK note portrays **Jakob Hurt** (1839–1907), folklorist, theologist and linguist. Hurt was a powerful influence in the development of a separate Estonian national identity. An educated man with a mission, he spent years on ethnographic treasure hunts, with the help of student volunteers, recording stories, songs, folklore and dialects. Hurt is remembered by Estonians for his motto: 'Estonians will never be great in number, but we can be great through our spirit'. For a small nation, not yet independent, this hope in a better future was a great consolation.

Chess has a place in Estonia's cultural history – the 5EEK note has a portrait of **Paul Keres** (1916–75) who, as an International Grand Master and prominent chess theorist, went the furthest as an Estonian in the world of chess. A major chess talent, he was often denied access to championships since the Moscow authorities did not like the idea of an Estonian on the world stage.

The 2EEK note shows **Karl Ernst von Baer** (1792–1876), anthropologist, naturalist and geographer. Von Baer's name features prominently in the history of embryology. He discovered the mammalian ova – the main achievement of his many contributions to biology. Baer's studies were used by Darwin in his theory of evolution. The reverse of the note gives a view of the University of Tartu, founded in 1632 and the site of Baer's activity as a scientist.

Art was represented on the 1EEK note by painter, teacher and cultural historian **Kristjan Raud** (1865–1943) but this note has now been replaced by a coin. Raud, one of the founders of the Estonian National Museum, illustrated the Estonian epic saga *Kalevipoeg* ('Son of Kalev') in his distinctive style. The images of Kalevipoeg fighting representatives of evil are seen as mirrors of Estonia's struggle against various occupiers. Raud also completed an impressive selection of paintings depicting Estonians from the era before the arrival and occupation by the Baltic Germans in the 13th century (in the style of national romanticism). There is a selection of his work in the Estonian Art Museum.

nation; J V Jannsen (1819–90), publisher of the first Estonian-language newspaper; and Jannsen's daughter Lydia Koidula, poet, playwright and symbol of the National Awakening. (See also box above.)

By the turn of the century, the country had very high literacy rates, although the overwhelming majority of the population lived on farms. It is not uncommon to hear elderly people recalling memories of the family sitting around a table in a candle-lit farmhouse while their grandfather read aloud from one of the first Estonian-language newspapers that hit the stands in the middle of last century. Literature came into its own during the inter-war independence period. One of the key themes is the farm boy who is bright and smart and can outwit the devil – that is, the Germans or the Russians, depending on who was overlord at the time. The other important theme is the Estonian sense of fairness and a stubbornness about what they think is right and just.

A survey in 1989 voted Anton Hansen Tammsaare (1878–1940) (see box page 50) as the writer who best depicted the local character. His *Tõde ja õigus* ('Truth and Justice') headed the list of best Estonian novels. This was followed by Oskar Luts's (1887–1953) *Spring*, an amusing tale about a one-teacher school at the turn of the century with a colourful array of characters playing childish tricks. In third place was Estonia's classic modern novel, *Hingede öö* ('Night of Souls'), written in Swedish exile in 1953 by Karl Ristikivi (1912–77). Ristikivi fled the Soviet occupation in 1944, and this novel is a surreal depiction of the fate of a refugee with no homeland.

Contemporary writer Jaan Kross's novels feature prominently in the top 20 favourites. Kross (born 1920) is just about the only novelist you are going to be able to read in a good translation. His soundly researched and readable historic novels such as *The Czar's Madman* have resulted in him being nominated several times for the Nobel Literature Prize. Kross weaves a story of principles, family and history, often using the theme of coping in an oppressive environment to reflect the struggle of Estonians over the centuries. Despite the watchful eye of the Soviet censor, he used the form of the historical novel to convey the difficulties arising from the choices that people make; in the Soviet era, readers transposed this message from history to refer to Soviet oppression. Kross's more recent works cover the recently ended Soviet occupation and the period leading to the re-establishment of independence. In 2003, he completed his autobiography.

Poetry has always been popular in Estonia. During the Soviet occupation it was also one of the few ways in which a political message could be successfully hidden from the censor. Many young poets are now active, but only one, Jaan Kaplinski, has had some of his work translated into English.

Music

While Estonia's glacier-flattened landscape may be relatively unvaried, it makes up for it with a remarkable variety of music. This is a place where music makes revolutions, and revolutions happen in music. The calibre of the different forms of music is clear, from the huge song festivals complete with choirs that number tens of thousands, to the silences interspersed with the sound of a small tinkering bell that you hear in the profound music created by contemporary composer Arvo Pärt.

Estonians have always liked to sing. There is a long folk music tradition, and in recent centuries a passion for choirs has been prevalent. The song festival tradition dates as a national event from 1869 in Tartu, which brought together

Estonian singers from across the country. The tradition expanded and eventually moved from Tartu to Tallinn. The modern festival has performers numbering 30,000 with audiences up to 100,000. In 1990, the first non-Soviet flavoured song festival was enjoyed by some 300,000 people waving the previously banned blue, black and white Estonian flag and singing with hope in their hearts.

Such large song festivals may seem Soviet in size, but the atmosphere is more like a county fair that has become national. For many people, it is a particularly special event, since even the smallest choirs from tiny places like Kaansoo (translated as 'leech-swamp'!) can compete with other choirs in the regional competitions, which select the best performers for the festival.

The festivals are held in specially constructed song festival grounds (*Laulu väljak*), situated just to the east of Tallinn centre, on the edge of the bay (close to Pirita). The festival grounds are worth a visit in their own right, because the size of the choral event cannot really be grasped without seeing the song bowl. The most recent song festival, probably the wettest in its 150-year history, was held in July 2004.

Between song festivals, the grounds provide a venue for other major events. A national Estonian youth song and dance festival is held in the years between the major song festivals, while rock concerts, especially international tours, also use the festival grounds, including in recent years the Rolling Stones and Elton John. A more folksy gathering is held at the annual beer festival, Õlle Summer, in July. The music ranges from folk to rock, with an emphasis on singing and dancing.

Tallinn is an impressive medieval city, and the medieval music played there is of a high standard. It is worth catching the Hortus Musicus ensemble, led by Andres Mustonen. They look medieval, play medieval and choose the best medieval venues (no shortage in Tallinn).

The avant-garde composer, Arvo Pärt, is Estonia's most well-known contemporary composer. Pärt's music has been described as an antidote to the neurotic age, depicting a simple but striking world, almost akin to the apparently simple but actually complex structure of a crystal. Pärt started his career in Estonia but was forced to emigrate since the Soviet authorities deemed his music unacceptable. He now lives in Berlin, but makes regular trips back to Estonia. One of the chief performers of his music is the world-class Estonian Philharmonic Chamber Choir (Kammerkoor). Under the direction firstly of Tõnu Kaljuste and now of Paul Hillier, they have premiered many of Pärt's works.

But Pärt is not the only creator of Estonian contemporary classical music. Veljo Tormis has used ancient Estonian and Finno-Ugric songs to produce some of the most amazing sounds, while other modern Estonian composers whose music is frequently performed in Estonia include Lepo Sumera and Erkki-Sven Tüür. Lepo Sumera died of a heart attack in 2000, aged only 50.

Estonia's more traditional classical composers, whose works are still performed, include Eduard Tubin, who wrote an impressive collection of symphonic works and Estonia's first ballet *Kratt* ('Goblin'). *Kratt* was being performed in March 1944 when the Russians bombed Tallinn, hitting the

Estonia Theatre. Survivors tell of the blaze in Tallinn's residential area and people in evening dress fleeing the burning theatre, as a background to the surreal sight of the main character, the 'kratt', running through the burning, snowy streets, his cape flowing. Also part of Estonia's classical music history is Rudolf Tobias, composer of *Jonah's Mission* (see box page 50).

Music performances are not restricted to summer events and Tallinn. There are a number of major annual festivals throughout the country – the Jazz Festival, the Viljandi Folk Music Festival, and the International Organ Festival held in atmospheric Estonian churches – as well as classical music outdoor performances in various small Estonian towns. Opera and operetta are popular and well subscribed, and there is an impressive frequency of classical music concerts and ballet. There is also a thriving local rock scene, which includes bands like Ice Edge (Jäääär).

After creditable performances in every Eurovision Song Contest since the re-establishment of independence (always making it into the top ten), Estonia finally won in 2001. An energetic performance of the song *Everybody* by the unlikely duo of Tanel Padar (local blond boy with cheeky punk looks) and Dave Benton (black Aruban-born Dutch, but now resident in Estonia) enthralled first the Estonian public and then the Eurovision jury. The May 2002 contest was therefore held in Tallinn.

Practical Information

WHEN TO GO

Estonia is warmer than many of its neighbours, thanks to the influence of the Gulf Stream. Harsh days do come each winter when temperatures can fall to 10°F (−15°C), but such bitter weather rarely lasts for more than a few days. In the summer, occasional heatwaves have brought temperatures of 90°F (30°C), but 65–75°F (around 20°C) is much more common. In December and January, with 18 hours of darkness, the days are so short that sightseeing outdoors offers little pleasure. October and March are excellent months with 12 hours of daylight, lower hotel prices, and few other visitors. October offers autumn colours throughout the country and March the chance to enjoy snow-covered forests, the frozen sea and more sunshine than in any other month. The frozen sea often makes access to the smaller islands easier in winter than in summer since roadways are marked on the ice. Estonia follows the Scandinavian tradition of dealing with snow on the main roads immediately, so driving is rarely a problem in winter. All major roads are quickly cleared, even on Saaremaa and Hiiumaa islands. In May and September there is little risk of cold weather and all outdoor facilities are open. By midsummer at the end of June, daylight lasts 18 hours, so July, the school holiday period in Sweden and Finland, is a very popular month for tourists. Fortunately for British visitors, August is no longer peak season so is ideal for those tied to school holidays. Throughout the year, rain tends to come in unexpected short sharp outbursts; always take an umbrella or a coat!

TOURIST INFORMATION OFFICES

Every town in Estonia has a centrally located tourist office with a wide range of leaflets on local attractions and they also sell maps, cards and guidebooks. Some can book hotels, guides and arrange car hire but most will refer such enquiries direct to suppliers or to local travel agents. Now that they are all on email, it is possible to contact them in advance for information but, because of very tight budgets, they are unable to post or fax material. The parks do not usually have their own information centres, but the nearest tourist information office will be able to provide details of facilities and accommodation. There are no tourist offices at the land borders or at Tallinn airport, but there is one at Tallinn harbour. The main tourist offices are as follows:

Haapsalu Posti 37; tel: 47 33248
Hiiumaa Hiiu 1; tel: 46 22233
Jõhvi Rakvere 13a; tel: 33 70568
Narva Pushkini 13; tel: 35 60184
Otepää Lipuväljak 13; tel: 76 61200
Paide Pärnu 6; tel: 38 50400
Pärnu Rüütli 16; tel: 44 73000
Põlva Kesk 42; tel: 79 94089
Rakvere Laada 14; tel: 32 42734
Saaremaa Tallinna 2; tel: 45 33120
Tallinn harbour Sadama 25; tel: 631 8321
Tallinn centre Niguliste 2; tel: 645 7777
Tartu Raekoja Plats 14; tel: 7 442111
Valga Kesk 11; tel: 76 61699
Viljandi Vabaduse 6; tel: 43 30442
Võru Tartu 31; tel: 78 21881

The email address of each office is the name of the town@visitestonia.com.
Therefore the address for the Haapsalu office is haapsalu@visitestonia.com.

RED TAPE

After independence, Estonia quickly set up western European-style customs and immigration at the Tallinn sea and airports, with red and green channels, the abolition of visas for many countries and a quick visa-issue service on arrival for others. Customs allowances are the usual litre of spirits, a bottle of wine and 200 cigarettes, but travellers from the EU can bring any quantities they wish for their personal use. From May 1 2004, crossing the Latvian border became much quicker. Hours however need to be allowed for crossing the Russian border except for travellers in public buses since these always jump the queue.

Visas

Visa procedures have now been standardised by the three Baltic states so citizens of Australia, Canada, the EU and Nordic countries, New Zealand, Switzerland and the USA do not require visas. South Africans still require visas, but a visa for one Baltic country is valid as well in the other two. Visa procedures for most African, Asian and Central American nationals are very complicated. Visa support is required from an Estonian travel agent and the visa has to be obtained in advance. Baltic travel specialists in Britain and in the United States can help with this. The procedure usually involves travel via western Europe or the United States to the nearest Estonian embassy or consulate (see opposite). Such visas are not valid in Latvia or Lithuania so visitors to these countries have to obtain separate visas by similarly cumbersome means. Estonian visas can no longer be obtained at Tallinn Airport or at land borders.

Travellers from all countries wanting to combine a visit to Estonia with one to Russia must ensure that their travel agent has pre-booked their accommodation in Russia and obtained the necessary Russian visa. Attempting to do this in Estonia is both time consuming and expensive. Russian visas in 2004 could no longer be obtained at the border although this was possible for earlier visits to Pskov. It is possible that this visa system will be re-introduced to stimulate tourism there but in general the Russian authorities have made obtaining visas more complicated and more expensive every year.

Estonian embassies and consulates overseas

The Ministry of Foreign Affairs website, www.vm.ee, carries details of all Estonian embassies and consulates, together with current visa regulations. There are about 30 Estonian embassies worldwide, and one or two new ones open each year.

Australia 86 Louisa Rd, Birchgrove, New South Wales 2041; tel: 2 9810 7468; fax: 2 9818 1779; email: eestikon@ozemail.com.au

Canada 958 Broadview Av, Toronto, Ontario M4K 2R6; tel: 416 461 0764; fax: 416 461 0353; email: embassy.ottawa@mfa.ee. *Estonian consulate:* 5th floor, 1199 West Hastings St, Vancouver, British Columbia V63 3TS; tel: 604 408 2673; fax: 662 3457; email: hjaako@discoverycapital.com

Finland Itainen Puistotie 10, Helsinki 00140; tel: 9 622 0260; fax: 9 622 0261; email: embassy.helsinki@mfa.ee; www.estemb.fi

France 46 rue Pierre Charron, Paris 75008; tel: 1 56 62 22 00; fax: 1 49 52 05 65; email: embassy.paris@mfa.ee; www.est-emb.fr

Germany Hildebrandstrasse 5, 10785 Berlin; tel: 30 254 60600; fax: 30 254 60601; email: embassy.berlin@mfa.ee; www.estemb.de

Ireland Riversdale House, Ailsbury Rd, Dublin 4; tel: 1 219 6730; fax: 1 219 6731; email: asjur@gofree.indigo.ee

Latvia Skolas 13, Riga 1010; tel: 781 2020; fax: 781 2029; email: embassy@riga.mfa.ee; www.estemb.lv

Lithuania Mickeviciaus 4a, Vilnius 2004; tel: 2 78 02 00; fax: 2 78 02 01; email: embassy.vilnius@mfa.ee; www.estemb.lit

South Africa 16 Hofmeyr St, Welgemoed 7530; tel: 21 913 3850; fax: 21 933 2579; email: irknipe@iafrica.com

UK 16 Hyde Park Gate, London SW7 5DG; tel: 020 7589 3428; fax: 020 7589 3430; email: embassy.london@estonia.gov.uk; www.estonia.gov.uk

USA 2131 Massachusetts Av, Washington DC 20008; tel: 202 588 0101; fax: 202 588 0108; email: emb.washington@mfa.ee; www.estemb.org. *Estonian consulate:* 600 3rd Av, 26th Floor, New York 10016; tel: 212 883 0636; fax: 212 883 0648; email: nyconsulate@nyc.estemb.org

The Estonian Foreign Ministry is keen to establish honorary consulates to make the country better known outside capital cities. In Britain, the first one was opened in August 1998 in Cheltenham (St James's House, St James's Square, Cheltenham, Gloucestershire GL50 3PR; tel: 01242 224433; fax: 01242 226712; email: jpb@bpe.co.uk) and is responsible for the west of England. In 2004 a second one was opened in Paisley (27 Ben Lui Drive, Hawkhead PA2 7LU; tel: 0141 889 5113; fax: 0141 848 7455; email:

pestprotect@cqm.co.uk) and others will doubtless follow in Wales and the north of England.

Foreign embassies in Tallinn

Canada Toom-Kooli 13; tel: 627 3311; fax: 627 3310; email: canembt@zzz.ee
France Toom Kuninga 20; tel: 631 1492; fax: 631 1385; email: france@datanet.ee; www.ambafrance.ee
Germany Toom Kuninga 11; tel: 627 5300; fax: 627 5304; email: saksasaa@online.ee; www.germany.ee
Ireland Vene 2; tel: 681 1888; fax: 681 1899; email: embassytallinn@eircom.net
Latvia Tönismägi 10; tel: 627 7850; fax: 627 7855; email: gints@latvia.ee
Lithuania Uus 15; tel: 631 4030; fax: 641 2013; email: amber@anet.ee; www.hot.ee/lietambasada
Russia Pikk 19; tel: 646 4169; fax: 646 4178; email: vensaat@online.ee. Ruutli 8, Narva; tel: 35 60652; fax: 35 60654; email: konsot@narvanet.ee (consulate). Ulikooli 1, Tartu; tel/fax: 7 403024 (consulate)
UK Wismari 6, Tallinn EE 0001; tel: 667 4700; fax: 667 4275; email: information@britishembassy.ee; www.britishembassy.ee
USA Kenntmanni 20; tel: 668 8100; fax: 631 2025; email: tallinn@usemb.ee; www.usemb.ee

Apart from Canada, no British Commonwealth countries have embassies in Tallinn so the British Embassy handles emergency consular work for them.

TOUR OPERATORS
Overseas
As there are no Estonian tourist offices in the English-speaking world, Estonian embassies abroad keep up to date with the main tour operators and their particular specialisations. Those who have extensive experience in handling individual and group tours on a year-round basis to Estonia include:

Australia
Well-connected Tours Suite 3, 11–13 The Centre, Forestville, NSW 2087; tel: 2 9975 2355; fax: 2 9451 6446; email: info@wctravel.com.au; www.wctravel.com.au

Canada
Valhalla Travel and Tours 120 Newkirk Rd, Unit 25, Richmond Hill, Ontario C4C 9S7; tel: 800 265 0459 or 905 737 0300; fax: 905 737 0304; email: info@valhallatravel.com; www.valhallatravel.com. Valhalla have regular group tours to the three Baltic states and to Finland. They also operate individual programmes.

UK
ACE Babraham, Cambridge CB2 4AP; tel: 01223 835055; fax: 01223 836766; email: ace@study-tours.org; www.study-tours.org. Operate a study tour to the three Baltic states each year and sometimes tours that combine Estonia and Finland.
Baltic Holidays 40 Princess St, Manchester M1 6DE; tel: 0870 757 9233; fax: 0870 120 2973; email: info@balticholidays.com; www.balticholidays.com. Originally Lithuanian

Holidays, they now offer individual and group tours to all three Baltic states.

Exodus Travel 9 Weir Rd, London SW12 0LT; tel: 020 8675 5550; fax: 020 8673 0779; email: sales@exodus.co.uk; www.exodus.co.uk. Cycling and soft adventure tours to Estonia and Latvia.

Martin Randall Travel Voysey House, Barley Mow Passage, London W4 4GF; tel: 020 8742 3355; fax: 020 8742 7766; email: info@martinrandall.co.uk; www.martinrandall.com. Extensive programme of group tours to the three Baltic states for those interested in art, architecture and music. Some are linked to the music festivals.

Naturetrek Cheriton Mill, Cheriton, Alresford, Hants SO24 0NG; tel: 01962 733051; fax: 01962 736426; email: info@naturetrek.co.uk; www.naturetrek.co.uk. Birdwatching tours to Estonia.

Operas Abroad The Tower, Mill Lane, Rainhill, Prescot, Merseyside L35 6NE; tel/fax: 0151 493 0382; email: info@operasabroad.com; www.operasabroad.com. Individual arrangements, including tickets, for music festivals in Estonia.

Regent Holidays 15 John St, Bristol BS1 2HR; tel: 0117 921 1711; fax: 0117 925 4866; email: regent@regent-holidays.co.uk; www.regent-holidays.co.uk. Operate an extensive programme of group tours, weekend breaks and individual arrangements to Estonia and its islands all through the year. Combinations are also possible with Finland, St Petersburg, Pechory/Pskov and the neighbouring Baltic states.

Scantours 47 Whitcomb St, London WC2H 7DH; tel: 020 7839 2927; fax: 020 7839 5891; email: info@scantours.co.uk; www.scantours,co.uk. Group tours to the three Baltic capitals, arrange weekend breaks and can make individual travel arrangements combined with Denmark, Finland or Sweden.

Specialised Tours 4 Copthorne Bank, Copthorne, Crawley, West Sussex RH10 3QX; tel: 01342 712785; fax: 01342 717042; email: info@specialisedtours.com; www.specialisedtours.com. Arrange short breaks to Tallinn which can be combined with Helsinki, and a 'Classical Baltics' group tour to Tallinn, Riga and Vilnius. They also offer tailor-made individual arrangements to Estonia.

Vamos Travel Fernwood House, Brindley Brae, Kinver, West Midlands DY7 6LR; tel: 01384 878125; email: info@vamostravel.com; www.vamostravel.com

USA

Amest Travel 16 Ocean Parkway #19, New York 11218; tel: 718 972 2217; fax: 718 851 4175; email: info@amest.com; www.amest.com

Value World Tours Plaza del Lago Building, Suite 202, 17220 Newhope St, Fountain Valley, CA 92708; tel: 714 556 8258; fax: 714 556 6125; email: vmmail@vwtours.com; www.vwtours.com

Vytis Tours 40–24 235th St, Douglaston, New York 11363; tel: 800 778 9847 or 718 423 6161; fax: 718 423 3979; email: vyttours@earthlink.net. Individual and group tours to all three Baltic states.

In Estonia

The following is a selection of local operators in Tallinn who work with tour operators abroad. They can also make arrangements on the spot throughout Estonia for visitors who have not pre-booked. Their public offices all close on Sunday and on Estonian national holidays. Outside

Tallinn, tourist offices often do this work in their own town, or will refer enquiries to a nearby local travel agent. There are no hotel booking agencies at Tallinn airport.

Estonian Holidays Pärnu 12; tel: 631 4106; fax: 631 4109; email: holidays@holidays.ee; www.holidays.ee
Estravel American Express Travel Suur-Karja 15, 10140 Tallinn; tel: 626 6233; fax: 626 6262; email: incoming.team@estravel.ee; www.estravel.ee
Via Hansa Rüütli 13; tel: 627 7870; fax: 627 7871; email: tallinn@viahansa.com; www.viahansa.com
Wris Tours Toompuiestee 17a; tel: 631 2057; fax: 641 8016; email: wris@wris.ee; www.wris.ee

GETTING THERE

From 1965 until 1988, Estonia's sole link with the West was a twice-weekly ferry to Helsinki, yet it had daily flights to most of the then capitals of other Soviet republics. Now the situation is completely reversed, with minimal links East and an ever-increasing range of links to the West. By the summer of 2004, ferries (and helicopters) were leaving hourly for Helsinki, and Tallinn airport served 25 destinations abroad and two within Estonia.

By air

Estonian Air (www.estonian-air.com) has established itself prominently and profitably amongst regular travellers from abroad and the local population. Founded in December 1991, it had a difficult start attempting to compete with several well-known Western airlines but now offers punctuality and a good standard of service in both business and tourist class. The Russian aircraft inherited from Aeroflot were soon abandoned. In December 1995 the government decided to part-privatise Estonian Air, and Maersk Air bought a 49% share. This was sold in 2003 to SAS Scandinavian Airlines who had a similar stake in Air Baltic, the Latvian Airline. Maersk continued, however, to represent Estonian Air in several places abroad, including London. A massive expansion of their operation took place in 2002–2004, with new services to Amsterdam, Berlin, Brussels and Paris and extra flights on the routes already operated. It is likely that in 2005 other UK airports apart from Gatwick will be served by direct flights.

For short stays in Tallinn it is often cheaper to buy a tour than an airfare on its own. British visitors wanting to book an inclusive tour to more than one of the Baltic states can take advantage of one-way British Airways fares to Vilnius and Riga and a one-way inbound fare from Tallinn to Gatwick with Estonian Air. The phone numbers for the main Estonian Air offices are:

Amsterdam	10 2083 670	**Paris**	1 53 77 13 47
Copenhagen	3333 8211	**Riga**	7 214860
Frankfurt	61 05 20 60 70	**Stockholm**	5450 4655
London	020 7333 0196	**Tallinn**	640 1163
Moscow	744 1241	**Vilnius**	273 9022

Foreign carriers have been as active as Estonian Air in promoting Tallinn. Finnair, Lithuanian Airlines and SAS Scandinavian have been there since the beginning but recent other entrants include Air Baltic, Air France, Austrian, CSA Czech Airlines, LOT Polish Airlines and Lufthansa.

These all offer connections beyond their home base and the chance to 'open-jaw' for visitors wishing to fly into one Baltic capital and out of another. For British travellers, they also between them serve Birmingham, Manchester, Glasgow and Edinburgh. The CSA schedules allow enough time for a day to be spent in Prague en route to Tallinn.

Not surprisingly, the EU 'open-skies' policy has brought the no-frills airlines to Tallinn, although it took several months for Tallinn Airport to reduce its taxes to an acceptable level for them. EasyJet (www.easyjet.com; tel: 0871 750 0100) is starting daily services to Tallinn from both Stansted and Berlin in November 2004. At the same time, Ryanair (www.ryanair.com; tel: 0871 246 0000) is starting flights from Stansted to Riga, which may help travellers wanting to travel in Latvia as well.

Avies Air (tel: 605 8022; email: info@avies.ee; www.avies.ee) provides domestic flights between Tallinn and the islands of Hiiumaa and Saaremaa. As these now operate twice a day and are heavily subsidised by the Estonian government, the 30–45 minute flight is an attractive alternative to a four-hour bus journey. **Air Livonia** (tel: 44 75007; email: info@airlivonia.ee; www.airlivonia.ee) operates about three times a week between Pärnu and the islands of Ruhnu and Saaremaa. In fact this is the only way to reach Ruhnu and once a week it is normally possible to spend a day there, flying out from Pärnu in the morning and back in the evening. Again the flights are subsidised by the government.

UK and US tour operators who specialise in travel to the Baltics can usually offer a range of discounted air fares to Tallinn; the best reductions are sometimes available only as part of a package tour that includes hotel bookings. Fares outside the peak summer season are always lower; between November and March, Estonian Air offer particularly attractive prices to encourage short-break tours to Tallinn.

Tallinn airport

Tallinn is the only Estonian airport with regular international flights although in the summer there are services from Visby in Sweden to Saaremaa Island and from Finland to Tartu. In the future there may well be flights from Finland to both Saaremaa and Hiiumaa islands. For full details of Tallinn airport and its services, see page 84.

By helicopter

Spring 2000 saw the introduction of an hourly service between Helsinki and Tallinn, which links the two cities in 18 minutes. At first it operated Monday–Friday but a full Saturday service was added in 2001. It takes off from the roof above the Linnahall Concert Hall next to the seaport. Various fares are offered, but discounts always apply from Tallinn on early-morning flights and from Helsinki on evening ones since the majority of tickets are still sold in Helsinki. Tickets can be booked through local travel agents and directly with the Copterline office at the terminal (tel: 610 1818; email: copterline@copterline.ee; www.copterline.ee).

By ferry

Competition between an increasing number of companies on the Tallinn–Helsinki route ensures a year-round comprehensive service, supplemented in the summer by catamarans which reduce the journey time to 90 minutes. Most ferries take about three to four hours and in good weather the views of Helsinki and Tallinn make this journey really worthwhile. The Port of Tallinn website (www.ts.ee) gives full details of all services to Helsinki, Stockholm and St Petersburg. Eckerö, Silja, Tallink and Viking are the main ferry companies; Linda Line, Nordic Jet Line and Tallink Autoexpress run the catamarans. As fares and schedules change frequently, tickets are best bought from agents in either Helsinki or Tallinn who will know the full range available. Estonian currency can be bought on the boats or on arrival at the port but change a minimum amount this way since exchange rates are better in the town. The port is served by local buses and metered taxis, but is almost within walking distance of the Old Town.

By train

Rail services within Estonia and to the neighbouring countries have consistently declined since independence and are unlikely to be of any use either to business travellers or to tourists. At the time of writing, there is little likelihood of this situation changing. As most international services are overnight, long delays at borders prevent any hope of sleep. There are daily services to Moscow (18 hours) and irregular ones to St Petersburg (11 hours). Tickets for these trains can and should be pre-booked abroad since the Russian visa will specify dates of entry and exit.

By bus

This is the easiest and cheapest way to reach Estonia from Russia and Latvia. Public buses always have priority over other traffic at land borders so delays there are minimal, but they are long enough to provide a respite for chain-smokers. Most services are operated by **Eurolines** who also have services via Lithuania and Poland to western Europe. There are four services a day from Tallinn to Riga (5 hours), two via Riga to Vilnius (10 hours) and three to St Petersburg (9 hours). The Riga buses stop en route in Pärnu and there is also a separate daily service from Tartu to Riga with an en-route stop in Valga.

Tickets bought in person at the bus station are cheap (about £8/US$14 to Riga, about £10/US$18 to St Petersburg) but inevitably are much higher if pre-booked through travel agents since they have to send a courier to the bus station to buy the tickets. Nonetheless, pre-booking is advisable particularly at weekends and around national holidays. It is not possible to book round-trip tickets so on arrival it is advisable immediately to book the next sector.

Eurolines have appointed agents in Germany and Britain to sell their intra-Baltic services so tickets are available outside Estonia at reasonable prices. Eurolines bus schedules are on their website: www.eurolines.ee.

By car

Entry into the EU has considerably reduced waiting time at all the previously tiresome borders that drivers need to cross between Germany and Estonia. There is also less risk of theft, but it is still advisable to leave a car overnight in a guarded car park. All registration documents for the car still have to be shown at each border crossing. The ferries from Helsinki and Stockholm are convenient but expensive. Car-hire rates in Estonia started to drop in 1996 and this trend is set to continue. Travellers to Saaremaa or Hiiumaa can make considerable savings by asking their travel agents to arrange car hire separately on the islands and travelling by bus to and from Tallinn. This also avoids the difficulty of pre-booking the car ferries from the mainland. Drop-off charges are high for cars taken in one Baltic country and left in another so it is more economical to hire a new car in each country and to travel by bus in between.

GETTING AROUND
By train

Buses are quicker and more frequent but, for train buffs, there are services from Tallinn to Narva, Tartu and Viljandi, and Valga. The last comprehensive rail timetable for the whole country was printed in 1939; in the Soviet era such information was a state secret and now there are no longer the resources to print one. Timetables are, however, shown on large display boards at each station. Tickets for international services to Russia can and should be pre-booked abroad since the Russian visa will specify dates of entry and exit. Domestic tickets can only be bought at stations and fares are low, about £6/US$9 from Tallinn to either Narva or Valga. There are no passes for rail travel so each ticket has to be bought separately. Most services operate just twice a day to bring workers to and from their factories and offices, but occasionally a service may fit a visitor's need too. The website (www.edel.ee) is only in Estonian which perhaps proves the point that foreigners are unlikely to want to take a train in Estonia.

By bus

Domestic bus tickets can also be pre-booked but, apart from those to the islands during the summer, this is rarely necessary. An extensive network operates from Tallinn to all major cities and also cross-country. Most of the nature reserves are on bus routes with a sufficiently frequent service to plan a half- or full-day trip based on them. For the longest distances, fares are no higher than 160EEK (£7/US$11). There is competition on the main routes from Tallinn so fares to Pärnu and to Tartu vary from 40EEK to 90EEK. It is fortunate that even the highest fares are very cheap by British and American standards. Few timetables are printed but services are clearly posted in bus stations. All companies use the same bus stations and en-route stops. Do check timings before booking as sometimes an express service leaving later may arrive earlier than a service with many en-route stops. There is an excellent website for Estonian bus services, www.bussireisid.ee, but note that it only lists direct services and cannot suggest connections where needed. The four letters õ, ä, ö, ü come at the end of the alphabet so Jõhvi will be listed after Juuru but before Järva. Pärnu will be listed after Porva but before Pääskula. The site is only in Estonian but the following language guide should suffice to find information from it:

Lahtekoht	place of departure
Sihtkoht	destination
Soidu paev	day of trip (E–Mo, T–Tu, K–We, N–Th, R–Fr, L–Sa, P–Su)
Sorteerida	sort
Valjumiskella jargi	time of departure
Otsi	search
Tuhjenda	clear

The search will bring up a timetable from which you can glean the following information:

Soidu Algus	departure
Soidu lopp	arrival
Kestus	duration
Liine nr	route number
Liine nimetus	route
Bussifirma	bus company
Soidupaevad	days of operation
Hind	price

By bicycle

Estonia is a very flat country, with Suur Munamägi, the highest 'mountain', being only 318m. The weather is often appropriate for cycling, with temperatures during much of the tourist season fluctuating only between 10° and 20°C. Main roads should normally be avoided as there are no cycle tracks and the scenery is not particularly varied. Longer distances can be covered by bus (dismantled cycles are accepted in the hold) and then local excursions carried out from each country town or within one of the national parks. The islands of Saaremaa and Hiiumaa are ideal for cyclists as motor traffic is minimal and sightseeing stops come every few kilometres. The suggested itineraries given in these chapters are suitable for cyclists as well as for motorists. Cycle hire is not yet well-developed in Estonia. If you do want to hire, contact the relevant local tourist offices before setting off (see page 56).

By car

It is not necessary to buy an international driving licence for Estonia although you must carry the original vehicle registration document (V5). Speed limits are strictly enforced and are usually 90km/h on the open road and 50km/h in built-up areas. Changes are clearly indicated.

The definition of drinking and driving is so tough that it is not worth drinking alcohol at all before driving. Do also bear in mind that the effects of evening drinking may not have worn off by the following morning. Roads are generally straight, wide and well maintained; driving is often a pleasure in Estonia as the traffic is minimal. Petrol/gas costs about £0.40/US$0.75 a litre, less than half the UK price.

Car hire

Estonian tour operators (see pages 59–60) can arrange car hire through their partners abroad, both self-drive and with a driver. Cars can be delivered at Tallinn airport and at the harbour. Rates are high for short durations, around £50/US$80 a day for up to two days, but this drops to £32/US$50 for rentals of over a week. In Saaremaa, pre-booked cars cost around £31/US$50 a day for any duration but, if cars are available on the spot, Tallinn prices are likely to be charged. Reckon on a drop-off charge in Rīga of £65/US$105 and in Vilnius of £75/US$120. Because of the high demand during the short summer season, it is very difficult to hire on the spot, but out of peak season these firms can help at the last minute. The following are the main organisations for car hire:

Avis Liivalaia 13; tel: 667 1500
Budget Tallinn airport; tel: 605 8600
Hertz Tallinn airport; tel: 605 8923
Tulikarent Tihase 34; tel: 612 0012

Taxis

Taxis in Tallinn (see page 84) have a poor reputation. Outside the capital, though, dishonesty is very rare. Many journeys will come within the flag-fall rate of 25–35EEK. They are always available at the main bus stations but do not wait at border crossings. There are also ranks at obvious central locations if these are some distance from the bus station, as in Tartu or Haapsalu.

Maps

For details of maps and atlases available in Estonia and overseas, see *Appendix 2, Further Information*.

WHERE TO STAY

Tallinn now has a wide range of hotels from two- to four-star and is beginning to offer bed and breakfast and hostel accommodation as well. Tourists staying in hotels will normally book these through tour operators before they arrive but details of hostel and bed and breakfast accommodation can be obtained from the tourist board office on Town Hall Square and at their office in the harbour. The main office on Town Hall Square keeps office hours so cannot help with visitors who arrive in the evening. An agency in Tallinn that arranges both short- and long-term lets of rooms and apartments all over the three Baltic states is **Rasastra** (Mere 4; tel: 661 6291; email: rasastra@online.ee; www.bedbreakfast.ee).

ESTONIAN FOOD

Maila Saar

Our information on Estonian eating habits dates back to the middle of the 19th century when standards of nutrition started to improve as a result of land reforms. At that time, the main meal was supper, consisting of porridge or soup served with bread and salted herring. Meat was a delicacy, usually served only on Thursday and Sunday.

Meat became more common early in the 20th century and a basic hot meal would consist of pork slices, potatoes and a sauce. Bread remained a major item of food, being considered sacred, and even stale bread was never thrown away. Rye bread was the most common and wholemeal rye is still one of the most popular kinds, with black bread also often being eaten. Black and white puddings can be regarded as the most well known national dish, with pork fat, onions and spices being added, together with blood for the black pudding. Sweet dishes were prepared only for festive occasions, with honey an essential ingredient. Beer has always been a popular drink and there are now breweries all over the country.

During the first independence period between 1918 and 1940, traditional food gradually gave way to more sophisticated urban cooking. Foodstuffs began to be imported and exported, with Estonian ham and butter being greatly appreciated in Britain. Spices were now a regular adjunct to most Estonian dishes and coffee became a popular drink, which it still is. Estonians drink it black, but cafés will serve it with milk for foreigners.

Pärnu and Kuressaare also have a wide range of hotels but the choice is much more limited in Haapsalu, Tartu and Viljandi. Several small towns such as Otepää, Paide and Rakvere have a good choice of three-star hotels and this standard is being developed in the national parks.

Three- and four-star hotels charge rather less than similar hotels in western Europe and two-star hotels are much cheaper. In the higher categories in Tallinn, rooms tend to cost £50–80/US$80–130 a night for a twin; about £10/US$15 less in Pärnu. Two-star hotels in the capital charge about £25/US$40 for a twin and elsewhere charges rarely exceed £15–20/US$25–35. Rates always include a buffet breakfast. There are few hostels outside Tallinn as the two-star hotels which exist in even the smallest towns cater for this market. As many two-star hotels are renovated into three-star ones, they tend to be replaced by more basic hostels, which are installing en-suite facilities to warrant a two-star description.

Farmhouse accommodation is rarely sold to foreigners as access requires a car and few families speak any language apart from Estonian and Russian. Bed and breakfast is beginning in Tallinn but, given the cramped accommodation most Estonians have to accept, few families have spare rooms to let in this way. Camping has never been particularly

Cafés are easy to find in all towns and villages and they serve a wide range of cakes – fruitcake, chocolate cake and curd cake – often with whipped cream. As the tax on alcohol is so low in Estonia, it is often tempting in a café to enjoy a glass of Vana Tallinn, Estonia's national liqueur. The recipe of spices used to make it are of course a secret but Drambuie is probably the nearest in taste to it of Western liqueurs. The close contact with western Europe has brought wine to Estonia but its price is still too high for most local people and beer remains the main alcoholic drink.

With the range of foreign restaurants now opening in Estonia, it is rare to find the traditional dishes such as black pudding or baked potatoes with pork and sauerkraut outside the home environment. Only at Christmas and on Shrove Tuesday will restaurants return to their Estonian roots and serve these dishes, or perhaps bean soup followed by smoked pork. Bakers like to celebrate Shrove Tuesday with an ever-wider range of buns and cakes.

Although Estonia has a long coastline, fish is rarely eaten as a main course, but rather as an hors d'oeuvre, smoked or salted. 'Tallinn sprats' are small raw sprats preserved in brine and spices. They are spread on boiled eggs or bread and butter. Fish can also be mixed with cooked vegetable salads and a sour cream dressing. Wild mushrooms are the most popular ingredient for such salads. In the countryside, stewed turnips are a staple fare but potatoes and meat remain crucial. Vegetarianism is hardly known in Estonia. The bias towards savoury food is perhaps best summarised in an old Estonian saying: 'Better a salty morsel than a square meal of sweet'.

popular in Estonia as many town dwellers have tiny country cottages to which they can retreat most weekends. Others had holidays arranged by their trade unions to massive holiday centres on the coast. The possibility of sudden storms also reduces the chance of an enjoyable stay. Sites are, however, now being estabished beside Lake Peipsi on the Russian border and at Lake Vagula at Võru. Others will soon be available at Viljandi and in Lahemaa National Park. The websites of the local tourist boards should have up-to-date details; otherwise they can be emailed for this information.

The Estonian spelling of hotel is hotell. In email and website addresses, some will use the Estonian spelling and some the English one. Policy can change on this but hopefully all addresses quoted in the book are correct as at summer 2004. (There is a similar situation with museums as the Estonian spelling is muuseum.)

WHERE TO EAT

In the 2001 edition of this book, I wrote that it was hard to pay more than £12/US$18 for a three-course meal with beer or a soft drink. Whilst this is still a guide price throughout the country, in Tallinn it is now quite possible to pay more than double this in restaurants that aim to provide a totally luxurious ambience. Wine varies enormously in quality and in price but is now available throughout the country. As cafés are geared to Estonians earning around £300/US$500 a month, they provide excellent value for snacks and cakes. Estonian restaurants do not vary their prices between lunch and dinner, but the dish of the day, päevapraad, is often cheaper than other similar dishes on the menu.

SHOPPING

Wooden toys, bowls, spoons, candlesticks and tablemats are sold extensively in Tallinn and in Kuressaare market on Saaremaa Island. Tallinn porcelain is not promoted as much as it should be, although it is of a high, delicate standard. The few shops that do sell it will wrap it properly so that it survives a journey abroad. Hand-knitted sweaters and gloves and knitted socks are available in all sizes as shops need to cater for tall Swedes and Finns just as much as for the shorter local population.

Independence brought an immediate passion for Western pop music but this has now passed, so CDs are available of folk music and orchestral music from contemporary composers such as Arvo Pärt or earlier ones such as Rudolf Tobias. The Song Festival in July 1999 led, as expected, to the production of many choral CDs, and this will probably happen again after the July 2004 festival.

Duty on tobacco and alcohol is minimal, so cigarettes can be bought for less at any kiosk than at so-called duty-free shops. Most tourists return with a bottle of Vana Tallinn (Old Tallinn), a sweet liqueur guaranteed to enhance a dull fruit salad or a bland portion of vanilla ice-cream. With Estonia now in the EU, tourists travelling home to other EU countries can now take back as much drink and tobacco as they wish, provided it is for their personal use.

For a more precise memory of a visit to Estonia, there are many extensively illustrated photographic books with English texts (see also *Appendix 2, Further Information*).

Every Estonian town has a large department store in the centre selling these articles, but they are surrounded by specialist smaller shops with wider selections in their particular fields. Shops keep long hours to attract business and many are open on Sundays. There is an extensive open-air market along the streets near the Viru Gate in Tallinn. Stallholders are active year-round, however bitter the weather might be in winter.

ENTERTAINMENT

Informal music festivals take place throughout the country during the summer. Most famous are the Old Town Days in Tallinn in early June, the Classical Music Festival in Pärnu in early July, the Tartu Accordion Festival in mid July, the Folk Music Festival in Viljandi in late July and the White Lady Days in Haapsalu in August. Over the next few years, further more serious events are likely to be arranged during the winter. In early July 1999 the Song Festival took place in Tallinn and in the end around 150,000 people (10% of the Estonian population) attended. For the few seats available, tickets can be bought in advance through tour operators but standing room is open to all on a first come, first served basis.

There is no shortage of cultural activities in all major towns and tickets for concerts, ballet and theatre can normally be bought on the day without difficulty. Prices by Western standards are cheap – £5/US$8 will buy an excellent seat. In Tallinn, the Estonian Theatre and the Estonian Concert Hall are conveniently situated beside each other. By summer 2002, programmes were available on all the regional tourist information websites (see page 268).

MUSEUMS

Museums usually only open at 11.00 and close at least one day a week; many close on both Monday and Tuesday. Admission charges vary between 5EEK and 25EEK (£0.20/US$0.30–£1.10/US$1.70) with lower rates for the over 60s. For many years after independence, tickets were often issued with the rouble price overstamped, even though Soviet currency was withdrawn in 1992, as museums could not afford to print new ones. Museums are usually empty as these prices now deter local visitors. Very few have adequate brochures in English, although labels in English are now more common. Many of the postcards and leaflets offered for sale still date from the Soviet period. The elderly staff are often kind and helpful to the few visitors they receive but they speak only Russian and Estonian.

OUTDOOR ACTIVITIES

Well-organised outdoor activities are available in most of the national parks. There is no specific listing for location and costs of these activities or of accommodation possibilities. Fortunately, away from the northeast coast, Estonia suffers little from pollution, and strict regulation will ensure that this state of affairs continues. Ecotourism is taken seriously and is now enjoyed by many local visitors and tourists from abroad. Full information can be obtained from the **Ecotourism Initiative** (tel/fax: 372 44 43 779; email: info@ecotourism.ee; www.ecotourism.ee).

MONEY AND CREDIT CARDS

Estonia was the first of the Baltic states to abandon the Russian rouble, and the kroon (EEK) was re-introduced in September 1992. It was tied to the German Mark at a rate of 8EEK = 1DM, a rate which it has held ever since, becoming 15.65EEK = €1 in January 2002. It is likely that the euro will be introduced in Estonia in 2007; indeed, many prices are already quoted in euro, even though shops are only supposed to accept local currency.

Exchange booths are available all over the country and are often open seven days a week. Rates vary wildly and one that exchanges Latvian lats favourably may have a poor rate for sterling. Always avoid exchanging money airside at Tallinn airport, at the bus station and at the port. Banks tend to offer better rates and in summer 2004 the best rates for sterling and US dollars were

DOS AND DON'TS WHEN VISITING ESTONIA
Lembit Opik MP

DO plan what kind of visit you want before you go. Estonia can offer everything from an extrordinarily lively nightclub scene, to the silence of the country. Tallinn is the clubbing capital of the Baltic; 50km outside, and you're in silent countryside, still largely farmed in low-intensive ways.

DON'T plan a beach holiday. The Baltic Sea is c-c-cold. The beaches are fine, but you're playing with hypothermia if you intend to spend long periods in the water except, perhaps, in the height of summer.

DO visit Tartu. It's a university town, quite similar in character to Stanford or Oxford. The whole town suggests an air of scholarly thought, with bars worthy of Europe's great philosophers.

DON'T go to Estonia for a mountaineering or skiing holiday, although cross-country skiing is OK. There's one hill, which is about 300m high and it gets very busy when it snows.

DO visit Lahemaa National Park on the northwest coast. In Soviet days, Estonia acquired the USSR's first national park. Its sights and sounds embody the spirit of Estonia, with long unspoilt beaches, songbirds and forest almost to the water's edge. There are also wolves and bears.

DON'T forget your midge repellent. Estonian bugs were specially trained to bite while serving in the Soviet military in the dark days of communism. They're not too dangerous to health, the bites are very itchy.

DO ask Estonians about their history. Most have a strong bias one way or another, but the more you ask the more complete a picture you'll get of the nation's troubled past. It's a stark contrast to the highly upbeat Estonia of today.

offered by the Hansapank. Their branch in Tallinn at Viru 4 is the most convenient one for tourists and it is open Mon–Fri 09.00–18.00 and Sat 10.00–15.00. In 2004 the pound was worth around 23.40EEK and the dollar about 12.50EEK. Tavid at Aia 5 in Tallinn and Rüütli 2 in Tartu prides itself on the range of currencies it accepts so this is the place to off-load Tunisian dinars and Thai bahts. The Tallinn office is open 24 hours a day but between 19.00 and 09.00 during the week, and from 17.00 at weekends, their rates worsen considerably, often by 10%.

Notes are issued for 1, 2, 5, 10, 25, 50, 100 and 500EEK. Coins are issued for 10, 20 and 50 sents, and for 1 and 2EEK; these last two coins are replacing the notes of the same value. When changing money, do not accept 500EEK notes, as they are very difficult to change when small purchases are made – they play the same role as £50 notes in Britain or $100 bills in the

DON'T go on about the good old days of the USSR. This will not make you any friends in the Estonian or Russian community. They generally like being in the EU, especially after winning the Eurovision Song Contest in 2001.

DO try the local vodka. It's a national pastime to drink 'quite a lot' especially in the winter.

DON'T try to keep up with Estonian drinkers. They're professionals, so you do so at your peril.

DO go shopping. A few hours in Tallinn centre will quickly change any prejudices you may have about Estonia's 'sauerkraut and potato' culture.

DON'T take food parcels and digital watches over as presents. This is patronising and pointless, because the 'shortages' simply don't exist now.

DO go to a song festival. Estonian choirs are second to none. Any choral occasion is a mixture of traditional songs and deeply moving harmonic reflections of the spirit of independence. Estonians are also interested in cultural exchanges. If you suggest one, it is very likely to happen, but make sure who's paying for the travel first. They're very good at negotiating.

DON'T turn down the chance to visit a traditional sauna. The secret of a good sauna is the construction of the room itself. You'll usually get a few drinks in the sauna too: make sure they don't kill you with kindness.

DO try the herring. If you like rollmops, you'll have a feast at reasonable prices in almost any restaurant anywhere in Estonia.

DON'T go to Estonia if your idea of a perfect holiday is a vegan extravaganza. Estonians are still coping with the idea that some people don't eat meat, though attitudes are now changing. Remember, if you're desperate, there are lots of calories in a vodka and orange.

Lembit Öpik is Estonia's first-ever Member of Parliament in the United Kingdom

USA. They are a sign of conspicuous consumption for rich foreigners and the local 'nouveaux riches'. As Estonia is relatively cheap for overseas visitors, there is rarely any need for notes above 100EEK. Credit cards are now widely used throughout the country and are a safe alternative to large amounts of cash. Passport numbers are sometimes requested when purchases are made with credit cards, so take a photocopy of the information page from the passport to avoid carrying around the passport itself.

Travellers' cheques can only be accepted at large branches of major banks and they will be refused elsewhere. Leave them at home! Cashpoints were first introduced to Estonia in 1996 and became so popular that by 1998 there were already three of them in Kärdla, the capital of Hiiumaa Island, which has a population of just 4,500.

HEALTH
with Dr Felicity Nicholson
No inoculations are required for Estonia as health standards are very high throughout the country. That said, travellers here as anywhere should be up to date with tetanus and diphtheria, which is now given as a combined vaccine that lasts for ten years. Hepatitis A vaccine is also recommended as standard. Travellers planning to visit more rural parts of Estonia from late spring to autumn should take ample supplies of insect repellent, and are advised to take precautions against tick-borne encephalitis. As the name suggests, this is spread by the bites of ticks that live in long grass and the branches of overhanging trees. Wearing hats, and long trousers tucked into boots, and applying tick repellents can all help. Likewise, checking for ticks after forays into grassy areas is sensible. Injections are available, and can be done within three to four weeks of travel.

Tap water in hotels is always safe to drink. Local hospitals offer a high standard of treatment for any emergencies. Most Western brands of medicine are available throughout the country.

SAFETY
Walking plays a major part of any tour in Estonia. Both in the towns and in the countryside many sites can only be reached and appreciated in this way. Whilst roads are usually well maintained, pavements rarely are, so be constantly on the lookout for pot-holes, ill-fitting manhole covers and loose paving stones or cobbles. In winter, falling or dripping icicles are a further hazard but the accompanying sunshine that usually gives rise to this provides ample compensation. Town streets are well lit at night, important in midwinter when there are only six to seven hours of daylight. Crime is less of a problem than in many other European countries and is very rare outside Tallinn.

Passports and unneeded valuables should be left in hotels; take the obvious precautions of not flaunting money and dressing modestly. Car theft is a problem at night so always use the guarded car park that most hotels have. Black market approaches are now rare as the Estonian kroon is a hard currency so anyone foolish enough to succumb to any offers on the street is likely to end up with worthless Belarussian roubles.

MEDIA AND COMMUNICATIONS
Local publications
Three local publications are crucial for any English-speaking visitor. *Tallinn in Your Pocket* appears every two months. It is a full, critical and often hilarious listing of hotels, restaurants, museums and shops. Its readers are assumed to be awake 24 hours a day. It is as comprehensive on nightlife as it is on breakfast cafés. Each issue has a supplement on another town in Estonia. Their website, www.inyourpocket.com, has extracts from the current issue and details of obtaining copies abroad. *The City Paper* covers Riga and Vilnius as well and combines a similar sharp critique in its listings with cerebral articles on

contemporary Baltic themes. Their website is www.balticsww.com. Each issue also has several articles on Baltic history. *The Baltic Times* is the weekly political paper, which is essential reading for all ex-pats in the area. It carries tourism pieces as well and is the best source of information on concerts and other performances. Its political articles often make for alarming reading for those not used to them as it gives extensive coverage to the many disputes within the fragile government coalitions that rule each of the Baltic states. Fortunately none of these quarrels have any relevance to tourism. All three publications are very reasonably priced and are available at most hotels, the tourist information centres and in bookshops. Tour operators abroad can often provide recent copies of them. *The Baltic Times*, *The City Paper* and *Tallinn In Your Pocket* are all available abroad on subscription.

Telephone and fax

Eesti Telfon has a monopoly on telephone services but it is not abused so charges for land lines are reasonable. Calls to mobile telephones, however, are very expensive. Public telephone boxes only use telephone cards which can be bought at most kiosks for 30, 50 and 100EEK. The 100EEK cards are better value as extra units are added free of charge. All telephone boxes have clear dialling instructions in English. Currently to phone abroad, dial 800 and then the country code. To call another town within the country, dial 82 and then the area code. Local calls rarely cost more than 1–2EEK and those to western Europe cost about 14EEK (£0.65/US$1) a minute with a slightly higher rate applicable to America and Australia. There are no phone boxes that take coins or credit cards. Cards are not needed for phoning the emergency services. Phone 01 for the fire brigade, 02 for the police and 03 for the ambulance service. As English may not be spoken, try to obtain local help for such calls.

Hotels, of course, charge more than the above rates, but their surcharges are usually reasonable and they do not charge for a minimum duration. Public fax bureaux are rare in Tallinn so faxes should be sent from hotels.

Telephone codes

The country code for Estonia is 372. Area codes for the major cities are:

Tallinn	6	Saaremaa	45
Haapsalu	47	Tartu	7
Narva	35	Viljandi	43
Pärnu	44		

Internet

Internet facilities are available free of charge in all public libraries, and in smaller towns this may be the only option. These libraries are usually open 09.00–17.00 on weekdays and on Saturday mornings. Larger hotels have business centres but they can often charge around 100EEK (£4/US$7) per half hour. Internet centres in central Tallinn charge around 60EEK

(£2.50/US$4.50) but elsewhere charges should be about half this. The cheapest internet centre in Tallinn is Matrix at Tartu 31, on the road to the bus station and the airport. It charges only 15EEK (£0.70/US$1.20) an hour and is open 24 hours a day. The clientele is largely teenagers playing computer games and looking at sites which their parents would probably try to ban at home.

BUSINESS

Since independence, Estonia has enjoyed a remarkably stable business environment. The currency has maintained its rate of 8EEK =1DM despite being freely convertible from its introduction in 1992. It is therefore now pegged to the euro at 15.65EEK = €1. A banking crisis in 1994 and the collapse of the Russian economy in autumn 1998 left their mark but the country suffered much less than Latvia and Lithuania when faced with similar difficulties. Estonia has no desire to work with its Baltic neighbours, particularly as its admission into the first wave of new EU entrants will in any case detach it from them. It sees itself as a Nordic country, modelled on Finland and Sweden. Trading relations with Britain have been particularly good, as they had been before the war, and tourists arriving in 1993 were surprised to see Mars bars, Scotch whisky and copies of the *Guardian* throughout the country, soon to be followed by books, cars and management consultants. The market of 1.5 million native consumers is of course a small one but it is enhanced by an equal number of tourists each year, many of whom consume luxury goods.

In the 1980s Estonia pioneered devolved management, in so far as this was possible in the Soviet era, so could adapt more easily to Western markets than many of the neighbouring republics. A policy of encouraging foreign investment introduced immediately after the re-establishment of independence has been firmly maintained since then and will certainly not be changed. The liberal visa policy, low rates of taxation and the harmonisation of the legal framework to meet EU requirements have all helped to attract foreign investors. Whilst some Estonians may regret the increasing shareholdings taken in their banks by Swedish ones, others will see this as the ultimate accolade and a sure sign of long-term security. Some will hope in due course to use Estonia as a springboard into Russia, seeing its role as similar to the one that Hong Kong used to play towards China.

Business negotiations in Estonia have never suffered from the time-wasting rituals encountered in many developing countries. Small talk is not encouraged, nor is lavish entertaining. Blunt speaking is the order of the day since time costs money in Estonia, just as much as it does abroad. If time is tight, meetings can easily take place in the evenings and at weekends. Partners of Estonian Air offer two- and three-night business packages to Tallinn, presumably on the basis that negotiations should not need to last longer.

The **Estonian Investment Agency** works actively abroad and is represented in most embassies. Its website is www.eia.ee.

SUGGESTED ITINERARIES
A long weekend in Tallinn
Day 1   Ideally this should be spent entirely in the Old Town. A walking route is suggested in the Tallinn section (see page 98)
Day 2   Aegna Island, Pirita Harbour, Maarjamëe Museum and Kadriorg Park
Day 3   Rocca al Mare in the morning; an indulgent afternoon in the Old Town cafés
Day 4   Full day excursion to Lahemaa National Park

One week by bus
Day 1   Tallinn Old Town
Day 2   Morning bus to Narva (about 3hrs). Afternoon in Narva to visit the castle
Day 3   Morning at seaside resort of Narva-Jöesuu. Afternoon bus to Tartu (about 3hrs)
Day 4   In Tartu to visit the university and the Estonian Folk Museum
Day 5   Morning bus to Viljandi (about 2hrs) to visit Castle Park. Afternoon bus to Pärnu (about 2hrs)
Day 6   Morning in Pärnu to visit the churches. Afternoon bus to Haapsalu (about 1hr) to visit the castle and Railway Museum
Day 7   Return to Tallinn (about 2hrs)

Two weeks by bus
Day 1   Tallinn Old Town
Day 2   Tallinn: Aegna Island, Pirita, Maarjamäe Museum, Kadriorg Park
Day 3   Morning bus to Palmse in Lahemaa National Park (about 2hrs). Afternoon at Palmse
Day 4   Lahemaa National Park
Day 5   Morning bus to Rakvere (about 2hrs). Afternoon in Rakvere
Day 6   Morning bus to Narva (about 3hrs). Afternoon in Narva
Day 7   In Narva and Narva-Jöesuu
Day 8   Morning bus to Tartu (about 3hrs). Afternoon in Tartu
Day 9   Whole day in Tartu
Day 10   Morning bus to Pärnu (about 3hrs)
Day 11   Morning bus to Kuressaare (about 3hrs including ferry crossing). Afternoon in Kuressaare
Day 12   Whole day by bus around Sõrve Peninsula with a stop at Sääre
Day 13   Morning bus to Haapsalu (about 3hrs including ferry crossing)
Day 14   Return to Tallinn

Two weeks by car
Day 1   Tallinn Old Town
Day 2   Around Tallinn: Paldiski, Rocca al Mare Open-Air Museum
Day 3   Lahemaa National Park with overnight at Palmse or Käsmu
Day 4   Morning in Lahemaa. Afternoon via Kohtla-Järve, Jöhvi and Pühtitsa Convent to Narva

Day 5   Narva and Narva-Jöesuu
Day 6   Via Iisaku, Lake Peipsi and Alatskivi to Tartu
Day 7   Tartu
Day 8   Põlva, Värska, Saatse, Obinitsa, Võru
Day 9   Valga, Tõrva, Viljandi, Pärnu
Day 10   Ferry to Saaremaa Island and drive to Kuressaare
Day 11   Tour around the Sõrve Peninsula
Day 12   Tour around main island to include Vilsandi Nature Reserve, Panga
         Cliffs, the Angla Windmills and Karja Church
Day 13   Ferry back to mainland and drive to Haapsalu
Day 14   Return to Tallinn

Part Two

The Country

LONDON GATWICK TO

Tallinn

* Nine flights every week
* Non stop
* Great fares
* No advance purchase
* No minimum stay

ESTONIAN AIR
www.estonian-air.com

For more information contact your travel
specialist or call us on 020 7333 0196.

Estonian Air international flights from Tallinn:
Amsterdam, Berlin, Brussels, Copenhagen,
Dublin, Frankfurt, Gothenburg, Hamburg, Kiev,
Moscow, Munich, Oslo, Paris, Stockholm, Vilnius.

Tallinn

HISTORY

Written records on Tallinn date only from the 12th century although it is clear that a small port existed well before then. In 1219 the Danes occupied Tallinn and much of what is now northern Estonia, on the pretext of spreading Christianity. The name Tallinn dates from this time and in Estonian actually means 'Danish city'. Although this name was chosen to suggest only temporary occupation, it has been maintained. The first German merchants settled in 1228 and they were to maintain their economic domination until 1939, even during the long periods of Swedish and Tsarist rule. Their elaborate coats of arms, displayed in the Dome and Niguliste churches, were a formal expression of this power. When, for instance, the Swedes surrendered to the Russians in 1710, the capitulation documents confirmed that German would remain the official language of commerce. Reval, the German name for Tallinn, is sometimes seen in English publications; it probably comes from Revala, the old Estonian name for the surrounding area. A more colourful explanation is that it comes from the two German words Reh and Fall, meaning the falling of the deer as they attempt to escape the Danish occupation.

Peter the Great visited Tallinn on 11 different occasions, so crucial was the city as an ice-free port to his empire. In 1711 he joined Christmas celebrations in Town Hall Square. He instigated the permanent expansion of Tallinn beyond the city walls by building Kadriorg Palace near the coast about two miles from the Old Town. The previous history of constant warfare at least in the vicinity of the town had led to all buildings being makeshift wooden houses which could easily be burnt as a preliminary defence to the city. Tallinn was then to enjoy 200 years of peace and increasing prosperity. Architecturally, though, the Old Town has always remained the centre of Tallinn and its main attraction. Gert Walter, a Baltic German who settled in East Germany and could therefore return to Tallinn during the Soviet period, describes the Old Town as having half a per cent of the surface area of Tallinn but giving it its entire magic.

The completion of the railway link with St Petersburg in 1870 turned Tallinn into a major city. The port was enlarged to handle the increasing volume of goods that could now be brought there and factories were established to take advantage of the larger markets. In the 20th century, most

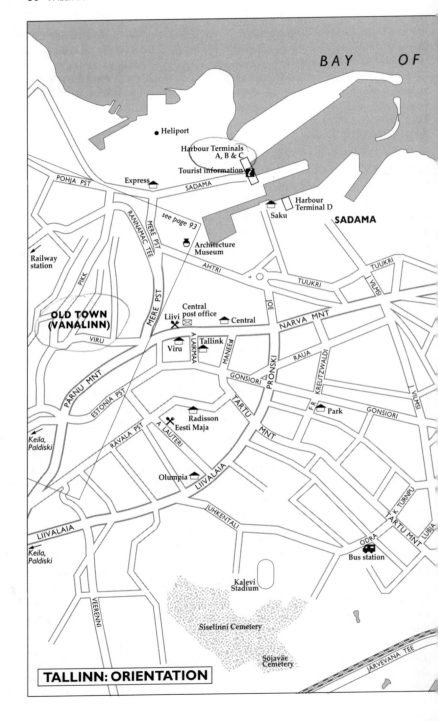

BAY OF

• Heliport

Harbour Terminals
A, B & C

Tourist information

Express

SADAMA

see page 93

Harbour
Terminal D

Saku

SADAMA

POHJA PST

RANNAMAC TEE

MERE PST

Railway
station

PIKK

Architecture
Museum

AHTRI

JOE

TUUKRI

TUUKRI

VILMSI

OLD TOWN
(VANALINN)

VIRU

MERE PST

Liivi

Central
post office

Central

NARVA MNT

Viru

A LAIKMAA

Tallink

MANEEZ

GONSIORI

PRONSKI

RAUA

KREUTZWALDI

VILMSI

PARNU MNT

ESTONIA PST

RAVALA PST

A LAUTERI

Radisson
Eesti Maja

TARTU

MNT

F R

Park

GONSIORI

Keila,
Paldiski

Olumpia

LIIVALAIA

JUHKENTALI

K TURNPU

TARTU MNT

LUBJA

LIIVALAIA

Keila,
Paldiski

VEERENNI

ODRA

Bus station

Kalevi
Stadium

JARVEVANA TEE

Siselinni Cemetery

Sõjaväe
Cemetery

TALLINN: ORIENTATION

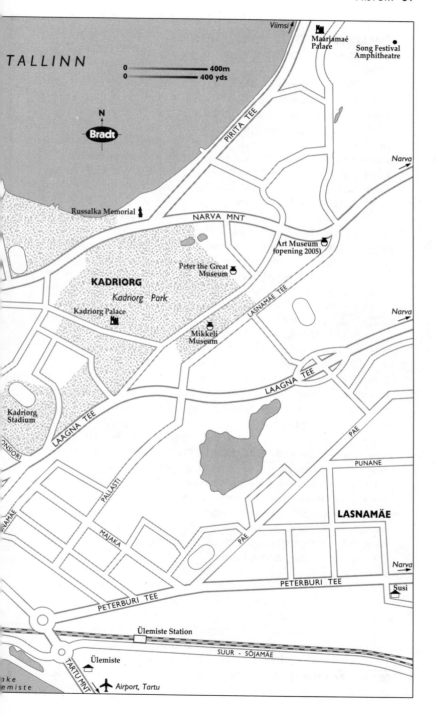

TALLINN

0 ——————— 400m
0 ——————— 400 yds

N
Bradt

Viimsi

Maarjamäe
Palace

Song Festival
Amphitheatre

Narva

Russalka Memorial

NARVA MNT

PIRITA TEE

Art Museum
(opening 2005)

Peter the Great
Museum

KADRIORG

Kadriorg Park

Kadriorg Palace

LASNAMÄE TEE

Narva

Mikkeli
Museum

LAAGNA TEE

Kadriorg
Stadium

LAAGNA TEE

PAE

PUNANE

LASNAMÄE

PALLASTI

MAJAKA

PAE

Narva

Susi

PETERBURI TEE

PETERBURI TEE

Ülemiste Station

SUUR - SÕJAMÄE

Ülemiste

TARTU MNT

Airport, Tartu

ake
emiste

TALLINN BEFORE WORLD WAR II

From 'Keepers of the Baltic Gates' by John Gibbons, written in autumn 1938

Tallinn fascinated me; it is like plenty of other cities with an old part on top of a hill and a new part down below. If that was all I had wanted, I need have gone no further from London than Lincoln. But it was the general atmosphere and the people which so struck me. Here was none of the wealthy prosperity of Stockholm nor the studied modernity of Helsinki. Instead I was seeing a melange that I had met nowhere else with a ferocious grasp at gaiety that was as far removed from the natural happiness of Latindom as from the unbending stolidity of Saxonhood and Scandinavia.

On top of the Tallinn hill, I was in a quarter that might almost have been an English cathedral close. The nobility used to live there, but now it houses government ministries whose gentlemen staff might almost have been English themselves, so perfectly do they speak our tongue. Up and down all Estonia there are plenty of similar gentlemen politely eager to show their hospitality to the stranger and to make a guest welcome to their land.

Coming downhill again, the streets were not the decorous promenades of cultured Finland. Here and there will be a chattering group of girls in what they think are the latest fashions of the Western world and then there could be a couple of old men in huge shabby coats that were probably first worn in Russian days now 20 years past. Everywhere there were students. In a land as new as prairie Canada one rather wonders how on earth they are going to find employment for all these anxious scholars.

By accident I found myself at what the guidebook calls the 'unimpressive Swedish Church of St Michael'. The architecture was indeed unimpressive – I only recall a lot of whitewash – but the congregation was the reverse. These people was so terribly and so whole-heartedly earnest. As the preacher droned on, even I of an alien creed could appreciate their attentiveness. There was no apparent oratory, no gestures, no ritual, nothing but the Word of God and they were following every word with an almost fierce eagerness. There is nothing indifferentist about Estonia.

events that would determine Estonia's future took place in Tallinn. Independence was declared there in 1918 and in 1991, German occupations were imposed there also in 1918 and again in 1941. The Soviets came in 1940 and then chased the Germans out in 1944. In the 20th century, the Russians and Germans between them occupied Tallinn seven times, and the country has been independent three times, although it has to be admitted that independence on the first occasion in 1918 lasted only for one day. Britain can claim considerable credit for ensuring that the next period of independence would last much longer – 20 years. Intervention by the Royal Navy during 1918–19 in the Gulf of Finland near Tallinn ensured that neither the Bolsheviks nor the Germans were able to conquer Estonia at that time.

The port always adapted to the political circumstances in which it found itself. During the first independence period from 1920 to 1940 it exported large quantities of timber and dairy products to Britain as the market to the new Soviet Union was lost. Passenger services linked it with all its Baltic neighbours. It would suffer a moribund 45 years from 1945 until 1990 with little international trade being allowed. The twice-weekly ferry service that operated for Finnish visitors from the 1960s rapidly increased to a boat an hour during the 1990s as the notorious 'vodka tourists' poured in, together with some other visitors who had broader interests. Whilst 2.5 million passengers a year come to Tallinn on this route, the port has to battle hard with Russian, Latvian and Lithuanian ports for the transit traffic in goods from Russia and Central Asia.

A DESCRIPTON OF TALLINN IN 1984

Kate Wharton

I spent last week in one of the saddest cities in the world, Tallinn in Estonia, famed for its medieval and 18th-century architecture. Extraordinarily, this tiny backwater of the Soviet Empire has been in the news recently as its people were warned by the voice of *Pravda*, Moscow's main daily newspaper at the time, that they were not Soviet enough. Suddenly the secrets of this benighted land began to emerge. So, last week, determined to find out about the real Estonia, I became the first Western journalist in the country for many, many months, and certainly the first since Estonia came back into the news.

At issue in Estonia is the enforced russification of their land and the disappearance of their language and all their customs. The blue, black and white flag of independent Estonia was banished in 1944. Today the Russian flag is everywhere. So is the huge figure of 40, accompanied by a hammer and sickle, to remind everyone that the yoke has been in place for 40 years and is intended to be there in excess of 40 x 40. Already more than half the population, 52%, is Russian rather than Estonian and by 1987, when the vast military harbour outside Tallinn is finished, the proportion will rise to 65%.

About 65,000 Estonians fled to the West in 1944. Thousands more were deported to remote parts of the Soviet Union and most of the present-day dissidents now rot in Russian labour camps. As Ernst Jaakson, Estonian Consul-General in New York, told me: 'There is hardly an Estonian family in existence that has not been separated from its loved ones or nearest relatives as a result of the Soviet occupation.'

Published in 'The Mail on Sunday', September 2 1984

Between 1945 and 1990 the city's population doubled in size to 500,000, about 30% of the total population of Estonia. Since then, Tallinn's population, like that of the whole country, has dropped considerably as women delay starting families and living on one's own becomes more popular. It is now around 380,000. The year 2002 was the first year since 1990 when more births than deaths were registered.

GETTING AROUND
Tallinn airport

The airport is only 3–4km from the town centre. It was originally built for the Olympics in 1980 and was then completely rebuilt in 1999 to cater for the increasing number of flights expected from abroad. The arrival of two flights at once used to cause great delays at immigration but, with Estonia's entry into the EU, passport stamping has stopped which greatly reduces queues for passport control. Departures are well streamlined so that check-in is only 30 minutes before take-off but this deadline is strictly enforced.

A local bus operates to Viru Square every 20 minutes. It stops en route at the bus station which is useful for those simply wanting to transit in Tallinn. The fare is 15EEK if paid to the driver. If tickets are bought individually at kiosks, they cost 10EEK, or a booklet of ten costs only 70EEK. Sadly these tickets are not sold by the kiosk at the airport so travellers arriving for the first time will have to pay the higher fare on the bus. The last bus is usually around 22.30, so too early for the evening flight from London or Copenhagen. Passengers arriving on these flights should pre-book a transfer through their travel agent as not many taxis serve the airport at that time. Taxis are plentiful earlier in the day and are metered. The fare into the town is likely to be about 100EEK or £4.50/US$8. Bus and taxi drivers are allowed to accept only local currency.

The exchange bureau airside has for years had terrible rates for buying local currency. Those landside are better, but more competitive rates are available in the town centre (see page 69). Kroon can now be obtained in many countries abroad, including Britain, so it is advisable to arrive with local currency if possible. There is no tourist office or hotel booking agency at the airport and as Tallinn hotels are fully booked at certain times of the year, reservations should always be made well beforehand. Flight arrival and departure information is available on www.tallinn-airport.ee.

Taxis

Tallinn taxis had an appalling press during the summer of 2004. Reporters posing as tourists tested out various companies and all were badly cheated. One of the companies tested had a 100% dishonesty rate. The main problem is the ease with which the meter can be switched from 35EEK to 100EEK and then be accelerated en route. Taxis which are ordered by phone are always cheaper and very rarely cheat. Ask the hotel or a local to advise. Most tourists in fact never need to use a taxi as so much is within walking distance of the main hotels.

Local buses/trams and trolleybuses

Many tourists to Tallinn never take either a bus or a taxi during their stay as the Old Town is very close to most of the hotels and the steep narrow roads conveniently restrict traffic to pedestrians only anyway. Such visitors, however, miss everything that is cheaply and easily accessible by bus outside the Old Town. There are competing bus companies so exact routes and numbers change from time to time but services are frequent and the public transport map *Tallinn Ühistranspordi kaart,* published by Regio, is reprinted sufficiently often to be up to date. Some stops have maps but not all do and the names of the stops listed in the timetables are unlikely to mean much to visitors. The tram and trolleybus routes are of course fixed. In spring 2004 the flat fare was 10EEK for individual tickets bought from kiosks or 15EEK for tickets bought on the bus. A book of ten tickets bought at kiosks cost 70EEK, so buying one of these halves the cost of travel. Passes are available for stays of four days or longer. (See also *Tallinn Card,* page 86.) Good bus services operate to Pirita and Rocca al Mare and also to the cheaper suburban hotels such as the Dzingel and Susi. Tram enthusiasts will be pleased at the number of places relevant to tourists which their routes pass. For details of tram routes, see page 271.

Leaving Tallinn

The long-distance bus station (*Autobussijaam*) is on Lastekodu, off the Tartu Road which leads to the airport. The enquiry number is 680 0900 but do not expect English to be spoken. There are no printed timetables but all services are listed on a large departure board showing arrival times and also buses for the return journey. Write down the destination, date and time to present at the booking office since few staff speak English. As a bus or taxi takes only a few minutes from the town centre, it is advisable to go a day ahead to book a specific bus and to check timings. Whilst in the winter and midweek it may often be easy to catch a bus without pre-booking, around the holiday periods and on less frequent services it is essential. Remember to book on an express for the longer journeys. Prices are very cheap – £6/US$11 to Saaremaa and Hiiumaa islands (including the ferry), Narva or Voru, or £4/US$7 to the nearer towns of Pärnu or Tartu. There is now competition on the major routes so travellers who can be flexible in their travel times may often be able to save on what are already very low fares by western European or American standards. A ticket has to be bought for each sector travelled, so a stop between Tallinn and Narva at Lahemaa National Park will require two tickets, not one. Stops of ten minutes are made at least every two hours, which allows time for a cigarette, use of the toilets and purchase of refreshments. Smoking is not allowed on buses.

On most routes, the first bus leaves around 06.00 and the last one around 21.00. To **Tartu**, they operate every half-hour, and the journey takes two hours. To **Narva** (three hours) the service is hourly. Buses go every two hours to **Pärnu** and **Viljandi** and the journey time in both cases is around two hours. Buses to **Kuressaare**, the capital of Saaremaa, operate six times a day and a space on the ferry is always guaranteed. Every town in Estonia, plus many villages such as those in Lahemaa National Park, has a bus service from Tallinn, so it is not usually necessary to change en route.

TOURIST INFORMATION

The two 'bibles' for any English-speaking visitor are *The City Paper* and *Tallinn In Your Pocket,* both of which are published six times a year. *The City Paper* covers Riga and Vilnius as well. It mixes cerebral but amusing articles on the local political scene with reminiscences on earlier times and detailed current listings. *Tallinn In Your Pocket* has extremely detailed listings on everything in Tallinn and each edition has a supplement on another Estonian town. It is particularly helpful for opening hours and current transport information. Both publications should be available at hotel kiosks and at the airport on arrival. Their irreverence is a welcome contrast to other more turgidly written local guidebooks. Serious Baltic tour operators abroad stock these publications and both have websites (see page 268). The *Baltic Times* is a weekly political newspaper covering the three countries. The fierce and bitter parliamentary debates it summarises contrast with the seeming stability of the world outside.

Tallinn Tourist Board has a shopfront office on the corner of Kullassepa and Niguliste which sells a good range of books, maps and cards. They always have up-to-date editions of *Tallinn In Your Pocket* and *The City Paper*. There is also a large reference folder with timetables for ferries to Finland, buses out of Tallinn and local railways. There is a similar office in the harbour. This office, like all other tourist offices around Estonia, has a website (see page 268). Visiting these sites before departure will save a lot of time on arrival.

The Tallinn Card

Vigorously promoted by the tourist board and in many hotels, the Tallinn Card will suit visitors keen to visit many museums and to travel to the outlying attractions. The cost includes a free sightseeing tour, free use of public transport and free admission to all museums. For those still active in the evenings it also includes free admission to the Hollywood Nightclub. However, it has to be said that for those taking a more leisurely approach to their stay and who are based in the town centre, it may well be cheaper to pay as you go. No reductions in the cost are made on Mondays or Tuesdays when many museums are closed. Full details of what is included can be seen on www.tallinn.ee/tallinncard. From April 2004 the cost is 90EEK for 6 hours, 250EEK for 24 hours, 300EEK for 48 hours and 350EEK for 72 hours.

WHERE TO STAY

Tallinn now has about 60 hotels but they are often fully booked at weekends, during trade fairs and in the peak summer season. Pre-booking is therefore always advisable. Specialist travel agents abroad often have access to lower prices than those quoted by the hotels directly, and they may also have allocations at several hotels specifically reserved for them. February 2001 saw the opening of the Radisson and during 2002 and 2003 several smaller hotels opened in the Old Town and just outside it. The year 2004 saw the opening of the 200-room Tallink

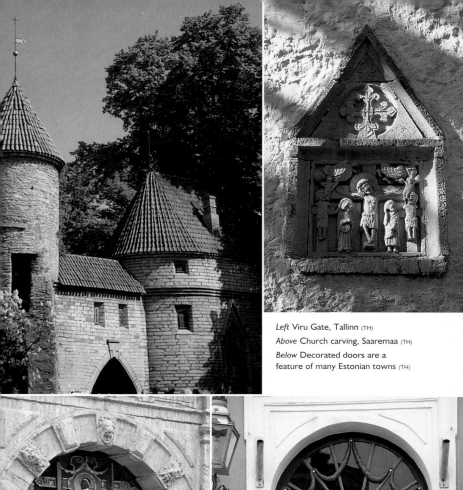

Left Viru Gate, Tallinn (TH)

Above Church carving, Saaremaa (TH)

Below Decorated doors are a feature of many Estonian towns (TH)

Above Palmse Manor,
Lahemaa National Park (TH)

Right Old fishermen's huts,
Lahemaa National Park (TH)

Below Coastal landscape,
Lahemaa National Park (TH)

Hotel opposite the Viru Hotel, L'Ermitage next to the National Library and the Ülemiste beside the airport. Visitors wanting to 'outfinn the Finns' will be able to stay at the port at the Saku Hotel, named after Estonia's most famous brew. A glass will be offered at check-in and crates will be available for sale to take onto the nearby boats. It cannot be long before many major chains not yet represented in Tallinn (such as Hilton and Holiday Inn) establish themselves here.

The recommendations that follow are obviously rather arbitrary and omission of a hotel should in general be taken as resulting from lack of space rather than necessarily as a criticism. An ethical tour operator will be able to warn visitors away from the fortunately few hotels that have degenerated into brothels, which sadly cannot be listed as such here. It can be assumed in all cases that the rooms in the hotels mentioned below have private facilities, that the hotel accepts credit cards, and that it has a restaurant and bar. Many hotels have saunas which guests can use free of charge. Baths are rare in Estonian hotels, even in four-star establishments, so should be specifically requested.

Prices

In luxury hotels expect to pay around £125/US$190 a night, in first class £70/US$120 and in tourist class £35–60/US$60–100. The more expensive hotels sometimes reduce prices at weekends and in July, the local holiday season, whereas the cheaper hotels usually increase them then. Prices always include buffet breakfast.

Rock-bottom accommodation is hard to find in Tallinn, as is bed and breakfast. There is neither the wherewithal nor the will to make Tallinn backpacker friendly. Most Estonian families do not have a dining-room, let alone a spare bedroom, so cannot rent out rooms. Rundown buildings which elsewhere might be converted to hostels are in Tallinn quickly transformed into offices or exclusive private houses. The increasing number of small hotels that are opening is again unlikely to stimulate demand for inferior accommodation at a not much lower price. The *Tallinn In Your Pocket* website (www.inyourpocket.com) always has an up-to-date list of hostels and agencies for arranging long-stays in private houses.

Luxury

Parkconsul Schlössle Pühavaimu 13/15; tel: 699 7700; fax: 699 7777; email: schlossle@consul-hotels.com; www.consul-hotels.com. For several years, this hotel was in a class on its own but competition finally came in 2003 with the opening of the Three Sisters (see below). A townhouse owned by many successful Baltic Germans over the years, the Parkconsul Schlössle was converted into Tallinn's first truly luxurious hotel and any senior government minister from abroad has always stayed here. With just 27 rooms, it still maintains the air of a gracious private residence. There is a small conference centre, but it seems incongruous. The hotel is a setting for constant but unostentatious indulgence, for cigars rather than cigarettes, for champagne rather than wine. The restaurant, like all the best ones in Tallinn, is in a cellar and has an extensive menu. For those able briefly to abandon all this indulgence, the hotel is within walking distance of all the attractions in the Old Town. Double 3,350EEK.

Three Sisters Pikk 71; tel: 630 6300; fax: 630 6301; email: info@threesistershotel.com; www.threesistershotel.com. Perhaps because it is so luxurious, the hotel does not bother with an Estonian name as no Estonian could afford it. It is clearly aiming to rival the Parkconsul and is to some extent modelled on it. Both buildings have a history of over five hundred years and both can claim famous rather than notorious owners. Here a library is the dominating public room and a member of staff escorts guests into the lift for the one-floor journey down to the restaurant. Having 23 rooms, one even with a piano, the atmosphere of a 19th-century townhouse can still be maintained. Computers and plenty of other 21st-century paraphernalia are available if needed, but it seems a pity to let modernity intrude. Estonians who wish to impress their friends on the cheap come for lunch here and linger over a £5/US$8 club sandwich. Foreigners come in the evening for pumpkin soup, pork with chanterelle mushrooms and a particular rarity in Estonia, homemade ice-cream. Double 5,550EEK.

First class

Barons Suur-Karja 7; tel: 699 9700; fax: 699 9710; email: barons@baronshotel.ee; www.baronshotel.ee. For every bank that closes in Tallinn, a new hotel opens, but in this case it is on the same site. Thirteen different banks in fact occupied the building during the 20th century. Some doors as a result do seem excessively secure. Visitors will find it hard to believe that Barons opened in 2003 rather than 1903, since the panelling, the minute lift, the sombre colour schemes and the illustrations of Tallinn are all from the earlier date. So is the name of the road: 'karja' means 'to herd', as cattle used to be led to pasture along it. Whenever renovation is carried out, more and more papers from the early 20th century come to light. The view from many rooms and from the restaurant over the Old Town will again keep the 21st century away. For once it is sensible to go upstairs to eat in Tallinn, rather than downstairs. Do however avoid Friday and Saturday nights here, when the hotel is an oasis of quiet against a backdrop of raucous behaviour in the surrounding bars. No rooms have baths but the suites have Jacuzzis. Double 2,500EEK.

Domina City Vana-Posti 11–13; tel: 681 3900; fax: 681 3901; email: city@domina.ee; www.dominahotels.com. As one of the few hotels to open in 2002, the Domina, with its Old Town location, its size and its standards, was bound to succeed. It is a pity that only six rooms have baths as well as showers, but the computers built into the television sets will be more than adequate compensation for most visitors, and the British will like the choice of Sky as well as BBC television. The Italian management is reflected in the ample use of marble in the reception area and with the range of wildly abstract art in the restaurant. What is distinctly not Italian is the fact that two whole floors are non-smoking. Like all good restaurants in Tallinn, the one here is built into a brick-lined cellar. Lovers of Soviet memorabilia should note the red star on the roof. Double 2,400EEK.

Meriton Grand Toompuiestee 27; tel: 667 7000; fax: 667 7001; email: hotel@grandhotel.ee; www.grandhotel.ee. Travellers who came to Tallinn in the early 1990s will remember the grim Hotel Tallinn that used to besmirch this site. Luckily all traces of it were removed before this new hotel opened in 1999. Being immediately below the Old Town and having 165 rooms, it appeals both to business travellers and to tourist groups. It is tempting to spend much of a stay in this hotel in the lift, since it offers one of the best views of Toompea Hill at the top of the Old Town. British tourists are drawn by the high proportion of rooms with baths. Double 3,000EEK.

Olümpia Liivalaia 33; tel: 631 5333; fax: 631 5325; email: olympia@revalhotels.com; www.revalhotels.com. Built originally for the Olympic Games in 1980, this hotel is now the firm favourite of foreign business visitors to Tallinn. With the range of restaurants and conference facilities it offers, some never leave the hotel during their stay in Tallinn. They are often joined by the local ex-pat community which has a particular affinity for the '60s' music played in the Bonnie and Clyde nightclub. At weekends and during the summer, rates drop to attract tourists paying their own way. All 400 rooms are now at least of four-star standard and the reception staff work very quickly during the arrival and departure 'rush hours'. The restaurant on the top floor offers excellent views of the Old Town and many rooms do so as well. The newspaper shop always stocks up-to-date British newspapers, a rarity in Tallinn. Tourists who want to arrive or leave in greater style than a local taxi is able to provide can hire the hotel's 9m-long Lincoln which costs about £50/US$80 an hour. Double 2,300EEK.

Reval Park Kreutzwaldi 23; tel: 630 5305; fax: 630 5315; email: sales@revalhotels.com; www.revalhotels.com. Formerly the dreaded Kungla Hotel which could barely claim two-star status, the site transformed itself within a few weeks during the summer of 1997 and has never looked back. It has pioneered rooms for non-smokers, for the disabled and for those with allergies as well as round-the-clock gambling, fortunately in a casino with a separate entrance. Rooms are larger here than in most other hotels and the restaurant has very low prices for excellent food. Walking to the Old Town is just about possible and indeed essential as the surroundings are very bleak. The guarded car park is free of charge to hotel guests. Double 2,000EEK.

St Petersbourg Rataskaevu 7; tel: 628 6500; fax: 628 6565; email: stpetersbourg@consul-hotels.com; www.consul-hotels.com. The St Petersbourg is under the same management as the deluxe Schlössle Hotel and suits those who want a comfortable Old Town address and who do not miss luxury. Its location near to many famous clubs and restaurants appeals to visitors who can dispense with sleep for much of the night. It is one of the very few hotels in Tallinn to offer a baby-sitting service. Double 2,500EEK.

Santa Barbara Roosikrantsi 2a; tel: 640 7600; fax: 631 3992; email: st_barbara.res@scandic-hotels.ee; www.scandic-hotels.com. The austere limestone façade from the turn of the century hides a very professional operation which is run by the Scandic group who also operate the nearby Palace Hotel. The cellar restaurant is completely German, with no intrusion from Estonia or anywhere else. It has 53 rooms so staff get to know all the guests, many of whom are now regulars, which makes the hotel difficult to book for first-time visitors. Double 1,600EEK.

Scandic Palace Vabaduse Väljak; tel: 640 7300; fax: 640 7299; email: palace@scandic-hotels.com; www.scandic-hotels.com. The hotel brochure claims it has offered 'excellent service since 1937' and this is probably true. Although many other hotels now match its facilities, Estonians are very loyal to it as the hotel was one of the few links from the first independence period that remained throughout the Soviet era. Embassies were briefly set up in the hotel in 1991 before foreign legations could reclaim their pre-war buildings. It is now equally conveniently situated for tourists interested in the Old Town and business visitors needing the government ministries. In 1997 President Meri opened the new Presidential Suite which will doubtless remain one of the most expensive in Tallinn at £250/US$400 per night, but the remaining 86 rooms are more modestly priced. The hotel is run by the Scandic Hotel Group that also operates the Santa Barbara in Tallinn and the Ranna in Pärnu. Double 2,600EEK.

Tallink Laikmaa 5; tel: 630 0800; fax: 630 0810; email: hotel@tallink.ee; www.tallink.ee. This hotel, with 349 rooms, opened in May 2004. All rooms have air conditioning and showers, with baths being limited to the deluxe rooms. Aiming to appeal to both business and leisure traffic, it does not vary its prices at the weekend. The décor is rather bland, both in the rooms and particularly in the corridors, but with its location so close to the Viru Square shopping centre, the port and the old town, few guests will spend much time in the hotel. Double 2,000EEK.

Viru Viru Väljak 4; tel: 630 1390; fax: 630 1303; email: reservation@viru.ee; www.viru.ee. Being the centre of the tourism trade for much of the Soviet era, the enormous Viru initially found it hard to redefine its role in the face of competition and ever-rising standards. By 2000 it had finally undergone a complete renovation and can now serve both business clients and fastidious tourists. It has become very biased towards Finnish clients, some of whom can provide unwanted liveliness late on Friday and Saturday evenings. Its location is excellent for the Old Town and for local shops. Tourists determined to have a bath rather than a shower are more likely to succeed here. Although the hotel already had over 400 rooms, it opened an extension with a further 100 rooms in spring 2004. Double 2,500EEK.

Tourist class

Central Narva mnt 7; tel: 633 9800; fax: 633 9900; email: central@revalhotels.com; www.revalhotels.com. This hotel became an immediate favourite of tour operators from abroad when it opened in 1995 as it had no Soviet past to eliminate. Staff were immediately aware of the demands and eccentricities of Western tourists, who have been catered for in the café/restaurant ever since. The hotel offers disabled access and one room in the new wing is adapted for use by disabled guests. It is within easy walking distance of the Old Town and the main post office. Having opened in what was then a rundown part of town, the surrounding area is becoming increasingly attractive, with more shops and restaurants opening every year. Double 1,500EEK.

Dzingel Männiku 89; tel: 610 5201; fax: 610 5245; email: hotell@dzingel.ee; www.dzingel.ee. Situated in Nõmme, Tallinn's most exclusive suburb, the Dzingel is in fact one of the town's simplest and largest hotels. Regular long-stay visitors find its facilities perfectly adequate in view of the low prices charged and many tourists are happy both in winter and in summer with its quiet location beside a pine forest. Modernisation in 2002 made a great difference. The bus journey north into the town centre takes about 20 minutes. It is one of the few hotels where the staff happily and openly speak Russian although they can manage basic English. The restaurant is dull and surprisingly expensive but there is a late-night supermarket in the same block which can provide the ingredients for a varied picnic. Double 700EEK.

L'Ermitage Toompuiestee 19; tel: 699 6400; fax: 699 6401; email: info@nordichotels.ee; www.nordichotels.ee. Opened in summer 2004, L'Ermitage is one of the closest hotels to the Old Town to offer free car parking to its guests. Each floor has a separate colour scheme and the fourth floor is entirely furnished in wood so is allergy-free. There are 80 twin rooms and, on the 6th floor, 11 singles which all have good views. TV sets are small but do receive the BBC. Double 1,700EEK

Imperial Nunne 14; tel: 627 4800; fax: 627 4801; email: info@imperial.ee; www.imperial.ee. Like the Konventa Seta in Riga and the Rūdninkų in Vilnius, this hotel is built into the town wall, which is therefore being preserved as part of it. Although on one of the few real roads in the Old Town, the location is quiet, except in the restaurant/bar where the same tape of Irish music is played loudly 24 hours a day. Rooms vary greatly in size and protruding beams sometimes add more of the medieval ambience than some guests would wish. Double 2,200EEK.

Meriton Old Town Lai 49; tel: 614 1300; fax: 614 1311; email: hotel@grandhotel.ee. This 40-room hotel opened in March 2004 and is under the same management as the Meriton Grand, but has deliberately been pitched at a very different clientele. Those who normally shun two- or three-star hotels may well accept such a standard here, given the view that most rooms have either over the Old Town, of St Olav's Church, or towards the harbour. There is also the added appeal of the hotel being built into the city wall. Being on the edge of the Old Town, the place is quiet yet with a reasonably central location, within walking distance of many museums and shops. It is worth paying the slightly higher costs for the rooms on the fourth floor, with their larger size, their baths rather than showers and above all for the views. The basement rooms make up for the total lack of a view with the skilfully implanted use of the old city wall. Double 1,000EEK.

Mihkli Endla 23; tel: 666 4800; fax: 666 4888; email: mihkli@anet.ee; www.mihkli.ee. The location on one of the main roads leading from the town centre is certainly drab and the hotel itself used to be as well. From around 1998, however, serious attempts were made to improve the décor and the staff and these have been largely successful. It is within walking distance of the Old Town and on the doorstep of the National Library. Long-stay visitors are now here and locals use the restaurant, both of which are always a good sign. The repeat business that the hotel enjoys is also evidence of a complete turn-around. The live music at the weekends in the restaurant is of a consistently high standard and is well soundproofed from the rest of the hotel. Double 900EEK.

Old Town Maestro Suur-Karja 10; tel: 626 2000; fax: 631 3333; email: maestro@maestrohotel.ee; www.maestrohotel.ee. Having opened in 2001, this small hotel now has its regulars who want straightforward furnishings, peace and quiet and yet an Old Town location. Rooms are much bigger than might be expected from a converted townhouse but the lift is much smaller – it can take only one person with a case at a time. The road is traffic-free but that does mean wheeling cases along the cobbles on arrival and departure. The reception area doubles up as a bar, which adds to the family atmosphere. The sauna and the business centre are, surprisingly, side by side on the top floor. Photographers should bring their cameras for the unusual views over the town from the staircase and from the sauna. Double 1,800EEK.

Pirita Convent Guesthouse Merivälija 18; tel: 605 5000; fax: 605 5010; email: pirita@osss.ee; www.piritaklooster.ee. For anyone determined to have quiet at night, this is undoubtedly the place to go for. The nuns stay up for late-comers so ideal guests are those who have dinner here and then go to their rooms. The yachting harbour of Pirita is 3km northeast of the town and the ruined convent with this new guesthouse is set well back from the main road. Prices, too, are provincial rather than Tallinn. Tourists with a car will be happy with the space here and others will be pleased that after 500 years a religious order is finally active on the site again. Double 1,000EEK.

Sakurock Sadama 25c; tel: 680 6600; fax: 680 6601; email: sales@sakurockhotel.ee; www.sakurockhotel.ee. No-one who stays at this hotel, opened in June 2004 right beside the docks, will forget the experience. Being named after Estonia's best-known beer, it is perhaps not surprising that two free glasses of the stuff are offered to every guest and that the sign asking the staff to delay cleaning the room does not say 'Please do not disturb' but simply 'Piss off'. The lamp stands are made from beer cans, as is the montage that supports the bar. The room phones are only house phones; if you are too old to have a mobile for your other calls, then stay away. About half of each door is taken up with a painted room number for the benefit of those who might return with somewhat restricted vision. There are 113 rooms but only 4 are doubles; sharing a bed is not what you come to a Saku Hotel for, even though the 6 rooms without a window might suggest the opposite. An enormous array of pizzas is offered day and night to help absorb the beer and of course the beer is only sold wholesale. It would be silly to return to Finland with only a sensible quantity. Don't tell your mother if you are coming here and probably best not to tell your girlfriend either. Double 1,900EEK.

Skane Kopli 2c; tel: 667 8300; fax: 667 8301; email: skane@nordichotels.ee; www.nordichotels.ee. Being just over the railway and the tramlines from the Old Town, this hotel is literally on the wrong side of the tracks. Yet gentrification cannot be far away and in the meantime guests can enjoy prices that are half of those charged by hotels just 500m away. No rooms have baths, but all have BBC television. Try to get a room on the third floor rather than on the second since when the hotel opened in summer 2003 only the former had soundproofing. Double 800EEK.

Susi Peterburi 48; tel: 630 3300; fax: 630 3400; email: susi@susi.ee; www.susi.ee. An estate agent would probably describe the location as 'unprepossessing' since it is surrounded by factories and a petrol station and is on the wide St Petersburg motorway. It is literally the high point of Tallinn at 55m above sea level. On May 14 1343, the St George's Night rebellion took place here. It had started further north on April 23 and this was the nearest point to Tallinn that Estonian forces would reach. Over 10,000 were killed in a desperate attempt to overthrow the Teutonic Knights. A plaque in the hotel lobby commemorates the battle, as does the park on the other side of the road where there are several further monuments. The hotel is more comfortable and more modern than any of the other tourist-class hotels outside the centre and is easily accessible by tram. The pictures displayed on its staircase put many of Tallinn's museums to shame. There are oils, lithographs and watercolours showing contemporary and historical Tallinn; other pictures are of country scenes. They are well lit and sensibly framed and of course can be seen 24 hours a day. Should the lift break down, this gallery is more than adequate compensation. The hotel suits many groups as parking is easy, as are access to the airport and the Tartu road. Double 1,000EEK.

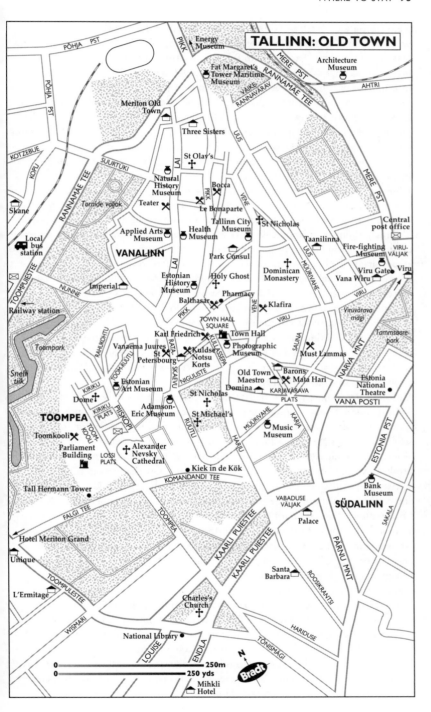

TALLINN: OLD TOWN

Taanilinna Uus 6; tel: 640 6700; fax: 646 4306; email: info@taanilinna.ee; www.taanilinna.ee. Perhaps they were daring, perhaps they were foolish, but in June 2002 Tallinn saw its first hotel with Russian-speaking reception staff and with brochures in English and Russian. The spelling 'Hotell' was the only concession made to Estonia at the time, although the website now has an Estonian section. Visitors who do not care about this will like the prices, the location in one of the few quiet streets in the Old Town and the use of wood rather than of stone. The terrace sadly looks out on to the back of a supermarket and a dreary block of flats but in future years this view may well change. The wine cellar is an unexpected bonus in a hotel of this size and category and is most welcome given the lack of other watering holes in the immediate vicinity. Double 1,500EEK.

Ülemiste Lennijamaa tee 2; tel: 603 2600; fax: 603 2601; email: sales@ylemistehotel.ee; www.ylemistehotel.ee. This new hotel beside the airport opened in July 2004 and was an instant saviour for passengers who rashly arrived in Tallinn without reservations. With so many late-evening arrivals and early-morning departures, it will be a convenient location for many people. The regular airport bus stops outside the hotel and takes about 10–15 minutes from there into the town centre. As the hotel has 132 rooms, it can cater for large groups and has the parking space for both coaches and private cars. Space is the theme, too, in the entrance, the lobby and in the rooms. It is worth paying extra for top-floor rooms with a view over the lake. Tourists from the EU eager to take advantage of Estonia's shopping opportunities will find the location next to a major shopping centre very convenient. Prices charged in Rimi for alcohol, tobacco and chocolate and in Jysk for linen, handiwork and kitchen tools are much lower than those charged in the town centre. Double 1,200EEK.

Unique Paldiski mnt 3; tel: 660 0700; fax: 661 6176; email: info@uniquestay.com; www.uniquestay.com. Tallinn hotels have tended to copy each other once a successful formula has been found. The larger ones inevitably copy models from abroad and the smaller ones try to recreate a 1930s' ambience even though modern technology is around if guests need it. When the Unique opened in spring 2003, it clearly wanted to break away from anything that had ever been tried before. Each room has its own flat-screen computer which can be used free of charge around the clock. It also has tea and coffee. The lighting in the corridors comes from the floor rather than the ceiling. Orange rather than green or brown is the predominant colour. Originally restricted to 17 rooms, the hotel added another 50 in April 2004. Several of these, the Zen rooms, are as original as their predecessors, with whirlpool baths adjustable lighting, and gravity-free chairs. This will also be the first hotel in Tallinn with an Estonian restaurant! The chain plans to expand both within Tallinn and to the neighbouring Baltic states. Double EEK1,400.

Vana Wiru Viru 11; tel: 669 1500; fax: 669 1501; email: hotel@vanawiru.ee; www.vanawiru.ee. Viru St is always full of tourists but most will not know of the existence of this hotel as its entrance is at the back. It was one of the very few hotels to open in Tallinn during 2002. Its vast marble lobby suggests luxury but in fact the 80 rooms are of a standard size and mostly with showers rather than baths. Few have good views but with a location beside the city wall, one can forgive anything. Groups will like the convenient coach park right beside the entrance. Double 1,700EEK.

WHERE TO EAT

There is now such a choice of restaurants in Tallinn that it is invidious to attempt a shortlist. Every major nation is represented and more unusual ones include Argentina, Georgia, Lithuania and Scotland. Hawaiian and Thai food appeared for the first time in 2000, Czech and Arabic food followed in 2002 and by 2003 Russian food had also staged a comeback, having been completely rejected in the years immediately following independence. All restaurants and bars have to provide a non-smoking section. In April 2004 there was serious discussion about following the Irish and banning smoking altogether.

Detailed descriptions of restaurants appear in *The City Paper*, shorter ones in *Tallinn In Your Pocket*. A dark entrance, down poorly maintained stairs in a side street, is usually a clear indication that good food and value lies ahead. Bright lights at street level should be avoided. Exploration need no longer be limited to the Old Town; competition there is driving many new entrants to open up in the suburbs. At the time of writing, nobody has opened a revivalist Soviet restaurant, though the success of such ventures in Riga and in former East Berlin must in due course tempt some embittered members of the Russian-speaking community in Tallinn.

Most of the following restaurants have been open for several years and are popular with tourists, ex-pats and local residents. I have, however, deliberately tried to include some that are not well known abroad and which cannot afford to advertise. Apologies in advance to the many other excellent restaurants that, with more space, would also have been included. Websites are listed so that menu planning can begin abroad and not just at the table. Restaurants are on the whole very good at keeping these up to date, and for those in a rush it is possible to pre-book not only a table but also the meal. Eating in hotels is popular in Tallinn and some of their restaurants are covered in the hotel descriptions in the previous chapter.

Budget

Prices listed below give an indication of costs for three courses without wine. (In November 2004, €1 = 15.65EEK, £1 = 23.85EEK, and US$1 = 13.00EEK.) The cost of wine varies enormously between restaurants, and is often as high as in Britain or the USA. Sticking to beer saves a lot of money – and it is, after all, an Estonian national drink. A small beer is 0.3 litres and large one is 0.5 litres. On Old Town Square and in the immediate vicinity, reckon to pay about 35EEK for a small beer and 45EEK for a large one. Elsewhere 20EEK and 30EEK are the more normal charges. Excluding drink, expect to pay about 90EEK for a two-course lunch and 250EEK for a three-course dinner.

Restaurants

Balthasar Raekoja Plats 11; tel: 627 6400; www.restaurant.ee. Garlic dominates every course here, even the ice-cream, but above all in the salads. Whilst other dishes do appear on the menu, they tend to be as appetising as a vegetarian option in a steakhouse. Opening in early 2000, the restaurant took over the top floor of the former pharmacy (see page 107) and has kept as much of the original wooden furnishings as was practical. With the restaurant's views over the Town Hall Square, it is tempting to linger here but it also offers a quiet respite over lunch between morning and afternoon sightseeing tours. The range of short drinks at the bar can be equally tempting at other times of day. 350EEK.

Bocca Olevimägi 9; tel: 641 2610; www.bocca.ee. A passer-by on the pavement here who happened to notice the plain glass windows with the two canvas panels behind them would not believe that during 2003 Bocca got more publicity abroad than all other Tallinn restaurants put together. Only the cars parked outside suggest considerable opulence inside. Critics liked the modern minimalist layout against the medieval backdrop of very solid limestone. They liked the changing lighting schemes – and the fact that plenty of modest pasta dishes were available if octopus and veal seemed unnecessarily extravagant. 400EEK.

Le Bonaparte Pikk 45; tel: 646 4444. The formal restaurant at the back and the easy-going café at the front are both French through and through. The décor is very domestic and totally unpretentious. The care and flair all go into the food, which is still too rare in Tallinn, whether it is a simple cake in the café or an elaborate paté at the start of a serious meal. Other unusual touches are the individual towels in the toilets and coat-warmers for visitors in winter. Prices in both the restaurant and the café are fortunately very Estonian. 350EEK.

Controvento Katariina käik; tel: 644 0470; www.controvento.ee. Uniquely in Tallinn, this restaurant could maintain a review written when it first opened in 1992. It has retained the same menu, the same décor and probably many of the same clients, who want no-nonsense home cooking in an Italian bistro and no attempts to emulate temporary culinary fads. Prices have had to increase somewhat but they remain modest in comparison with the competition in the Old Town. 250EEK.

Eeslitall (The Donkey's Stable) Dunkir 4; tel: 631 3755; www.eeslitall.ee. In the early days after independence, this restaurant was an immediate indication of changing times. Whilst its easy-going service, French sauces, enormous menus and wine lists may now seem normal for Tallinn, it then set a trend which other restaurants took several years to emulate. Young and old both dine happily here (an unusual combination in Tallinn), although only the young would consider staying in the spartan hostel of the same name upstairs. The whole building closed for renovation in late 2003. 150EEK.

Eesti Maja Lauteri 1; tel: 645 5252; www.eestimaja.ee. Do not expect quick service here or even staff with much English, but instead be ready for enormous portions and rich food at each course. It will be hard to spend more than £6/US$10 a head and many eat their fill for much less. The vegetable soup makes a good meal in itself at lunchtime. The building also houses *Global Estonian*, an English-language bi-annual magazine well worth buying for the tough interviews they give to local politicians willing to meet them. 150EEK.

Karl Friedrich Raekoja Plats 5; tel: 627 2413; www.restaurant.ee. The grand location on Town Hall Square might suggest ostentation and prices to match but fortunately this has not happened. Each floor caters for a different age-group but it is the top floor that is recommended; the long walk up and down is well worthwhile. Oldies should book well in advance for a table overlooking the square and enjoy a lingering lunch or dinner. Its fish salads are to be recommended and it has its own beer, called Karl Friedrich. 350EEK.

Klafira Vene 4; tel: 667 5144; www.klafira.ee. If Soviet Russia has been banished for good from Estonia, the Tsarist aristocracy is making an effective comeback here instead. Perhaps they were wise to wait until 2000, nine years after the re-establishment of Estonian independence, before doing so. Their food is strictly Russian, their wine is sensibly French. That rich Estonians are firstly willing to come and then secondly even to speak Russian to the staff shows the high standards the restaurant has set. Allow a full evening here and do not consider the cost beforehand. It will be expensive by Estonian standards, but not by London or New York ones. 350EEK.

Kuldse Notsu Kõrts (The Golden Pig) Dunkri 8; tel: 628 6567; www.schlossle-hotels.com. Although this restaurant belongs to the luxury St Petersbourg Hotel next door, the two establishments have nothing in common. This country restaurant, with low ceilings and long wooden tables, seems pleasantly incongruous in the middle of the Old Town. However, this is precisely its appeal. It offers varied Estonian fare – thick mushroom soups, pork in innumerable guises and apples in almost as many. Drink apple juice or beer rather than wine. Few tourists venture in, but many Estonians do and this must be its best recommendation. 250EEK.

Liivi Steakhouse Narva mnt 1; tel: 625 7377; www.steakhouse.ee. Everything is wonderfully predictable here, so this is the place to be unadventurous. All styles of steak are on the menu and they can be accompanied by a wide range of red wine. The starters are patés and soups and the sweets apple-pie or ice-cream. Being situated opposite the Viru Hotel in a complex that also houses the main post office, the clientele is very varied but always conventional. 300EEK.

Mata Hari Suur Karja 11; tel: 631 4900; www. matahari.ee. Regular visitors to Tallinn will remember the Crêperie sans Nom in Müürivahe and will be glad that the same French cooking is available here, despite the change in name and address. It provides a welcome oasis of peace, sobriety and gastronomy in a street now notorious for offering the exact opposite. Some magazines have wrongly listed it as a café. Whilst it certainly functions in that role in the morning and afternoon, the meals are always substantial. 200EEK.

Must Lammas (The Black Sheep) Sauna 2; tel: 644 2031; www.mustlammas.ee. For years this Georgian restaurant was called Exit but it changed its name in early 2001. Luckily little else has changed. All guests are greeted with portions of firewater and strips of salted beef as the menus are handed out. Eat meat, meat and more meat all evening, topped, if you did not have lunch, with some ice-cream drenched in brandy. Start with stuffed vine leaves and move on to beef and pork stews. Vegetarians keep out. 250EEK.

Olde Hansa Vanaturg 1; tel: 627 9020; www.oldehansa.com. Ignore the silly name and the silly costumes worn by the staff but enjoy the candles (there is no electric light) and the genuinely Estonian live music. Some tables are for two but don't venture in for a quiet, intimate evening. This is really a party venue so come as a group and with a very empty stomach. Portions are enormous, even for soup and ice-cream. 250EEK.

Peppersack Viru tänav 2; tel: 646 6900; www.peppersack.ee. Johan Peppersack was one of Tallinn's best mayors when Estonia was ruled by the Swedes in the 16th and 17th centuries. He fought the occupiers for money and for autonomy with a tenacity that no other mayor could equal in the subsequent 400 years. He would not have tolerated the mess Polish restorers, local Estonians and the Soviet occupiers got into when they tried and failed to restore the building in time for the 1980 Olympics. The compromise between Polish baroque and the former Gothic is still there. Perhaps it is better to look at the live entertainment, which can feature fencers, troubadours or martial artists. (Check the website if it matters which.) The menu is extensive but many find it easiest just to order one of the feasts at a fixed price which includes three courses and drink. 250EEK.

Sultan Väike-Karja 8; tel: 644 4400. After successful ventures in north London, the owners came to Tallinn in 2004 to introduce one of the few cuisines and environments still unknown here then. Do not be put off by the ground-floor bar but head straight downstairs into genteel Istanbul. Dining tables are at various heights and the subdued lighting does not encourage minute study of the menu, but this hardly matters as most clients just discuss what they want with the staff. 150EEK.

Teater Lai 31; tel: 646 6261. Coming into this basement from the stairs will often seem like an intrusion, so glued to their cigarettes and to television are the staff and their close friends. However, walk through to a back alcove and the gathering will be interrupted to bring a mixed Creole and Estonian menu. Start with the grilled dishes from the former and finish with the pancakes from the latter. Do not expect any tender loving care here but the cheapness and the variety of the menu will be ample compensation. 200EEK.

Toomkooli Toomkooli 13; tel: 644 6613. Those who are not deterred by the awkward location at the back of the Old Town are rewarded on arrival with an extensive international menu and wine list but prices that have stayed Estonian. Minimal music and very heavy wooden chairs give a more formal air to the surroundings than is now common in many Tallinn restaurants, but in a town now so geared to the young, this should be taken as a compliment. 350EEK.

Vanaema Juures (Grandma's Place) Rataskaevu 10/12; tel: 631 3928. This is probably Tallinn's most famous restaurant but not even a visit from Hillary Clinton has gone to its head. The valid and repeated descriptions of it – good home cooking, a traditional décor and a cosy atmosphere – degenerate into cliché but few would dispute them. The furnishings and photographs from the previous independence period (1918–40), together with discreet music from that time, deter the young and raucous, but others will immediately appreciate the originality of total Estonian surroundings. Unfortunately, Grandma has not got around yet to having a website. 300EEK.

WHAT TO SEE

Tourists tend to concentrate on the Old Town but many modern buildings are of interest too. The main sights in the Old Town can be covered in one day but more time would be needed for other visits. A route for a day-long walking tour is suggested and then another day should be allowed for Pirita and Kadriorg. Several sights outside Tallinn warrant a half-day on their own. For museum opening times, see page 69.

A walking tour through Tallinn

The tour starts at the final Soviet architectural legacy to Estonia – the **National Library** (Eesti Rahvusraamatukogu) – begun in 1986 and completed in 1993. It is situated on the intersection of Endla and Tonismägi close to the Mihkli and Santa Barbara hotels. Its predecessor was opened in 1918 in the parliament building on Toompea and had 2,000 books, a number that only increased to 6,000 during the 1930s. After World War II, the history of the library mirrored that of the country as a whole. Its bleakest period was until 1953 when most of the collection was of Russian books translated into Estonian. On Stalin's death, the library was renamed after one of Estonia's most famous authors, Friedrich Kreutzwald, a clear sign of a more liberal climate. By 1967 funds were specifically allocated for books in the Estonian language and in 1988, shortly before this new building was supposed to open, it was renamed the National Library and the formerly restricted sections were opened to all. The design seems to symbolise *glasnost*: light streams in through many massive windows, and large open shelves display a wide cross-section of the two million books stored there. It will remain a grandiose memorial to massive public sector investment. Yet it was almost not completed. The fading Soviet government was not eager to continue funding projects outside Russia and the new Estonian one was faced with bills it could not pay. On June 28 1989, between four and five thousand volunteers joined the building works under the slogan 'Dig a grave for Stalinism'. The director, Ivi Eenmaa, later to become mayor of Tallinn, single-handedly fought Moscow and then each new Estonian government for adequate funds and was finally able to open the library on February 22 1993, two days before National Day.

Day tickets can be bought in the entrance hall, which is decorated with prints by one of Estonia's most famous contemporary artists, Eduard Wiiralt. To encourage regular use, the library has several music rooms, shops, a café and even piped music. On a bitter winter's day, tourists may wish to await a change in the weather amongst the many English-language books and journals now available there. As one of Estonia's many adaptations to entry into the EU, there are also large French, German and Scandinavian reading rooms. Normally, however, visitors should head straight for the 8th floor to view two contrasting Tallinns. To the north and east is the Tallinn of the posters – the spires, turrets and golden domes. In the other direction is a part of the town best seen at this distance, consisting of abandoned factories and fading tower blocks, with minimal intrusion of any colour.

Cross the road to **Charles's Church** (Kaarli Kirik). In its almost Episcopalian simplicity, it is the perfect antidote to what is to come later in the walk. It is a massive and austere late 19th-century limestone building which seats 1,500 people. At a time when Russian rule was becoming more oppressive, its size discreetly symbolised Estonian nationalism. The name comes from an original wooden church built in the late 17th century during the reign of the Swedish King Charles XI. Although the church took 20 years to build, the large altar fresco was completed in ten days in 1879 by the well-known artist Johann Köler.

On leaving the church, turn right into Kaarli and then take the first road on the left, Toompea. Immediately on the left is the entrance to the **Occupation**

TALLINN IN 1960
Michael Bourdeaux

For 15 years after World War II, Tallinn was a closed city, nestling amongst the forest of defensive (offensive) weaponry trained on the NATO countries. Suddenly in 1960 it was opened to Western visitors. I was lucky enough to have been a student at Moscow University at the time, so in May 1960 I was perhaps the first British visitor. Diplomats kept away until independence in 1991 because according to the bureaucrats a visit would have implied recognition of the Soviet occupation. I not only went there by train from Leningrad but stayed illegally in a private house for the first and only time during the 25 years that I knew the Soviet Union. Far from being worried that I would bring trouble on their heads, the occupants barred the exit and refused to let me out until I had agreed to stay for three nights, having found my photograph displayed on their wall!

How did this come about? In 1958 the Soviet authorities allowed a few hand-picked theological students to study abroad. One from Riga and one (Pastor Kaide Ratsep) from Tallinn arrived at Wycliffe Hall, Oxford while I was there. As I was a graduate in Russian, we gravitated towards each other. The next year, the door suddenly opened to me to study in Moscow as a member of the first-ever exchange programme with the USSR and I finally met Pastor Ratsep there when he was in transit to London. I promised I would call on his family if ever the opportunity arose.

It did. On arriving in Tallinn, I took a suburban train to the (as it still is) upmarket suburb of Nomme with its large wooden houses among the trees, looking more like Scandinavia than the Soviet Union. Maps of any practical use were unobtainable, being considered items of military intelligence, so I had to ask my way to the Ratsep's house. A rare Russian speaker eventually pointed me down one of the many paths cut into sand and I found a two-storey house separated from its neighbours by a wooden fence and a strip of pine trees. I knocked on the bright green door. A man with grey hair put his head out of an upstairs window before coming down. We had no common language, but I mentioned the name of the person who turned out to be his son. He invited me in, and there on the wall was the photograph of the Wycliffe Hall student body of 1958.

Museum. It could only be built thanks to funds provided by an Estonian American, Olga Ritos, who fled abroad in 1944 after both her father and her uncle had been killed by the Soviets. When the museum was formally opened in 2003 by her and the Prime Minister Juhan Parts, they cut not a ribbon but barbed wire. The pathetically inadequate clothing of the prison camps is perhaps the most moving exhibit, though the sight of small cases into which thousands of Estonians had to pack belongings for their Siberian exile must run a close second. A red star and a swastika are always shown side by side as in Estonian eyes the Russians and the Germans were equally guilty. Do allow

He simply would not allow me to leave and I somehow understood that I must await the return of his daughter-in-law. I was anticipating a conversation of a few words, knowing how elementary Kaide's knowledge of English had been when he arrived in Oxford. On the contrary, Enid Ratsep was bilingual, having been born in free Estonia of an English mother. The family at home had always spoken English, a tradition not entirely dead in 1960. Their 12-year-old daughter spoke it quite well. Later I would meet Enid's brother who sang me Harry Lauder songs while marching me through the streets of medieval Tallinn. Thirty years later I reflected on whether this might have been a preview of the Singing Revolution. I could hardly believe I was in the Soviet Union. Lampshades and bedspreads were of British pre-war manufacture. I slept in Kaide's study with a bookcase of German and English theology behind my pillow.

All of us, as if by common agreement, steered clear of the topic of the Soviet occupation but the family thoroughly organised my time for the next three days. After eight months in drab winter Moscow, the elan of ancient Tallinn in its bright spring colours took me into a new world. A visit on Sunday to Kaide's Lutheran Church, St Charles Church, left mixed impressions. Strangely, the family did not want to accompany me. This huge church was about half full, with 40% of the congregation younger people, a far higher proportion than one saw in Russia. I tried to see the pastor after the service, but the corridor was blocked by dozens of young people waiting outside his door. None of these, to my surprise, would speak to me, although most must have known Russian. I surmised they were waiting for religious instruction, illegal under the Soviet system at the time, and were unwilling for a foreigner (or a Russian if they took me for one) to intrude.

On my final day, having purchased an air ticket to Riga, I was waiting on the tarmac beside a small aeroplane. An official came up to me, demanded my documents, took me inside and told me my intended flight was illegal for a foreigner. 'Our rules are less strict than yours in Britain for Soviet citizens,' he said. 'When I was there, I was prevented from visiting many places. You can go where you like, but not always by your chosen route. Visit Riga by all means, but you must do so by train via Leningrad.'

plenty of time to watch the videos, all of which are in English, as they bring to life the drama and terror of both occupations as well as the occasional lighter sides of life which were possible under them.

There are also display cases showing day-to-day life in Estonia under Soviet rule. It seems hard to believe that most Estonians knew nothing else until 1991. The cellars are now being used to display statues from Soviet times, which had all been pulled down when Estonian independence was restored in 1991. One is of Viktor Kingissepp (1888–1922) who was executed after attempting a *coup d'état* in Tallinn in 1922 and the other is of Mikhail Kalinin

(1875–1946), a close colleague of Stalin whose death was commemorated by giving his name to the former German capital of East Prussia, Königsberg. One name is however missing. A statue of Stalin that had survived since 1956 could not be included; being 4m high, there was no way it could be brought into the museum for display.

At the first crossroads, note the simple **monument** to August 20 1991, the date Estonia declared independence during the failed Moscow coup. Had it been necessary, Estonians were ready to use the walls and towers to defend the Old Town from possible Soviet attack but the quick collapse of the coup and the immediate recognition by the USSR of Estonian independence prevented this. Looking ahead is a monument that dates from the 15th century, **Pikk Hermann** (Tall Hermann Tower). It has withstood numerous invasions and remains intact. Its height of nearly 50m is supported by foundations 15m deep. The first Estonian flag was flown from here in 1884, 34 years before the country was to become independent. Subsequent conquerors always marked their success by raising a flag here. A German guidebook printed in 1942 lists 12 major dates in Tallinn's history, the last being August 28 1941 when the German flag was raised over Pikk Hermann. During the Soviet occupation, the Estonian SSR flag was flown, but the Estonian national flag returned in 1989. It is raised at sunrise and lowered at sunset, except at midsummer when it is not lowered at all on the night of June 23/24. The blue in the flag represents the sky, black the soil, and white the aspirations of the Estonian people.

Turn right down the hill (Komandandi) to **Kiek in de Kök** (Peep in the Kitchen). The reason for the name becomes obvious as one climbs the 45m to the sixth floor and peers into more and more houses; only the steeples of St Nicholas and St Olav are higher. From its initial construction in the 15th century until completion in the late 17th century, the tower grew in height and width with walls and floors as thick as 4m, but ironically, after a Russian attack in 1577, it never saw military action again. The last time it was prepared for war was in the 1850s when the Russians feared a British invasion during the Crimean War. On the top floor, note the model of the 'plague doctor' with a waxed tunic and cape impregnated with herbs. He carries a cane with which to touch patients to avoid any risk of infection. The main exhibition on the top three floors covers Tallinn's military history. The lower floors are now used as an art gallery. Kiek in de Kök does not have any catering, but the nearest tower to it, **Megedi**, can be recommended in this respect. This tower, like most in the city wall, dates from the late 14th century and was continually enlarged during the 15th century. From around 1800 when its defensive potential declined, it was converted into a barracks. In 1980, the top floor became a café which uses the name Megedi, and the ground floor a restaurant, called Neitsitorn.

On leaving Kiek in de Kök turn back up the hill and turn right into Toompea, which ends in the square between the **Parliament building** and the **Alexander Nevsky Cathedral**. The juxtaposition of these two buildings appropriately contrasts official Estonian and Russian architecture. The one is simple, small and functional, the other elaborate, and deliberately powerful. Ironically, the Tsarist power that it represented was to last only a further 17 years. Entering the cathedral represents a symbolic departure from Estonia. No-one speaks Estonian and no books are sold in Estonian. It is a completely Russian architectural outpost dominating the Tallinn skyline and was built between 1894 and 1900 at a time when the Russian Empire was determined to stifle the burgeoning nationalistic movements in Estonia. It was provocatively named after Alexander Nevsky since he had conquered much of Estonia in the late 13th century. The icons, the mosaics and the 15-ton bell were all imported from St Petersburg. Occasionally plans are discussed, as they were in the 1930s, for the removal of the cathedral as it is so architecturally and politically incompatible with everything else in Toompea, but it is unlikely that any government would risk the inevitable hostility that would arise amongst the Russian-speaking population of Tallinn.

The Parliament building, most of which dates from 1921, is one of very few in the Old Town to have seen frequent reconstruction, the last one resulting from a fire in 1917 which may have been started by the Bolsheviks. The façade is a simple classicist one, and all the stone and wooden materials are local. Earlier buildings on this site had usually served as a governor's residence although, in the late 19th century, the building became a prison. The earliest fort was built on this site in 1227 and the northern and western walls date from this time.

The most famous room within the building is the White Hall, with a balcony overlooking the square. The current décor, with white cornices and a yellow ceiling, dates from 1935. From 1922 there had been a more elaborate neo-classicist design, including ceiling mirrors and elaborate panelling. The current Parliamentary Chamber was rebuilt in 1998 and members of the public can attend debates there, but no interpretation from Estonian is provided. There are 101 members of Parliament, often representing as many as ten different parties. Visitors are forbidden to enter 'with cold steel, firearms and pungent-smelling substances'.

Continue up the hill along Toomkooli with the post office on your right. By the end of 2004, this street should be completely restored, the first one to be back to its 1920s glory. Straight ahead, on Kiriku Square, is the **Dome Church** (Toomkirik), sometimes called St Mary's Cathedral. Work started soon after the Danish invasion in the early 13th century and the first church was consecrated by King Waldemar II in 1240. It was slowly enlarged over the next four centuries as funds became available but much of the interior was destroyed in the fire of 1684 which devastated the whole of the Old Town. The Swedish King Charles XI imposed a special tax for the rebuilding of Tallinn and within two years the church had been largely restored. The baroque spire was added in 1778 so in all the church has an architectural history of over 600 years. The altarpiece, painted in 1866, is the work of the Baltic-German artist Eduard von Gebhardt. The organ, probably the most powerful in Estonia, was made in Frankfurt an der Oder in 1913 so is the last to have been imported from Germany before World War I.

The Dome Church was the religious centre for the main families of the Tallinn Baltic-German community; their coats of arms cover the church walls and their tombstones cover the floor, although a few are of Swedish origin. At the back of the church are two tombstones commemorating the butchers and the shoemakers guilds. The most impressive tomb, which is beside the altar, is that of the French mercenary Pontus de la Gardie, who served in the Swedish army in many battles with the Russians. In the north aisle is a monument to Samuel Greig, a Scots admiral who served in the Tsarist navy from 1763 until his death in 1788. The inscription expresses the sorrow of Catherine II at his death. Like many Scots predecessors and successors, he had a distinguished career in this navy. He helped to destroy the Turkish fleet at the battle of Chesme in 1770 and to build up Kronstadt into a major naval base. Next to this monument is one to Adam von Krusenstern, the Baltic German who led the first Russian expedition to sail around the world, in 1803. Note the two globes, both of which omit New Zealand.

Turning left out of the church, the **Estonian Art Museum** dominates the opposite side of Kiriku Plats. Although it looks as though it was built as an art gallery, it was first used in the 19th century as the headquarters of the Estonian Knighthood, a major business guild. During the first independence period (1920–40) it was the Foreign Ministry and for much of the Soviet period served as the National Library. The names of the 19th- and 20th-century artists displayed here are sadly unknown outside Estonia, but many styles will be recognised by visitors. Both in the Tsarist period and under independence, most Estonian artists of note studied in Paris so the prevalent style there is reflected in their pictures. Konrad Mägi (1878–1925) is the most famous landscape artist and his pictures here are of many regions in Estonia. There is no catalogue available in English at present, perhaps because the collection will move to a new National Museum planned to open in the Kadriorg Park area in 2005.

Turning sharp right from the museum along Toom Rüütli leads, after 150m, to the main viewpoint across Tallinn. It is inevitably crowded during the tourist season so an alternative can be recommended along Rahukohtu, on the corner of Rüütli. Rahukohtu also starts on the right-hand side of the gallery. To reach the lower town, it is necessary in either case to return along Piiskopi towards the Russian cathedral and then to walk down the steps of Lühike Jalg ('Short Leg'), rather a misnomer as there are in fact about 100 steps. At the top, though, are several tempting cafés, souvenir shops and well-maintained toilets which can provide a respite before continuing the walk. Before starting the descent, look to the left along Pikk Jalg ('Long Leg'). The façade which commands one of the best views over Tallinn is modelled on the main building of Tartu University. Perhaps appropriately, in view of the current strength of the Estonian economy, this imposing building houses the Ministry of Finance.

On the right at the end of Lühike Jalg is the **Adamson-Eric Museum**. Adamson-Eric (1902–68) was without doubt the most famous Estonian artist who worked during both the independence period and the Soviet era. This house has no links with him, although before being used as a museum it did have workshops for coppersmiths. The museum opened in 1983 and the collection is based on around 1,000 works bequeathed by his widow. These cover his whole life in both painting and applied art. Gifts from abroad have recently been added to the collection. Labels are in English. Adamson-Eric's parents were able to pay for long periods of study during the 1920s in both Paris and Berlin. Elements of Fauvism and Cubism can be seen in many of his pictures but he was equally drawn to the Bauhaus and worked closely with Walter Gropius, George Grosz and Otto Dix. On his return to Estonia he first specialised in portraits, then added landscapes and broadened into applied arts. In this field, his work became as diverse as his painting. Around 1930, he began with tapestries and textiles and then added ceramics and metalwork to his range. Shortly before the war, he diversified even more, starting to work with leather and to design stage sets. He retreated with the Soviet army in 1941 and managed to maintain his artistic integrity despite the stringent demands of Soviet officialdom. With the inevitable lack of materials for applied art at this time, he concentrated again on painting. In 1949, the political tide finally turned against him and he was expelled from the Communist Party, forced to give up his posts and sent into factory work. Although released in 1953 on Stalin's death, his health had deteriorated and he suffered a stroke in 1955. His reaction was simply to learn to paint as well with his left hand as he had previously done with his right! His health slowly improved and he was able to add porcelain painting and tile design to his work in the field of applied art. He remained active until shortly before his death in 1968. Several of his paintings that were in western Europe during the Soviet era have now been given to the museum.

Continuing down the hill, the steps become a road which continues to a junction. To the left is Rataskaevu and to the right, Rüütli, both roads which house some of Tallinn's most famous restaurants. Ahead is **St Nicholas Church, Niguliste**. It is unusual in Tallinn in having been a military installation as well as a church with ample hiding places and secret exits to the city walls. In common though with other churches, it was first built in the 13th century and then expanded over the next 400 years. The original spire dated from 1696 and, being outside the town walls, the church was spared from the 1684 fire. It was, however, badly damaged during the Soviet air raid on Tallinn of March 9 1944 and the spire was only restored in 1984. Fortunately the carvings, chandeliers and pictures, many dating from the 16th century, had been removed before the raid. They are all now on display again and are particularly valuable given that so much similar work was either destroyed in the 1684 fire or suffered from neglect in more recent times. The interior of the church was slowly restored during the Soviet period from 1953 onwards. A small exhibition describes this work but captions are only in Russian and Estonian. St Nicholas has kept its role as a museum and concert hall so has not been reconsecrated. The life of St Nicholas is portrayed in the altarpiece, over 6m wide and painted in Lübeck by Hermen Rode between 1478 and 1482. Note the one very modern addition – a stained-glass window by the contemporary artist, Rait Prääts, whose glass can also be seen at the National Library and the Sakala Conference Centre.

On leaving the church, turn right to the memorial to the writer Eduard Vilde (1865–1933). The illustrations depict scenes from his novels and plays. The two stones represent an open book. Between 1918 and 1920 he served as Estonian ambassador in Copenhagen and Berlin, convincing both governments that an independent Estonia was here to stay. The Tallinn Tourist Information Centre is on the other side of the road. Proceed down the steps to Harju and then turn right again. This bombed site has deliberately been left as it was after the raid of March 9 1944. The inscription commemorates the 463 people killed by the raid. In June 2002 a referendum was held in Tallinn about the future of this site. Only 2% of the population turned out to vote, but 87% of them wanted to keep the site as a memorial and not let it fall into the hands of developers. Ahead is the bookshop Felix & Fabian, but on the corner of Harju and Kuninga note the plaque to the writer Juhan Smuul (1922–71), who lived here as the building belongs to the Writers Union. (He also lived on the island of Muhu; see page 243.) Despite winning both Stalin and Lenin prizes and being chairman of the Writers Union, Smuul was a genuinely popular writer at the time which is why the plaque has not been removed. Hopefully his works will soon be republished. Jaan Kross (born 1920), Estonia's most famous contemporary writer, still lives in this complex and is fit enough to reach his fourth-floor flat without a lift. (In Soviet times, only buildings with five floors or more had lifts installed.) Returning along Harju and then Kullassepa brings one into Raekoja Plats, or Town Hall Square. Just before reaching the square, it is worth turning right for a few minutes into the small alley, Raekoja. The building on the right, which now houses the **Photographic Museum**, was the town's main prison until the early 19th century. Estonia has always had a strong photographic tradition and this museum displays not only cameras produced in the country but photographs from the 19th and early 20th century. It is fortunate that many pictures from the first independence period have survived. The basement is a gallery for the display and sale of contemporary photographs.

Town Hall Square (Raekoja Plats) is similar to many in northern Germany as it was the commercial centre for the Baltic Germans. In the 16th century, the Germans accounted for about 1,500 of Tallinn's total population of around 5,000. They maintained all positions of authority, ruling from the Town Hall and the surrounding buildings. The square was the centre for all major events in the town, happy and tragic. Carnivals, weddings and Christmas have all been regularly celebrated here and the Tallinn Old Days Festival, held each year in early June, recreates the carnival atmosphere with its musical and artistic events. What was probably the world's first Christmas tree was displayed here in 1441. Yet the square was also the site for frequent executions and floggings, its grimmest day being in 1806 when 72 peasants were executed following a failed uprising. Nowadays it is hard to imagine such a background as work and punishment have given way to total relaxation. Cafés surround the square and spread into it during the summer. Since 2001, a Christmas market has taken place here throughout December. The Café Tristan and Isolde, in the Town Hall building but with an entrance from the square, is hardly noticed by tourists so offers a quiet respite from all the activity elsewhere, as well as much lower prices.

One of the few buildings on the square that has kept its original function is the **pharmacy**, which dates from 1422. Tour guides often like to point out that this is 70 years before Columbus discovered America. The coat of arms of the Burchart family, who ran the pharmacy for 400 years, can be seen over the entrance. Amongst the medicines they dispensed which are unlikely to find contemporary favour were fishes eyes, lambswool and ground rubies, but patients were at least offered these potions with a glass of hot wine to help digestion. In 1725 Peter the Great summoned Burchart to St Petersburg, but he died before Burchart could reach him. In 2000 the pharmacy was extensively refurbished.

The **Town Hall** is the only late-Gothic building still intact in Estonia, dating largely from the 15th century. The exterior and the interior are equally impressive. It was the administrative and judicial centre of the town and the extensive range of woodwork and paintings in the Council Chamber mainly reflect judicial themes. Six centuries of Tallinn's history have been determined in this room and, with the restoration of independence, its role will now increase. For much of this time, there were clearly ample funds in the public treasury, as is shown by the opulence of the candelabra, the money-chests and the size of the wine cellars. One of the carvings on the magistrates' bench of David and Goliath is often taken to symbolise the relationship between Tallinn Council and its nominal masters on Toompea in the Old Town. The Council Chamber has always been heated, unlike the neighbouring Citizens Hall. Dancing, eating and drinking at winter receptions tended to be particularly vigorous to compensate for this. The original weathervane on the top of the spire, known as Old Thomas, was destroyed in the 1944 raid but the rest of the building was spared. German architects, artists and craftsmen were employed for the Town Hall and all documents were written only in German, even during the long periods of Swedish and Russian rule. Only the tapestries have a non-German origin, being Flemish. The originals are not in fact displayed any more, because of their fragile condition, but two exact copies woven over a six-month period in 2003 by the British company Hines of Oxford now hang in the Citizen's Chamber. Both are over 8m long and show scenes from the legend of King Solomon.

A large exhibition in the basement opened in 2003, and it is worth braving the extremely narrow staircase down to it. Plans and photographs of the square are shown as it has been, as it might have been and as it may be, together with many fragments unearthed in recent excavations. Do use the toilets here as they have been skilfully placed within the foundations.

Another exhibition opened in summer 2004 in the attic behind the clock. Its main exhibit is a model of Tallinn as it was in 1825, but more important is the fact that it has been cleared. Restoration that started in 1952 finally came to an end 52 years later. It generated 273 tons of debris, much of which had been stored here. Some of the smaller, more valuable finds in wood, earthenware and textiles are now on display alongside the model.

It is sometimes possible to climb up the spire; the view from the top offers excellent shots of the Old Town for photographers but the stairs are steep and in poor condition so this is only recommended for the fit and determined.

Across the square, opposite the Town Hall, are several short streets which lead to Pikk. On the corner of Mündi and Town Hall Square is a millennium clock which counted down the seconds until midnight on December 31 1999. Saiakäik is the smallest street in Tallinn. Take either of these and turn right to the junction of Pikk and Pühavaimu for the **Holy Ghost Church**. That it does not face due east suggests that there was already a complex street layout by 1300 when building began. It was the first church to hold services in Estonian and the first extracts from the catechism in the Estonian language were printed for use here in 1535. The 1684 fire destroyed much of the interior and the original spire. The next spire was for many years the oldest in Tallinn, dating from 1688. It was badly damaged in a fire in 2002 but was quickly replaced. Of the same age inside the church is the large wooden clock on the north wall, carved by Christian Ackermann from Königsberg. Spared from the fire was the folding altar carved in 1483 by the Lübeck artist Bernt Notke. Only the organ is modern, dating from 1929; it is one of the few in Tallinn's churches built by an Estonian and not imported from Germany. To the left of the altar, the white ensign and the plaque below it commemorate the British sailors who gave their lives between 1918 and 1920 fighting the Bolsheviks.

Cross Pikk for the Ajaloomuuseum, the **Estonian History Museum**. The building is as impressive as any of the contents, perhaps more so. Dating from 1410, it was the headquarters of the Great Guild and has changed little since. Visitors who arrive when the museum is shut can at least be consoled by the sight of the 15th-century door knockers. Exhibits inside are well labelled in English and concentrate on archaeology and costumes. Of more contemporary interest is the coin collection and a section on the founding of the local freemasons in the late 1770s. They were later banned by Alexander I in 1822. As you turn left into Pikk, the new Russian embassy is on the left and on the right is Maiasmokk, a café that has deliberately stayed old-fashioned both in décor and in prices. (Tea in 2004 was 8EEK/£0.35/US$0.60 and cakes 12EEK/£0.50/US$0.90.) The name translates appropriately as 'sweet tooth'. The café is thought to be the origin of an Estonian definition of communism as being 'marzipan every day'. In summer 2004 the Kalev Chocolate Museum was due to move here. Whilst it does give a thorough coverage of the different production techniques used in its 200-year history, the real interest is in the political history shown in the designs on the boxes issued during the Soviet period. It was also the only factory allowed to produce chewing gum at that time. Pikk has two of the few notable **Jugendstil buildings** in Tallinn, both designed by Jacques Rosenbaum. Number 18, next to Maiasmokk, has a flamboyant Egyptian theme; number 25 on the corner of Hobusepea is more modest. Number 61, built across Pagari, and probably the blandest building in the Old Town, was the KGB headquarters in Soviet times, and now houses the Interior Ministry. Unlike its opposite number in Vilnius, it has not been opened to the public. Next on the left is **St Olav's Church** (Oleviste) named after the king of Norway and now a Baptist church. When first built in 1267, its 140m-high steeple made it one of the tallest buildings in the world. This steeple caught fire in 1820, having been struck by lightning, and its replacement 'only' reaches 120m. Since 2002 it has been open to the public during the summer. It is still, however, a major feature of the Tallinn skyline. Much of the interior of the church was destroyed in the subsequent fire, as it had been in an earlier one in 1625. The rebuilding, completed in 1840, provides a contrast to most other churches in Tallinn for its plain interior. Tsar Nicholas I donated a large bell in 1850 and his generosity is noted in an inscription written, with no trace of irony, in German. The organ dates from this time but the chandeliers are earlier and have been donated from other buildings.

A few yards further down on the right is **Fat Margaret's Tower** which houses the **Maritime Museum** (Meremuuseum). Outside is a plaque unveiled by Prince Andrew in May 1998 which commemorates British naval involvement in the battles between Estonian forces and the Bolsheviks from 1918 to 1920. The tower was built between 1510 and 1529. Some walls are as much as 6m thick. In 1830 it became a prison but after being stormed in 1917 it was left as a ruin for the next 60 years. Polish restorers, famous throughout the former Soviet block, finally came to the rescue in 1978. Climb to the roof for very photogenic views of St Olav's and the town gates. The museum covers shipbuilding, cartography, port-construction and fish-breeding. There is a recent exhibit on the *Estonia* which sank off the Finnish coast on September 28 1994 with the loss of 850 lives. A model of one of the boats has political interest. It was named first after Viktor Kingissepp, leader of the underground Estonian communist party in the early 1920s and then in 1990 was renamed after Gustav Sule, who was Estonian javelin champion in the 1930s.

Turn right out of the museum and leave the Old Town on Suur Rannavarara, the continuation of Pikk. On the right is the monument to those who died in the *Estonia* tragedy in 1994. It can be interpreted in a number of ways, perhaps symbolising the boat breaking into two or the total divide between life and death. Cross Pohja Puiestee to the disused power station, now ironically the **Energy Museum** (Energeetikamuuseum). Built originally in the late 1920s, it then had some claim to Jugendstil influence but many subsequent alterations have completely removed any hint of beauty and style. For tourists who never had the chance to visit Tirana's 'Albania Today' or Chinese museums during the Cultural Revolution, this is a splendidly flamboyant substitute. Ironically for an energy museum, many of the lights do not work but those that do illuminate graphs that all start at zero in 1945 and shoot up to the stratosphere throughout the 1950s, 1960s and 1970s. Engineers will be interested in the various meters and generators on display. The only hint of modern Estonia is in an occasional photograph. The basement could not provide a greater contrast with all its striplights working and its displays of contemporary abstract art. Modern Estonia does indeed have energy but it is now portrayed more metaphorically than literally. Demonstrations of the machinery take place several afternoons a week. Check at the entrance for details.

Return into the Old Town and walk behind Fat Margaret along Uus. Number 31 is the Scottish club, in fact a restaurant open to all which has the best-maintained lawn in Estonia. Next door is a whisky shop, a clear testimony to Tallinn's affluence and passion for Western consumer goods. It is hard to believe that until 1989 whisky was only available in foreign-currency shops. Turn right into Olevimägi and then left into Vene. On the left is a smaller, but no less Russian version of the Alexander Nevsky Cathedral, **St Nicholas Russian Orthodox Church**. Again no concessions are made to Estonia; everything is written, spoken and sung in Russian. It dates from the early 19th century. On the right at number 17 is the **City Museum** (Linnamuuseum). As with the History Museum, the building is as of much interest as the contents. Having escaped the fires that ravished so many buildings in the Old Town, this 14th-century merchant's house still has examples of 16th-century wooden panelling, windows and furniture. Many of the exhibits would now be regarded as politically incorrect in the West as they concentrate on the accoutrements of the rich; life below stairs and outside the guilds and churches is ignored. Part of the museum is quite understandably called the 'Treasury', given the quantity of tapestries, silverware, pewter and porcelain displayed there. Nonetheless the collection shows the breadth of industry and culture that developed in Tallinn from 1860 onwards. The arrival in 1870 of the railway from St Petersburg led to an increase in the population from 30,000 to 160,000 by 1917. One anniversary the Estonians were forced to celebrate in 1910 was the 200th anniversary of the Russian conquest. The museum was closed in 2000 for extensive renovations. It now shows videos of pre-war and Soviet Estonia, of the 1944 bombing, the 1980 Olympics and the 1989 demonstrations that would in due course lead to independence. Allow at least an hour to see all of these. A room of Soviet posters has also been added, together with an early 20th-century kitchen. In the portraits of Tallinn's mayors, note that the first Estonian one, Voldemar Lender, only took office in 1906. The café on the top floor is unusual in only offering homemade food. This museum is well labelled in English and the postcard sets they sell are excellent value.

On the right are the ruins of the **Dominican Monastery**, founded in 1246 but destroyed during the Reformation in 1524 when the monks were forced to flee. Extensive archaeological excavations were carried out between 1954 and 1968 when the ruins were first opened to the public. Take a torch and wear sturdy shoes as the surviving ambulatories are poorly lit. Of most interest are the stone carvings by the 16th-century Dutch sculptor Arent Passer. Chamber-music concerts take place here during the summer. On leaving the monastery, turn left into Vene and left again into Katariina Kaik. This tiny alleyway is where local ex-pats buy their souvenirs of Tallinn, as few tourists find it. Turn right at the end into Müürivahe, which runs below the city wall. Elderly Russians have stalls here, selling woollen sweaters, gloves and socks both in midsummer and in midwinter. The walk ends at the junction with Viru Street. To the left is the 15th-century Viru Gate, as formidable as the fortifications seen at the start of the walk. To the right is McDonald's; will it also last five centuries?

Elsewhere in Tallinn

Visitors with more time can see many other museums. Close to the Viru Gate at Vana Viru 14 and opposite the Viru Hotel is the **Fire-Fighting Museum**. Like the Energy Museum, it has not changed since the Soviet era so combines the didactic with the heroic. Dolls' houses show every possible cause of an accident in each room. Macabre photos abound of charred bodies, exploding television sets and open fires out of control. A panel lists medals awarded to local firemen until 1988 but none are listed after that year. It is a cruel comment to suggest that heroism in the Estonian fire service ceased at the restoration of independence in 1989. A number of horse-drawn and early motor fire engines are displayed. Although captions to all exhibits are only in Estonian and Russian, the staff hand out translation cards in English and German.

Back in the Old Town, in Lai, are the **Applied Arts Museum** at number 17 and the **Health Museum** at number 28–30. The former still sells the Soviet guidebook which boasts that the exhibits 'are really wonderful, conspicuous in their originality and can bear comparison with the best items of the world'. Exhibits from the Soviet period are now on the upper floors, and modern ones on the ground floor, so visitors can judge the changes for themselves and whether such hyperbole applies to either era. In all fields the collections are extensive and show the Estonian dedication to pottery, weaving, glassmaking and woodwork that has surmounted all political regimes.

The Health Museum is one of the few totally contemporary museums in Tallinn and uses a range of models, toys, visual aids and colourful charts to show both adults and children the importance of healthy living. It is a brightly lit and well-thought-out display, a vivid contrast to many other museums. It may well be the only museum in the country with a hands-on element – two exercise bicycles are available for visitors. One section has been translated into Russian – that on sexually transmitted diseases.

Next to the Applied Arts Museum is the **Natural History Museum** at Lai 29, much of which is in fact contemporary rather than historical. Whilst there is an impressive collection of stuffed animals, of far greater interest is the collection of photographs of the Estonian countryside, all well lit and well labelled in English.

The **Theatre and Music Museum** at Müürivahe 12, despite its name, only covers music. A violin-maker's workshop has been reconstructed and the display covers most instruments of the orchestra, all of which have at some time been made in Estonia. The production of violins and pianos has a long and distinguished history in Tallinn. Very few labels are in English but fortunately this does not matter too much given the self-explanatory nature of the exhibits. Estonians are often accused of taking themselves too seriously;

from the cartoons on the stairs, it is clear that musicians at least do not. No famous 20th-century conductor is spared portrayal in irreverent clothes. One violinist, Hugo Schuts, is even drawn in a bathing costume.

Just outside the Old Town, behind the railway station at Kotzebue 16, is the **Dolls' Museum**. Opened in 1985 as a memorial to one of Lenin's closest colleagues, Mikhail Kalinin, it nonetheless even then had a small collection of toys. Kalinin is now forgotten and toys have taken over completely. The collection of dolls and dolls' houses goes back as far as the 18th century, but there are also board games, teddy bears and general toys from 1900 onwards since this is one of the few elements of Estonian life unaffected by the changing political environment. The walk from the Old Town offers a completely changed architectural environment; Tallinn on the wrong side of the tracks becomes a town of poorly maintained wooden houses and an abandoned factory. The market beside the station is worth a stop of a few minutes. Excellent light refreshments are available at prices well below those elsewhere in the town and the choice of clothes, CDs and gadgets is a good reflection of mass Estonian taste.

A walk from the Viru Gate along either Pärnu mnt or Estonia pst, and then along Kaarli pst back to the National Library, passes the main buildings that remain from the end of the Tsarist period and the first independence period, from 1900 until 1940. Jugendstil, neo-classicism and functionalism are all represented here and it is to be hoped that developers do not get permission to make drastic changes. The **Estonian National Theatre** was in fact designed by a Finnish architect, Armas Lindgren, and opened in 1913, although the rebuilding that followed the bombing of Tallinn in 1944 was carried out under the Estonian architect Alar Kotli. The money for the original building was raised by private subscription and the Tsarist authorities attempted to block the project. They did briefly succeed in preventing the Estonian language from being used in any production. In 1918 the Estonian National Assembly met there.

On the opposite side of Estonia pst from the theatre is the **Estonian Bank Museum** which was modernised in the summer of 1998. The political history of the country is mirrored in this museum through the currency. In 1928 the kroon was tied to the British pound but it floated after 1933 when Britain had left the Gold Standard. The current building dates from 1935 and manages to combine elements of neo-Gothic, neo-Renaissance and functionalism. In its predecessor, Estonian independence was proclaimed on February 24 1918 and in this one, a temporary government was formed in September 1944 between the German and the Russian occupations.

The **Sakala Conference Centre** behind the bank is best known for the stained glass of Rait Prääts whose work can also be seen in St Nicholas Church and in the National Library. This area is likely to be developed soon with many office and hotel projects now under consideration. On Vabaduse Väljak (Freedom Square), the Palace Hotel and the Town Hall beside it both date from the 1930s. Their size and the imposing nature of similar buildings along Pärnu mnt testify to the confidence of the regime at the time. Behind them are a number of functionalist buildings that survived the 1944 bombing raid. There was a statute of Peter the Great in the square from 1910 to 1923, when it was removed. Nobody knows what happened to the top, but the metal from the base was used to mint Estonian coins.

Until 2003 a walk again from Viru Gate across Viru Square gave an appropriately unflattering picture of the construction that took place between 1960 and 1980. Looking back towards Narva mnt, the **Viru Hotel** was a major eyesore and the inevitable result of conflicting Soviet policies in the early 1970s. On the one hand, tourists needed to be admitted to Tallinn to boost the country's international image; on the other, they must not be allowed serious contact with the local population. An isolated tower block was obviously the answer, and until 1980, when some of the Olympic Games were held in Tallinn, the Viru was the only hotel for foreigners. Many probably only saw Tallinn from the bar on the 22nd floor. Estonians console themselves with the knowledge that the Viru Hotel did at least spare them a 'Stalinist cathedral' which was one proposal for this location, or an enormous memorial to Mikhail Kalinin which was another. Kalinin, a member of Lenin's Politburo, lived in Tallinn for three years between 1901 and 1904 whilst he was banished from St Petersburg. A Soviet guidebook published in 1987 blames the lack of 'artistic and economic means' for the failure of both projects. One published a year or two later might have given the true reason: the intense local opposition. A more modest statue of Kalinin was instead erected on Tower Square, a park between the Old Town and the railway station. Behind the Viru Hotel is a department store built in the 1960s. In the Soviet period it was crudely divided between a shop for the local population and one for foreigners. Both were flagships in their different ways. The local shop was better supplied than most in St Petersburg and Moscow and the notorious 'Berioshka', which took only precious *valuta* (hard foreign currencies) in exchange for vodka, wooden dolls and fur hats, was the only Soviet shop that thousands of tourists would ever enter. Before the war, the main Tallinn synagogue stood on this site.

The current **synagogue** shares premises with the **Jewish School** on Karu, near the harbour and was opened in December 2000. It is the only active synagogue in Estonia and replaced a temporary building used in Soviet times, on Magdaleena Street in the southern part of the city. Sadly, the occasional brutal attack on the premises has meant that they carry no outside identification. The building is now the headquarters for the small Jewish community in Tallinn. Visitors, both Jewish and non-Jewish, are welcome to visit the synagogue.

This area was completely transformed in 2004 when a new shopping centre opened on what had previously been the square, with a bus station underground and a walkway to link it to the original Kaubamaja. The exterior of the Viru Hotel was brightened up and extended. If, in the old days, some people never left the hotel, perhaps today they will never leave the square. There are about 70 different shops and ten different restaurants. Tallinn had known out-of-town shopping malls for a few years before 2004, but this is the first one in the centre. Early signs are that it is a success and not just patronised by Finnish tourists.

Returning towards town, Karu becomes Ahtri which skirts the harbour. Very dwarfed by the huge boats that ply between Helsinki and Tallinn, the icebreaker **Suur Töll** still stood out as a boat seemingly moored here for good. Having been delivered to the Tsarist navy in 1914 from the Stettin shipyards in Germany, it would inevitably have a complicated history over the next eight years, being based in Tallinn all that time. The Finns and Estonians who operated it wanted to prevent its fall into either White Russian or Bolshevik hands and, under the Tartu Treaty signed between the USSR and Estonia in February 1920, it was finally given to the Estonians. It could break ice a metre thick when launched, and it was still doing so with the same equipment in the late 1980s. Visitors can see the engines, the living quarters and the two separate kitchens from which food for the officers and for the men was prepared. In 2003 the boat was closed for restoration and it was expected to open again at a new location in late 2004.

EXCURSIONS FROM TALLINN
Rocca al Mare Open Air Museum

This deserves a half day to itself, ideally in balmy summer weather. Take the 21 or 21b bus from the railway station and also take a sweater as protection against the wind on the many non-balmy days. A winter excursion on a sunny day is worthwhile to get some impression of what most Estonians used to endure month in, month out, every winter. Visitors at midsummer on June 23 can enjoy the all-night celebrations held here. The name in Italian means 'cliff beside the sea' and was given by the original owner of the estate when it was bought in 1863. The museum was founded in 1957 and first opened to the public in 1964. The descriptive panels throughout are in English. It now consists of around 70 buildings and when complete should have a hundred. The aim is to show all aspects of Estonian rural architecture, with houses of both rich and poor. Most date from the 19th century but one of the chapels was built in 1699. The whole of Estonia is represented – windmills are of course from the island of Saaremaa but in contrast there are fishermen's cottages from Lake Peipsi on the Russian border. Even the poorest families managed to afford a sauna since to Estonians it is as crucial to living as a cooking pot. The interiors have all been appropriately furnished with kitchen utensils, weaving looms and chests of drawers. Amongst the more unusual buildings are a tabernacle from the Herrnhut movement, a strict offshoot of the Lutheran Church. Future plans include the restoration of a Swedish cottage – about 8,000 Swedes lived in Estonia before World War II. There is already a Swedish church here, brought from the formerly Swedish-speaking village of Sutlepa. The exterior is 17th century and the interior 19th century. Inside there is a permanent exhibition of drawings from all the other Swedish churches in Estonia. In bad weather, finish your tour at the Kolu Tavern. Kolu is a village between Tallinn and Tartu. The tavern still has two separate bars, one originally for the gentry and one for the peasants. It serves filling, hot food such as pea soup and mashed potatoes with bacon, but do not expect any concessions to the 21st century; it remains firmly in the 19th, although a more conventional restaurant will in due course be built for more fastidious diners.

Paldiski

Since independence, an uneasy quiet has descended on this former Soviet naval base situated 40km west of Tallinn. Unusually for Estonia, a regular train service operates from here to Tallinn, with eight services a day, the journey lasting a little over one hour. However, individual tourists would be well advised to take a car and guide for a half-day excursion as several en-route stops can be made. Estonians are more than happy to see the back of the Russian sailors but have yet to find a new role for this harbour. A daily car-ferry service to Kappelskär in Sweden started in summer 2000 and the switching of cargo services from Tallinn is being considered.

Peter the Great inspected the site personally in 1715 before authorising the building of a harbour which was originally planned as the largest in the Russian Empire. He was not to live to see its final completion which was not until 1768 as financial problems had led to frequent delays. Much of the labour was supplied by prisoners; so many died of ill-treatment that Paldiski became known as the 'second Siberia'. In September 1939 the USSR imposed a mutual assistance pact on Estonia under which Paldiski was seized as a naval base. In May 1940, shortly before the full occupation of the country, all Estonians were expelled from the town, a practice that would be repeated all too often from 1945 in many other towns and villages along the coast. Paldiski is now the largest Soviet blot on the Estonian landscape; only the dustbins, brightly coloured and modelled on penguins with their beaks open, provide relief from piles of rubble, barbed wire and ransacked blocks of flats. The first building to be seen on the way into the town is the former prison, but it can hardly be distinguished from much of what follows. When the Russian forces finally left in September 1995, having been granted dispensation to stay after independence, a population of around 4,000 was left with only 10% of them speaking Estonian. The remainder were Russian-speaking civilians. A curtain behind a window, an occasional light or even the sight of an occasional human being, shows that life has not totally died out here but the slogan in the town's English-language brochure, 'A Town with a Future', seems a joke in particularly bad taste. However, in 2000 a new hotel was opened, the **White Ship** (Valge Laev) at Rae 32 (tel: 674 2095; www.weekends.ee). 'Welcome aboard' mats are behind each entrance, a porthole is on the door of every room and maritime memorabilia cover all the walls. It would be possible to commute into Tallinn from here and when Tallinn hotels are full, late bookers will have no choice.

Returning to Tallinn, two very contrasting stops can be made. Shortly after independence, a monument was erected in the forest at **Klooga** to commemorate the massacre of 2,000 Jews there on September 19 1944, just before the German withdrawal. The small Estonian–Jewish community had already been killed by then; these victims were largely from other Eastern European countries. The former village of **Tabasalu** is now the first of Tallinn's suburbs. Most of the inhabitants have much more money than sense or taste. The money stands out, but it is well protected by high walls and rottweilers. A few poultry farmers remain on the outskirts of the village but it cannot be long before they are bought out.

Aegna, Pirita and Kadriorg

Allow a full day to visit the island of Aegna, the yacht harbour at Pirita and the park at Kadriorg. Boats to and from Aegna operate out of Pirita harbour from a small jetty beside the café east of the river, not from the larger jetty beside the hotel and yacht club. Several buses serve Pirita from the town centre and the journey takes about ten minutes. Boats leave for Aegna around nine in the morning, at midday and in the early evening. Check timings at the tourist office or via a hotel reception before setting off and do not forget an umbrella in case the weather suddenly changes. Tickets cost 80EEK (£3.50/US$5.50) for the round trip.

Aegna

Aegna is so quiet that even Estonians are prepared to turn off their mobile phones, and neither the Germans nor the Russians were able to leave their mark. Conifer trees abound, as do minute beaches, and the few open areas have been made available for camping. Much of the island can be seen in the three hours allowed by the morning boat schedule though a full day of peace and quiet is what most local visitors seek. Paths are clearly marked and a detailed map is displayed at the harbour.

Pirita and Viimsi

Pirita was built as the Olympic village for the yachting and sailing events of the 1980 Olympics. For a precious three weeks, Tallinn briefly returned to being an international city. An array of consumer goods, Western newspapers and direct international telephone dialling suddenly came to Tallinn and left equally suddenly when the Games were over. Only the buildings have remained and they are so obviously of Soviet design that the harbour hardly seems to belong to modern Estonia. On returning to Pirita, visitors of Estonian origin may wish to take the 34 bus for 2km inland to **Metsakalmistu**, the **Forest Cemetery**. Most famous Estonians are buried in this pine forest, including the writer A H Tammsaare, the poetess Lydia Koidula and the chess player Paul Keres. Since independence, the body of Konstantin Päts, president until the Soviet occupation, has been returned and he is now buried here together with his immediate family. He died in a Soviet psychiatric hospital in 1956. The body of General Laidoner, however, still lies in 2004 in a communal grave in Vladimir Prison where he died in March 1953, despite strong pressure from the Estonian government for it to be formally identified and returned. Laidoner was Commander-in-Chief for much of the pre-war period and his former house on the Viimsi Peninsula, about 5km from Pirita, is now the **Laidoner Museum**.

The most moving exhibit is a French–Russian dictionary given to him during his imprisonment in 1944; he used several pages of it to compose his political testament. It ends, in English, with the words 'Estonia, with all thy faults, I love thee still. Johan Laidoner'. Considering how jealous Stalin was of his reputation, it is remarkable how many items associated with him and with this house have survived. During Soviet times, the KGB had taken it over in order to break completely the links with Estonian independence.

The museum was greatly expanded in 2001. With the help of the Imperial War Museum in London, there is now a British Room, covering the navy's role in helping to establish Estonian independence in 1918–20. It is expected that many more exhibits will soon come from Britain. This would be appropriate in view of Laidoner's often-quoted remark, 'Without the arrival of the British fleet in Tallinn in December 1918, Estonia and the other Baltic States would have found themselves in the hands of the Bolsheviks.' The Poles have likewise opened a room in honour of Marshal Pilsudski who played a similar role to Laidoner in ensuring his country's independence from Russia.

Other visitors will head for the main harbour and the entrance to the *Lembit* submarine, beside the petrol station. No brochures are available but the sailors on board speak reasonable English and their enthusiasm on meeting the few English-speaking visitors who bother to come more than compensates for any linguistic failings. Two submarines were originally commissioned from Barrow-in-Furness by the Estonian navy in 1936. *Kalev*, the second one, was sunk in October 1941, by which time both had been taken over by the Soviet navy and taken from Tallinn before it fell to the Germans. The *Lembit* saw service throughout World War II, being used mainly to attack German cargo ships en route to Sweden. Its torpedoes had a range of 12km and it could sink below the surface for up to 24 hours. Its speed reached 60km/h. It remained in service until 1955, after which it was used for training. The Soviets made no attempt to conceal the British origin of the submarine so many of the original features remain. The *Lembit* was closed for restoration in 2003 and was likely to reopen at a new site in 2005.

The walk back to the centre of Tallinn is two or three miles. Cross the main road from the harbour to the site of **St Birgitta's Convent**. Although the convent is included in most sightseeing tours, walking here can be a precarious experience as the surroundings of ruins are so badly maintained. The convent lasted intact for only 170 years, from 1407 until the siege of 1577 when it was largely destroyed by troops of Ivan IV in the Livonian Wars. The outline of the main body of the church, the western gable together with the vestry, cloister and refectories, is clear. Minor restoration and excavation work started in 1960 and was brought to a close only in 2001. The new convent on the north side was completed in 2000 and part of the building is used as a hotel (see page 92).

Staying on the land side of the main road, after half a mile is the **Soviet War Memorial**. It could hardly be anything else, given its size and the military themes of the bronze statues. The Estonians carry out minimal maintenance here but, as with all Soviet war memorials, they are not removed and Russians congregate on the days of the old Soviet holidays such as May Day and November 7. On other occasions, bored teenagers hang around drinking and smoking. The text is particularly offensive to Estonians as the monument is dedicated to 'Fighters for Soviet Power'. It was completed only in 1975. A Soviet guidebook excuses this long delay by claiming 'at last Estonian artists had enough skill and adequate economic means to complete such an ensemble'. The obelisk dates from 1960 and commemorates the hurried departure from Tallinn of the Bolshevik fleet in 1918 when German forces occupied the town. Inland from the memorial, a German cemetery has now been reconsecrated and this is being properly maintained with the support of the German government. References here are to 'defensive battles' as the most appropriate way of describing resistance to the Soviet forces.

An even more dominant landmark from the Soviet era is the **TV Tower**, about a mile inland from Pirita on Kloostrimetsa. Going there by bus, expect to be surrounded by elderly Russians with flowers, since the Russian cemetery and crematorium are nearby. The few tourists who now visit the tower also seem to be Russian. This is a pity as it does provide an extensive view of the town and port not available elsewhere. The entrance is as flamboyant as one would expect: the windows are of stained glass, with portraits of valiant industrial workers; covered aisles surround basins of fountains and they in turn are surrounded by lawns. However, nothing has been maintained properly (except for the lifts inside) so moss and weeds become ever more prominent. Nobody has bothered to put Estonian signs in the lift or to change the menu in the revolving tower restaurant from smoked fish and chicken kiev. Even the telescope still takes kopek coins.

A few hundred yards further along this road is **Maarjamäe Palace**, which has probably had one of the most turbulent ownership histories of any site in Tallinn. Maarjamäe means 'Mary's Hill' but the German name, Streitberg ('Hill of Strife'), was for many centuries more appropriate. The only consolation is that the blood shed here spared Tallinn itself from many battles. The final one took place in the early 18th century as Russia seized the Baltics from the Swedes during the Northern Wars. To set the seal on his conquest, Peter the Great established Kadriorg Park as a summer residence, so many of the St Petersburg nobility felt obliged to followed suit. Those who could not immediately afford the luxury of a suitable building, subsidised it with a factory, so lime kilns and sugar refineries adjoined the manor houses. The sugar was sold in Riga and St Petersburg and the plant was run on British coal. A fire in 1868 destroyed much of the factory and it was never rebuilt. In the 1870s, when the estate was bought by Count Anatoli Orlov-Davydov from St Petersburg, the rebuilding he ordered came to deserve the title 'palace'. Terraces, a gateway decorated with copper eagles, and the Gothic tower gave it an almost regal air. The Dutch Consulate bought it in the 1920s when the Orlov-Davydovs emigrated to France and continued its use as a summer residence. It was to lose its appeal in this role when in 1926 the road to Pirita was built across the grounds, cutting off the manor house from direct and private access to the sea. However, the road brought with it commercial potential realised in a hotel and restaurant called the Riviera Palace. In 1937 the Estonian air force took it over as a training school and they are sadly responsible for the dreary façade at the front of the building. From 1940 until 1975, when Maarjamäe became a museum, the Soviet military used, but did not abuse it. During the 1980s, Polish restorers finally brought the building back to its turn-of-the-century glory, turning their attention to the chandeliers, fireplaces, parquet floors and ceilings. It is ironic that one of the last Soviet legacies to Tallinn should be the perfect surroundings for a museum which chronicles Estonian independence. A further legacy can be seen at the back of the building – remnants of Soviet statues too bulky to move to the Occupation Museum.

Although few labels are in English and the one available guidebook is now badly out of date, this is without doubt the best museum in Tallinn. New rooms are constantly being added, exhibits are generously displayed, layout is sensibly planned and there is the complete absence of benign neglect that seems to permeate so many other Tallinn museums. It covers Estonian history from the mid 19th century until the present day. It amply contrasts the lifestyles of rich and poor and shows the diversity of industrial products and international contacts that the country enjoyed during the first period of independence between the two world wars. It even had a thriving tourist board whose brochures displayed here sold Estonia as 'The Cheapest and Most Interesting Country in Europe'. One room opened in the summer of 1998 is devoted to the life of Konstantin Päts, Estonia's president between the two world wars. On more contemporary themes, the anti-Soviet guerrilla movement and the return to independence are covered movingly but not bombastically. Amongst new themes covered in rooms opened since 2000 are the battle for Tallinn in early 1918 and the German occupation from 1941–44.

Continuing towards the town centre is one of the few late-1950s constructions of which Estonians can be fiercely proud – the **Song Festival Amphitheatre**. It has the massive grandeur to be expected from that time but is not wasteful of materials and does not dominate the surrounding area. The parabola provides cover for 5,000 singers and up to 20,000 more have often taken part. The most famous recent festival took place in 1989, when the previously banned national anthem, the *Song of Estonia*, was sung by an audience of around 300,000 people, 20% of the entire population of the country. In winter, the steep slope at the back of the parabola provides Tallinn's only ski- and toboggan-run. Note the plaques at the top of the slope which commemorate each of the Song Festivals held every five years since 1869. The 2004 festival was commemorated by a statue at the top of the auditorium to Gustav Ernesaks (1908–93), who did more than anyone else to keep the Estonian element alive in the Song Festivals held during Soviet times. The tower was opened to the public in 2000, and gives photographers good shots of the Old Town and the port combined.

Returning to the shoreline, at the junction of the roads to Pirita and to Narva, note the **Russalka** (Mermaid) **Memorial**, which commemorates the sinking of a battleship with this name in 1893. It depicts an angel looking out to sea. The sculptor, Amandus Adamson, is one of Estonia's most famous, and perhaps because of this monument he was granted official respect in the Soviet period and a memorial bronze bust of him stands in Kadriorg Park. The park is the next stage of the walk and one corner is just behind the Russalka Memorial. The park, and **Kadriorg Palace**, which forms its centrepiece, was built immediately following Peter the Great's first visit to Tallinn in 1718 with his Italian architect Niccolo Michetti. Sadly it was not completed by 1725 when Peter the Great died and no subsequent Tsar ever showed the commitment that he did. In fact Catherine I never came to Tallinn again after his death. Perhaps the description often given of the palace as a 'mini-Versailles' is fair, as what was carried out does show some French and Italian influence. A fire destroyed much of the interior in 1750 and it was subsequently never again used by the Russian royal family. Kadriorg Palace became the official residence of the Estonian presidents, but now houses the **Foreign Art Museum**, the collection being mainly Flemish and Baltic German. However, the room devoted to Soviet art from the 1920s is likely to be of most interest to visitors. The designs on the porcelain show the most immediate break with the past as all the themes are 100% political. It would take another ten years before painting was similarly controlled. Some of this porcelain was prepared for the first Soviet Art Exhibition held in St Petersburg in 1923, by which time the St Petersburg Imperial Porcelain Factory had become the State Porcelain Factory. It came to be known as 'agitation porcelain'. Many rooms have been restored to their original 1930s layout, when President Päts lived here. The Danzig-baroque library is the most elaborate room and was only completed in 1939, a year before the Soviet take-over.

Kadriorg Park is a year-round joy for local people and tourists alike. In winter the combination of sun and snow amidst the trees and sculptures offers a peaceful contrast to the hectic commercial life of Tallinn just a few hundred metres away. Spring brings out the blossom of the cherry and ash trees, summer the swans, the squirrels and the fountains and autumn the blends of gold and red as the trees shed their leaves. In 2004 serious work started to restore the formal gardens that used to surround the palace. A cottage in the park used by Peter the Great during the construction of the palace now poses as a museum but the paucity of exhibits perhaps redefines the word 'minimalist'. A bare main room, a few photographs and some haphazard items of furniture would be best concealed from tourists entitled to expect much more.

A hundred metres back towards town, on Weizenbergi opposite the main entrance to Kadriorg Palace, the **Mikkeli Museum** will quickly restore the enthusiasm of a visitor. This building was the palace kitchen but in 1997 was opened to house the collection of Estonia's most fortunate private art collector, Johannes Mikkel. Born in 1907, he was able to start buying during the first independence period when departing Baltic Germans and Russian nobles abandoned enormous quantities of paintings, porcelain and prints. He was allowed to trade during the Soviet period and enhanced his collection with items bought in the Caucasus and Central Asia. There is no predominant theme, but the quality and taste of every item stands out, be it a piece of Kangxi or Meissen porcelain, a Dürer woodcut, a Rembrandt etching or any one of his 20 Flemish paintings. Folders in English are available in every room with descriptions of all major exhibits, and modern lighting ensures that each item is viewed as well as possible.

On leaving the museum and turning left, a slight detour can first be made to the far side of the lake behind the Mikkeli building. The splendidly isolated house at Roheline 3 is the **Eduard Vilde House Museum** where Estonia's most prolific writer, both at home and in exile all over Europe, spent the final six years of his life between 1927 and 1933. Typically for most established Estonians at that time, the furnishings are simple and there are many empty spaces. Return to Weizenbergi to continue back into town. At the corner of Poska on the left, house number 20a has some baroque imitation of the palace although it was built only in 1939. A good place to rest is the Café Omabi on the other corner. Apart from one microwave, modern Estonia has passed it by so the food is freshly prepared for each order, there is no menu in English and no piped music. Beside it is Kasitoo, a souvenir shop sensibly patronised by overseas Estonians as its prices are not geared to cruise passengers or Finnish day trippers. Weizenbergi lasts a further 300m or so before joining Narva mnt. Every house is probably now owned, or was before World War II, by a famous Estonian. Ladas or small Toyotas may be parked in the street, but considerable wealth is discreetly hidden behind the lace curtains. The turn-of-the-century, four-storey houses display hints of Jugendstil, whilst the wooden ones are characteristic of middle-class suburbs throughout Estonia. On a neighbouring street, Koidula, one of the largest wooden houses belonged to Estonia's most famous author, A H Tammsaare, who died in March 1940. In his honour it is now the **Tammsaare Museum** but labelling is only in Estonian and Russian. The only English translations of his work were published in Moscow in the 1970s and are now out of print. The exhibition has hardly been changed since the Soviet era so presents him as far more of a 'man of the people' than was really the case. Tammsaare is depicted on the 25EEK note and it is perhaps significant that it is his farm that is pictured on the reverse, not this town house. Some downstairs rooms are now used for modern art exhibitions, which contrast a much-needed splash of colour to the gloom upstairs.

At the junction of Weizenbergi and Narva mnt there is a taxi rank and bus stop. A large Methodist church has recently been built on the far side; otherwise Narva mnt from here back to the Viru Gate is totally devoted to Mammon. There is no point in describing any of the buildings since they are mainly being pulled down to give way to glass skyscrapers. This area will soon be Tallinn's Wall Street or Square Mile. A Japanese restaurant has already opened to ensure a serious and affluent gastronomic ambience.

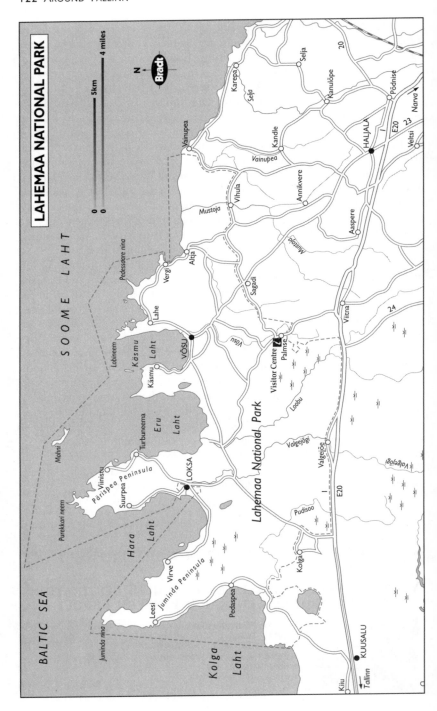

Around Tallinn

LAHEMAA NATIONAL PARK

Situated along the north coast of Estonia, about 100km from Tallinn en route to Narva, Lahemaa National Park and the buildings within it show both the Baltic-German and the Soviet occupation at their most benevolent. The von der Pahlen family, which owned Palmse Mansion, the architectural high point of a visit to the park, contributed to Estonia for two centuries with their administrative, commercial and academic activities. Whilst to the west, the Soviets would blight the outskirts of Tallinn with shoddy tower blocks and to the east ransack the coast with oil-shale exploitation, Lahemaa, the Land of Bays, was given the status of a protected national park in 1971 and great efforts were made to support and enhance the wildlife of the area. Similar support was given to restoration of the manor houses and fishing villages. The boundaries of the park stretch for 40km along the coast and include several islands. Most Estonians, and all foreigners, were forbidden to enter the park because of its proximity to the coast but this did at least prevent any tourist and industrial development. Building work is now restricted to the minimum necessary to grant access to visitors and to provide for their stay. For details of flora and fauna, see *Natural history*, page 32.

Getting there

Given the distances between major sites, hiring a car or joining a group tour is the best way to travel around the park; cyclists can bring their bikes on the many public buses that link the villages of Võsu, Käsmu and Palmse with Tallinn and Rakvere. Within a full day, it is possible to cover most sights and then return to Tallinn but now that several hotels have opened in the park, a more leisurely visit with at least one overnight stop can be recommended.

A bus service operates twice daily from Tallinn to Palmse and Sagadi, more frequently to Võsu and Viitna. There is also a twice-daily bus service from Haljala into the park. Many of the buses going east from Tallinn to Narva stop at Viitna and Haljala. A limited bus service operates within the park, but stops are always conveniently situated close to the manor houses or in the village centres.

Where to stay and eat

Hotel Park Palmse; tel: 32 23626; fax: 32 34167; email: info@phpalmse.ee; www.phpalmse.ee. This hotel was built in 1995 in the former distillery to Palmse manor house. The 30 rooms are simply furnished in wood, as is the dining room and the beer cellar. Being off the road, quiet is assured and there are plenty of short walks in the lovely grounds of the manor. Double 990EEK.

Hotel Sagadi Sagadi; tel: 32 58888; fax: 32 58880; email: sagadi@sagadi.ee; www.sagadi.ee. This ten-room hotel opened in 1998 in the house of the former farm manager, at the side of the main manor house and above the Forestry Museum. Several rooms are family ones, with bunk beds, so offer a cheap but comfortable stay for those planning several days of walking in the park. A local bus stops outside the manor and the hotel has a reasonably priced taxi service. Double 900EEK.

Merehotell Võsu; tel: 32 99279; fax: 32 99242. This is by far the biggest hotel in the park, with 75 rooms. It is situated on the edge of the village, in a pine wood about 100m from the sea. It will suit those wanting access to the sea, walking and some evening entertainment. It also caters well for children and has very reasonable long-stay rates, even in high season. As it dates from the Soviet era, rooms are larger than might be expected but the décor is totally bland. Double 600EEK.

Pension Merekalda Neeme 2; tel/fax: 32 38451; email: info@merekalda.ee; www.merekalda.ee. This guesthouse is a cluster of buildings beside the bay just outside the village. There are eight rooms, some large enough for families, and the grounds provide an ample lawn for children and gentle access to the hotel's own beach. Outside school holidays, it is a very quiet location. Whilst breakfast is provided, other meals are not, so a car is essential to reach shops and restaurants. Double 800EEK.

Kolga Hotel Kolga; tel: 32 77477; fax: 32 77270; email: kolgahotell@email.ee; www.kolgahotell.ee. This 17-room hotel has been converted from the former stables beside the manor house and offers the highest standard of rooms in the park. It also has cheaper ones, with shared facilities. Sadly the location is spoilt by a long-term restoration project for the manor house which will last several years. The nearby walks and imposing views are lacking here. Double 900EEK.

Touring the park

Leave the St Petersburg Highway from Tallinn to Narva at **Viitna** and then drive through **Palmse**, **Sagadi**, **Altja**, **Võsu**, **Käsmu** and **Kolga** before returning to the main road 18km further west. Drivers starting from the east or south will come off the main road at Haljala and begin the tour at Sagadi. Viitna is best known for its coaching inn, which dates from 1791. Like so many buildings in Estonia, it was destroyed at some stage in its history by fire; what is surprising is that the fire here was in 1989. Let us hope that it is the last serious fire to blight Estonian architecture. The inn appeals most in midwinter with its open fire and substantial portions of food, but at all times of year offers a good respite from the dull drive between Tallinn and the Russian border at Narva. It is no longer a hotel, but in the days of horse-drawn transport it served this function, being a day's ride from Tallinn. The inn was clearly divided into two sections so that masters and servants would not eat together.

Palmse Manor

The manor is 6km off the main road, the perfect distance to ensure easy access but equally to ensure a totally calm natural environment. It is without doubt the most impressive manor house in Estonia and the 15 years of restoration between 1971 and 1986 have left a lasting and appropriate memorial to the von der Pahlen family. The main building and the surrounding gardens were begun in 1697 but the Northern War between Sweden and Russia halted construction. It was completed in 1740 and then work started on the other buildings. The family lived here until 1923, when the estate was nationalised in accordance with the Land Law of 1919. The land was then divided amongst ten families and the house became a convalescent home; after World War II the Soviet administration converted it into a pioneer camp for young people. The other buildings had all been left to decline and by 1972, when restoration began, were in such poor condition that it was necessary to consult drawings and photographs from the turn of the century to see their original format. Different histories like to typecast both the architecture of the manor house and the landscaping of the gardens. The former has been labelled French, Dutch and Italian, the latter English and Chinese. None of these are helpful as the von der Pahlens wanted a tasteful, solid and modest environment both indoors and outdoors and used largely local materials. They had no desire or need for ostentation as they all had highly successful careers in many different fields. They distilled as profitably as they ran the Baltic Railway Company; their paintings are as worthy as their botanical research. Apart from one episode in 1805, their 200-year rule passed without peasant unrest and the famous Estonian writer of the 19th century, Friederich Reinhold Kreutzwald, puts this down to the relationship between the family and their farmers being similar to that between parents and children. They shunned military activity and the only sign of Prussian patriotism is the name they gave in 1871 to one of the paths through the wood – Parisian Way – following the defeat of the French by the Prussian army the previous year.

Apart from one chair in the main bedroom, and the chandelier in the reception, none of the furniture is original but the items which have been collected from all over Estonia are similar to those the family would have used. The chairs in the concert hall have all been recently produced, but follow the original designs. The late 19th-century music box is still in working order and plays 24 different pieces, mainly dance music. The drawings and charts on the first floor are by the 20th-century artist Olev Soans (1925–95) although many are modelled on 19th-century originals. On the balustrade are two monograms, one from the von der Pahlen family in 1785 and one added two hundred years later to commemorate the restoration in 1985. The tiled stoves throughout the house are original, as are the two granite obelisks which guard the entrance. In 2004 the basement wine cellars were reopened and they give considerable space for the display of 19th-century kitchenware and furniture. To the left of the main building is a small wooden one which looks like a small chapel. It has the German name 'Kavalierhaus' which defies translation into English but was where the younger people congregated. Now it would be a computer centre by day and a disco by night but, in the early 19th century, sedate dancing could take place for much of the day. Its current use is as a discreet souvenir shop. To the right of the main building is the former bath house, which has now been converted into a café.

Further left is the orchard and the greenhouse, testimony to several generations of botanists in the family. Sadly the greenhouse no longer cultivates the plums, apricots and pineapples which used to enhance the family meals. The distillery has been converted into a hotel and although it serves a wide range of Estonian spirits, none are now produced within the confines of the park. The former stables are now an information centre for the whole park and the shop there sells a wider range of maps and guides than does the souvenir shop. Particularly useful in this respect are two leaflets, *Viru Bog Nature Trail* and *Lahemaa Birds*. A walk along the lakeside is worthwhile, if only for the view back to the main house, but it can then be extended by taking one of the many different trails through the woods. Of sociological rather than architectural interest is the monument to the von der Pahlens erected in 1933 by the ten families who took over their land which shows the affection with which they were still regarded a decade after their departure. More impressive, although untouched by humans, are the erratic boulders, the massive lumps of granite that cluster in several places in the woods.

Sagadi

Sagadi is a 6km drive from Palmse and its **manor house** is very different. Local writers prefer it to Palmse, making comparisons with the chateaux on the Loire and even with the Garden of Eden. Travellers arriving with such expectations will definitely be disappointed, but those with a more open mind will see how a typical Baltic-German family lived and ruled. The land was owned by the von Fock family from the 17th century, but the current building, and those immediately surrounding it, date largely from the 1750s. Construction was not therefore hindered by the Northern War which halted work at Palmse. The façade was rebuilt in 1795, with the addition of the balcony. The von Focks had a variety of business careers, largely in shipbuilding and in forestry, but none reached the eminence of the von der Pahlens. The family lived in the building until 1939 although, following the Land Law of 1919, the estates were nationalised and the main building became a primary school. It kept this function until 1970, and soon afterwards full restoration of the whole estate began. Some of the furniture is original but, as at Palmse, many pieces have been brought from other houses which were not restored. The carpet in the banqueting hall is from Aubusson in France and belonged to President Konstantin Päts. The **Forestry Museum** used to be in the main house, but has recently been extended and is now in an annexe. Some labels are in English.

Altja

The fishing village of Altja is 8km from Sagadi. It has never been much more than a hamlet but it suffered under the Soviet regime when fishing, its sole livelihood, was banned and the population dropped from around 120 down to merely 20. Subsistence farming was hardly a substitute as only potatoes could grow in the sandy soil and the grazing lands supported only a minimal number of cattle or oxen. Fishing is now being revived and the excellent inn, which tourist groups use, provides employment during the summer. Although outsiders, even Estonians, were not allowed access to the coast at that time, restoration of the wooden buildings started in 1971. The inn dates from the early 19th century and, for most of its life, women were not admitted except on March 25, Lady Day. Most of the buildings are not in fact inhabited but are netsheds for storing boats and fishing equipment. There are several walks along the coast, and paths have been cleared between the erratic boulders. Given the isolation and, in the winter, the desolation of this village, it is hard to picture it a hundred years ago as an affluent port where the fishermen and boatbuilders could enjoy coffee and wine.

Võsu

Eighteen kilometres to the west lies the seaside resort of Võsu, popular throughout the summer with Estonian families. It was quite a grand resort in the 19th century but has since broadened its appeal, families in the 1920s coming here by ferry from Tallinn. Yet it is never overcrowded and the pine woods that back on to the beach make for pleasant short walks both in the summer and on a bright winter's day in the snow. For a grotesque Soviet experience the restaurant opposite the Merehotell can be 'recommended'. It does not merit a name so is simply called *Soogisaal* ('eating hall'). For bleak décor, surly staff, lack of hygiene and poor food, it has no equal anywhere in Estonia.

Käsmu

The village of Käsmu is a further 8km along the coast. When built in the early 19th century, it was often known as 'millionaire's village', such were the profits made from salt smuggling. In the 1920s smuggling shifted to alcohol when Finland attempted to impose prohibition. Finland gave up this aim in April 1932 and Käsmu suffered considerably. A macabre end to this traditional role came in June 1940 when many likely victims of Soviet hostility were smuggled out of Estonia before the whole country was occupied.

Käsmu is clearly no ordinary fishing village and this early prosperity shows signs of returning as affluent Tallinn businessmen buy up the former captains' houses. The main building is the **Maritime Museum** which previously served as a navigation college during the first period of independence and then as a coastguard station in the Soviet period. The large watchtower beside the building of course dates from the latter, when swimming was banned after 21.00, such was the supposed risk that escapes to Finland might be made under the cover of darkness. The museum has two unique features in that there is no admission charge and it is open at any time. The owner, Aarne Vaik, spent 20 years collecting material surreptitiously for the museum when there was no chance of displaying it. At present the collection concentrates on the 1920s and 1930s but it will be extended through World War II and the Soviet period. A natural history section to cover sea fauna and flora is also being planned. One item of particular interest to British tourists is the £1 note from 1919; with all local currencies at that time being so insecure, sterling was the only acceptable currency for maritime insurance.

Beside the village church is the **Baron Dellingshausen Memorial**, perhaps unique in being built by him to feign his death. He was implicated in the failed plot to kill Tsar Alexander II in 1881 and fled to Germany with this memorial as a safeguard against the police looking for him. The false tomb was soon discovered but the baron was able to die of natural causes in the safe environment of Potsdam. The building now houses a photographic exhibition of local people at work and at home, all the pictures having been taken in 1999.

Kolga

Kolga is 30km west of Käsmu so can be visited on the way back to Tallinn. The estate was originally a monastery, but in 1581 the Swedish king gave it to his French army commander Pontus de la Gardie as a reward for his military prowess. He himself hardly used it as he was drowned in the Narva River four years later in 1585, but the property stayed in his family until the mid 17th century when Christina de la Gardie married the Swedish Admiral Otto Stenbock. The 'Stenbock era' was to last until 1940 when the family returned to Sweden at the time of the Soviet occupation. Sadly the estate was then allowed to degenerate and only in 1980 did maintenance and restoration begin. Much remains to be done but a visit is still worthwhile as it is easy to picture how impressive the whole area must have been. The classical columns surmounted by the Stenbock coat of arms were built at the turn of the 18th and 19th centuries when the family was at its most prosperous, thanks to its successful distilling and farming. It is to be hoped that such prosperity quickly returns to the area.

Viinistu

Visitors who turned up in this village during the 1990s would have found a village that modern Estonia had completely ignored. Thanks though to a former manager of Abba, the continuingly successful Swedish pop group, it has suddenly become mainstream.

Jaan Manitski, who was born here in 1943, could chart his family links to the area stretching back 400 years, so when the family fled to Sweden in 1944, they always hoped to return. He did so in 1989 when, having made a fortune, he decided that money was no longer of great importance to him. He compared it to cow dung: something useful in small doses but which stinks in larger quantities. His first work in Viinistu was growing mushrooms; he then had a short spell as Estonian foreign minister where he caused havoc in the accounts department when he left by not bothering to claim his last month's salary. He is now part-owner of Estonia's major daily paper *Eesti Päevaleht* but what he will definitely be remembered for is the Viinistu Art Museum, which opened in 2003.

As Estonian museums are obliged to have an admission fee, and Manitski could not prevent this even in a private collection, he provides coffee and biscuits for the 10EEK he is forced to charge. Visitors are rewarded with the best collection of 20th-century Estonian art in the whole country, and in particular with works by Konrad Mägi (1878–1925) and Eduard Viiralt (1898–1954). The collection is being extended and several rooms are devoted to temporary exhibitions, some of which will undoubtedly shock more sensitive visitors, who may prefer to limit their viewing to the permanent collection. The building is beside the sea and a hotel nearby is due to be opened in 2005. Rich Estonians who patronise the arts are very rare; as more business people enjoy the success that Jaan Manitski did, let us hope they follow in his footsteps.

Jäneda

Readers of *An Estonian Childhood* by Tania Alexander, and H G Wells enthusiasts, will need no further incentive to come to this house, about an hour's train journey or bus ride from Tallinn. Although there is a railway station called Jäneda about 2km from the house, it is often quicker to take a suburban train to the last stop on the line at Aegviidu and then to arrange transport from there, as it is only 6km away.

The building dates from 1913 when it replaced an earlier one destroyed in a fire. It was modelled on the Red House in Bexley Heath, just outside London. In its early days, when still in the Russian Empire, it usually provided respite from those escaping from the Bolsheviks in Petrograd, later to be Leningrad. A British naval attaché, Dennis Garstin, composed the following ditty, anglicising the name Jäneda to Yendel:

> At Yendel girls begin the day in optimistic negligée
> Followed hot-footed, after ten, by the pyjama-radiant me.
> I'm always sad in Petrograd.
> My nicer thoughts meander back, back to Yendel.
> Oh to be in Yendel for eternity.

He was only one of many men to be seduced by Jäneda in several senses of the word. Maxim Gorky and H G Wells were amongst these others. H G Wells in fact completed his autobiography here in 1934 with the words: 'I am finishing this autobiography in a peaceful and friendly house at a small lake in Estonia.' However, the owner of the estate had himself been murdered in the grounds in 1919. He was the father of Tania Alexander. The house she describes, and to which Wells refers, Kallijärv, is not this main one but a smaller one about a kilometre away beside the lake.

In 1928, an agricultural school was founded in the main and adjoining buildings by Konstantin Päts, who would later become president of Estonia. In Soviet times, the current (2004) president of Estonia, Arnold Rüütel, studied here and agriculture has remained his major interest. The school continues to this day and some of its students work in a hotel which has just been established on this site (tel: 38 49 770; fax: 38 49 751; email: info@janeda.ee; www. janeda.ee/mois).

The museum in the main building covers the history of the estate between 1920 and 1940, with many documents fortunately being saved from then. It also covers the Soviet period of the agricultural college, with the appropriate array of red banners and portraits of Lenin and Stalin. As in so many institutes in Soviet times, the Stalin memorabilia was only hidden after 1956 and was never destroyed, though few can have imagined that it would later be brought out for ridicule rather than for devotion.

RAPLA, TÜRI AND PAIDE
Combining a visit to these towns and the surrounding villages makes a congenial tour of a day or two. Alternatively, the area can be visited en route from Tallinn to Tartu.

Getting there
Both Paide and Türi enjoy a frequent bus service north to Tallinn and south to Tartu and Viljandi. There are also east–west services which stop in both towns en route from Narva to Pärnu. Rapla has a less frequent bus service but is almost unique in Estonia in having a good train service from Tallinn. The station is in fact about 2km from the town centre but local buses meet each train. Car hire is a sensible option for travelling in this area as some of the places recommended away from these three towns are not on major bus routes.

Rapla
There can be few if any other towns in northern Europe where an archaeological dig produced two contemporary 11th-century coins, a penny minted in England under William the Conqueror and a dirhem produced under Emir Daisam in Azerbaijan. Yet Rapla was already sufficiently cosmopolitan then for many traders to stay. It has to be admitted that the region then went into decline for 700 years until Catherine II took the area seriously again. By the late 19th century, it had become sufficiently grand for German Chancellor Bismarck to pay several private visits. He was a university friend of the local Baltic-German landlord, Alexander Keyserling, whose manor house Raikküla is a few kilometres outside the town. The main oak tree there has been named 'Bismarck Tree' as the two of them used to sit and chat underneath it.

Rapla has always been at the forefront of Estonian nationalism, from the St George's Day rebellion in 1343, through peasant uprisings in the 1850s and the anti-Tsarist movement in 1905 to support for the Forest Brothers in their guerrilla warfare against Soviet forces after World War II. Estonians are proud of two separate achievements of Rapla, one in Tsarist times and one in Soviet times. Despite the size of the town, neither a Russian Orthodox church nor a statue of Lenin was ever allowed to grace the landscape. The long-term links the town is happy to mention are those with Britain. It enjoyed several centuries of timber and flax trading with Scotland and the design of early iron crosses found in the cemetery suggests that the first Christian influences might have come from there rather than through the Teutonic Knights. In the 19th century, to free themselves from German or Russian names given by their landlords, several Estonian families took British place names instead. Bristol, Glasgow and London still, as a result, feature in the local telephone book.

From an architectural point of view, the Soviet era seems to have largely passed the whole town by. This makes a short stop here particularly attractive and, for those with more time, there are many manor houses within the county which are now sufficiently restored to warrant a visit. The county also represents a microcosm of Estonian history. The Antarctic explorer, Adam Johann von Krusenstern, was born in 1770 in Hagudi, 10km to the north of Rapla on the Tallinn road. The 19th-century playwright, August Kotzebue, came from Jarlepa, to the northeast of Rapla. Otto Tief, prime minister for just one day in 1944 before he was deported to Siberia, came from **Alu**, a village just outside Rapla which has one of the best-preserved, 19th-century manor houses. Although Lennart Meri, president from 1992 to 2001, had no links with Rapla, the community is pleased that he made up for this by marrying a Rapla girl. Jüri Rumm is not a name to be found on any book jacket or in any political history of Estonia, but his fame as a 19th-century horse thief has given him legendary status and a recent film will ensure this renown continues. His cover job was as a servant at Kehtna Manor, 10km south of Rapla, but he only really came to life after dark. Monuments, museums and houses throughout the county commemorate these and many other famous Estonians linked to the area.

The town of Rapla is famous for its two-tower **Mary Magdalene Church**. This church is unique in another respect – it has never been destroyed or burnt down so the rebuilding at the beginning of the 20th century came about simply through the wishes of the local people and as a result of their affluence. The church seats 900 in all; 500 downstairs and 400 upstairs. The congregation dropped to around 200 in 1949 when public displays of religion required the greatest courage. It increased in the 1980s to around 500 and then to 1,000 at independence. At no time in the Soviet era could Christmas trees have been taken into the building, but during more liberal times, the pine trees outside the church were sometimes decorated in late December. The plaques beside the altar note the landowners who contributed to the cost of the building. The peasants who actually built the church have scrawled their names under the supporting arches. The organ, installed in 1939, was probably the last pre-war one built in an Estonian church that survives. (One built in 1940 for St Peter's Church in Narva was destroyed during the fighting in 1944.)

The church at **Juuru**, 12km east of Rapla, has its origins more in politics than in religion. It was largely rebuilt in 1895 with Baltic-German money, to help reduce the spread of Russian Orthodoxy. This was the time when the Alexander Nevsky Cathedral was built in Tallinn, so where the Lutheran Baltic Germans could fight back, they did so. Much of the interior is earlier, the pulpit being by the 17th-century Tallinn wood-carver Christian Ackermann, whose work can also be seen in Rapla and in the Dom Church in Tallinn. Panels are based on those in the Holy Ghost Church in Tallinn. The cemetery dates from 1690, so just before the plague when burials in town had to be banned on health grounds. The stone crosses have inscriptions in Estonian.

The **Mahtra Peasants Museum**, also in Juuru, covers an uprising that took place near here in 1858 against the corvée which the Russians were still trying to collect from local peasants. In the end it was suppressed, but only after bitter fighting and the use of considerable Russian reinforcements. The museum describes the fighting with the help both of models and of memorabilia, which include the manacles in which the leader of the rebellion, Hans Tertsius, was held before being sent to Siberia. The museum opened in 1970; as the revolt was more economic than nationalistic, it had a useful role to play in the Soviet presentation of Estonian history.

Mahtra War is one of the most famous novels by Eduard Vilde, written as a newspaper serial in the 1890s for the *Postimees* newspaper. The racy style which such a work needed to bring in the readers each week has ensured the continued publication of the novel, and hence the interest in this uprising. The museum, however, covers more than just the battles. There is a good 'upstairs, downstairs' contrast between day-to-day life at the manor and in the cottages at that time.

A kilometre outside Juuru is **Atla Manor**, the centre for earthenware production in Estonia. Their products are available in shops throughout Estonia, and a selection can be seen on www.keraamika.ee, but are obviously cheaper here. As usual in Estonia, there is no hard sell.

Märjamaa is to the west of Rapla so can be easily visited en route to Pärnu. The church is unusual in many respects. Its walls are 2m thick although they were never actually used in defence. On the northern side there are no windows, although the variety of designs on the south side makes up for this. Most of the building dates from the end of the 17th century. Retreating Russians bombed and totally destroyed the interior in 1941 when they thought, wrongly, that Germans had taken it over as a base. An altar by Christian Ackermann was one of many valuable pieces destroyed then. Basic restoration started in 1960 and thanks to help from the Finnish town of Vihanti, more work has been done since the re-establishment of independence.

Where to stay

Rapla has no hotels, but plenty of guesthouses and several pubs with rooms. One of the nearest to the town centre is the **Joe** (Joe 31a; tel: 48 94600; email: lehar.adoma@neti.ee; www.joe.ee) which is probably the first in Rapla to have its own website.

Türi

Turi appeals to two probably conflicting groups of people – railway enthusiasts and horticulturalists. When Estonia had a serious commitment to a railway system, it was centred on Türi, and railway workshops still operate there. The **Town Museum**, which covers its history until 1940, concentrates on the 19th-century industrialisation. It has a lot of material on the railway system but from 2005 there is likely to be a dedicated railway museum here, with some of the material currently housed in Lavassaare (see page 220) being moved to Türi.

Garden fairs take place throughout May in Türi but there is clearly collective pressure on the entire population to take horticulture seriously.

They do, after all, have the space and the time necessary for this. A visit any time during the summer will show the results of this activity.

The **Broadcasting Museum** opened here in 2002, in the same new building that houses the Town Museum. The first Estonian radio broadcasts were made from here, in view of its central location. The technical equipment and the sets that reached the consumer from the 1920s until the present day are all shown, for both radio and television.

Parts of **St Martin's Church** date back to the 13th century and it has fortunately suffered far less than many others. It is seen by some as a symbol of Estonia since it is constructed of limestone and granite as well as brick. The brick tower is a much later addition, dating from the 1860s. Perhaps this combination of styles, materials and eras explains why it featured on the 2EEK stamp in 1995. The altar is by Christian Ackermann whose work can also be seen in Juuru and Rapla, and in the Dom Church in Tallinn.

Paide

Paide, halfway between Tallinn and Tartu, makes a pleasantly quiet interlude between Estonia's two busiest cities. Paide means 'limestone' in Estonian and the German name for the town, Weissenstein, is the same. A visitor in 1923 enjoyed the peaceful atmosphere, ascribing it to the fact that the town 'had neither communists, nor capitalists, only "petits bourgeois"'. He would not be disappointed were he to return now, since the architecture of the 19th-century Town Hall Square has remained largely intact and the octagonal tower **Pikk Hermann**, blown up by the retreating Soviet army in 1941, has now been fully restored. A walk to the top offers an extensive view of the surrounding countryside, some of which can also be enjoyed from the café on the first floor. It shows quite how flat so much of the countryside in this area is. The tower has no permanent displays but a range of different temporary exhibitions; in winter, the heaters on each floor are most welcome.

The original collection of the **Järvaamaa Museum** dates from 1905 and the museum has been in this building for 45 years, but was extensively refurbished in autumn 2000. One of the founders was the mayor Oskar Brasche who had inherited a chemist's shop originally founded in 1796. He donated the complete interior of this shop to the museum. Another room portrays farming life in the late 19th century, when the abolition of serfdom made peasants largely self-reliant. The local wood was made into jugs, plates and chests, leather into shoes, and flax or wool into clothes. The use of metal was limited to knives, chisels and axes. With schools teaching in Estonian from 1835 onwards, they would all be literate. Another room shows how a more fortunate family spent their ample leisure time, in this case singing around the piano, all dressed to the nines. Like several recently restored museums, Paide no longer sees the need to eradicate the Soviet period. The 'Golden Sixties' are portrayed with smiling farmers receiving their prizes. A sitting room has been recreated so realistically that even the regulation bowl of coarsely wrapped boiled sweets has not been forgotten.

Where to stay

Hotel accommodation is much cheaper here than in Tallinn or Tartu and as
both are little more than an hour's drive away it is possible to stay in Paide and
still have a full day for sightseeing in either city. Although a very modern
town-centre hotel, the **Nelja Kuninga** (Four Kings) (Pärnu 6; tel: 38 50882;
fax: 38 50167; email: neli.kuningat@neti.ee; www.estpak.ee) reverts back with
its name to 1343, the date of the first major uprising of Estonian peasants
against their still relatively new masters, the Teutonic Knights. The four
Estonian elders chosen to represent their community in negotiations were
imprisoned in Paide Castle and then murdered so were subsequently
honoured with the title of king. The restaurant is called the 'Golden Crown'.
Clients expecting regal standards will be disappointed; those happy with a
standard three-star hotel will be pleased, particularly when comparing the
prices with Tallinn.

Paide also has a guesthouse, the **Toru** (Pikk 42; tel: 38 50385; fax: 38 51884)
which is about five minutes' walk from the town centre.

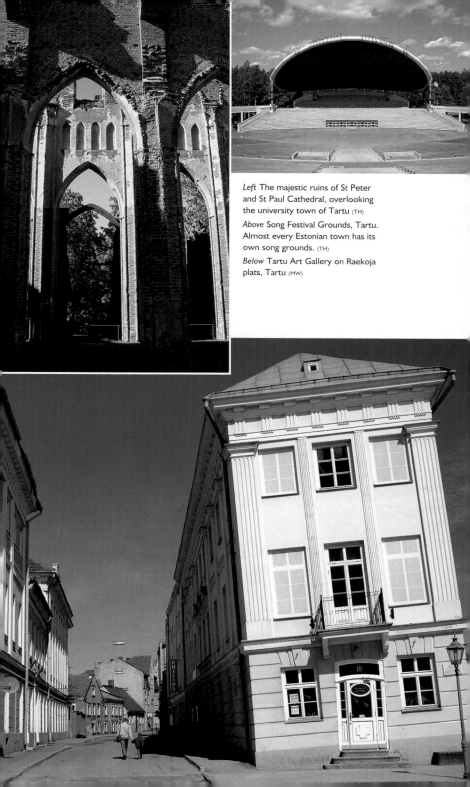

Left The majestic ruins of St Peter and St Paul Cathedral, overlooking the university town of Tartu (TH)

Above Song Festival Grounds, Tartu. Almost every Estonian town has its own song grounds. (TH)

Below Tartu Art Gallery on Raekoja plats, Tartu (MW)

Above Ruins of the castle at Viljandi, a backdrop for open-air theatre in the summer (TH)

Right Diesel train at the Russian border to the southeast (TH)

Below Holy Lake (Pühajärve), one of around 1,450 lakes in Estonia (TH)

North and Northeast Estonia

This area of Estonia has been largely ignored by tourists since independence, or at best raced through en route to St Petersburg. There are a number of reasons for this. During the Soviet occupation, many Russian settlers moved in and some towns still remain 90% Russian-speaking; their interests and commitments have therefore been eastwards rather than westwards. Decent hotels have been few and far between and industrial pollution severely harmed much of the coastal area. The larger hotels at Lake Peipsi were used to receiving allocated Soviet trade-union groups so never needed to promote themselves and could not adapt to the more fastidious requirements of middle-class Western tourists. However, since 1996 a determined effort has been made to tackle these problems and to spread the economic blessings of tourism that the rest of Estonia has enjoyed. The urban environments are now clean and strict controls ensure the maintenance of the national parks and the water flowing into Lake Peipsi. Visiting the area in 2003 was a very different experience from going in 2001. There are many new hotels, attractions are being built and some museums are actually looking for visitors, rather than seeing them as a tiresome intrusion.

RAKVERE

Rakvere is just off the main Tallinn–Narva–St Petersburg highway, about 100km from both Tallinn and Narva. Compared to most towns in Estonia, it has had a remarkably peaceful history, benefiting from membership of the Hanseatic League from 1300. It has stayed a quiet, but affluent county town, largely undisturbed by the changing political regimes. For horrendous violence, it is necessary to return to 1574 when a quarrel broke out between German and Scottish mercenaries, both serving in the Swedish army against the Russians. The Germans slaughtered most of the Scots and the few who survived that onslaught were taken prisoner by the Russians and then immediately killed.

Getting there and around

Considering the town's population of only 18,000, it is remarkably well served by buses to all parts of Estonia. In particular it is worth noting the buses that operate from here to several villages in Lahemaa National Park which enable

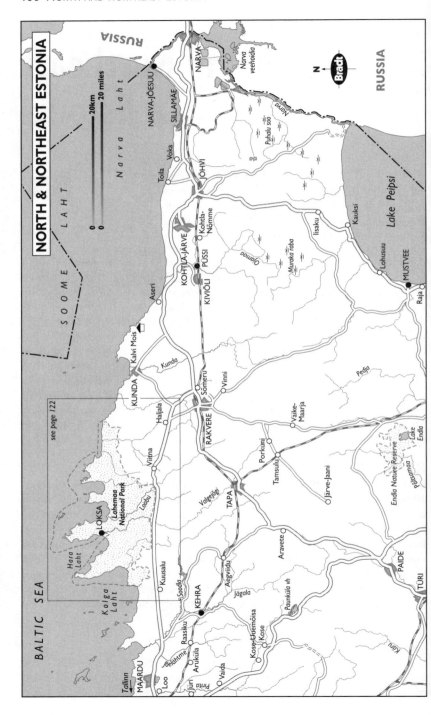

NORTH & NORTHEAST ESTONIA

RUSSIA

RUSSIA

N

20km

20 miles

0

0

SOOME LAHT

Narva Laht

BALTIC SEA

Tallinn

MAARDU

Loo

Jüri

Pirita

Oelahtme

Arukula

Vaida

Raasiku

Soodla

Kose-Uiemoisa

Kose

Kehra

Jägala

KEHRA

Paunküla vh

Aravete

Kuusalu

Valgejõgi

TAPA

Aegviidu

Kõru

TÜRI

PAIDE

Järve-Jaani

Tamsulu

Porkuni

Lake Endla

Endla Nature Reserve

Pätsamaa

Pedja

Vaike-Maarja

Vinni

Lohusuu

Raja

MUSTVEE

Lake Peipsi

Kauksi

Iisaku

Muraka raba

Qamaa

Puhatu soo

Narva veehoidla

NARVA

SILLAMÄE

NARVA-JÕESUU

Voka

Toila

JÕHVI

Kohtla-Nõmme

KOHTLA-JÄRVE

PÜSSI

KIVIÕLI

Aseri

Kalvi Mois

Kunda

KUNDA

Sõmeru

RAKVERE

Haljala

Viitna

Vihula

Loobu

Hara Laht

Kolga Laht

LOKSA

Lahemaa National Park

see page 122

visitors without a car to explore that area. Buses going south pass the Pandivere and Endla reserves. Buses to the east serve Kohtla-Järve, Narva and St Petersburg. Rakvere is also on the main railway line between Tallinn and St Petersburg, but no passenger trains have stopped here since 2001.

Where to stay and eat

Rakvere is a convenient base for exploring the nearby manor houses and castles, as well as Lahemaa National Park (see page 123). It has two excellent hotels:

Wesenbergh Tallinna 25; tel: 32 23480; fax: 32 23524; email: wesmo@neti.ee. Centrally located in a building now 100 years old, but which was fully restored in 1998, its 30 large rooms suit the business community who are its backbone throughout the winter. Some describe it as 'the end of civilisation' in view of their contempt for anything further east towards the Russian border. Double 850EEK. Next to the Wesenbergh is Estonia's only British pub, the **Old Victoria**, which imported all its furniture from Britain. Fortunately it sticks to Estonian prices so double measures of spirits cost about £1/US$1.80 and cottage or steak-and-kidney pie does not cost much more. Car drivers can sample tea with honey instead. If weather permits, the pub garden can be recommended, if only to try to spot each of 40 different species of flower grown there.

Villa Teresa Tammiku 9; tel: 32 23699; fax: 32 23432; email: aviisa@hot.ee. This small hotel has been carved out of an opening in a wood on the outskirts of the town, about 1km from the bus station and main shopping centre. It currently has only seven rooms but may well build an extension; one of the rooms has been adapted for access by the disabled. All rooms are named after German towns. One, Preetz, near Kiel, is where the owner was born. In 2003 the hotel only had Estonian TV. Double 700EEK.

Tourist information

The tourist office is very close to the bus station at Laada 14 (tel/fax: 32 42734; email: info@rakvere.tourism.ee; www.visitestonia.com/rakvere). It does not have a shop front but is on the first floor of an office block.

What to see

The **castle** dates originally from the 14th century but neglect and looting are more responsible for its current ruined state than any specific attack. It is now beyond restoration but in 2002 an extensive repair programme was begun and one can almost say that by 2004 it had become a theme park, with a Livonian dining hall and a chamber of horrors. It can now offer performances both inside and outside during the summer. Details of these performances can be checked on the castle website, www.rakvereteater.ee.

The 750th anniversary of the founding of Rakvere in 1252 was marked by the commission of a statue of a bison from Tauno Kangro, whose work is always provocative and always larger than life, particularly where the depiction of sexual organs is concerned. This bison is no exception, as it weighs seven tons and has a distance of 3m between its two horns. The plinth lists all the donors who contributed, and also gives a history of the castle in the languages of its many occupiers – Danish, German, Polish, Russian and Swedish. The

AN UNFORTUNATE DISCOVERY

A local legend ascribes the discovery of oil-shale as a fuel to a peasant who built a sauna from what he took to be a reliable stone. When planning a relaxing evening in front of his new stove, he was horrified to see it engulfed in the flames he had just generated. He suffered, but in the long term, Estonia would benefit from the discovery of 'combustible stone', which is the literal translation of the Estonian word for oil-shale.

Danes introduced stone buildings into Estonia in the 13th century. Before that, they were all of wood.

The **secondary school** on Vabaduse Tänev (Freedom Street) is an unexpected masterpiece of Estonian functionalist architecture and was fortunately just completed before the first Soviet invasion in 1940. It was unique at the time in building classrooms for specific subjects and in allocating space specifically for a gymnasium. Its special status continued to be recognised in the 1960s during the Soviet period when a swimming pool was added. For many years the **Rakvere Museum** (Tallinna 3) did not do the town justice but recent additions in the archaeological section, models of former burial mounds and a new section on the manor houses of the surrounding county now make a visit worthwhile. The value of a visit to the **Citizen's Home Museum** (Pikk 50) has never been in doubt. It has been owned and inhabited since the late 18th century by a number of successful small businessmen, each of whom added tastefully to the furnishings, upholstery and kitchenware. The museum opened in 1983 and ever since then donations from local people have helped to broaden the collection. Recent additions include workshops of a tailor and of a cobbler and many photographs from the 1920–40 period. Twenty-five kilometres south of Rakvere is the **Väike-Maarja Museum** (Pikk 10) in the village of the same name. It is unique in Estonia in its concentration on the Soviet period. This is because it was the most successful collective farm in Estonia and made its director Boris Gavronski famous all over the USSR. He came in 1967 and stayed until its end in 1990. Between 1979 and 1987 he increased monthly wages from the already high 250 roubles a month to the enormous 350 a month. A few exhibits are from earlier times and a 19th-century schoolroom has been recreated. As Väike-Maarja is on the Rakvere–Tartu road, it is easy to reach by bus from either town. For those travelling by car, it is worth making a small detour to the northeast on the way back to Rakvere by visiting **Porkuni**, a castle tower dating from the 15th century which houses the Limestone Museum. Many of the exhibits are of interest only to professional geologists, but plenty of others show how important Estonia's national stone has been in its history. The other buildings date from the 1870s and since the 1930s have continuously housed a school for the deaf.

TAPA

Tapa owes everything to the development of the railways in the 19th century. What was formerly a little village had the good fortune to find itself at the junction of the Tallinn–St Petersburg and Tallinn–Tartu railways which opened in 1870 and 1876 respectively. It then also became a major agricultural distribution centre, earning the nickname 'sausage town' from its importance in the meat trade. It suffered widespread bombing from the Soviets during their retreat in 1941 and before their return in 1944. More recently they have bequeathed an enormous military and air-force base which can be seen from the Paide Road. For those in a car, a short diversion is worthwhile to see it in its full horror. Although different, the destruction by the departing soldiers was as ruthless as that carried out by their grandfathers 50 years earlier. Anything with possible resale value was removed so no single thread of copper wire or a single piece of wood remains. Stolen petrol too bulky to take was poured into the ground, ruining the water supply and potential civilisation for several years afterwards. Only water supplies over 150m below ground could be regarded as safe. With the uncertainties surrounding Estonian rail privatisation in late 2001, the town now has to look to diversification into small-scale manufacturing and into agriculture to ensure its future. It has, however, no plans to abandon its coat of arms, a silver letter 'T' on a red background, symbolising the railway junction.

Getting there and around

The train takes about an hour to Tallinn, two hours to Tartu and 45 minutes to Rakvere. Buses also serve these three towns, as well as Rapla and Paide. Buses leave from the railway station which is appropriately located right in the town centre.

What to see

The **Orthodox church** (1904) and the **Methodist church** (1920) are both close to the station and show the divided ethnic loyalties of the town. Both are still well supported, financially and with good congregations. The **museum**, in Pikk, about a kilometre from the station, dates only from 1991, but has built up a remarkably diverse collection in that time and is constantly expanding. The railway theme of course predominates, with pictures, timetables, uniforms, ticket printers, gas lamps and even candle lights. There is also a banknote display covering 1920–40, ceramics and glassworks. Hopefully the departure of the Soviet military and the town's current transition can soon be covered.

Visits to the railway workshops can be arranged for specialist groups and much current and abandoned rolling stock can be seen from public areas including a Russian L-1361 steam engine built in 1950 and displayed here since 1975.

KOHTLA-JÄRVE

If any Estonian town aiming to attract tourists is likely to fall victim to music-hall jokes, it must be Kohtla-Järve. Its comprehensive English-language brochure admits that it has no ancient history or beauty, but hopes that visitors will realise that it has great potential. It then proclaims the rather ambiguous slogan that 'Kohtla-Järve is mostly open to the winds of change'. A small town before World War II, it was rapidly developed in Soviet times as an industrial centre with the expansion of the oil-shale mines. A new chemicals plant was established to use the raw materials that the oil-shale provides. Kohtla-Järve is now the fourth-largest town in the country, after Tallinn, Tartu and Narva. By the late 1980s, the town had become a byword for industrial pollution, and much early political activity in Estonia against the Moscow authorities was aimed at bringing this to the attention of the international community. This pollution has now been controlled, but the city buildings and the health of older residents will remain scarred for many years to come.

Such political activity did not come from the Russians, who moved into the area to work in the mines and factories, but from ethnic Estonians now living elsewhere. Most Russians in Estonia were happy at least to acquiesce in the moves towards independence; only in Kohtla-Järve were there serious attacks on, for instance, the increasing use of the Estonian language from 1988.

The artificial hills surrounding the town are from the layers of limestone that divide the beds of oil-shale and which are surplus to the requirements of the cement industry. The likely future of these hills is as artificial ski slopes or as hang-gliding centres, since the few natural hills in Estonia are a good 150km to the south and this area is assured of regular, substantial snow falls throughout the winter.

Getting there and around
Local buses regularly serve Jöhvi, Sillamäe and Narva. At Jöhvi it is possible to change to buses going to Tartu, Valga and Võru. There is no hotel suitable for foreign tourists here.

What to see
From around 2000, Kohtla-Järve and the surrounding towns really began to try to present themselves internationally. Earlier visitors to the **Oil-Shale Museum** were amused to see a Soviet exhibition that had not changed since the early 1980s with a beaming Leonid Brezhnev, ever-rising production figures and workers who never strike. The local government was of course sensible to close it down and rebuild the exhibition in modern surroundings in 2000 – it is now in the Town Hall – even if the result is more predictable. For those not interested in the technical side, several dramatic paintings and sculptures are also on display.

The functionalist **secondary school** is very similar to that in Rakvere, although built by a different architect. The large, rounded projection can be compared to that on the Ranna Hotel in Pärnu. The **Orthodox church** may well be unique in its functionalist design. The lack of any onion motifs or other similarities to what is normally expected in the design of Orthodox churches is clearly a reflection of anti-Russian feeling at the time it was built. The museum and the church are both on Jarvekula, the main street through the town. The school is on Spordi, a cross street to Jarvekula and close to the museum.

Even those who can only make a 'virtual' visit to the **Kohtla Mining Museum** (www.kaevanduspark.ee) will instantly see what progress has been made in the last few years. It is probably the only museum in Estonia to open seven days a week on a year-round basis and to open during the week at 09.00. Those who take the trouble to go, and visitors do so from all over Estonia, are rewarded with travel on the underground railways, the obligation to wear protective clothing and, perhaps less enticing, the chance to eat a miner's meal. Life outside the museum buildings is equally active, with the former slag heaps now converted into tracks for skiing, orienteering and motor cycling to ensure year-round use.

Where to stay

Alex Kalevi 3; tel: 33 96230; fax: 33 96241; email: alexhotell@hot.ee; www.alex.ee. A small modern hotel is most welcome in Kohtla-Järve; it only has ten rooms and some may feel there is overkill on the facilities offered to attract local people in as well. There are nine billiard tables and a casino that closes only 07.00–09.00. However these can easily be avoided by guests wanting a conventional stay, as can presumably the 'drug-shop' which the website offers as a nearby facility. Double 800EEK.

Kalvi Mois Tel: 33 95300; fax: 33 95301; email: kalvihotell@kalvimois.ee; www.kalvi-hotel.com. The location beside the coast, down an unmade track, about 30km from Kohtla-Järve and a similar distance from Rakvere is very appropriate. A fortification has been situated here for centuries and it hosted a wide range of activities, few of them legal or pleasant. The turbulent sea was a convenient source of instant shipwrecks and equally useful for the disposal of unwanted bodies. The tunnels were more important than the living rooms. The remains of earlier buildings can still be seen in the grounds and they were all destroyed in a fire in 1910, which of course remains unexplained. The von Stackelberg family wanted to put the past behind them and to live as other Baltic-German barons had done in Estonia for centuries, but with the building completed only in 1914, this was never to be. However, the basic fabric, a mixture of limestone, brick and granite survived the turbulence of the 20th century and luxury finally returned in 2002. Most people thought the new owners mad to open in such isolated surroundings but the hotel has rightly been a great success, mixing conferences, weddings, hunting parties and individual tourists. 'Kaffee und Kuchen' gives it a German touch, and afternoon tea a British one. Sporting facilities are offered, too, but this is probably a place just to relax and to enjoy the sea, of course from a distance. Double 2,500EEK.

TOILA

The village of Toila is situated on the coast 10km to the north of Jõhvi. Such is the intensity of feeling towards the pre-war President Konstantin Päts that the site of his summerhouse, although now destroyed, is still a centre of interest to local tourists. The palatial building was originally constructed at the turn of the century by a St Petersburg businessman hoping to present it to the Tsar in return for a title. The Estonian government bought it as a summer residence for the president in 1935 but it was destroyed by the retreating Soviet army in 1941. Only the terrace, the entrance gates, the long gravel drive encompassed by willow trees and steps to the garden remain, although a series of underground passages is also gradually being reopened. Yet the surroundings are of such unusual natural beauty that it is easy to forget the absence of the palace. The Püha River cuts a dramatically deep course through the estate to the sea, with a botanical garden formed on either side. Sheer cliffs stretch along the coast for several kilometres. An outdoor concert centre was completed in 1995 with seating for several thousand and only the absence of cheap accommodation prevents more visitors from coming.

Getting there
Buses run several times a day from Jõhvi and taxis for this short journey are not expensive. A driver/guide is worthwhile for Toila and the neighbouring area. This can be arranged as part of a tour or on the spot at the tourist office in Jõhvi.

Where to stay
Toila Sanatoorium Ranna 12; tel: 33 25233; fax: 33 25326; email: info@toilasanatoorium.ee; www.toilasanatoorium.ee. So international does this hotel want to be that its website is in four languages and its prices were quoted in euro in 2002, five years before Estonia was likely to adopt that currency. Probably people will meet here whose paths would never cross elsewhere. Russians will come on sentimental grounds, thinking it is still home. Finns will come because the basic costs and those for treatments are so much lower than those at home, or elsewhere in Estonia. Estonians will use it as a base for work or pleasure over the whole northeast. To Westerners it can be recommended for similar reasons. It offers enough on site for taking it easy, but is a useful base from which to drive, walk or cycle along the coast and to explore inland as well. Double 700EEK.

Where to eat
There is a good restaurant in Toila, the **Fregatt** (Pikk 18; tel: 33 69647). It has attracted a middle-aged clientele with its dependable steak, generous Irish coffee and the music of Roy Orbison. They are quite willing to turn off the music altogether, or to substitute contemporary Estonian music.

JÕHVI
Jõhvi is the capital of Ida Viru, the eastern county of Estonia. At first glance, it is tempting to write it off as a Soviet leftover, best driven through at the fastest speed possible. Certainly other towns in the area still have a completely Russian feel but Jõhvi is clearly trying to promote co-existence. This must be its future, with a population one-third Estonian and two-thirds Russian. The town is re-establishing an Estonian identity, without trying to hide a Russian past of half a century. This is seen in the variety of shops recently established and the enormous rebuilding programme underway in the town centre. The development of exports such as dairy products is, however, geared to Russia.

Getting there and around

The bus station is close to both the Town Hall and the Pääsuke Hotel. Perhaps because the local population are poorer here than elsewhere in Estonia, fewer people have cars so the public transport system is much more extensive. Direct services operate frequently all over the country, with hourly buses to Tallinn, Kohtla-Järve, Narva, Rakvere and Kuremäe and a service four times a day south to Tartu and Võru. The daily Tartu–St Petersburg bus stops in Jõhvi.

Where to stay

Paasuke Kaare 11; tel: 33 22268; fax: 33 70190. For years this was Jõhvi's only hotel, used largely by long-stay foreigners. From the outside it looks an extremely improbable hotel, being situated in an unlit, pot-holed side street and forming part of a very dreary block of flats. Although the public rooms continue this uninviting pattern, several of the bedrooms have been well renovated. It is a tradition built up amongst those who stay there that extra breakfast ingredients should be brought in to supplement the rather repetitive buffet that the hotel offers. Double 650EEK.
Wironia Rakvere 7; tel: 33 64200; fax: 33 64210; email: info@wironia.ee; www.wironia.ee. This 18-room hotel opened in autumn 2004. Despite its small size, it has a restaurant and conference facilities.

Tourist information

The tourist information office is at Rakvere 13a; tel/fax: 33 70568; email: info@johvi.tourism.ee; www.tourism.ee/johvi.

What to see

Architecturally, the Town Hall, which dominates the centre, can only be Estonian with its mixture of functionalism and classicism. Some neighbouring Soviet horrors can therefore be forgiven. The nearby **Lutheran church** has also survived the frequent changes in secular regimes and managed to win support from all of them despite the execution of two vicars, one in 1918 and one in 1941. This latter fact gives it the macabre distinction of being the only church in Estonia with two martyrs. The Soviets in a small way redeemed themselves by keeping the church open and by rebuilding the organ in the early 1950s. In 1984, they also rebuilt the tower, which had been destroyed by the Germans in 1943. As the church was as much a castle as a place of worship, it has a complex array of tunnels and hiding places. The pulpit has frequently been repainted, but the design is the original early 18th-century baroque. The altar is modern, but the six steps that lead up to it disguise a cover for an extended cellar which over many centuries housed supplies and hid troops. Now it hosts exhibitions and an audio-guide is available to give further background to the history of the church.

Kuremäe

Tourists who appreciate the Golden Ring around Moscow should travel the 25km south from Jõhvi to visit the largest Russian Orthodox church outside

Tallinn. **Pühtitsa Convent** at Kuremäe was completed in 1910 and seats 1,200 people; services are often full with most members of the congregation travelling long distances to attend. Six smaller churches, a museum and a formal garden were added later to the complex which is surrounded by a brick wall. Remarkably, the community of around 150 nuns and the buildings themselves were unharmed through all the changes in regime of the last hundred years. The museum chronicles this remarkably peaceful story. The surrounding land, which the nuns cultivate, produces enough to support the community and to cater for visitors, and the sale of tasteful souvenirs is beginning to ensure maintenance of the buildings. Note the cemetery just outside the compound. Wrought-iron crosses are frequently seen in northern Estonia but it is rare to find such a large number of fine examples in one single cemetery.

SILLAMÄE

At long last it is possible to picture Sillamäe as it was in the 19th century when Tchaikovsky was just one of many Russian musicians and artists who came here during the summer. Natural colour is returning with its trees and flowers and the pastel decoration on the larger buildings has now recovered from 40 years of pollution. The wide stone steps down to the seafront are clearly modelled on the Crimea. Architecturally, it is possible to use the word 'Stalinist' in a positive sense as the neo-classicist buildings in the town centre all date from the early 1950s, although one has to mention that many were constructed by German prisoners of war held in the Soviet Union until 1955. Two buildings from that time, the cultural centre and the cinema, have preservation orders on them.

It was the construction in 1928 of an oil-shale processing plant and its massive expansion after the war that led to the horrendous pollution of the 1970s and 1980s. As uranium was processed here for the Soviet military, the town was closed even to most Estonians. Adjusting suddenly to environmental concerns, to the free market and to Estonian as a working language has been very difficult, but from around 2000 progress has been clearly seen. The port is being developed, training colleges are being established and, although Russian grandees from St Petersburg are unlikely to return, there is no reason why tourism should not be promoted. The museum gives a vivid and extensive picture of the town in Soviet times. It even has a 'red' room festooned with banners, tapestries and statues. Some exhibits go back to the 1930s and some of those from the 1950s are not all that different from what a British museum of that era would show – television sets with doors, wind-up gramophones and radiograms with legs. The population is Russian-speaking, although all signs are in Estonian. A few road names that would not be acceptable elsewhere in the country have been kept here, such as one that commemorates the spaceman Yuri Gagarin.

Where to stay and eat

Krunk Kesk 23; tel: 239 24076; fax: 239 24165; email: orders@krunk.ee; www.krunk.ee. Although Narva is the third-largest town in Estonia, it still does not have a business-class hotel, so this hotel really serves that function as Narva is only 24km away. It offers the full panoply of conference facilities, satellite TV, internet connections in every room and a restaurant with a wide menu. All this has been taken for granted for years elsewhere in Estonia, but not in the northeast, so this hotel was most welcome when it opened in 2001. Double 700EEK.

NARVA

Narva could only be a border town. It is dominated by its fortress which always defended it, until the 20th century brought aerial bombardment. The Narva River now separates the town from Ivangorod in Russia and ever-larger border posts on both sides reinforce this. During the first period of independence, between 1920 and 1940, the frontier was about 8km further east but most Estonians are now reconciled to this new border, although it has not been formally agreed between the two governments. At times of tension in Russia, such as during the currency crisis of autumn 1998, the clear division that the river provides between the two countries is probably welcomed in Tallinn. When Estonia joined the EU and NATO in 2004, this welcome spread well beyond Tallinn. Local residents have to be more ambivalent as the population is almost entirely Russian-speaking and, of the 14 schools in the town, only one teaches in Estonian. Perhaps this ambivalence is best shown in the statue of Lenin that is still on display in the castle grounds: although hardly in a prominent position, he looks firmly eastwards across the Narva River to Russia. He has presumably abandoned any hope of his ideology returning to the land behind him. Were he able to turn round, he would find a large McDonald's and a German pub serving Irish beer. He would not have been happy to know that, in a petition circulated in September 1998 over the river in Ivangorod, the local population asked to rejoin Estonia.

A rushed visit to Narva can be made in a few hours, as a break en route from Tallinn to St Petersburg, but it is worth spending the night there to allow for time to visit the town properly. A visit can be extended to include the seaside resort of **Narva-Jõesuu.**

History

Narva's history goes back as far as that of Tallinn, as both cities were built up following the Danish occupation in the 13th century and the two cities would witness many successes and defeats in parallel as conquerors and defenders quite rightly saw both as equally important. Both cities would look back to the 200-year Swedish era of the 16th and 17th centuries as the most benevolent occupation and the most successful commercial era, prior to independence. The architectural legacy of that era in Narva is now restricted to a few buildings as so much was lost in World War II and in subsequent development. Peter the Great realised the potential of Narva as a harbour, just as he did with Tallinn, and developed it accordingly. In 1700 he lost a battle with the Swedes there but four years later he was able to seize the town.

In the 19th century Narva developed quickly into a major industrial centre. This was in due course to centre around the **Kreenholm Manufacture**, a strange translation which stuck through all regimes until 2000 when the current Swedish owners changed it to **Krenholm Textiles** at the same time taking out one 'e' from Kreenholm to give the name a more Western flavour. It was established in the 1850s and was soon to employ 10,000 workers. Its founder was one of the most successful industrialists amongst the Baltic Germans, Baron Ludwig Knop. His constant presence in any new industrial development gave rise to the ditty: 'In any church there is the pope, in any plant there is the Knop.'

In 1870 the opening of the St Petersburg–Narva–Tallinn railway provided a great stimulus to the business but then, in 1872, Kreenholm was the site of one of the first strikes in Tsarist Russia, with workers protesting against the 14-hour day imposed by management. Workers were again active in the 1905 and 1917 uprisings. Kreenholm's textile production, however, survived under all regimes, winning in the Soviet era the Order of Lenin and the Order of the October Revolution. In 1994, the factory was sold to the Swedish company Boras Walfveri and by 1999 was profitable, selling largely to western Europe, with Estonian management and a Russian-speaking workforce. Some of the lessons learnt came from the first independence period of 1920–40, when the border with the Soviet Union was as closed to trade as is the current one with Russia. At that time the labour force dropped from 10,000 to 2,500. In 2003 the factory had to start laying off workers again in order to compete with factories in Asia, but in 2004 its workforce consisted of 3,400 employees.

The end of World War I would see many battles in the vicinity of Narva but not actually in the town itself. The success of the Estonian forces in driving back the Bolsheviks enabled them to impose a harsh territorial settlement on the nascent Soviet Union in the Tartu Treaty signed in February 1920. In contrast, from January to July 1944, Narva suffered one of the most intense bombardments of World War II as Soviet forces retook it from the Germans. It became known as 'Women's City' since so few men survived the battle and the women had been evacuated as the fighting started. Even with massive post-war immigration, by 1960 the population was 70% female and 30% male. Much of the town was destroyed, although it is now felt that more could have been restored had the Soviet government wanted to do so. Warsaw could have provided a model and the town is now seeking foreign investment to make whatever amends are possible in one or two streets.

The Soviet era saw a return to massive industrial expansion with the construction of a hydroelectric power station and several furniture plants, using the locally mined oil-shale, with disastrous effects on the local environment. The resort of **Narva-Jõesuu**, protected from this pollution, appealed to the 'nomenclatura' and to the trade unions, so its continued future as a health centre and summer beach resort was assured. The early 1990s, when independence was restored, was an uncertain period in Narva as most of the population found themselves stateless in a foreign country, being of Russian origin and unable to speak Estonian. Whilst Narva remains poor by Estonian standards, the dire conditions over the river in Ivangorod and the surrounding countryside reconcile the local population to being cut off from

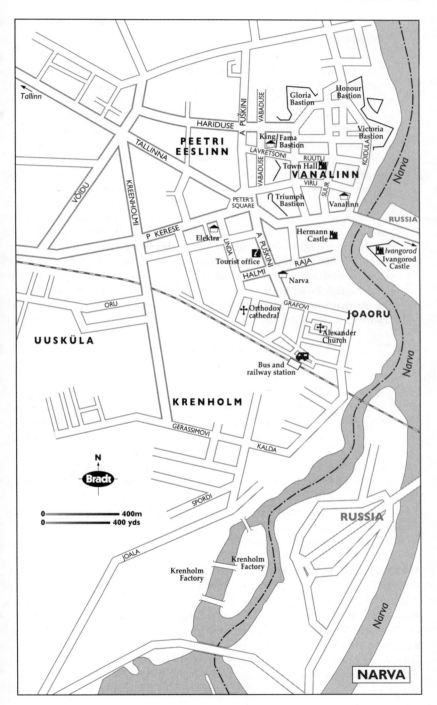

BATHING IN PRE-WAR ESTONIA

Ronald Seth

Where the pine forest comes right down to the edge of the shore, it is possible to bathe without costumes, the women on the right, the men on the left. This is a custom which has been inaugurated at most Estonian seaside resorts. I was told an amusing story by an English woman writer, whom I met later in the summer. She and her son found themselves at Narva-Jõessu on their way back from a visit to Finland. They went down to the beach armed with costumes and towels, and sat down on a bench wondering if it were permissible to undress on the beach. They did not know the regulations and were all the more chary because they could distinguish a policeman hovering in the distance. As they sat there in uncertainty, two young men came along and sitting on the next bench a few yards away, took off all their clothes and ran down to the sea nonchalantly naked. After that, there was no further need for scruples at all. It is of no use, a woman who has wandered on to the wrong part of the beach, complaining to the authorities of the indecent behaviour of the men. It is their own fault if they go there and are shocked. [Nude bathing was apparently common in pre-war Estonia although this is no longer the case.]

Extract from 'Travels in Estonia' published in 1939

their former neighbours. Each year more can meet the language requirements for Estonian citizenship and potential new industrial developments will hopefully reduce unemployment. Krenholm has shown how a totally Soviet environment can quickly adapt to Western demands. Estonia's accession into the EU caused great problems for the Russian-speaking community in Narva as border controls on both sides became even tougher than they had been for the previous 12 years. It is perhaps significant that all the signs to the border are bilingual, not in Estonian and Russian but in Estonian and English. One English word now current in Estonia – 'secondhand' – has more poignancy in Narva than elsewhere. It describes a shop full of goods that no serious dealer would handle so is really a sheltered flea market.

Getting there and around

Narva is very well served by local and express buses. When travelling to Tallinn or Tartu, it is important to book an express rather than a much slower bus that stops en route. There are frequent services to Narva-Jõesuu on the coast. Three Tallinn–St Petersburg buses a day stop en route at Narva and there are also buses that start in Narva and then cross the border into Russia. It is possible to catch the overnight Tallinn–St Petersburg train in either direction at Narva but with its departure times of 01.00 or 03.00, this is not ideal. There is also an overnight train to Moscow which currently leaves at 21.00, but the return train arrives in Narva at 05.00. With the cut-back in Estonian rail services in 2000 and 2001, Narva now has no day trains at all so the booking office is open between 17.00 and 05.00 rather than the other way round.

Where to stay and eat

Most tourists staying in Narva use the small **Hotel Vanalinn** (Koidula 6; tel: 35 22486; fax: 35 24120; email: vanalinn@hot.ee), a converted 17th-century townhouse within walking distance of the castle and overlooking the river to Russia. The best views can be enjoyed in winter. The majestic monuments to Tsarist power stand out through the snow, which also covers much of the current dereliction. Appropriately for a fortress town, the restaurant is in a well-bricked cellar. Double 500EEK. Business people tend to use the higher standard **Elektra** (Kerese 11; tel: 35 22024; fax: 35 31607; email: hotel@nev.ee), which is about 500m from the castle but which only has ten rooms, so is often fully booked. The hotel uses the smaller of the two entrances which leads up to a reception on the first floor. The other caters for local people paying, and often disputing, their electricity bills. The guesthouse is overlooked by the power station. Because there is nowhere else to stay in Narva, it is important to pre-book before arrival. Double 600EEK.

In 2005 the hotel situation should be different with the reopening of the **Narva Hotel** (Pushkini 6; tel: 35 99600; fax: 35 99603; email: hotel@narvahotell.ee; www.narvahotell.ee), which has been closed since the end of the Soviet era. At the time of writing the only information available is that it will have 51 rooms and the building will be totally renovated.

The **Kohvik Aleksandr** (Pushin 13) is conveniently situated next to the tourist office. It serves meals, snacks and drinks all day. The **German Pub** (Puskini 10; tel: 35 31548) is both restaurant and pub and serves Guinness and Murphys as well as the predictable German and Estonian brands. The **King** (Lavretsovi 9; tel: 35 72404; email: vestaking@hot.ee; www.hotelking.ee) is probably Narva's best restaurant, admittedly from a limited choice. In 2002 the restaurant started to let rooms and became a hotel. The staff speak good English, they are well trained and the menu is extensive, yet it would be hard to spend more than £6/US$9 on dinner there. The brass instruments hanging on the walls offer a novel and unexpected décor. Sadly, they are not used for the live music at weekends but the 'King' (Elvis Presley) is well played as is more modern music when it is requested. Double 800EEK. Around Peter's Square (Peetri Plats) there are plenty of cafés where substantial meals can be had for little more than £2/US$3. Expect more leisurely service than elsewhere in Estonia, but a welcome absence of mobile phones. The **castle** has an excellent restaurant but it only serves pre-booked groups. Tourists travelling to St Petersburg often have lunch there en route.

Tourist information

The tourist office is at Puskini 13; tel: 35-60184; fax: 35-60186; email: info@narva.tourism.ee.

What to see

Narva Castle dates from the 13th century and amazingly, for the first hundred years, survived as a wooden structure. Some of the current brickwork dates from the 14th century, but the 50m-high **Herman Tower** and the final extensions were built in the 16th century. This final strengthening followed the building of **Ivangorod Fortress** over the river. No other castle in Estonia is as well preserved, except perhaps for Kuressaare on Saaremaa Island. It is a town within a town, and when necessary could be self-sufficient for months on end. Allow at least two hours for walking around the ramparts and exploring the **museum**. Inevitably, the museum has concentrated on military history but soon should have more material on the Soviet period. Some rooms are usually devoted to temporary exhibitions of modern art. Extensive renovation is currently in hand so sometimes certain areas are closed to visitors. Guides are happy to point out the contrasting neglect of Ivangorod Fortress. Just to the north of the castle is the modern road bridge to Russia, but on the other side, now incorporated into a riverside park, are nine massive bastions built by the Swedes as a further defence against the Russians. This is now a peaceful area, ideal for a walk on a summer's evening. As the castle ramparts are open all day, photographers may well wish to return on several occasions to record different views. The back of the 5EEK note shows Narva and Ivangorod Castles. The range of subterranean passages beneath the park still remains to be fully excavated.

There are no regular tours of the factory at Krenholm Textiles, but these can be arranged with prior notice. Visitors will see how much use of the former infrastructure has been salvaged and adapted to EU safety requirements. Some new machinery has of course been imported, but not as much as one might expect. For once, most signs are in Russian, so that they are sure to be understood! The current workforce is around 3,500 and likely to stay at that level. The presence of a Swedish consulate next to the factory suggests further involvement elsewhere in the town. It is on an island in the river as the waterfall beside it used to provide its power. The outside of the building, which suffered little damage in the war, is best viewed from the pedestrian bridge which is one of the border crossings to Russia. This vantage point also offers good views of the river for photographers. The factory shop beside this bridge sells pillowcases, tablecloths, flags, aprons and oven gloves at well below normal Estonian prices. It is, however, only open Monday–Friday and does not accept credit cards.

Returning into the town along Pushkin, note one of the few other large buildings that survived the war, the **Vasili Gerassimov Culture House**. The interior was repaired during 2001 and returned to being an enormous centre for plays, films and concerts. Gerassimov was one of the leaders of the strike at Kreenholm in 1872. The 17th-century **Town Hall**, of baroque design, was restored in the early 1960s. An account written in 1938 describes the doorway as 'typical of Swedish Narva' but sadly it is now unique in this context. Two other buildings of note also escaped serious damage in the war, the **Orthodox cathedral** and the **Lutheran church**. The foundation stone of the Orthodox cathedral was laid by Tsar Alexander III in 1890. It is located beside Krenholm and was designed by the same architect, Pavel Alish. The massive new Russian consulate is now situated beside the Lutheran church.

The town council is hoping to raise US$5million to restore the old town centre, which would encourage more visitors, while those who already come might stay longer. In due course it may be possible to make visa-free day trips to Ivangorod on the other side of the Narva River, but at present the Russian consulate in Narva is as strict and as expensive as any other around the world.

NARVA-JÕESUU

The road to Narva-Jõesuu on the coast follows the river for 14km. In the summer this trip can be done by boat. On leaving the town, the road passes several memorials and cemeteries. As elsewhere in Estonia, the Soviet ones have been left but those dedicated to independence fighters in 1918 have been restored and others erected in memory of those deported in 1941 and 1949. There is also a cemetery for the many German soldiers killed in 1944. Pine forests, the widening of the river and soil turning to sand announce the approach to the resort. It is not now an affluent town and does not seem to be addressing the problem in the way that its neighbours are. It certainly was prosperous during the 19th century when it was as popular as Haapsalu or Pärnu for the St Petersburg aristocracy. During the first independence period it had an equal appeal to the Tallinn élite. The allocated places were highly sought after during the Soviet era as the slightly Western feel it could offer was appreciated by all those unlikely ever to travel abroad. Its earlier history had been very different. Legend has it that its 17th-century German name of Hungerburg was given to it by shipwrecked German sailors unable to find any food in the vicinity.

The beach is about 13km long so is never crowded. The town is very spacious, full of villas and small hotels built amongst the pine woods. There are no high-rises. On hot days in July, it could almost be Mediterranean.

Getting there
See under *Getting there and around* for Narva, page 148.

Where to stay and eat
In contrast with other towns in this area, there has, however, been little new building or upgrading since the mid 1990s. One exception is the **Hotel-Spa Narvajoesuu** (Aia 3; tel: 35 99529; fax: 35 99525; email: info@narvajoesuu.ee; www.narvajoesuu.ee) which has clearly tried, and succeeded, in recreating the ambience taken for granted here in the 1930s. Everything it offers is clearly four-star; it stands out in a town where mediocrity and even decrepitude is becoming standard. Double 860EEK. One of the few completely new hotels to open here since 2000 is the **Minister** (Jüri 5; tel: 35 99530; fax: 35 99541; email: info@minister.ee; www.minister.ee). Double 750EEK.

LAKE PEIPSI

Estonia's largest lake, and the fifth-largest lake in Europe, now forms the border with Russia so it faces an uncertain future. In Tsarist times, the Estonian side provided refuge for the Old Believers, persecuted in larger cities from the 17th century until the end of the Tsarist era in the 20th century for their disaffection with the Orthodox Church; they were allowed to live in relative peace in the isolated border lands. They maintain customs abandoned by the 'modern' Church but even within this community there are differences in their degree of 'oldness'. At Mustvee, for instance, the church has electricity, but at Raja only beeswax candles are used. Men and women are always kept apart in their services. Nowadays it forms a sort of refuge for a new generation of Old Believers, who cannot cope with the pace and new direction of contemporary Estonia. In Soviet times, the Estonian side supported fishing and a large number of trade union holiday centres. The villages tend to divide themselves into Estonian and Russian speaking and this is reflected in the architecture too. Russian communities are much more open whereas Estonians want their privacy. If you see a hedge, the house behind it will belong to an Estonian-speaking family. From the border at the Narva River around to Raja, south of Mustvee, the villages are 'Russian'. From Kasepää southwards, they are Estonian. The 2,000 population of Mustvee is equally divided. A recent census found 1,000 Estonian speakers and 1,000 Russian speakers but it did not say which they use amongst themselves. *Mustvee* means 'black water', and it describes the colour of the river as it reaches the lake after passing through several swamps.

Fishermen must now be careful not to stray across the border in the middle of the lake and are having to survive on a limited catch. They also run allotments growing cucumbers and onions. The structures of the old collectives have remained although these are now voluntary associations of fishermen who realise they can make more money this way than by attempting to operate totally on their own. The fresh yellow paint on many of their houses, which matches the dandelions that grow in profusion here, proves the point. The small towns along the lake such as **Lohusuu** and **Mustvee** have both Lutheran churches for the native Estonian population and Orthodox ones for the Old Believers. In fact, a hundred years ago, there were seven churches in Mustvee and four are still in use, despite the small population. The Orthodox is the oldest, dating from the 1860s; the Lutheran and Baptist ones were both built in the 1870s, and the current Old Believers one was completed in 1930, although they had had a church here since 1795. None have regular opening hours so the best opportunity of seeing the interiors is around the time of a service.

The Old Believers Church at **Raja** was destroyed in the war, as there was considerable fighting in this area in 1944 and only the campanile remains. Worship now takes places in the icon-painting school where there is a regular exhibition of recent work. This school was founded in 1880 and has continued its work through all changes of regime in Tallinn and Moscow.

Hopes that Russians would return in large numbers for holidays were dashed by the 1998 financial crisis there. Increasingly strict visa regulations following Estonia's entry into the EU in 2004 have been a further disincentive. For Russian-speakers happy to relive Soviet holidays from the 1960s, the trade union centres provide spartan but adequate accommodation and a base for exploring the small lakeside villages. Beaches, though, are few and far between; the best is at **Kauksi** on the north shore of the lake. Even in summer, an eerie quiet pervades much of the coast and foreigners may be stared at, given that they are so rare. It is hard to think of a greater contrast to Tallinn with its 24-hour activity. A convenient trip can be made 12km inland to the village of **Iisaku** to see what will soon become one of the best museums in Estonia; it already puts to shame many in Tallinn and Tartu. Housed in a former school, it expands month by month and, with clear labels in English, it already offers an extensive introduction to the natural history of the area and to life in the countryside since the early 19th century. Uniquely for Estonia, it opens at 09.00 instead of the more usual 10.30 or 11.00. Amongst recent additions (2002–04) are a Soviet room and a costume collection.

About 25km south of Mustvee is the largest village on the lake, **Kallaste.** Perhaps if relations with Russia improve it may become a large tourist centre as it offers beaches and a potential yachting harbour, although at present no hotel. The walk through the village offers two unusual sights – a series of redstone caves along the shore and two buildings in the centre, the Town Hall and the Agricultural College. Both feature classical pillars, not what would have been expected from the early 1950s when they were built. An equally unexpected architectural monument, **Alatskivi Castle**, can be seen 8km south of Kallaste. The owner, Arved von Nolcken, produced his own design, following a long visit to Britain in 1875. He engaged Russian bricklayers and builders from Latvia; only the carpenters were local Estonians. Even the tiles for the stoves were brought from Riga. He took as his model for the gables and towers the royal palace at Balmoral, in Scotland, which in turn was based on 16th-century Scottish castles. The tall entrance hall with fireplaces, extending upwards through two floors, is presumably based on a Robert Adam design. The outside drive was originally lined with lime trees, which added an English rather than a Scottish element. The building was completed in 1885 but was only used as a serious residence until von Nolcken's death in 1909. His son used it as a hunting lodge, and then during the first independence period it was first a school and then a border-guard station. The Soviets ran a collective farm from it. Only in 2003 did serious reconstruction begin so hopefully by 2005 the interior will be as impressive as the exterior.

Two roads go south from Alatskivi; the main one turns inland to Tartu and the other goes eastwards back to the shore of Lake Peipsi. The next village along the lake, after 8km, is **Kolkja**, where an Old Believers Museum opened in 1998. It shows their costumes, their religious artefacts and above all their simple standard of living which is so apparent when driving along this shoreline. The fish-and-onion restaurant in the village can be recommended. It does not serve coffee, only tea, and sugar is never added. Sweet things can, however, be eaten as part of the meal.

Taking the Tartu road, the next village after 3km is **Rupse**, the location of the Liiv Museum. Juhan Liiv (1864–1913) is one of Estonia's most famous poets, and he grew up on this farm. Most of his life he suffered from schizophrenia and travelled listless around the country on trains until he was thrown off for not paying, and not being able to afford the fare. Sadly he destroyed much of the poetry he wrote but enough remains to ensure his continuing reputation, and some of his drafts are here. Visitors can also see the room he shared with his very conventional brother (who became mayor of Rakvere) and the outside sauna which was also used for roasting meat and washing down corpses. A Liiv prize is awarded to a young poet every year and they leave a handwritten copy here of the winning poem. The museum opened in 1962 and expanded considerably in the late 1980s towards the end of the Soviet era. In 2005 it is likely that a room will be opened commemorating the 100th anniversary of the birth of the composer Eduard Tubin, who grew up nearby.

Getting there and around
As in other poorer parts of Estonia, good public transport makes up for the lack of cars. Several buses a day run from Tartu to the lake and along the shore to Mustvee. Others link Mustvee with the northeastern towns of Jõhvi and Narva and there is also a route along the lake to Mustvee, inland to Rakvere and then to Tallinn. Tartu–St Petersburg buses stop at Mustvee.

Where to stay
As the area still really caters only for local tourists who have their own summer houses here or rent rooms from friends, there is little commercial accommodation. However, the **Aarde Villa** (tel/fax: 77 64 290; email: info@aardevilla.ee; www.aardevilla.ee) opened in 2002 at the village of Sääritsa, about 10km south of Raja, off the main road but directly beside the lake. It was a border-guard station in the pre-electronic era and guests can climb up the former lookout tower. There are extensive gardens with facilities for both adults and children and for those who like to catch their own supper, fishing expeditions are organised on the lake.

Greylag geese

Central Estonia

TARTU

Unlike Tallinn or Pärnu, Tartu is not a town of instant charm. Arriving on any of the dreary approach roads does not suggest the imminence of a famous university town or of one where Estonia gained its statehood. Yet intellectually and architecturally it is the centre of Estonia. Its university cultivates an Oxbridge/Ivy League tradition but has combined it with the radicalism of Berkeley or the London School of Economics. Estonia's most famous scientists, without exception, studied and taught here and its most famous patriots, whether against the Tsar, the pre-war President Konstantin Päts or the Soviet regime, likewise spent their formative years in Tartu. The 200km distance from Tallinn suited both sides. Political activists could be more daring and the government could feign liberalism, safe in the knowledge that its detractors would not be a threat to the capital. With independence and democracy now safe in Estonia, Tartu will have to take up new causes. It introduced parking meters to the country in 1992 but a more lasting testimony to the first period of renewed independence must be in the offing.

It is only from around 2000 that Tartu started to take tourism seriously. Museums were moved from gloomy suburban locations to properly adapted buildings in the town centre. Hotels too came into town and started to promote themselves vigorously. Pedestrian precincts appeared and so did signs in English. Only in 2003 was the squalid bus station and the equally squalid Hotel Tartu beside it modernised. Tartu can therefore now offer a savoury arrival and departure. Whether such travel could involve the railway station or the airport was still under discussion in 2004.

Tartu now has a diverse programme of festivals that take place all year round except in July and August (when the hotels fill up anyway). If it matters whether you turn up for the cross-country ski marathon, the break-dancing finals or student rag week, check their dates on www.kultuuriaken.tartu.ee before contacting your tour operator. This site also gives the programme at the Vanemuine Theatre, which spills out on to the Town Hall Square when weather permits during the summer. One thing unites all these programmes: even if they were not designed as such, they are a perfect deterrent to stag parties, which stay firmly in Tallinn as a result.

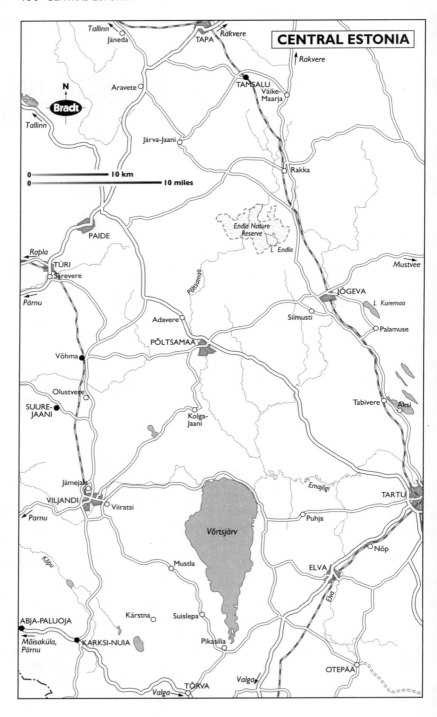

History

The university was founded in 1632 but the town has a much longer history. Its location at the crossroads of the north–south link from St Petersburg to Riga and the east–west one from Tallinn to Pskov has given it written records since 1030. Until recently the Emajõgi River also had a serious role in trade. The town's future outside the university will depend largely on relations with Latvia and Russia. If trade continues to decrease with these two countries and EU membership stimulates more contact with the West, Tartu's location to the east will make it less competitive than towns along the coast.

Although Tallinn was always spared fighting within the city, Tartu sadly was not, and during the 16th century was a constant battleground between the Russians, the Baltic Germans, the Poles and the Swedes. Three more recent calamities hit the town – its destruction by Peter the Great's armies in 1708, a fire in 1775, and then World War II when both the Russian retreat in 1941 and their return in 1944 caused considerable damage. As the earlier town was largely built of wood, what the visitor now sees dates only from the late 18th century onwards. In the small streets around the Town Hall Square, the 20th century is not obtrusive. It is easy to visualise a thriving market town, which was its role for many centuries. A full day is needed to cover the town centre and the university, and a further half day to visit a selection of the museums. The parks beside the river offer relaxing walks and concerts in the summer.

Tartu University

The importance of the university can be seen in the determination of each new conqueror to make their mark on it immediately. Conversely, bands of lecturers sometimes moved the university to temporary safety when the town of Tartu was threatened. When it first opened in 1632, it was the second university in the Swedish Empire, Uppsala being the first. It is thought that there was only one ethnically Estonian student in the university at that time. Twenty years later, because of the Russo-Swedish War, it moved to Tallinn for ten years and when the Russians attacked again in 1700, it moved to Pärnu. Most of the faculties were housed in Pärnu fortress, just above the gunpowder cellar. Before Pärnu fell to the Russian armies, the archives for these turbulent 70 years were taken to Stockholm and many of the academic staff, being Swedish, returned with them. The issues these archives cover have a very modern ring to them. The possibility of war with Russia is mentioned, as is the constant need to remind students to be loyal to the Swedish king. There are also concerns that scientific discoveries should not threaten theological teaching. Far more worrying for many of the staff, however, were the lack of pay, difficult landladies, leaking roofs and disputes with the military over room allocations.

Peter the Great had originally planned to reopen the university either in Pärnu or in Tartu but the founding of the Academy of Science in St Petersburg in 1724 put paid to this. Both Pärnu and Tartu submitted plans to refound the university on various occasions during the 18th century, but these were unsuccessful; it would only reopen nearly a hundred years later in 1802, as a reaction to the French Revolution. The Tsarist authorities panicked at the ideas that students sent to study in western Europe were bringing back with them and from 1798 such studies were banned. In the best Tartu tradition, however, the result was that such ideas simply reached Estonian students more quickly than they otherwise would have done as the teaching staff were unwilling to acquiesce in the reverent approach that the Russians and the Baltic Germans had wanted.

The university now had a comparatively stable century ahead of it. Funding from the state was adequate and provided for all the main buildings that were needed on its re-opening. Even a botanical garden was included. It was lucky that the Napoleonic Wars started only after the completion of Tartu University otherwise funds would never have been found for it. The town was to grow with the university, the population increasing from 3,500 in 1802 to 8,500 in 1826. The teaching staff were drawn from all over Europe, with the majority having a German background as this was to be the language of instruction. If one member of the faculty deserves special mention, it must be Karl Morgenstern who ran the library for 37 years from 1802 until 1839. By joining the book exchange association of the major German universities, he ensured that Tartu became a mainstream European university. His successors, German and Russian, expanded this work so that by 1917 there were 180 exchange partners including several in Japan and the United States. Morgenstern was also accomplished at what would now be called public relations and persuaded many wealthy patrons to donate books and antiquities to the library and to the classical museum that he founded.

The period of peace between the Napoleonic Wars and the Crimean War again ensured immense financial support for the university, equalling that given to Moscow. The building of the railway links to Tallinn and St Petersburg in the 1870s and then to Riga in 1887 brought considerable expansion to the university, the number of students increasing from 600 in 1865 to 1,700 in 1889. The year 1889 also marked the start of greater control from St Petersburg and, with the use of Russian as the language of instruction, the Russian name for Tartu, Jurjev, replaced the German name of Dorpat at the university. The Estonian name Tartu was used only after independence in 1919, when Estonian also became the language of instruction. The Ministry of Education took direct control of academic appointments, so much of the autonomy previously enjoyed by the university was withdrawn and many of the German-speaking staff left. One embittered historian wrote that 'the bright flame of German science went out because it was smothered by barbaric Slavic hands'. The two protagonists for the soul of Tartu University during the 19th century, the Baltic Germans and the Russians, clearly saw the battleground as simply between themselves. The occasional Estonians who managed to enter were expected to integrate and put their peasant background behind them.

The German army seized Tartu on February 24 1918, and on March 7 decreed that tuition in German instead of Russian would be instituted with effect from March 20. After protest, this deadline was extended by a further

TARTU IN 1941

Ants Oras

The Red Soldiers marching in the streets to the tune of one of the four or five songs they seemed to know were a very neglected, listless lot. A large proportion of them were illiterate. Soon after the occupation, delousing stations were set up for them, an establishment with which we were made familiar for the first time. The Red Commanders, as the officers were still called, dressed more smartly but they were obviously unaccustomed to living in a 'bourgeois' environment, even after its Sovietisation. Having been assigned some of the best living quarters in our town, they found themselves out of their depth in dealing with such gadgets as bath taps, lavatory chains or electric lights. In one flat, a Soviet officer used his bathroom as a pigsty in which he reared a large sow. In spite of protests from inmates of the floor below, he refused to see the inappropriateness of his conduct. The Red wives adapted themselves more easily to their new surroundings, however. Being well provided with money, they stormed our shops, always buying the most expensive articles, although their taste was more gaudy than ours. Though they generally avoided red, of which they must have had a surfeit at home, their dresses looked exotic in their many-coloured richness. Their make-up was very marked and most of our perfumes were too subtle for them. An unexpected feature was their religiousness. The Orthodox churches were crowded with women fresh from Soviet Russia, whereas the men stayed away.

Ants Oras was a lecturer at Tartu University who fled to Sweden in 1944

two weeks. The university reopened in full at the end of April 1918 with a complement of 60 staff, 30 of whom had been recruited from German universities. This would however be the shortest 'interregnum' in the history of the university. Following the armistice of November 1918, the German military had to withdraw. In the meantime, many academics left with the retreating Bolshevik forces to found a university in exile at Voronezh. Most of the artefacts and books they took with them have remained there, even though the Soviet government agreed their return under the Tartu Treaty of 1920.

The new Estonian government wisely took its time before reopening the university in December 1919, with the Prime Minister Jaan Tönisson carrying out the formal ceremony. To begin with, about half the lectures were given in Russian and half in Estonian, but Estonian quickly became the predominant language. The new country immediately had at its service an internationally respected university. Former staff happily came back from exile to work there and were soon joined by many foreign experts; by 1930, the teaching staff had reached 400. For 20 years, the university was pleasantly normal, teaching local students in their national language.

From 1940 to 1945 the situation was not merely abnormal, but vicious. The Russians dismissed and deported many of the leading faculty members; the Germans treated the replacements they appointed even worse in 1941, when several were sent to concentration camps. In 1944, most senior members not sympathetic to the Russians had just enough time to flee to Sweden. Only 22% of the staff en poste in early 1940 were still there in the autumn of 1944. On all three occasions, the occupiers had detailed plans for running the university, cynically realising that it had to be neutered if they were to control Estonia effectively. The Soviet regime did make large funds available immediately on their re-occupation to rebuild the university following the destruction much of the town had suffered during the war. Constant expansion was planned throughout the Soviet era with student numbers doubling from 3,500 in 1950 to 7,000 in 1978. A computer centre was established in 1976 and a history of the university printed in 1982 talked proudly of 'modern methods of management' being used in the running of the university. The 350th anniversary in 1982 was fervently and formally celebrated with a massive budget provided for further new buildings.

Anyone now prominent in Estonian public life was educated at Tartu under the Soviet system but the academic rigour of the courses and the subtlety of the teaching in most cases made the political background irrelevant. What was missing was contact outside the USSR; Tartu was a closed city so initially Westerners could not travel there at all and later only for the day from Tallinn.

Undergraduates had no chance to be taught languages by native speakers or to keep up to date with Western research. One of the first tasks of the new administration since 1989 has been to 'internationalise' the university again without allowing its Estonian identity to suffer. Lecturers from many EU countries, rather than from just one, ensure this necessary diversity. Wandering amongst the students and perusing the notice boards, it is hard to realise that the current transformation took less than eight years. Reading the English-language brochures or browsing the website (www.ut.ee) shows immediately what has been achieved.

Getting there and away

Tartu is well served by buses to all major towns in Estonia. They run every half-hour to Tallinn and most are non-stop, taking about two and a half hours. Buses operate several times a day to Rakvere, Narva, Võru, Valga, Viljandi and Pärnu. Eurolines have a daily morning bus to Riga, which stops at Valga, and it returns in the evening. Eurolines also operate a daily service to St Petersburg via Narva. From the totally dilapidated station, two–three trains a day run to Tallinn, but these are much slower than the buses as they have lengthy stops at every village en route. There are no scheduled services from the airport, only occasional charter flights. Sightseeing boat trips operate along the Emajögi River in the summer, as do ferry services to Piirissaar Island. Sometimes there are services to Värska as well. Full details of all boat and ferry services are on www.transcom.ee. Negotiations started with the Russians in 2001 to resume what had been a very

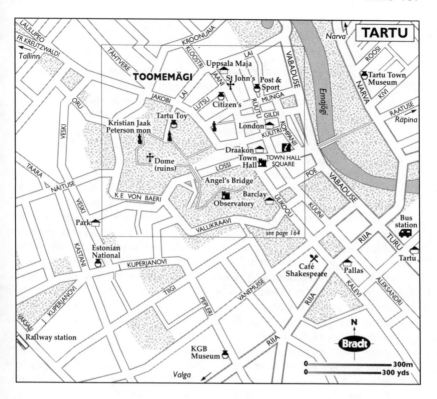

popular trip in Soviet times – a boat from Tartu to Pskov – but by summer 2004 the Russians had still not provided the visa exemption which would be needed for such trips to be viable so the Estonians have no plans to attempt future negotiations unless there is clear evidence of a Russian *volte-face*.

Where to stay

Aleksandri Aleksandri 42; tel: 7 366659; fax: 7 366646; email: aleksandri@hot.ee; www.hot.ee/aleksandri. This guesthouse about 15 minutes' walk from the town centre opened in 2002. Bathrooms, toilets and a kitchen are shared between two rooms; otherwise it could be classed as a hotel. Rooms are large and the road is quiet. Double 500EEK.

Barclay Ulikooli 8; tel: 7 447100; fax: 7 447101; email: barclay@barclay.ee; www.barclay.ee. When it opened in 1996, it was undoubtedly the best hotel in Tartu, but complacency set in and eight years later it gives the feeling that the façade, the interior and the staff could all do with a face-lift. The wooden panelling is bland and there are no pictures in the restaurant. However, prices have now dropped dramatically, so its regular business visitors are likely to stay loyal and will appreciate the very quiet yet central location. Double 1,600EEK.

Draakon Raekoja Plats 2; tel: 7 442045; fax: 7 423000; email: tonyas@solo.delfi.ee; www.draakon.ee. This welcome addition to the Tartu hotel scene opened in summer

A STUDENT IN SOVIET ESTONIA

Tina Tamman

I was a university student in Soviet Estonia for five years, which was then the standard length of studies. I was offered no choice of subjects, but I was happy at the time and remember this period fondly. In independent Estonia it is no longer fashionable or even acceptable to praise the Soviet period but I certainly benefited from the system.

The university had an excellent library which opened at 08.00 and closed at 22.00, seven days a week. When I came to write a thesis in my final year on the American writer William Saroyan, there was nothing available in Estonia and all the books and reviews had to be ordered from a library in Moscow. This service was quick, efficient and free of charge.

I benefited, too, from sharing a room at the university hostel, at first with ten other girls but after a few months I managed to transfer to a smaller room which I shared with only three others. Inevitably this brought the four of us very close, and we liked this. We learnt to be considerate. We had lots of parties with loud singing when there was something to celebrate and quiet periods when one of us had to study. From those parties, I still remember the Armenian brandy and the enormous piles of aubergine sandwiches: Bulgarian tinned aubergine paté was the cheapest sandwich filler in those days.

Bedclothes in the hostel were changed once a fortnight. This did not, however, get rid of the bedbugs, which were widely believed to have been brought in by some Russians. I remember once waking up in the morning to see a dead bedbug on my pillow; I had apparently squashed it in my sleep. There was warm water in the showers, which worked most evenings, and there were lockable shower cubicles. In the communal washrooms, the water was icy cold, particularly in winter, and everybody washed in full view of each other. The toilets were often blocked and the communal kitchens filthy. Everyone took turns to clean the kitchens – some better than others! Quite a lot of cooking and eating was done in groups. The most popular dish was sautéed potatoes, which required only potatoes and cooking fat. Meat was beyond the reach of most students.

We did not pay for the hostel and most students received a grant of 35 roubles a month, which just about paid for the food; help was needed from parents for anything beyond this basic level. In contemporary Estonia the grant system has been largely abolished, and student loans introduced.

Although I was reading English, this involved studying Marxism–Leninism

2000. Wth 65 rooms, BBC television, and a location beside the Town Hall, it soon became popular with British visitors. It has made a serious effort to cater for the disabled, with no narrow staircases and all facilities being wheelchair-accessible. Double 1,700EEK.

Ihaste Pallase 25–27; tel: 7 331060; fax: 7 331048; email: info@ihastehotell.ee; www.ihastehotell.ee. Hardly in Tartu at all, being almost in the countryside, this new and a host of related subjects. Even physical education was compulsory. I was excused from Russian as I had done very well in it at secondary school. The strangest subject was 'safety in factory work', although none of us was expected to work in a factory. About a hundred of us would dutifully copy down what the lecturer told us; I remember him particularly drawing a lathe on the blackboard. I had never seen one in real life and have not done so since.

English studies were arranged in small groups of around 12 students. It was very formal, with an awesome English grammar book written by a Russian and published in Russia. All our language teachers were Estonians who had never been to England. Our literature teacher was an English communist who emigrated to the USSR, and then married an Estonian poetess. Literature for him ended before World War II and we were never taught anything about post-war writing.

There was no shortage of activities in Tartu. The town had an excellent theatre, as it still does, combining drama, opera and ballet. There were coffee-shops of the German and Austrian kind where we could linger. We could not afford butter on bread or sugar in coffee but we would talk long into the night, sometimes able to stretch to a glass of Hungarian wine.

By contrast in the autumn we would be sent to a collective farm to work. This was hardly fun as it rained often, the potato fields became soggy and the potatoes heavy. The work was at the expense of our university studies and may well account for the fact that I never really mastered the basics of Latin.

We were guaranteed a job at the end of our university course regardless of our exam results. Since I had been reading English, I was offered a job as an English teacher, as were the other 25 of us. Take it or leave it, but sign on the dotted line for the minimum of two years – that was the principle. It is a day I still remember well. It was well organised and, with hindsight, even reassuring, but so demoralising at the time. I refused to sign at first but was told that I had no option, although I was not interested in a teaching career.

It has been reassuring in the years since that many of the students with whom I read English and shared accommodation have had very satisfactory careers as teachers after all. They did not seem enthusiastic at the time but later grew to like their teaching jobs.

Independence has changed a lot in people's attitudes; present-day pupils are willing to learn and their parents are even willing to pay for extra lessons. It is a far cry from the days when nobody in Estonia wanted to learn English because there was nothing one could do with one's language skills.

hotel is an entertainment centre in its own right, with a bowling alley, billiards, a dance floor and horse-riding nearby. A local bus does go into town, but the hotel is best suited to groups with their own coach or to car drivers, since it has guarded parking. Double 900EEK.

Kantri Riia 195; tel: 7 383043; fax: 7 477213; email: info@kantri.ee; www.kantri.ee. Located 5km from the town centre, this hotel cultivates a manor-house feel with its

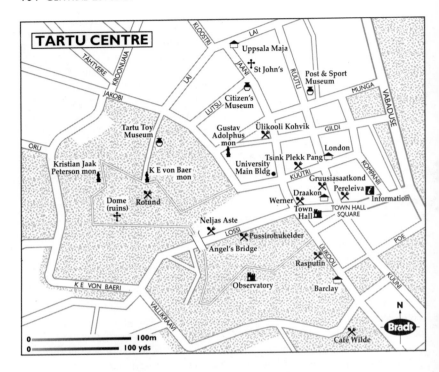

small number of rooms and ample surroundings, although it is in fact a completely new building. Double 850EEK.

London Rüütli 9; tel: 30 5555; fax: 30 5565; email: london@londonhotel.ee; lwww.londonhotel.ee. A very conventional business hotel in the town centre which opened in 2003. It provides an excellent location in winter, with everything else on the doorstep, but in the summer, life on the streets might last a bit too long for comfort. The hotel should not be judged by the appalling standard of English in its brochures. Its Kokoko café adopts the pleasant American custom of only charging for one cup of coffee with refills being free of charge. Double 1,700EEK.

Pallas Riia 4; tel: 7 301200; fax: 7 301201; email: pallas@pallas.ee; www.pallas.ee. Pallas is the name of a famous art college that was on this site before the war. The hotel is a completely new building, above a department store but worth the ascent to the second floor. The lobby and the rooms are decorated with paintings from its former pupils. The 'star' works of art, by the director of the school, Ado Vabbe, are understandably exhibited in the suites. Double 1,300EEK.

Park Vallikraavi 23; tel: 7 427000; fax: 7 434382; email: info@parkhotell.ee; www.parkhotell.ee. Situated in University Park, this two/three-star hotel attracts regular visitors with its quiet location. It had the misfortune to open in 1940 but in March 1964 welcomed a guest whose visit to Tartu will never be forgotten by those old enough to remember it. Finnish President Kekkonen was the first Westerner to see Tartu after the war and he spoke Estonian throughout his stay, to the consternation of his hosts – most of whom spoke very little, or none. (His skiing was equally proficient and therefore alarming to his local minders.) Many Estonian exiles felt he had sold out to the USSR, but an equal number of others, and certainly Estonians who had stayed in the country were pleased to see any possible links with the outside world, however controlled they would be from Moscow. A room in the new hotel, renovated in 2000, is named after President Kekkonen. Regular visitors like the quiet location and the lack of any evening entertainment. It is a hilly walk of 15 minutes to the town centre but after a snowfall or during a long summer evening, this can be very congenial. In Soviet times of course it was a way of ensuring no casual contact took place between any visitors to the university and local students. Double 1,200EEK.

Tartu Soola 1; tel: 7 314300; fax: 7 314301; email: info@tartuhotell.ee; www.tartuhotell.ee. Many hotels in Estonia still have a Soviet exterior, but this one still had a Soviet interior in 2000. Restoration of this archetypal Soviet hotel began in 2001 and was fortunately completed in 2003. It is now, by one room, the largest hotel in Tartu, having 62 rooms compared to the Pallas with 61. It is basic, but does not pretend to be anything else, and is within ten minutes' walk of the town centre. The location beside the bus station is convenient on arrival and departure. Double 1,000EEK.

Uppsala Maja Guesthouse Jaani 7; tel: 7 361535; fax: 7 361536; email: uppsala@uppsalamaja.ee; www.uppsalamaja.ee. This is a little corner of Sweden, installed in central Tartu by its Swedish twin city in 1996, although the house dates from the 18th century. It has had a varied series of owners, including a butcher whose hooks are still on display. There are five bedrooms, with shared facilities, and a kitchen and library. It can be recommended for long-stay visitors. Double 1,000EEK.

Where to eat

When this book first came out in 1999, writing on Tartu restaurants and cafés was disappointingly straightforward: anything reasonable was automatically included. By early 2004, an entire listings magazine could have been devoted to this topic. Tartu does not have or need the variety that Tallinn offers, but there is now sufficient choice that anyone staying for several days need never return to an earlier venue, although this is likely to be a pleasure. Pretentious luxury has not yet come to Tartu, but good cooking from anywhere famous for its food certainly has done. Prices given here are for three courses without wine.

Café Shakespeare Tel: 7 440140; www.shakespeare.ee. Not surprisingly, this is situated in the Vanemuise Theatre. Following the Western pattern, theatres are now eager to encourage visitors to come at times when there are no performances, just as much as when there are. The exterior is drab, but the varying exhibitions and the equally varied menu make up for this. Quite a lot of ad hoc entertainment is provided by the actors who double as waiters here – Vanemuise was, after all, the God of Song in Estonian mythology. Being in 'theatreland' the restaurant/café is open until midnight during the week and 02.00 on Friday and Saturday. 170EEK.

Café Wilde Vallikraavi 4; tel: 7 309765; web: www.wilde.ee. You do not have to be under 30 to be admitted here, but it probably helps! The excellent range of cakes and open sandwiches, the unusually fresh coffee, the gentle service and the academic décor is somewhat marred by constant loud music. Note the griffin logo around the walls, this mythological winged lion being the protector of publishers. A quick escape to the English-language section of the bookshop beside the café is recommended as soon as the excellent food has been consumed. The café is named after Peter Ernst Wilde (1732–85), a doctor, veterinary surgeon and publisher who printed the first medical textbooks in Estonian here and won the rare privilege of being allowed to publish uncensored. Outside the restaurant, two other Wildes are remembered. A bronze sculpture pictures an imagined meeting between Oscar Wilde and a contemporary Estonian author Eduard Wilde (1865–1933), a similar 'enfant terrible'. This was unveiled in 1999 to commemorate the centenary of Oscar Wilde's death in 1900. 190EEK.

Gruusiasaatkond (Georgian Embassy) Rüütli 8; tel: 7 441386; www.gruusiasaatkond.ee. Like the Contravento in Tallinn, this restaurant has built up a regular clientele who it is hoped will safeguard it from change. The Georgian menu is sufficiently extensive to warrant several visits and the décor sufficiently bohemian to ensure that prices stay low and that Tartu's small financial community stays away. 160EEK.

Neljas Aste (The Fourth Instance) Lossi 17; tel: 7 441264; www.neljasaste.ee. It is an encouraging comment on the lack of crime in Estonia that space could be found in the law courts to open a restaurant. It is one of many setting up just outside the Old Town, so within easy reach of hotels and offices but able to offer much lower prices. The dishes here have provocative names but innocent ingredients: Dictatorship of the Proletariat is simply a herring salad. 120EEK.

Pereleiva Rüütli 5. Probably the most central coffee-house in Tartu, and certainly the one with the best baking. It stays open until 19.00 during the week but on Saturdays and Sundays follows the irritating Tartu habit, shared by all shops, of closing at 16.00, even in the height of the tourist season. 130EEK.

Pussirohukelder (Gunpowder Cellar) Lossi 28; tel: 7 303555; fax: 7 434124; web: www.pyss.ee. For much of the 1990s this was a grand, medieval restaurant built sufficiently deeply below the city walls to ensure that mobile phones would not work there. Although it made no attempt to hide the brickwork when it reopened in 2001 as a very lively pub and discotheque, the age range of the clientele has dropped at least one generation. The menu is limited, though reasonably priced, and vegetarians are as unwanted as ever, but who need worry about food in such surroundings? The website address says it all. 150EEK.

Rasputin Ülikooli 10; tel: 7 305996; www.hot.ee/kassisilm. Deep red is obviously the predominant colour here, rather than the crimson of later Soviet times. The menu must be one of the longest in Tartu but it is rare to find anything unavailable. As every dish is prepared individually, don't come in a rush, but to enjoy a whole evening, sometimes to the background of live Russian folk music. Forget milk with tea here and drink it with honey or jam plus sultanas. 120EEK.

Rotund Toomemagi. Located at the top of University Hill, the restaurant is an appropriate reward for the steep walk from the town. In summer it spreads out of its tight, octagonal surroundings into the park, but not being open late in the evenings spares it from wilder students. A good place to seek refuge from a sudden Baltic storm. 130EEK.

Thai Pikk 40; tel: 7 402509; www.hot.ee/nostalgia. Several restaurants have now had the courage to open across the river in what used to be a gastronomic and architectural wasteland. It is now neither, and clubs are beginning to open here too. It cannot be long before a hotel follows suit. 120EEK.

Tsink Plekk Pang Küütri 6; tel: 7 303411; www.pang.ee. Whilst Chinese food in Tallinn still has to make its mark, it came instantly at a high level when this restaurant opened in 2002. It has all the surroundings that in the context of Chinese food assure quality – noise, a bland décor and rough service. 120EEK.

Ülikooli Kohvik (University Café) Ülikooli 20; tel: 7 435457. This restaurant is on the first floor with a view over the main university building. I think it is unique as a café in Estonia for not having piped music, but I would be delighted to be proven wrong on this point. It serves mugs of tea from an urn for £0.04/US$0.06 but the more fastidious can have a Liptons teabag for only three times this price. The food is a conventional selection of meat dishes and salads with a small choice of sandwiches and cakes. 110EEK.

Werner Ülikooli 11; tel: 7 441274. Although in the heart of the student area, this is a café where nobody need be ashamed to admit their age. The 19th-century prints of Tartu on the walls provide an ambience for looking backwards rather than forwards. Buillon with pie followed by salmon pancakes make an excellent lunch. Chess sets are provided free of charge for those who wish to linger. 120EEK.

Tourist information

In summer 2001, the local tourist board published a series of guidebooks in English to the town and the surrounding area with suggested walks, cycling and riding tours. *Tartu Today* is published twice a year and is the best source of current information on exhibitions and museum opening hours. The tourist board have an office/shop conveniently located on Town Hall Square (Raekoja Plats 14; tel: 7 442111; email: tartu@visitestonia.com; www.tartu.ee). It sells a wide range of postcards, small souvenirs and maps for the whole of Estonia. The Tavid currency exchange office at Rüütli 2 offers competitive rates for over 50 currencies, and their list shows how extensively Estonians now travel on their holidays.

What to see
A walk around Tartu

A tour should start at the **Town Hall Square.** This north side of the square has a number of well-preserved, late 18th-century buildings whereas those on the south side are largely 20th century. **Number 18** is famous on two counts: it belonged to the family of General Barclay who successfully repulsed Napoleon, and it has a lean because it was built on swampy foundations. It is now used as an art gallery for Tartu artists famous during the first independence period. Although the **Town Hall** gives the impression of careful planning and its façade has survived in total from its construction in 1789, there was much dispute about its size, use and layout. A suitable design for the fountains at the front of the Town Hall was only resolved in October 1998. The one chosen, of an embracing young couple, clearly breaks with the more staid tradition of earlier Estonian sculpture. Town Hall Square stretches from here to the river and was formerly a market. The first stone bridge in the Baltics, a gift to the town from Catherine II following the fire of 1775, used to cross the river here. It was destroyed in World War II but an appeal launched in 1992 hopes to raise sufficient funds to rebuild it soon.

A short walk along Ülikooli brings the main **university** into view. The façade may well seem familiar after a few days in Estonia; it is depicted on the back of the 2EEK note and was copied in Tallinn Old Town by the main building overlooking Pikk Jalg ('Long Leg'). The architect, Johann Wilhelm Krause, later became famous in Estonia, but this was his first major work, completed in 1809. The building now houses the main student assembly hall, the administration, and the **Museum of Classical Antiquity.** Posters in the entrance hall advertise all the concerts and plays taking place in the university. The collection in the museum is far more extensive than its name suggests. Whilst there are original Greek works and many plaster cast copies as well, the museum also has on display two Egyptian mummies and several hundred Russian icons, many recently seized from smugglers. There is one of four death masks of the German philosopher Immanuel Kant, which was presented to Karl Morgenstern, the founder of the collection. The museum first opened in 1803, just a year after tuition began again at the university. The **Assembly Hall** is acoustically one of the best concert halls in Estonia; Liszt and Schumann performed here in the 19th century and were followed more recently by every favourite Soviet pianist and violinist. It had to be rebuilt following a fire in 1965 which was caused by badly maintained electric wiring.

In the attic above the Assembly Hall, one of five original **student lockups** remains. These were based on models from Göttingen and Heidelberg and date from the early 19th century when German influence was at its strongest. Specific sentences were laid down for any of the misdemeanours students were likely to commit. Insulting a cloakroom attendant warranted five days, insulting a woman only four. (Female students were not accepted at the university until 1915.) Smoking on university premises and returning library books late were regarded equally, both leading to a two-day sentence, but swearing was four times as evil since it carried an eight-day sentence. The austere furniture and surroundings are no worse than many students at liberty would have endured in their lodgings. The graffiti on the walls testifies to the wide range of talent amongst those detained here. The incorrect Latin, however, was bequeathed by Soviet restorers after the 1965 fire.

Coming out of the university building and turning left along Jaani, note at the junction with Gildi the **statue of Jaan Tõnisson** erected in 2001. Tõnisson had many senior political posts in the 1920s and was also editor of Estonia's most famous newspaper, *Postimees*. A hundred metres further down Jaani is **St John's Church** (Jaani Kirk) which should be completely restored by summer 2005. Visitors in the early 1990s found it difficult to imagine that it had once been one of the most imposing Gothic buildings in the Baltics, with 2,000 terracotta statues adorning both the inside and outside walls. The building was badly damaged in August 1944 as the Germans retreated in the face of the Soviet armies. The church was neglected for most of the Soviet era, with much of the nave collapsing in 1952. Rebuilding work finally started only in 1989 under Polish supervision with the aim of reopening the church as a concert hall. Polish restorers had a worldwide reputation at the time in view of what they had achieved in Warsaw. Estonians took over in 1991 with the aim of restoring the church to its original state when about half of the original 2,000 terracotta statues will be displayed. Christmas 1997 could be celebrated for the first time since the war as the roof was completed that year. The copper steeple and the bells followed in 1999. A single window was commissioned in 2000 from Urmo Raus, a stained-glass designer who had by then settled permanently in France. (In 2004 he had a major exhibition in Chartres.) This window has now been withdrawn; some people disliked the abstract design, others the fact that the artist no longer lived in Estonia and they wanted the work to be done locally. Visitors will therefore now see totally plain glass with frames of stainless steel.

Opposite the church is a nondescript office building with a warning sign in Estonian and English – *Varise Misohtlik*, 'Liable to Fall Down'. This was a transit prison in 1941 and 1949 for those due to be transported to Siberia, and about 100 executions took place here in each of those years. In the neighbouring small streets are several stone and wooden houses that survive from the 19th century; fortunately these are being restored and not torn down. Crossing Lutsu the next building of note on the left-hand side is number 16, the Town Citizen's Museum, a recreation of a townhouse from 1830.

To continue the tour, return to the back of the university building where there is a new statue of the Swedish King **Gustav Adolphus**, the founder of the university in 1632. The statue is new because the earlier one was removed in the Soviet period. This one was unveiled in 1992, during the first royal visit to Estonia following the restoration of independence, by King Carl Gustaf of Sweden. A stiff ten-minute walk now follows to reach the monuments at the top of the hill behind the university. A walk in this area shows the university at its most serious and at its most carefree. Two memorial statues immediately stand out, one of **Karl Ernst von Baer** (1792–1876) who is seated with a book open in his lap. As the founder of embryology, he is Tartu's most famous scientist and also equally famous as an explorer. He was one of very few Baltic Germans to integrate with Estonians and to learn the language. A rather sour portrait of him adorns the 2EEK note. This seriousness does not prevent students using his statue as a site for wild fraternity and sorority parties, with dancing and bonfires. Those who can afford it wash him with champagne. The other statue is of Estonia's first poet, **Kristian Jaak Peterson** (1801–22), who is standing, clasping a stick. It is claimed that he walked from Riga to Tartu to study here, such was his enthusiasm. He died of tuberculosis at the age of 21, but despite hardly reaching adulthood, he proved that poetry and serious prose need not be written only in German. His work covers a wide range of topics, including religion, music and the natural world, but he was sadly ahead of his time. Ironically, one year after his death, some poetry he wrote in German was published in Leipzig, but it was another hundred years before his poems in Estonian saw the light of day. Behind the Peterson statue is **Kissing Hill**, a surprisingly open area for lovers to congregate; the tougher male students traditionally show their affection by carrying their girlfriends here from

Angel's Bridge, a distance of about 200m. This bridge was built as a memorial to Georg Friedrich Parrot, the first chancellor of the university when it reopened in 1802.

The hill is dominated by **Tartu University History Museum,** housed in the shell of the former St Peter and St Paul Cathedral which had been originally built in the 13th century. When completed it was the tallest church in Estonia and, from pictures that survive, one of the most imposing Gothic ones in the Baltics. Wars and fires soon took their toll, and by the early 17th century the entire interior had been destroyed. Much of what remained was looted and the site even degenerated into a rubbish dump. In 1807 the choir was restored and rebuilt as the university library, a role it would maintain until 1985 when the present museum opened. Extensive renovation was carried out both in the independence period and during the Soviet occupation. The collections cover all the scientific and medical fields in which Tartu showed particular expertise and most rooms have labels in English. A range of artists have painted all the highlights of the 19th century, while photographers have played the same role in this century. One large map shows the worldwide extent of the Tartu Diaspora. The role of the Jewish community is documented in a chart which covers the period from 1865, when Jews were first allowed to live in Tartu, through to the 1890s, during which time the quota system which restricted the number of Jewish students rose from 5% to 20%. This quota was abolished only in 1916. Jewish studies were banned by the Russians in 1940 and the few Jewish staff who remained at the time of the German invasion the following year were all arrested and murdered.

The **Observatory** was built shortly after the reopening of the university in the early 19th century and was designed by Johann Wilhelm Krause, the architect of the main university building. Until World War I it was probably the best in Europe, having registered 120,000 different stars. A small exhibition inside covers the history of the observatory and displays several telescopes. This exhibition has hardly changed since it first opened in the 1890s, so shows the best of 19th-century astronomy and telescopes which were actually used then. Several came from England and Germany. The exhibition was formally closed to the public in 1993, pending a planned restoration, but can be visited on request. An English-language catalogue of the telescopes can be consulted on www.obs.ee. The observatory had remained in use until 1964, when a new one opened outside Tartu at Toravere. The view from the roof is the best over Tartu but admission to it is not always possible. The Estonian flag flies from this roof 24 hours a day; unlike the flag on Hermann Tower in Tallinn, it is not lowered at sunset.

There are several routes back to the town from the university. The quickest is along Lossi to the back of the Town Hall. The nearby Barclay Plats should not be missed. In its centre is the statue of **General Barclay de Tolly**, who successfully fought Napoleon.

Museums

Two museums, the **Classical Antiquities** and the **University History,** have been described in the walk above. Tartu has 14 others but, unlike Tallinn, takes most of them seriously. Four of likely interest to foreign visitors are described here. All are usually open from 11.00 to 18.00, Wednesday to Sunday (closed Monday and Tuesday), but tour operators can make arrangements for group visits on closed days.

The **Estonian National Museum** (Kuperjanovi 9; tel: 7 421311; fax: 7 422040; email: erm@erm.ee; www.erm.ee) should serve as a model for others in Estonia; it is sad that more foreign tourists do not visit. Layout, lighting and description have all been properly thought out and, given the paucity of English-language books about Estonia, this is the best introduction to take their place. The 19th century is particularly well documented and temporary exhibitions enhance what is shown in the main collections. The museum covers not only Estonians, but other nationals who have lived there such as the Baltic Germans, the Russians and Swedes. Recent additions include a room on the Soviet period and photographs of many of the country's manor houses. Note in particular the pictures of bomb damage for 1941, of the final shopping queues in 1991 at the end of the Soviet era and the montage of Stalin on a gallows daringly put together in 1941. Do open the drawers upstairs to see the displays of gloves woven in all areas of the country, The total collection of tankards amounts to 3,000 but of course only a few can be exhibited at any one time.

Opposite the museum is the largest fraternity house of the university; such organisations were banned in the Soviet period but have enjoyed a revival since then. The university assures visitors that in this building 'old strict discipline has given way to modern liberty and the best man is not one who drinks most beer but the one who does it best and shows most sociability'. The railway station is a walk of around 300m from the museum. It is sad that what was such an extensive wooden building has been allowed to fall into complete decay and it is an equally sad commentary on the contemporary state of rail passenger services that there are usually more pigeons than people using the station.

Tartu Toy Museum (Lai 1; tel: 7 461777; www.mm.ee) opened in 1994 although the building dates from 1770. Its collection, based entirely on voluntary donations, is mainly traditional, but modern toys are being added. In political terms, this is a classless museum with the porcelain dolls of the rich claiming the same space as the rag dolls and wooden horses of the peasants. The products of craftsmen and of the large factories are given equal space. It is hoped to extend the collection of board games and mechanical toys as more gifts are received. Tasteful wooden toys are sold in the museum shop. The interior was renovated in 2003 when a collection of puppets was added and animation films began to be shown.

The **Sport Museum** (Rüütli 15; tel: 7 300750; www.spordimuuseum.ee) opened in 1963 and, given Soviet support for this activity, much of the material was collected then. This building opened in 2001. A collection had in fact been started in 1934 so photos, medals and sportswear go back to the turn of the century. Many of the early posters are therefore in German. This building also houses the Postal Museum, which does not limit itself to stamps. Postmarks are of equal significance in the political history of Estonia, as were the interventions of censors for almost all previous regimes. Note the stamps issued in Otepää from July 22 to August 12 1941 when the Russians had fled and the Germans had not yet had time to impose their own postal system. The shop here has a varied selection of postcards for sale at prices lower than elsewhere in Tartu.

The building which now houses the **Tartu City Museum** at Narva mnt (tel: 7 461911; www.tartu.ee/linnamuuseum) dates from 1790 when Tartu's architecture was at its height; after the fire of 1775 buildings were in stone, and were made to last and to impress. The architect Johann Walter, who also designed the Town Hall, was clearly briefed to make this the most lavish private residence in Tartu and to base the design on the contemporary French style of Louis XVI. However it did not stay long in private hands and the next two centuries would see it being used as a printing press, a school, a hostel and then finally a cultural centre during the Soviet period. For the first ten years after the restoration of Estonian independence, this museum was housed in totally inadequate premises near to the university, but in 2001 it finally moved here, to a building that can do justice to the collection. The museum is fully equipped for the disabled.

The highpoints here are the model of Tartu in 1940, before any bombing, and the actual table at which the Tartu Treaty was signed. It was by this treaty, signed in 1920, that the Soviet Union recognised Estonian independence and its borders. Earlier exhibits cover 14th-century painted glass cups, and clocks, silver and textiles from the Swedish period in the 17th century, and the coin collection – around 7,000 in all – is the most extensive in Estonia. Films from the first period of independence and from the Soviet era are shown regularly.

The **KGB Museum** opened in 2003 in its former local headquarters at Riia 15b (tel: 7 461717; www.tartu.ee/linnamuuseum), although the entrance is in fact on Pepleri. The exhibition has really come about through the efforts of Enn Tarto who as a dissident had three different spells in prison during the Soviet era, totalling 15 years in all. Despite this, he was fortunately able to be an active parliamentarian during the 1990s. Visitors can see the cells as victims knew them and also an exhibition of Estonian resistance during the Soviet era.

The **Estonian Agricultural Museum** (tel: 7 412397; www.epm.ee) is at Ülemurme, 6km south of Tartu, but buses going to Põlva and Võru all stop there. As its name implies, it is by far the largest museum in the country on this theme and even determined city dwellers should be interested by the diversity of its collection. It is far from being a collection of rusty tools, an all-too-common occurrence in this field. It has machinery, models, space, diagrams and effective lighting to show what has and what has not succeeded in Estonia over the last 200 years. It is fortunate that so much survived the war, including tractors imported from America in the 1930s. Visitors are welcome to picnic in the grounds and admission is free of charge on the first Sunday of the month.

VILJANDI
History
Both history and geography have been cruel to Viljandi. No major military conflict has passed the town by and major fires in 1682, 1765, 1894 and 1905

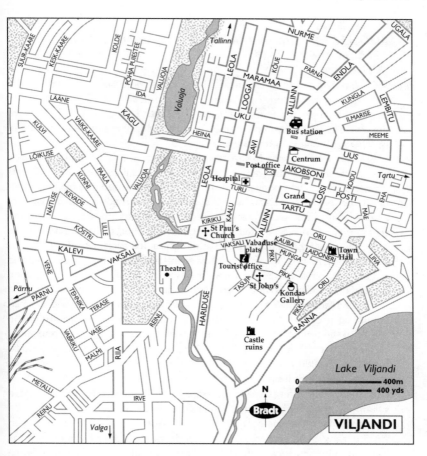

caused just as much damage. The lack of a large river and more recently of a railway junction has denied the town the prosperity it could otherwise have enjoyed. Being founded in the 12th century, its history is in fact older than that of Tallinn. Fortunately, much of its rich architectural legacy has survived, so a walk around the town centre offers a cross-section of most Estonian styles and materials. The foreign conquerors – the Germans, Poles, Swedes and Russians – have also all left their mark. Probably Viljandi's richest period was in the late 18th century when a population of just a thousand supported three goldsmiths and two wigmakers. It is now best known in Estonia for various athletics competitions that take place there, some in the town and some around the lake. A full music programme, much of it centred on the open-air concert hall in the castle, is offered during the summer.

Getting there

Express buses run hourly to Tallinn, and slower services also run hourly to Pärnu and Tartu. Journey times are around two hours in each case. The Pärnu

AUGUST MARAMAA: MAYOR OF VILJANDI
1919–21 and 1927–39

Carol Pearson

Viljandi may claim to be an ancient settlement some 700 years old but the town as we see it today grew up in the space of just 20 years and was largely the vision of one man: August Maramaa. 'I want,' Maramaa said, 'to develop Viljandi into a perfect town in a free nation, the pulsating centre of prospering business and manufacturing life.'

In 1919, when August Maramaa was elected as the first mayor of Viljandi, this vision was still some way off. First he had to deal with the realities of post-Tsarist Estonia. The population of the town had increased, the budget was in difficulties, new schools and hospitals were needed, roads and canals were in a poor state, unemployment was rising and so was poverty. Job-creation schemes were therefore used to put the unemployed to work paving roads and excavating around the lake and at the site of the ancient castle. Two new schools and a hospital were built, followed in 1932 by a home for the aged and a children's home. The layout of the town was modernised, an industrial zone created near the station and Tallinna Street turned into a shopping centre.

Mayor Maramaa felt strongly about environmental matters and in 1928 he set up a department of 'Cleanliness and Beauty'. The streets in the centre of the town had to be cleaned twice a day, it was decided, and snow cleared within three days. During 1929, schoolchildren were encouraged to help plant 20,000 pine trees around the town. Special attention was also paid to Lake Viljandi since Maramaa's long-term aim was to turn the town into an inland health resort. Trees were planted, the shore was repaired, a swimming pool, restaurant and tennis court were built.

August Maramaa was born near Tartu in 1881. He moved to Viljandi in 1906, having been sacked as a teacher from a school in Vastemoisa for 'revolutionary activities' – probably efforts to gain Estonian independence from Tsarist Russia. He became mayor of Viljandi in 1919 and held the post for two years until he was elected to the first session of the *Riigikogu* (the Estonian National Parliament) representing the Social Democratic Labour Party. He continued as a town councillor over this period and became mayor for the second time in 1927.

buses serve Kaansoo, the entrance to Soomaa National Park. About three or four services a day run to Valga and Narva.

Where to stay and eat

Through the 1990s tourists just lunched in Viljandi but did not stay as there was no suitable hotel. In 1999 the Centrum opened, followed in 2002 by the Grand.

Centrum Tallinna 24; tel: 43 51100; fax: 43 51101; email: centrum@matti.ee; www.centrum.ee. Individual tourists will appreciate the location beside the bus station

Maramaa was well known for overseeing the details of each project. He would start his working day by walking around the town with a juniper stick in his hand checking everything was in order. When the Central Square and the Viljandi Hotel were created at the junction of Lossi and Posti in 1937, at least one senior engineer resigned because Maramaa wanted to do everything himself. Records show that he ordered the window glass, decided on the door panels and personally inspected all the finished work. In 1939, Maramaa refused to stand for re-election because he claimed there were too many restrictions on his ability to run Viljandi. President Konstantin Päts offered him a post as director of Tallinn Housing and he moved there for a few months.

When the Soviet Union took over the government of Estonia in June 1940, Maramaa returned to teaching at a school near Viljandi. Soviet soldiers stopped his car as he was driving home on January 11 1941 and he was arrested and then deported to Russia. He was executed on December 21 1941.

During the years of Soviet occupation from 1945, Viljandi, like much of Estonia, seemed to be frozen in time. Maramaa's 'pulsating centre' became a sleepy backwater inaccessible to visitors from the West. Shops and hotels closed, the infrastructure collapsed, houses and roads fell into disrepair and the lakeside complex was closed. At the same time, figures such as August Maramaa were removed from the history books. According to Soviet literature, this was necessary because the worst enemies of the working class were the 'superiors' of the local councils. It was alleged that local government officials speculated to become richer until thwarted by pressure from below. August Maramaa was indeed a wealthy man but most of his riches had come from Estonian-language text books and from a series of children's stories called *Maret and Jüri*. These were published at a time when Estonian schools had stopped Russian teaching and were desperate for books in their own language. In the early 1990s August Maramaa was finally reinstated as a significant figure in Viljandi's history. A statue has been erected outside the Town Hall and a road in the town centre has been renamed in his memory.

and about 100m from the Tourist Office. The ground-floor entrance could be larger and more inviting but, once on the first and second floors, there is ample space and comfort. Some rooms are allocated for the disabled and some for non-smokers. Double 900EEK.
Grand Lossi 29; tel: 43 55800; fax: 43 55805; email: info@ghv.ee; www.ghv.ee. Tourists using the swimming pool, the gym or the beauty salon here will find it hard to believe that during World War II this was a concentration camp disguised as a hospital and then during most of the Soviet period was an art college. It had a short spell as the Hotel Viljandi in the 1980s and early 1990s. In March 1917 the end of Tsarist rule was proclaimed from its balcony. Only from 1938 to 1940 had it

previously been a 'grand' hotel and its public areas are clearly modelled on that time. It reopened in 2002 and can surely look forward to a future of much longer than two years. Double 1,100EEK.

What to see

The town is dominated by the ruins of the **castle** which dates from the early 13th century. Three hundred years later it had become, in appearance, the best-defended fortress in Estonia, with two surrounding walls, but every new invader could in the end seize it. When the Swedes conquered the town in 1620, they decided it was no longer worth rebuilding, and over the next 250 years much of the stonework was looted. Only in the late 19th century did the Baltic Germans revive interest in the castle and they ensured the preservation of the basic structure that can still be seen. The excavations they began, and the creation of the surrounding park, continued during both the independence period and the Soviet occupation.

The **museum**, situated on General Laidoner Square, was completely rebuilt during 1998 and 1999. One room is dedicated to natural history, one to archaeology and one to local jewellery. Of most interest to foreign tourists is the model of the castle with illustrations of recent excavations. Note too the 19th-century prints on the wall in this room. The original archaeology section dates from 1878 but the museum was closed during most of the first independence period because of the Baltic-German bias of much of the material assembled during the late 19th century. The Germans reopened it in 1942 during their three-year occupation and it was maintained, largely as an archaeological collection, during the Soviet period. Carvings and fragments from the castle form part of this collection. Fortunately, the later material that both the Germans and the Soviets found offensive was hidden and can once again be displayed. These include 19th-century photographs and documents from the many Estonian literary organisations active at that time. Models of the town at different periods are on show, together with one of the castle before it fell into decline. A second floor added to the museum in 2002 covers village life from Tsarist times until the end of the Soviet period. It has models of collective farms and also documents relating to the Estonian army in 1918. Householders with three–four rooms had to give passing soldiers one pair of underwear; those with five rooms two pairs and two pairs of slippers; and those with six or more rooms three pairs and three pairs of slippers. The building itself is of stone, one of the few dating from the late 18th century. Until 1940 it was used as a chemist's shop.

The building now known as **St John's Church** dates from the late 18th century, as revealed by the hints of baroque in its design. Several previous churches had been built on the site but they were all completely destroyed. It remained in use as a church at the beginning of the Soviet occupation but from the mid 1950s was used as a granary. The chandeliers and wooden furnishings were all dispersed to other churches which remained open. Nonetheless, extensive archaeological excavations were carried out during this period and it was restored during the 1980s with the aim of being reopened as a concert hall.

The foundations of earlier churches can be seen in the basement. In 1989, at the end of the Soviet era, permission was granted for the building to return to the church and the first service was held at Christmas 1991. It was reconsecrated in time for Christmas the following year.

The former vicarage of St John's Church is now the **Paul Kondas Gallery** (Pikk 8; tel: 43 33968; www.kirikyyt.ee) which makes amends for this artist (1900–85) whose work was never publicly exhibited during his lifetime. It opened in 2003. Kondas was a teacher for all his working life and only took up painting seriously in his retirement when he was very much a recluse, respected openly abroad but not recognised officially at home. Frivolity and colour are the hallmarks of his work, but in some topics such as theft from government offices and nudity he went well beyond what could be officially sanctioned in Soviet times. He was also skilled at allegory. A painting nominally about the bombing of Dresden clearly shows Tallinn after Soviet air raids in 1944. All the 26 works displayed in this gallery were painted after his 50th birthday.

St Paul's Church dates from the expansion of Viljandi in the late 19th century, before which St John's Church alone could serve people of the town and the surrounding countryside. (Between 1825 and 1867, the population increased from 1,000 to 3,000.) Baron Ungern Sternberg, famous mainly in Hiiumaa, also owned some land here which he donated for the construction of this church. It was built between 1861 and 1866 under the supervision of two architects, Franz Block and Matthias von Holst, whose neo-Gothic design was to be used again in Riga where they both later practised. The church remained open during the Soviet period and the German organ, installed in 1866, was extensively restored in 1966.

The **Town Hall** at Linnu 2 is small given the current size of Viljandi and was a private residence when originally built in 1768. The baroque façade clearly dates it from this period although it was extensively restored in 1932. There are many 19th- and 20th-century stone buildings in the town worthy of note. Tallinn 16, dating from the 1850s, is an opulent former private house with an elaborate Italian façade. Tallinn 6 was built 20 years later and was famous as the office of *Sakala*, one of the first newspapers printed in Estonian. The **secondary school** at Uueveski 3, like St Paul's Church, is late 19th-century neo-Gothic. The **old water-tower** in Laidoner Square, constructed in 1911, is certainly the most surprising and memorable construction in central Viljandi. It has a red-brick base of 30m topped by an octagonal wooden tower, but is no longer in use. The office building at Tartu 5 was completed in 1939 and is unusual for the quantity of glass used. Tallinn 5, now the **House of Culture**, is one of the few totally Soviet buildings in Viljandi. It can almost be described as Stalinist.

Most wooden houses were destroyed by fire, but a few remain. The former German clubhouse called 'Casino' at Posti 11 was built in 1843 to serve the large Baltic-German population but miraculously survived all the subsequent changes in regime. A much more modest, and slightly earlier, house is at Posti 2. Note here the cornices and the decorations on the front door. Posti 23 is plainer still but is revered by Estonians as the house of one their most famous but impoverished playwrights, August Kitzberg, who lived at this address in the 1890s.

PÕLTSAMAA

Põltsamaa is famous for what it was and for what it never has been, rather than for what it is now. As a capital city for Ivan the Terrible's vassal state, it suffered badly in the fighting between Russia, Poland and Sweden in the 1570s. The months of June 1578 and June 1941 were equal in the terror and destruction caused. The town was at its most prosperous in the 18th century when production of porcelain and glass was started, as was a printing industry. The castle, with a Gothic exterior and a rococo interior, dated from this era. A newspaper in Estonian was published for the first time here in 1766. Its aim was to teach Estonian peasants healthy living. No railway ever came to Põltsamaa so it missed possibilities for expansion in the late 19th century but this meant that it also missed out on Russian factories and a Russian population moving in after World War II.

Getting there

The town makes an excellent stop en route from Tallinn to Tartu. Buses serve both cities, as well as Paide and the county capital of Jõgeva. Although Jõgeva itself is of little interest, buses go from there to Palamuse, Siimusti and Mustvee and to other tourist centres in the county. In the 1920s and 1930s Põltsamaa had several hotels and restaurants along the main road to serve transit traffic but now that this road bypasses the town, it is only seen by those who really want to come.

What to see

The **Rose Garden** beside the remains of the castle was a sensible alternative to redevelopment after the war. It claims to have 3,000 plants and 800 different species. Only the shell of the **castle** now remains but it hosts both classical and pop music festivals, and summer markets. Beside it is the **museum** which surprisingly opened only in 1997. There are plenty of pictures of the castle as it used to be and much on the local hero Karl August Hermann (1851–1909), who combined songwriting with editing the local newspaper. Visitors who want to do more than look can try out the weaving looms and spinning wheels or play the harmonica.

Few people in the entourage of Konstantin Päts, the pre-war president, escaped deportation and then death in Russia. Even fewer are alive and active today. In Britain famous cooks seem to last only as long as football managers. Päts's cook, Elle Reeder, began her broadcasting career when Fanny Craddock was a household name and she carries on in the Jamie Oliver era, although she was 85 in 2004. Her 50 years in the public eye are described through her broadcasts and books.

The rebuilding of **St Nicholas' Church** owes everything to the persistence of the pastor Herbert Kuurme who was still active, in his 90s, in 2004. Although the population of the town is only 5,000, it has the largest active

Lutheran congregation outside Tallinn. He manoeuvred the Soviet authorities so skilfully that restoration could start in 1947, decades before it was considered in other churches, and he was always sure of a large congregation, despite the political statement that such activity made in those days. The church had been briefly closed before, but that was in 1895 when two fat ladies from the congregation blocked the entrance to a German pastor trying to take over from an Estonian one. The 1941 damage was caused by German advances, not by Russian retreats, and the tower fell into the body of the church. The walls of both the castle and the church survived as many are 4m thick. Several of the interior furnishings came from the University Church in Tartu, which after the war was converted into a library.

PALAMUSE

Every Estonian knows Palamuse through the children's book *Spring* by Oskar Luts (1887–1953). Like the best of such work, it gives a stability and timelessness totally absent in the real world. The school Luts attended in the 1890s is now the Parish School Museum, restored as he would have known it and opened in 1987 to celebrate the centenary of his birth. (His death was hardly marked as he died two weeks after Stalin in March 1953, at which point no other deaths could be mourned.) The book is currently not available in English so we must just take the word of Estonian commentators that the author was their Mark Twain. A picture of Tsar Nicholas II looks down on the classroom but more unexpected is the larder, a room of the same size, as pupils had to bring their food for the long winter with them. Another room is therefore the dormitory. The main punishment was detention, during which Russian poetry had to be learnt by heart. The former staff room has been converted into a museum about the Civil War in 1918, when Estonia fought to establish its independence from both the Bolsheviks and the White Russians.

St Bartholomew's Church is the oldest on the mainland of Estonia, dating from 1234, with only some on Saaremaa claiming a longer history. Most of what is seen now dates from a restoration in 1929 but the tower dates from 1800 and the altar and pulpit from 1693, much having been destroyed earlier that century in the Livonian War. The extent of the secret passages in the foundations shows how much this was a fortress as well as a place of worship.

Siimusti

The ceramics factory in the centre of the village, Siimusti Keramika, was founded in 1886 and took advantage of the narrow-gauge railways which linked the local clay pits to the national railway system, which in turn could provide an extensive distribution outlet. This must be one of the very few Estonian institutions that carried on unperturbed through every change in regime. Perhaps as most of their earlier work was very utilitarian no political objections could be made to it. The workforce that stood at 90 in Soviet times has inevitably been downsized to 35 but the design team must have been enlarged given the range of products and patterns now on offer. With typical Estonian modesty, the shop is not even in the same building as the factory, so there is no hard sell.

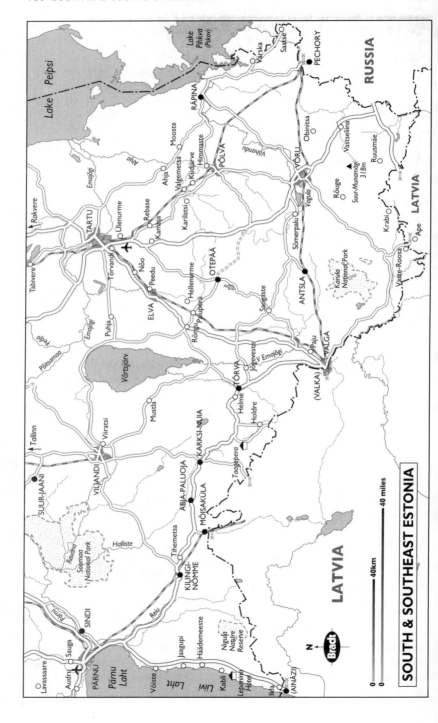

SOUTH & SOUTHEAST ESTONIA

South and Southeast Estonia

OTEPÄÄ

When other towns in Estonia shutter themselves up for the winter, Otepää bursts into life. It is the country's skiing and ski-jumping capital and the centre for other winter sports as well. The Estonian Olympic teams train here, often under floodlights as all the ski- and toboggan-runs are illuminated. In midwinter, daylight can be down to six hours. The main skiing centre, Tehvandi, is on the edge of the town; there are many others a little further away. An earlier name for the town – Nuustaku – comes from the German *Nusstage*, as a favourite autumn occupation was collecting nuts from the surrounding hazelnut woods. The current name means 'bear's head', which walkers in the countryside will appreciate: it is the name of the hill on which the town is built and its shape can probably justify this description. Visits in spring and summer are equally worthwhile, when both the town and the surrounding countryside are quieter. Descriptions of it in pre-war literature encouraged Jean-Paul Sartre to battle with the Soviet authorities for permission to visit Otepää and in the end he succeeded. Alexander Solzhenitsyn recovered in Otepää from his imprisonment in Siberia and wrote the *Gulag Archipelago* in the town.

Getting there

There is no bus station in Otepää but the stop is on the main square beside the Town Hall where the tourist information office is situated. Tickets are sold on board; the most regular service is to Tartu, a journey time of around an hour. For other destinations a change is usually needed there, although the occasional bus goes directly to Tallinn, Valga or Võru.

Where to stay

Through much of the 1990s, Otepää could benefit from the poor level of accommodation available in the nearby towns of Tartu, Valga and Võru. It was the only base for exploring southeast Estonia. These other towns have now caught up, but Otepää still excels in its sport facilities, particularly for ski-jumping so hotels now work on keeping their guests within the town. They have successfully built up a conference business to ensure equal occupancy at weekends and during the week.

Bernhard Kolga 22a; tel: 76 69600; fax: 76 69601; email: hotell@bernhard.ee; www.bernhard.ee. As the Otepää area likes to present itself as 'Little Switzerland', the hotel's name is no surprise. Not only was the hotel purpose-built, but much of the surrounding area was as well, and this process is continuing. An artificial lake 'opened' at the same time as the hotel in 1997 and golf courses and riding trails are now following. Unusually for Estonia, the hotel has an indoor swimming pool. All rooms face south, over the lake, and some have kitchens for families wishing to self-cater. The hotel does not only promote itself as a country retreat; the restaurant is a gallery for the local artist, Johannes Viga, who died in 1997. Two of the suites are named after famous Estonian composers who have stayed there, Arvo Pärt and Veljo Tormis. The website shows the current restaurant menu and Estonian dishes always predominate. Expect a lot of herring, trout, ham, peas and beans. Double 1,200EEK.
Karupesa Tehvandi 1a; tel: 76 61500; fax: 76 61601; email: karupesa@karupesa.ee; www.karupesa.ee. Until 2003, the hotel was run by Scandic Hotels who operate the Palace in Tallinn and the Ranna in Pärnu, but they then sold it to one of Estonia's best-known skiers, Andrus Veerpalu. Whilst of a high standard, it does not claim to be in the same league of luxury as these two hotels, although the wine list in the restaurant might well match them. It is next to the ski centre about 2km from the town centre and ski hire can be arranged. Double 800EEK.
Pühajärve (Holy Lake) Tel: 76 65500; fax: 76 65501; email: pipk@pipk.ee; www.pyhajarve.com. This hotel took a long time to adapt from the Soviet environment to independent Estonia, but it has at long last succeeded. Both the exterior and the interior are now inviting and in 2001 the lakeside area was cleared and a jetty built so that boat trips on the lake are now available. In 2003 the stables were converted into a bowling alley and a swimming pool. The feel of the manor house that it once was has returned, despite the 70 rooms it now has. Treatment at the health centre can be booked on a daily or long-term basis. For those not concerned with their health, a basement pub opened in 2000. Double 850EEK.

The town and surrounding countryside are full of opportunities for bed and breakfast and farmstay accommodation. The tourist information office (www.visitestonia/otepaa.com) has an extensive list. It also has maps of the ski-trails and walks for the summer visitor.

What to see and do
It is appropriate that the town's most famous visitor since independence has been the Dalai Lama who sought solace in 1991 at **Holy Lake** (**Pühajärv**), situated just outside the town. A plaque commemorates his visit. This lake has been a protected area since 1929 and unholy behaviour is limited to the occasional raucous party on a long summer's evening and to one weekend in June when a rock festival takes place. The lake has the country's best inland beaches and warmest water for swimming. Walkers can follow the 16km path around the lake. The nearby rivers are well stocked with trout, pike, perch and eel.

    Otepää church had an important role in Estonian history. The blue, black and white flag of the Estonian Students Union was unfurled here in

Above and left Novel windmills on Saaremaa (TH)

Next page Kuressaare Castle, Saaremaa (TH)

1884 and amazingly this first flag still exists and is displayed in Tallinn from time to time. In 1922 the design was adopted as the national flag. The interior of the church is often closed but is worth seeing if possible for the ornate wooden roof and organ. The organ was built in Tartu by Ernst Kessler, a Baltic German whose work can still be seen in several other churches in Estonia.

The **Independence Memorial** in front of the church is in fact the original, which was hidden during the Soviet era. The two panels beside the entrance door that explain the history of the flag were cemented over by the Soviets, but were uncovered again in July 1989. A flag had in fact been unfurled at the church as early as October 1987 and similar daring was shown in Võru around the same time. The three still-small oak trees at the side of the church were planted after a meeting of the three Baltic presidents in 1992. The stained glass around the church is being renewed as and when funds can be raised. Services are held every Sunday during the summer only.

The **Flag Museum** which opened in 1996, and the **Skiing Museum** which opened in 2001, share premises in a former vicarage. The pastor who lived there for many years in the late 19th century was Jakob Hurt, very famous in Estonia for his role in the 'National Awakening' movement. As well as covering the origins of the flag, and the struggles in 1918 and in the late 1980s to get it accepted, the Flag Museum shows all the efforts of the Estonian communities abroad during the Soviet occupation to keep alive knowledge of it.

The Skiing Museum opened with three rooms but will clearly expand. The earliest ski exhibited dates from 1870 but it is the clothes that will surprise visitors most; it was only in the 1950s that women gave up dresses for trousers. There is a full video display of Estonia's most famous skiers in action on the Otepää ski jump and wax models of those from the pre-video age. Before metal skis replaced wooden ones, Estonia was a major ski production centre.

The former **Soviet Culture House** is a rare positive legacy from the 1950s. Few towns in Estonia, or anywhere else, with a population of around 3,000 can boast such an impressive community centre, particularly as the town also has a theatre. The main hall seats 200 and few days go by without a performance there. The surrounding rooms display art by local children. Design and furnishings throughout are modest and practical. In the same building a Soviet museum and restaurant called **Punataht** opened in 1998. It caters for the number of Estonians now willing on occasion to laugh at the Soviet past, as well as for the younger generations and foreigners of all ages who never knew it. Their publicity warns that it is 'Not for too serious people'. No concessions are made to the present – the clocks are on Moscow time as they had to be during the occupation. Music is provided by rousing bands of Young Pioneers and portraits of Brezhnev's last cabinet look down on a décor that would be recognised anywhere from Tallinn to Vladivostok. On display are the black-banded newspapers produced in Russian and Estonian on the death of Stalin and the array of kopek coins which covered most expenses in the USSR when the pound and the rouble were nominally worth the same. Two 'political' menus are available: the 'proletarian' one offers beetroot and cabbage salad for £0.40/US$0.60 whereas the 'nomenklatura' one offers eel and salmon salad for £2.50/US$4.00. Sadly, the restaurant was closed in early 2001 for not meeting EU health requirements. It always seems about to reopen but still had not done so by summer 2004.

Twenty-five kilometres south of Otepää on the road to Valga is **Sangaste Castle,** misleadingly described in most local brochures as being a 'copy' of Windsor Castle. It is in fact a mildly eccentric, red-brick, neo-Gothic manor house with very basic accommodation unlikely to appeal to most regular tourists, let alone the British royal family. For many years it served as a children's holiday home and as it has scarcely been refurbished since then, it can be recommended for a short coffee break, but not for anything else. It was built in 1874 for the famous Baltic-German scientist Count Magnus von Berg by the architect Otto Hippicus, who also designed Charles Church in Tallinn – and this is where to look for parallels. Models for the design are likely to have been Minley Manor in Hampshire, Peckforton in Cheshire or Welfen near Hanover. The large reception/meeting rooms on the ground floor exhibit hunting trophies, so perhaps there is a hint of the English countryside here. Von Berg became famous for work on the cultivation of rye and the high-yielding type he grew now bears the name Sangaste. A few grains of it are still scattered on his tomb every year. In the park at the back of the castle is an oak tree allegedly planted by Peter the Great. This park is often also called an 'English garden' but is in fact largely a play area for children with a wood in the background.

TÕRVA AND HELME

The local tourist board offers Tõrva as a centre for 'intellectual holiday-makers' and this is an apt description of what is offered. Few major events in Estonian history passed the town by, yet its lakes, forest walks and caves provide easy-going relaxation. Tar was produced here in small quantites from the late 19th century, and *tõrv* is in fact the Estonian word for tar. It was clearly profitable for the 2,000 or so people who lived there then, since they have left a remarkably diverse range of houses and gardens. More recent building has fortunately kept these high standards. In line with this intellectual tradition, it was an opera that really made the town known outside Estonia. On August 29 1998, to commemorate the 100th anniversary of the birth of George Gershwin, his *Porgy and Bess* was performed in front of an audience of 7,000. Tõrva's two hotels were built for this event and have been able to trade on its success ever since, although Tõrva and Helme combined only have a population of 6,000.

In 2001 Tõrva signed a twinning agreement with Crowhurst in Surrey, the first such link between Estonia and Britain. It commemorated Leo Lupseck who grew up in Tõrva but came to Britain as a refugee after the war. From 1983 until his death in 2000 he served as chairman of Crowhurst Parish Council.

Getting there

There are several buses a day to Viljandi, Pärnu and Valga and these three towns provide a wide range of connections to other towns in Estonia.

Where to stay

De Tolly Karja tn 6; tel: 76 33349; fax: 76 79202; email: detolly@hot.ee; www.hotelldetolly.ee. About a kilometre from the bus station, set back from the road and surrounded by a private garden. Although a new building, there are hints of Jugendstil in some of the design, a characteristic of several large buildings in Tõrva and in neighbouring Valga. A boating lake is nearby. Double 800EEK.

Pigi Linna Valga tn 17; tel/fax: 76 68727; email: heelix.pigilinna@mail.ee. Within walking distance of the bus station. It does not have a restaurant, only a café, but the enormous billiard room is considered more than ample compensation by many visitors.

Taagepera Tel: 76 76390; fax: 76 35590; email: hotell@taageperaloss.ee; www.taageperaloss.ee. The opening of this converted manor house in June 2003 will doubtless transform tourism in this area. It is in a village of the same name 18km west of Tõrva, just off the main road to Viljandi and Tallinn. South Estonia now has a country base for those wanting luxury for the same price as a standard hotel in Tallinn. Some visitors will use it as a base for walking and cycling, others for driving to and fro across the Latvian border now that EU accession has made this possible. Hunting pheasant, deer and moose is another possibility. The really self-indulgent need do nothing more than climb the tower to admire the view.

The building was completed in 1912 so was hardly used as a private residence. The architect was Otto Wildau (1873–1942) who also designed the neighbouring manor houses at Peetri and Holdre. He clearly took a free-and-easy approach to his work here and it remains the building for which he is best remembered. There is a complete lack of symmetry in the outside walls, with no main façade. Some of the stonework is polished, some left rough. Perhaps foreseeing future wars, he ensured that there was minimal use of wood, that the manor was built on a hill and that the view from the 40m tower would give ample warning of the approach of hostile forces. Wildau was arrested by the Russians in 1914 and exiled to Kazan. When released in 1919 he did not return to the Baltics but took up a job with the Commerzbank in Salzemen near Magdeburg where his work can still be seen, as it can also be in bank buildings in Gelsenkirchen and Strasbourg. Double 1,000EEK.

What to see and do

Tõrva Church/Chamber Hall (Kirik-Kammersal in Estonian) was built as a Russian Orthodox church in 1905 although it is hard to tell this from the largely Gothic exterior. Bombing destroyed much of the interior in 1944 and in Soviet times it was used only for concerts and art exhibitions. In 1990 the building was given to the Lutherans but, as its name suggests, it now has a dual role as the religious community is too small to support a church on its own.

The ruined **castle** at the neighbouring village of **Helme**, 3km from Tõrva, still shows the power of the Teutonic Knights who built it at the end of the 13th century. Nearly 300 years later, it fell briefly into the hands of the Polish

Empire before being seized by the Swedes. They blew it up in 1658, to prevent it falling into the hands of the Russians and Lithuanians. It was never subsequently rebuilt. The **caves** at the back of the ruins were originally a natural phenomenon but were then widened to provide sanctuary from the wars raging all too often round the castle. They were also extended at the end of the 18th century when the local landlord planned a grotto based on those so popular in England at the time. Amongst the more original names given to one of the caves by the local community is 'Devil's Stomach'. Helme Church was bombed by the Russians in September 1944 because the tower was a German observation post. It has not been restored.

The **Barclay de Tolly Mausoleum** is near the village of **Jõgeveste**, about 6km from Tõrva. It commemorates one of the most famous Russian commanders who fought Napoleon in 1812 and 1813 and who culminated his triumph with a march through Paris in March 1814. His family was partially of Scottish extraction but from the 17th century had lived in what is now Latvia and Lithuania. Following the Russian conquest of Finland in 1809, he was the first Governor-General there until 1812. Jõgeveste was the estate of his wife's family and his body was brought back there after his death in East Prussia in 1818. The Mausoleum was completed in 1823 on the instructions of de Tolly's wife Eleanor von Smitten. She commissioned Apollon Shchedrin, a leading St Petersburg architect, to design it and its structure has remained intact since then, although the two coffins were opened during World War II. The exterior design suggests parallels to a Roman triumphal arch, the interior to a chapel with an altar recess where the bust of de Tolly is placed. The statue on the right is of Athena, the Greek goddess of war, and on the left the statue of a sitting woman represents the symbol of mourning. Outside are the tombs of de Tolly's son and daughter-in-law and a Soviet memorial to soldiers killed in the 1944 invasion of Estonia.

PÕLVA AND THE RUSSIAN BORDERLANDS

Although rarely visited by foreigners, the county and town of Põlva is very popular as a holiday centre for Estonians. Despite the proximity of the border, this is now more of a curiosity than a threat and, although a fence runs along the Russian side, it is hard to think of this as being NATO's frontline since April 2004. If there are guards, they are few and far between. Foreigners who do make the effort to come will find a calm pace of life, an extensive variety of architecture and scenery and many reminders of life a century or two ago.

Getting there

Buses go about once a hour from Põlva to Tartu and some of these continue to Tallinn. Local buses also operate hourly to Räpina and to Värska, with less frequent services to Saatse and Koidula. Three buses a day travel from Värska via Põlva and Tartu to Tallinn. Tartu provides connections to the rest of Estonia from this area.

Where to stay

Pesa Uus 5, Põlva; tel: 79 98530; fax: 79 98531; email: kagureis@kagureis.ee; www.kagureis.ee. It is sad that this hotel is situated in the only part of town that can be described as ugly, but it has a well-sheltered balcony and garden where meals are served in the summer and the trees block the view of surrounding blocks of flats. With 30 rooms, it can cater for individuals and groups. The bus station is within walking distance, as is a large swimming pool. Double 900EEK.

Värska Spa Värska; tel: 79 64793; fax: 79 64693; email: info@spavarska.ee; www.spavarksa.ee. Any potential visitor is strongly advised against looking at the website since it lists in great detail every possible illness the spa can cure. In fact most visitors are Estonians simply wanting the comfort of some spa treatment to enhance a conventional holiday. The hotel opened in 1980 and now that it has been modernised, will in due course no doubt try to follow the Saaremaa pattern of attracting year-round Finnish groups. Individuals should perhaps enjoy it whilst they can. There is a public computer should visitors be email obsessed, but it seems hardly appropriate in such otherwise relaxing surroundings. Double 1,100EEK.

What to see and do

All Estonians know Põlva for its **dairy** and most of the country's milk and cheese comes from this region. Põlv means 'knee' and the name comes from a legend about a girl allegedly buried into the church wall in a kneeling position. In 1840 the first temperance society in Estonia was founded here and in 1858 a precursor to the Tartu Song Festival took place.

The current **St Mary's Church** dates only from 1840 but the altar panelling and the picture it includes of the Last Supper dates from 1650; both were restored in 2001. The painting of the Resurrection dates from 1845 and is by Ludwig von Maydell, best known for his work in St Olav's in Tallinn and for his illustrations of children's books. Several vicars here achieved national prominence. Pastor Treublut served for 65 years from 1716 to 1781, a record nobody else has surpassed, although Herbert Kuurme in Põltsamaa (see page 178) may soon do so. Jüri Kimmel was vicar from 1945 to 1982 so had to serve entirely under the Soviet regime when it was at its toughest. He fought bravely to keep what church property he could, always sure of the support of an equally tenacious congregation, who resisted efforts from the local school to prevent their children attending; one headmaster in 1969 personally tried to chase 20 children out of the church during a New Year service. Pastor Kimmel died as he was about to hold a service.

The **Karilatsi Peasant Culture Museum** (www.miksike.ee/karilatsi) is 18km northeast of Põlva, just off the road to Tartu. The schoolroom was built in 1945 when it had 76 pupils. The number dropped steadily and by 1966 it was down to 21 so the school was closed in 1972. Many of the furnishings however date from around 1900. The school was comparatively affluent having a harmonium as well as a violin; most would have been lucky to have just a violin. The dried peas beside the oven were the basis of punishment; pupils had to kneel in great discomfort on them for 15 minutes with the intense heat at their side. The lunchboxes shown in the teachers' room were also the basis of punishment. They could be confiscated and returned only in the late afternoon.

The village shop has been rebuilt as it was in 1920–40 with a range of goods most of which would never have been seen there between 1945 and 1990. Estonian bitterness at the wasted years of the occupation is so easy to understand here.

Behind these buildings is a 'natural' map of Võru country, assembled by local children with clumps of trees for the forests, wooden tracks for the roads and a miniature railway line to link Põlva and Võru.

The museum is on both sides of the road. On the western side is a history of the local clothing industry showing how flax was made into garments. There are also threshing machines imported from Britain before World War I.

South of Karilatsi and west of Põlva is the **Varbuse Post Station** where horses were changed in Swedish and Tsarist times. By 2005 it should be open as the Road Transport Museum and will specialise in the 1950s and 1960s. There are many sculptured signs from this pre-vandal era as well as more basic ones too. To check progress here, visit the website www.maanteemuuseum.ee.

If the Estonian human population is still a cause for concern, the ant one certainly is not. Although nobody has actually counted them, there is little reason to doubt the figure of three million given as the population of the **Akste Ant Colony** about 12km northeast of Põlva. This reserve can only be visited with a guide and it is perhaps comforting to hear from him that community life there is as fraught as in any human one. The ants that get along with each other create hills 2m high; others concerned with privacy burrow similar distances underground.

It is rare to be frustrated at the lack of even gentle development in an Estonian town, but this must be the feeling of many visitors to **Räpina**, 30km east of Põlva. It should be the centre of tourism for the county but has no hotel. The late 19th-century manor house is one of the best preserved neo-classicist buildings in Estonia but now seems much underused as a horticultural college, although there can be good art exhibitions here. The papermill, which may be visited, once produced banknotes for Catherine the Great. The parks beside the river are well maintained with the care given to the lawns creating an almost English feel to them. The landscape artist however was German, Walter von Englehardt, who was director of the Düsseldorf Municipal Garden before World War I. The town offers a congenial break between Põlva and Värska. In due course it should become much more.

The town of **Värska** developed around the church, which was built in 1904. Note the cemetery beside the church, quite a rarity in Estonia, as following the plague in the early 18th century burial inside a church was forbidden on health grounds and isolated sites well away from the village were chosen instead. Once mineral water was discovered here, however, its role as a spa was assured. In recent years tourists have been attracted by the Setu Farm Museum which opened in 1994. 'Museum' is hardly the correct name for it, cultural centre or even theme park being more appropriate. (For a serious museum on the Setu community and background on them see under Obinitsa, page 192) One room does represent life for this community in 1920–40 but otherwise there is plenty of singing and dancing, the chance to try cooking on a log fire and the temptations of what must be the largest souvenir shop in Estonia. If you are short of towels and long dresses, this is the place to come, as prices are set for Estonians rather than for foreigners.

If it really is better to travel than to arrive, the road from Värska to Saatse certainly proves the point. The **Russian border** gets closer and closer and then actually crosses the road. For about 2km the road belongs to Russia and traffic is forbidden to stop on it. In 1992 the Russians, not normally conciliatory to Estonia in any way, agreed to the continuing use of this road by Estonians as it is the only link with the rest of the country for several villages. Traffic is not allowed to stop and it seems that nobody has yet broken down here or tried to use the road for illegal entry. The border has no particular rationale anywhere in Polva county, having been set in 1944 when it was only between two provinces of the USSR, not between western and eastern Europe. Until then, Estonian territory stretched several kilometres further east and south, as was agreed in the Tartu Peace Treaty signed by Estonia and the USSR in 1920.

Saatse has a museum which proudly boasts a collection of 15,000 objects but it has to be admitted that there are many similar and better-displayed collections elsewhere in Estonia. The building has had a very chequered history, even by Estonian standards. It looks like a modest private residence, but in fact was built as an officers' holiday home in 1908, then converted into a hospital. Between the wars and through the early Soviet period it was a boarding school, becoming a museum in 1963. However most visitors will want to stride through the woods here for further glimpses of the incongruous border. It is easy to approach and there is no problem with photography. The Russians mark their side very clearly with fencing; the Estonians limit themselves to the occasional border post. For those with a Russian visa, there is what has always been a quiet crossing point about a kilometre from the village. In 2004, as traffic began to queue for the best part of a day in Narva on the Tallinn–St Petersburg road to cross into Russia, it was thought that some drivers would prefer the 500km detour to this area just to be able to use one of these Põlva county crossing points without any delay.

VÕRU

Võru is unusual in Estonian terms in being a totally planned town that has retained its original layout. Catherine II supervised its design during the 1780s and little has changed since. The surrounding county, which borders on Latvia and Russia, is the only hilly area in Estonia, so attracts walkers and skiers. To Estonians, Võru is best known as the town where the famous 19th-century author Friedrich Reinhold Kreutzwald lived. Sadly, none of his work, not even his most famous epic poem *Kalevipoeg,* is currently available in English. His house, where he practised as a doctor, is now the **Kreutzwald Memorial Museum**, which surprisingly opened in February 1941 during the first Soviet occupation. His books were published extensively in a number of languages during the main Soviet occupation and, hopefully, contemporary Estonian publishers will take up this work again. The museum shows the high standard of living that professional people could enjoy during the 19th century, even in small towns. It now also houses paintings by two Estonian artists who spent most of their lives in exile, Juri Erik Hammer who lived in Sweden and Gunnar Neeme who lives in Australia. Võru is proud of its connection with Kreutzwald and is particularly conscious of its Estonian heritage. It is in no hurry to Westernise or expand so should remain for many years a congenial, small, county town.

Getting there

Some buses go directly from Võru to Tallinn, Narva and Pärnu but it is normally necessary to change in Tartu or Valga for onward travel to the rest of the country. There is an extensive local network going south to Rõuge and Vaste-Roosa and east to Obinitsa and Värska. No buses cross the Latvian border or the Russian border in this area. For travellers with a Russian visa, transfers can be arranged to the border at Koidula and then on the other side to Petseri. As Petseri is only about a kilometre from the border, it is almost possible to walk. The railway line at Võru no longer carries passengers.

Where to stay

The lack of a decent hotel deterred tourists for many years from visiting Võru but a former youth centre converted itself into a luxury hotel in 2000, just as a three-star hotel opened on the beach in the town centre.

The luxury hotel is the **Kubija** (43a Männiku; tel: 86 6000; fax: 86 6001; email: info@kubija.ee; www.kubija.ee) which has the most detailed website of any in Estonia, zooming in on any room detail a potential visitor may wish to examine. It is in a pine forest on the edge of the town, and with its range of sports and business facilities hopes that few guests will leave the compound during their stay. Double 1,000EEK.

All the wood and fabrics used in the hotel are from the local area. One of the suites in the hotel is named after Erki Nool, who won a gold medal for Estonia in the decathlon at the 2000 Sydney Olympics. In fact the hotel is rapidly becoming a shrine to Erki Nool. By 2003, a statue of him pole-vaulting had pride of place in the foyer and his collection of shoes was also displayed there. The hotel also opened a large sports centre to further link his name with them. There is a presidential suite, distinguished by the security room provided for his guards, but if the president and the Olympic champion should arrive at the same time, there is no doubt who would receive the most attention.

The Kubija has the only large restaurant in Võru which is used by local people and by those passing through – and, cynics might say, by those who need to recover from a visit to Russia. In the town centre, the **Hundijala**

Pubi at Juri 18b can be recommended for those who prefer a more casual (and cheaper) environment.

The three-star hotel is the **Tamula** (4 Vee; tel: 78 30430; fax: 78 30431; www.tamula.ee), a completely new building on the lake-shore, within easy walking distance of all the sites in the town. Although it only serves breakfast, there is a pub/restaurant next door with a lunch and dinner menu. All 22 rooms have a view over the lake and a balcony. A large car park and tennis courts cut the hotel off from the town, so a quiet environment is assured. Double 800EEK.

What to see and do

The **Town Museum** is the best in Estonia for coverage of the 1918–20 War of Independence, of the resistance to the Soviet occupation organised by the Forest Brothers and of the independence movement of the late 1980s. A model of one of the Forest Brothers' hide-outs has been rebuilt. One room is devoted to Frits Suit, the mayor of Võru throughout the first independence period from 1919–40. It has been a major challenge for his successors to emulate the diversity of cultural achievements that he instigated. The three Kriisa brothers, Jakob, Juhaw and Tannil were Estonia's most famous organ builders and the museum has reconstructed their workshop for exhibition.

The Catherine Church is named not after the saint, but after the Russian empress, who would approve of the way it still dominates the town landscape; surprisingly it is Lutheran and not Orthodox. It was built between 1788 and 1793 and mixes baroque and classicist styles. The architect was Christoph Haberland, well known for his work in Riga. The organ is of course the work of the Kriisa brothers.

The monuments to Estonian freedom fighters that were destroyed during the Soviet period were all quickly and extensively restored in this area. It was sadly necessary in 1995 to build another memorial which is in the square beside the Catherine Church. It is to the 17 town councillors who lost their lives when the *Estonia* sank off the Finnish coast in September 1994.

Võru has a good beach on Lake Tamula, where a music festival takes place each July. More activities are now being arranged in the winter and spring. In 2003 the new floodlit ski-centre at Suur Munamägi was opened, offering several routes for cross-country skiing. Kreutzwald is always commemorated in early December with readings of his poetry. May is the month for cross-country races and for dancing competitions.

BEYOND VÕRU

South of Võru are the two extremes of Estonia, both within the Haanja Nature Park. Twelve kilometres south on one road is **Suur Munamägi,** the highest 'mountain' in the Baltics at just over 300m, while a similar distance from Võru is the lake at Rõuge, with a depth of 38m. The tower at Suur Munamägi, a short climb from the road, was built in 1939 and added a further 30m in height. The date is significant as it was one of the last functionalist buildings to be completed before the Soviet occupation and was sited in an area that had no links with any of the occupying powers. The glass gallery on the top was added in 1970 as the growth of the surrounding trees would otherwise have blocked the view, which extends across innumerable forests and lakes, well into Russia and Latvia. The lower floors of the tower house a museum on nature protection. The tower and museum were closed in 2004 for renovation but should be open again in 2005.

A settlement at **Rõuge** dates back to the 5th century and seems to have been destroyed and re-established about once every century for the next 600 years until it was finally abandoned, not being revived again until the 18th century. The settlement was excavated extensively in early Soviet times in the hope of finding evidence of a very Russian environment but nothing was found. From then, research continued at a much slower pace, but has now been revived. The scenery here is totally different from the rest of the country, as the hilly environment offers a waterfall and fast-flowing streams, which in turn gave energy to a watermill which generated electricity for the village until 1956. Construction of the church began in 1730 and was continued until the 1920s as it was attacked in 1918. The organ is by the Kriisa brothers.

Another settlement only half an hour's drive from Rõuge has a very different origin. It is at **Vaaste Roosa** on the Latvian border and was where the Estonian and Latvian guerrilla movement, called the Forest Brothers, hid from their Soviet persecutors. Visitors who have seen the Cu Chi Tunnels in Vietnam will find many similarities. Life could continue for days underground with all evidence of exits and entries concealed. The area is of course isolated and well forested so hiding was easier than in the more open countryside further west. Tourists can in fact stay a night in a bunker and one is named after a former prime minister of Estonia, Mart Laar, since he did precisely that. Before entering politics, he was a historian and he has written the standard book on the Forest Brothers which is available in English.

There is now quite a holiday air in the surroundings of the bunkers and it is possible to have more conventional accommodation in the farmhouse beside them. The real temptation though is Metsakohin, or 'Rustle of the Forest', which is literally the local firewater. A lit match is put to each bottle when it is opened to prove its strength to sceptical visitors. A sign in the café pleads with guests to leave sober, quite a tall order after tasting this brew, and those who cannot manage to do so are offered free accommodation for the night. To check events and facilities here, visit www.metsavennatalu.ee

Visitors wanting to proceed south can cross the border here. Ape is the first town on the Latvian side and it is a short journey to Aluksne from there.

Thirty kilometres east of Võru is **Obinitsa**, centre of the local **Setu** community. The Setus are linked ethnically and linguistically to Estonia but many of their customs have a Russian origin. Although they would attend Russian Orthodox services, they would rarely understand the language and they maintained pagan customs for centuries after they had been dropped by both Estonians and Russians. It is probably because of their adherence to the Orthodox Church that they were allowed to build one in Obinitsa in 1952, at a time when religious communities elsewhere in Estonia were suffering particularly strong persecution.

Kreutzwald was the first Estonian to make any study of their communities but serious anthropological work only began in the 20th century. The current border between Estonia and Russia cruelly divides many families, particularly as Petseri/Pechory used to be their headquarters. Estonians now admit that they were neglected as a community during the first independence period, with a standard of living well below that in the rest of the country. The new Estonian government did however insist in 1920 that girls attend school, which previously they had not done. The Soviets saw little difference between them and the Estonians so Setu agriculture was collectivised in the same way. This did at least ensure that electricity finally reached the Setu community in 1962. Finnish organisations are now providing considerable support for the Setu and help publicise their cause outside Estonia. As there is no formal way of defining a Setu, estimates of the current size of the community differ, but about 1,300 is the number living in Estonia and 600 in Russia.

The **Setu Museum** in Obinitsa opened in 1995 and is built as a family house. It shows a 'Red Corner' with icons draped in red scarves. The wooden chest was for women to store their handicrafts, an activity they could learn without formal schooling. As a dowry the bride traditionally had to provide gloves, belts, bedspreads, shawls and long dresses. They would also have become skilled in ceramics by then. The museum has an extensive display of the very elaborate costumes the Setu women used to wear, and still do on festive occasions. Women who could afford it had silver breastplates and often other accessories in silver as well. These would be buried with her.

About 3km north of Obinitsa are the **Piusa Caves**. The sandstone here was excavated for over 40 years from 1922 to 1966 to supply Estonia's glass factories but now safer and faster open-cast mines are used for this. The caves have now been taken over by a large colony of bats but they do not object to occasional tourists walking around. Do bring a torch and do come as a group. There are no permanent staff on duty to deal with accidents or anyone getting lost.

From Piusa, it is possible to travel north to Värska and Põlva or east into Russia at the Koidula border crossing point.

INTO RUSSIA

The early 1990s in Europe is usually seen as a time of collapsing borders and easier travel. Along the new border between Russia and its Baltic neighbours, the situation was the complete reverse. Barbed wire now cut across formerly open fields and what had previously been a short local bus ride now became an expensive tour that had to be planned weeks in advance. For several years after the Estonian declaration of independence in August 1991, the actual location of the border was a matter of bitter dispute between Estonia and the Russian government. In 1998, the Estonians acquiesced to Russian demands and formally gave up claims to territory which had been theirs between 1920 and 1940. It has left several thousand Estonian-speakers on the Russian side and also split the **Setus**, a racial group that has affinities with the Estonians but sees itself as a different community. This territory included **Petseri**

Monastery (Pechory in Russian) and the ruined castle at **Izborsk**. On a two-to-three-day visit into Russia, they can be combined with a stay in **Pskov**.

Getting there

In 2001, a simplified visa system was operated for tourists to the Pskov region. Instead of having to obtain them abroad, they could be arranged at the border on the Võru–Pskov road, and tour operators who specialised in Russia were able to do this without difficulty. In 2002 this concession was withdrawn, although there were hopes in 2004 that it might be restored. Otherwise it is necessary, as for any trip to Russia, to apply for a visa abroad, once all the travel arrangements have been confirmed by the tour operator.

Thanks to a Finnish aid programme, both border stations are spacious, modern and impeccably clean. There are surprisingly no refreshment facilities available so iron rations should be taken to cover the hour or so that can be spent in queues on either side. Neither foreign exchange office accepts sterling, but dollars, euro, kroon and lats can easily be exchanged into and out of Russian roubles.

Tourists who include Pskov as part of a longer tour of Russia can reach Novgorod by coach in around three hours, or St Petersburg by train in about four hours. There are regular local bus services between Pskov, Izborsk and Pechory but none across the border. Individual tourists can pre-book a private transfer to Võru or Tartu since drivers with local agents on both sides usually have multi-entry visas to enable them to do this. There are regular discussions between the Tartu and Pskov authorities about restoring a boat service between both cities, which was a very popular summer trip in Soviet times. In 2004, as in previous years, the Russians were not able to make concessions on visas, even for day trips, so the boats could not operate.

Although, because of visa complications, very few tourists now reach Pskov, there is a tourism site, much better than many in Estonia, on www.tourism.pskov.ru, with full information on all hotels, transport and opening hours for the museums. The town site, www.pskov.ru, has a varied question-and-answer session with the county governor. These two sites are in English, but those listed below for the hotels are not.

Where to stay

Krom Metallistov 5; tel: 8112 39007; fax: 8112 167364; email: pskov@hotelkrom.ru; www.hotelkrom.ru. Double 800RUB.

Planeta Petseri village; tel: 8117 22537. Double 600RUB. The hotel was renovated in 2002, so although simple is now perfectly acceptable.

Rizhskaya 25 Rizhsky Prospect; tel: 8112 462223; fax: 8112 462301; email: hotel@svs.ru; www.pskov-hotel.narod.ru. It has all the advantages and disadvantages of Soviet three-star hotels. Throughout the large building, everything works adequately, there is good security, café prices are cheap and it is always clean but imagination in furnishings, menus and architecture is completely lacking. Do not expect satellite TV, a buffet breakfast bar or any useful tourist literature at reception. That their brochure advertises 265 'rums' and 20 'suits' shows how little contact they have recently had with the Western world. It is a ten-minute walk along Rizhsky Prospect to the Olga Bridge which crosses the Velikaya River to the Kremlin. Younger visitors may like to enliven their stay by crossing the road to the Jaguar Club. Double 900RUB.

The shell of a hotel which Intourist had started to build in the late 1980s on the river beside the Olga Bridge, nearly opposite the Kremlin, in 2004 still awaited a new investor to complete it.

What to see
Pskov
Visitors to Pskov have to redefine the concepts of 'old' and 'recent'. With a chronicled and architectural history going back 1,200 years, many 18th- and 19th-century buildings suddenly appear very contemporary. Most of what the visitor needs to see is within walking distance of the **Kremlin** and many will in fact not leave its boundaries, given the feast of what is there. The rows of tower blocks that besmirch the skyline of every Russian city, are restricted to the distant suburbs here, so they do not disturb visitors on a regular tourist itinerary. The Germans were less barbaric here than in other cities and more destruction was in fact caused by the Russian bombardment in 1944 than in the 1941 invasion. Perhaps to make amends for this, the area that suffered most, on the south side of the river opposite the Kremlin, was quickly rebuilt in the early 1950s in a neo-classical style. For once, the adjective 'Stalinist' need not be used in a pejorative sense.

Pskov has gained and suffered from being on the borders of the Teutonic and the Slav worlds. Membership of the Hanseatic League to the West, combined with road and river links to the East, ensured centuries of successful trading and relative political freedom. Exports were furs, flax and grain; imports were salt, fruits and paper. The Veché (Town Council) took upon itself powers more akin to those of a state. There are many variants on a story of how even Ivan the Terrible, who hoped to ravage Pskov in the wake of his conquest of Novgorod in 1570, was humbled into eating bread and water rather than Christian flesh. Three hundred and forty-seven years later, the last Russian Tsar, Nicholas II, was equally humbled, this time into signing his abdication warrant. Yet every war, from when Rurik of Novgorod started to expand his rule in 864, until the defeat of the Germans in 1945, could not but involve Pskov and its citizens. In fact, the years since 1945 probably represent the greatest period of peace the area has ever enjoyed. It now has to work out an economic future, largely independent of Moscow. Links are being established with many towns abroad, including Perth in Scotland.

This peace has led to the re-emergence of much silverware and of many paintings and icons which were hidden from view for centuries and which can only now be safely displayed again, either in the churches or in the **museum**. Pskov is proud of its distinctive art, which it maintained even when the city nominally became subservient to Moscow in 1510. In any century, this art would be more daring than anything Moscow produced, more colourful, more innovative and above all, more personal to the painter. There was no reluctance

A SERVICE AT PETSERI IN 1938

Petseri has a comparatively new look to it. There is a Lutheran church, built of red brick, an austere, ugly building, but the Eesti Pank (Bank) is quite an imposing structure. Estonia has no Defence of the Realm Act, so alcohol is obtainable all day long.

We climbed up an incredible number of stone steps to the small court in which stood the white church, with green domes. Outside the door sat a beggar, with no legs below the knees, muttering words I could not catch, but doubtless invoking the saints. He crossed himself, swaying backwards and forwards. I dropped ten sents into his hat.

The church itself is one mass of gilt and colours, chiefly ultramarine. It is not big, but had an air of expansiveness caused, I think, by the absence of seats. In the Russian ritual, the congregation stands when it is not kneeling. There are windows only in two walls, for the church itself is built into the sandstone of the hillside. I wandered around from shrine to shrine. These consisted of pictures, crucifixes, and groups of broken figures. They would have fetched little, I suspect, in a commission shop. To the peasants, however, and perhaps to the priests as well, they provided straws at which to clutch in an otherwise puzzling world. One or two peasants came in and approached several shrines, kneeling before one here, kissing a picture there, and then stroking the foot of another one. Altogether it seemed a little overdone, this bowing before idols, yet the peasants did it with an air of simple devoutness. I found myself thinking of Soviet Russia, now trying to get on without a religion, and found myself realising what these people must have felt like when they broke the bonds of the tyrannising Church. I could understand their determination to have no religion at all.

The service began. I could not understand the liturgy. Most of it took place behind a gilt grating; from time to time, curtains were drawn back. There was much incense, which smelt like rather a cheap brand and an old priest sang a very long gospel slowly. The monks looked odd, with their long flowing hair, greased and parted in the middle. The young men wore

to incorporate Byzantine, Lithuanian or German themes or to use green rather than gold and red as a major colour. What the museum now shows is as much a reflection of recent political and military upheaval as of the local artistic tradition. There are 700 icons of which only a minute percentage have been on display since the museum opened in 1918. Some left Pskov towards the end of the Civil War in 1920, others were removed in the early 1930s during the increasingly hostile attitude of the Soviet government towards religion, others were looted by the Germans during their wartime occupation, others were withdrawn to Moscow at the same time. Their survival is as remarkable as their artistry.

Approached from any direction, the **Kremlin** appears more powerful and formidable than its Moscow namesake. Its location at the confluence of two rivers reinforces this impression. Photographs should be taken from all sides, in nothing on their heads, but the senior brothers wore a mantilla-like headdress of black. All the monks wore black, short cassocks, displaying a large portion of Russian boot below. They were all not just threadbare and shabby, but indescribably dirty. The whole service was sung. I had heard the Don Cossacks in London, and thought them phenomenal. Here in this church, I heard voices as immensely deep, powerful and tuneful. The Russians have titanic voices which are deeply moving.

The service over, we returned once more down the stone steps into the courtyard. The wall of the building that formed one side was whitewashed. Just under the eaves, angels with outspread wings were painted in gorgeous colours. It all looked so attractive and bright and clean, with the sun giving the colours their full beauty, in striking contrast with the persons of the monks. The whole monastery was splashed with brilliant colours, in all odd corners and nooks there being some holy figures painted. The clock-tower with its 13 bells formed the corner, with the red and white painted library. It contains gifts from Ivan the Terrible and many other Russian tsars.

On Petseri station that evening, as we were waiting to return to Tartu, I saw a peasant woman dressed in a long white coat, edged with red embriodery. Around her neck hung a necklace made of silver chain and old Russian kopeks. We agreed a price of ten kroons. I then hurried to the bookstall to buy a postcard to send to my wife. I wrote: 'Have been extravagant, but got a treasure for you. I don't think you will be angry when you see it.'

From 'Baltic Corner', by Ronald Seth, published in 1939, when Petseri belonged to Estonia. The 'Defence of the Realm Act' referred to was legislation introduced in Britain in 1917 which closed bars and wine merchants during the afternoon. The aim was to curtail drunkenness amongst workers in the munitions industry. These regulations were to stay in force for about 60 years so Britons travelling abroad would often comment on the pleasures of day-long access to alcohol.

particular from the Olga Bridge which crosses the Velikaya River and from the Sovetskaya Embankment, beside the Pskov River. Unlike the Moscow one, it was never seized in battle and it retains the walls built in 1323. Excavations, however, have found evidence of settlements going back as far as the 4th century. This Kremlin has also not been converted to suit car users so retains a medieval feel. The major site within the complex is the **Trinity Cathedral** with its 72m painted dome. The building dates from the 17th century, but some of the icons are 100–200 years older. It is worth visiting the cathedral during one of the daily services to see the intensive religious fervour of the congregation. The **Administration Chamber** was only restored in 1995, but this has been carried out so effectively that it gives the impression of having ignored all the occupations with which Pskov has been plagued. All formal ceremonies took place here and at other times it was used as an enormous office. Certain tables were always reserved for specific senior officials and for ambassadors.

The Pskov Museum is about 2km from the Kremlin, on the same side of the river. It is divided into two clear sections. The new building, visible from the road, dates from 1978 and exhibits Soviet painting. Some works could not be anything else, others show an individuality which has perhaps been inherited from the equally iconoclastic religious artistry of the previous six centuries. There is also a Soviet history section here, which becomes more self-critical with the passing years. The older building at the rear, although a former merchant's house, is called the **Pogankin Palace**, and it contains the icons and jewellery that could not be housed in the churches as well as photographs of the town in the late Tsarist era around 1900.

The **Mirozhski Monastery** is the one major historic site well away from the Kremlin, being 2km upriver on an isolated hillside. It is on the UNESCO World Heritage List and the original bulding may well predate the Kremlin. The first records are from 1156 and they refer to construction having started in 1140, and to Greek workers being employed. The artistic bias towards Constantinople has continued to this day and may explain the hostility often felt at the hands of different Moscow regimes. As, however, the surrounding stone wall was only built in the 19th century, the monastery suffered from every invasion over the previous 600 years in a way that the Kremlin did not. That a bomb which landed in 1944 did not explode is described as a miracle.

The monastery was only spared from flooding and from damp because of its height above the river and this has kept some of the icons in excellent condition. More important, it has kept the wall frescos largely intact, with 80% of them surviving from the late 12th century. They could have been destroyed in the 18th century when they were covered over in whitewash. There are several theories on why this was done. Maybe some people thought the frescos too faded. Perhaps their Byzantine feel would be taken as offensive to Moscow which was then exerting greater influence both in politics and in religion.

The biblical scenes they represent, such as the Ascension, the Last Supper and the Crucifixion, can now easily be made out. The restoration that brought this about was begun in 1969 and represents a long-term and positive legacy of the Soviet Union. Whilst the work continues, neither international support nor any local initiative can equal what was done during those first 20 years. About ten monks currently live at the monastery and several are skilled icon painters; they can often be seen at work in their studios.

The **railway station** is best known as the site where Tsar Nicholas II abdicated in 1917. He was planning to return from the front to St Petersburg but his train was blocked by revolutionaries; they then forced him to sign the document they had prepared. Later he would be taken with his family to Ekaterinberg where they were subsequently executed. The **Railway Museum** nearby covers the history of the Warsaw–St Petersburg line on which Pskov was the third station to be completed. Probably the history of the railways in the area can be more closely documented than any other field, such is the number of engines, uniforms, timetables and even medical kits that have been salvaged.

Izborsk

The ruined fortress at Izborsk is about 30km from Pskov and a similar distance from the current border crossing to Estonia. Between 1920 and 1940, it was just on the Estonian side of the froniter. The small museum has collected together the 1,300 years or so of archaeological history that the site now represents and is particularly strong in bronze and stone weapons. It also offers some 19th-century memorabilia of the surrounding village. This has recently been restored and could soon become a major site for day trips; there are several picnic areas both inside and outside the fortress, and walks in the hills and beside the river. Botanists have counted over a thousand different flora within walking distance of the village. Cafés and guesthouses are beginning to open. Pancakes in particular can be recommended.

Pechory Monastery

A visit to Pechory Monastery requires almost as much time below ground as above ground, with the caves playing an equal role in its history to the churches. On many occasions the caves were a refuge; for over five centuries they have always in addition been a burial ground not only for the monks but also for the local great and good. The family names Kutozov, Pushkin and Musorgski are probably the most famous to be seen here. Women are also buried here as their contribution to the work of the monastery has always been credited. The caves now contain around 10,000 graves and there is space for many more. Some are absolutely basic wooden coffins, but many are individual works of art, both in wood and in silver. The dry, sandstone surroundings ensure preservation. Candles are provided by the monks for the tour, but visitors may use their own torches if they prefer.

The complex now contains nine churches with 80 monks in residence, a drop in the number from 200 during the Soviet era. Ironically one has to return to the 16th century to find another period when the figure was this high. The monastery also employs many lay women and men. Building started in 1473 but most of what remains is from the early 18th century. The most famous monk was Abbot Cornelius who was beheaded on the orders of Ivan the Terrible in 1570. The pathway down to St Nicholas Church is sometimes called 'The Blood-Soaked Road' as, according to one story, his head was rolled down it immediately after the execution. Peter the Great was a frequent visitor and probably was the last one allowed to smoke there. A special chapel was allocated to him for this purpose. Vladimir Putin, the current Russian prime minister, now follows in his footsteps and is believed to attend confessional from time to time. In any case, he certainly ensures the financial support needed to keep the complex at a standard both Peter the Great and the pre-war Estonian governments would have recognised. The defensive walls fell somewhat into decline between their two eras when the Tsarist border moved to the coast. It was the Soviet regime that restored them in the 1960s when ample central government finance was combined with a more liberal view of religion. The complex is best seen and best photographed from the garden on Saints Hill behind St

Nicholas Church. The Saints Tree dates from the 16th century, so is nearly as old as the original buildings.

Contemporary visitors may be surprised at the opulence in the monastery compared to the poverty in the surrounding village. Both the Yeltsin and the Putin regimes have poured money into the monastery, perhaps to show dedication to the Russian Orthodox Church or perhaps more to reinforce its legal status to the large number of Estonian tourists who come to Russia for a few hours specifically to see it. (There is a border crossing close to the village but its use is largely restricted to local residents on either side.) By prior arrangement, groups can visit the Setu school in the village, which teaches in Estonian and is partially funded by the Estonian government.

VALGA

For some two hundred years, the border town of Valga has, to put it mildly, had a bad press. In the 19th century travellers wrote of squalor and mental deficiency in both the Estonian and Latvian populations. In the 20th century, both during the first period of independence and very recently, travellers complained of visa and currency problems, of long delays for connecting trains and buses, or of not being able to cross the border at all. In Tsarist times and earlier, it did not much matter that the town had a mixed population of Estonians and Latvians but this was crucial during the struggle for independence at the end of World War I when both wanted to claim it. Most of the town is in Estonia, although the Latvian side forms a compact town, Valka, in its own right.

There was a serious risk of war between both sides until Sir Stephen Tallents from the British Foreign Office managed to impose a border running through the town. He did not enjoy the mission and never returned, quite happy to rely for reports on its success from equally cynical observers. Tallents then went on to pioneer public relations, at first with the post office and then at the BBC. Tallents House, the post office building in Edinburgh opened in 2001, shows how respected he still is in this field, as does a medal which carries his name awarded by the Institute of Public Relations. He was the first president of the institute when it was founded in 1948.

Valga has one other link with Britain, through someone whose life took a totally different course from that of Tallents: the communist writer Salme Palme Dutt. Born in 1888, she was of the generation able to be active as the revolutionary movement spread amongst factory workers from the 1905 uprisings onwards. She suffered exile in Siberia for her activity and then moved to Finland. She came to Britain in the 1920s and remained active as a journalist in the Communist Party right up to her death in 1964.

Valga prides itself on the many pioneers who came from the town who were of Estonian ethnic origin. Mats Erdell (1792–1847) was the first Estonian to own a manor house. Johannes Martson became mayor of Valga in 1901, six years before Tallinn had an Estonian in this position. Alfred Neuland (1895–1966) was the first Olympic gold medallist at the Antwerp Games in 1920. He returned to Valga and set up a flower shop. Hella Wuolijoki

(1886–1954) would never have tolerated such a quiet life. She left Valga for Helsinki in 1905 and witnessed the first salvos of the Russian Revolution there. She wrote radical plays, by then in Finnish, ran oil and timber companies and just avoided being executed as a spy by the Soviets in World War II.

The restoration of independence to Estonia and Latvia led to a firm border being re-imposed and the two towns breaking all links. Even hospital patients cannot now be brought across. Ironically it was the British in 1999 who made the first move to bring both sides together again when the British Council established a joint English-language school. This was followed in 2001 by the opening of a joint tourist office and an exhibition of paintings by Estonian children in the Valka Museum. Sadly the Latvians moved out the following year and now have a separate office again on their side of the border. Perhaps the divisions between the two countries are best shown by the lack of Estonian–Latvian dictionaries. The latest one produced in Latvia dates from 1967 and in Estonia from 1959. The Soviet military presence previously made Russian the predominant language in both parts but Russian-speakers now represent less than 50% of the population on both sides of the border.

Getting there
Valga has excellent bus links to Tallinn, Tartu, Viljandi and Võru, and also services to the surrounding villages. Buses stop in the station forecourt and tickets are bought in the station. There are five or six services a day to Tallinn, a journey which takes four hours and which stops en route in Viljandi, which is roughly halfway. Four buses a day go to Tartu, a journey of two hours with an en-route stop at Otepää. The bus journey to Võru, which also takes two hours, is the most scenic with several en-route stops in the Karula National Park.

Crossing the border
No local buses now cross the border, nor do any passenger trains, but Eurolines operate a daily bus service each morning from Tartu to Riga which stops in Valga and a return service each evening. Having crossed the border, it does not make any en-route stops in Latvia. Valka on the Latvian side does not have a railway station in the town but there is an excellent service four times a day to Riga from Lugazi, about 5km from Valka, and a local bus connects with each train. The fare to Riga is only £1.50/US$2.20 and the journey takes three hours. This train passes through Cesis and Sigulda, both likely stops for tourists visiting Latvia. In contrast with Estonia, local trains in Latvia are more comfortable and reliable than buses. However, there are three buses a day to Riga and eight to Smiltine. The Riga service stops en route at Valmiera, where other connections can be made.

Most contemporary travellers do not see the town at all, as they cross at the main international border on the Tartu–Riga road about 2km from the centre. A new joint border crossing, with one large building, opened in 2000 and replaced a ramshackle selection of wooden shacks that had done service for the previous ten years. Valga is, however, worth seeing and, now that international

OVER THE BORDER
Owen Rutter

When I visited Valk, the barbed-wire entanglement which had previously marked the boundary had been taken down, but I was told at an inn on the Latvian side that special police permission was necessary to cross the dividing street, that the penalty for going without a permit was a fine or one day's imprisonment, and that the sentries would stop me if I tried to pass.

As I believe in conforming to the regulations (however tedious) of a country in which I am a visitor, I set off to find the police station. I had walked some distance through the rather uninteresting town and was just beginning to think that the police station was a long way when, looking up to see what street I was in, I saw the strange word 'tan' instead of the familiar Latvian 'iela' – street. It seemed that I was in Estonia. To make sure, I went into a shop and bought some chocolate. The Latvian money I tendered in payment was refused. This was Estonia, the good lady said uncompromisingly and in Estonia one paid in Estonian kroon. No she could not change my lat. I could either pay for the chocolate in the proper currency or give it back.

Then came the question of how to get back to Latvia. After what I had been told, it seemed highly probable that I might shortly find myself lodged in an Estonian (or Latvian) gaol. The prospect of either was unpleasant. I retraced my footsteps until I saw ahead of me a sentry-box. There seemed no life about it so I sauntered by and glancing in as I passed, I saw that it was empty. Standing in the middle of the cobbled roadway, with one foot in Latvia and the other in Estonia, I took a photograph of that crooked street, and then hurried on, keeping to the Latvian pavement.

Extract from 'The New Baltic States'. The author visited Valga in 1924; 'Valk' is the German name for the town which fell on both sides of the border.

travellers can cross in the town itself, first or last impressions of Estonia and Latvia can be much more positive. The border appears in various guises. In the countryside, it may be almost unmarked; in the town, it is sometimes vicious with barbed wire, and sometimes more gentle with a low barrier and a couple of border guards happy for English-language practice. One of the roads now blocked at the border is ironically called *Sopruse*, which is the Estonian for 'friendship'.

Where to stay
Apart from being a possible transit stop for tourists en route to Latvia, Valga can be considered as an alternative to Tartu or Otepää when hotels there are full or too expensive. A large hotel, the Kuperjanov, is due to open in 2005.

Sade Jamma 1; tel: 276 41650; fax: 276 61017. For years, the one hotel in Valga. The name means 'spark', a translation of the Russian *Iskra* which was the title of the clandestine newspaper founded by Lenin in 1900. Surprisingly, nobody has bothered to change the name yet, which is perhaps a reflection of the easy-going pace of life in Valga. For the £10/US$15 or so that the hotel charges for a room, it is good value and some will find the number of rooms with baths rather than showers another pleasant Soviet legacy. Double 300EEK.

Jaanikese Motell Valgamaa 68225; tel/fax: 76 68745; email: info@jaanikese.ee; www.jaanikese.ee. Situated in splendid isolation beside a new motorsport centre. Its brochure claims to cater for guests 'looking for excitement' but, as motor rallies are few and far between, those who want peace and quiet are more likely to be satisfied. Double 600EEK.

Tolli Tolli 1; tel: 52 35515 (owner's mobile); fax 52 35853; email: seba@uno.ee. The first serious entertainment centre in the Valga/Valka region to realise the potential of the under 40s. Considering the stress on youth elsewhere in Estonia, it is surprising they have been ignored for so long here. The hotel rooms are, however, well soundproofed and in another building. The building is right beside the gully that marks the border between the two countries and it is hard to believe that many Latvian guests observe the warnings about not crossing except at designated points. Double 450EEK.

Where to eat

For many years, there has been one serious restaurant in the town, the **Conspiraator** (Vabaduse 29; tel: 76-61489), highly recommended for its wide menu and low charges. Normally in Estonia one expects prices to be 20 years 'out of date'; here they revert to the 1960s. It also does not play loud background music, a pleasant relief in comparison to most restaurants in Estonia, so plotters wanting to live up to the name of the restaurant must presumably speak more quietly here than they would normally. In 2003 a second serious restaurant opened beside St John's Church. The **Horan** (Kesk 16; tel: 76 41655) offers a great variety of Korean and Chinese food. In any town, its menu and its prices would be welcome; here it is even more so, given the lack of choice elsewhere and the surprise at finding it in such a small town. For lighter meals in a more casual environment the **Voorimehe Pubi** (Kuperjanovi 57; tel: 76 79627) can be recommended. It was once a coaching inn and the décor looks back to the times when guests arrived on horseback rather than by car.

What to see

Valga is fortunate that a castle was never built here so it avoided the battles that repeatedly destroyed so many other Estonian towns. A number of wooden houses survive from the 19th century and others date from the 1920s and 1930s when the industrial wealth of the town increased and produced a number of elegant private houses. The **railway station** is a peaceful architectural anachronism where visitors may well first arrive, although this is more likely to be by bus rather than by train as it also serves as the bus terminal. The station was built by German prisoners of war in 1949 (they were allowed back to Germany only in 1955) so has all the flamboyance, space and

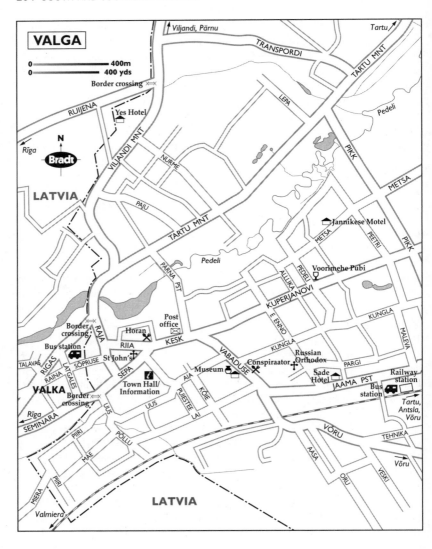

light of Soviet buildings from that era. There must be few other towns with a population of 15,000 that can boast a station with chandeliers and a balcony. The station only comes to life properly in the middle of the night, when the daily Moscow–Riga trains pass through, as otherwise it is used only for a declining number of domestic services. Yet its well-maintained toilets are open all day and can be welcome after the four-hour bus journey from Tallinn. Let us hope that similar standards soon spread elsewhere in Estonia. About 100m into town from the station is a restored 2-6-2 steam engine from the 1950s.

Crossing Jaama, taking Enno and then turning left into Pargi, the area is dominated by the Russian Orthodox **Issodor** Church. It dates from the 1890s when the two recently opened railways to Tartu and to Pskov brought many Russian speakers to the town and increased the congregation to around 5,000. Most of the building costs were met by the central Russian government and can be seen as part of its campaign to minimise religious and linguistic dissent in the Baltic region. Although many Russian-speakers left after Estonian independence in 1920, taking all the church records with them, the congregation stayed at this number because of the support for the church amongst the Estonian Orthodox community. The building suffered badly during the Soviet era when, although it stayed open, it was not maintained or guarded so fell victim to neglect and vandalism. There are currently insufficient funds for the serious restoration that is desperately needed.

Returning to Jaama, next on the left is Valga's major employer, the food-processing plant. Turning right into Vabaduse and passing the hospital on the left, then comes the **museum**. The building dates from 1911 and was converted first into a restaurant and then into a theatre during the first independence period. More recently it was a bank, as is clear from some of the strong doors that now guard the exhibits. The original museum collection dates from 1955 but much of the display was destroyed in a fire in 1988. Local enthusiasm and generosity meant that when it reopened here in 1999, the new collection was much more extensive than the earlier one had been and could include many items and topics that were banned in the Soviet period. The ground floor is devoted to the natural history of the region and is particularly strong on fossils and skeletons. The first floor concentrates on the urban environment and it has pioneered the use of wax models which other Estonian museums are now following. The two most prominent ones here are of Johannes Martson, mayor shortly before World War I, and Marta Parna, headmistress of the girls' secondary school at the same time. The significance of this is that both were the first ethnic Estonians to have these posts. Elsewhere, even then, senior positions were taken by Russians or Germans. Exhibits and models show the changes in day-to-day life since the mid-19th century. The most moving section recreates the Magadani Camp in Siberia where many local residents were deported in 1941 and again in 1949. In the future the exhibits will be extended to cover the establishment of the border in 1920.

Behind the museum is the **Zenckeri Villa** built in 1902 which, during the 20th century, was to house every form of authority and political grouping prominent in Estonia. Parties both for and against pre-war President Päts had, at different times, their headquarters here. The Estonian, Soviet and Nazi military have all used it, as have the Communist Party and the Young Pioneers. In 1989, it hosted the first public display of the Estonian flag since the start of the Soviet occupation. Continuing to be ahead of its time, as early as 1996 when the building was a public library, it offered the local population their first access to email. If Estonia is ever renamed @stonia, Valga can claim the credit.

Turning left into Kesk at the end of Vabaduse, the **Town Hall** is on the left-hand side after 200m. It is one of the most impressive wooden buildings in the town and its façade is regularly painted. It now houses the **Valga Tourist Office** which is open seven days a week in the summer. Many of the souvenirs they sell reflect a joint role, as they incorporate both national flags. It has a wider range of booklets in English than might be expected, devoted mainly to the work of local architects and artists. They also have a lot of material on northern Latvia.

St John's Church, opposite the Town Hall, stands out for its unusual oval shape and was designed by the Riga classicist architect Christoph Haberlandt in 1780. Because of financial constraints, the building was only completed in 1816. The organ, built by the German Friedrich Ladegast in 1867, is still in excellent condition, partly because the church remained open in the Soviet period. It can be heard at Sunday services and sometimes at concerts during the week. Worship in Estonian started here in 1880; it had previously been in German. The granite monument is a replacement for one erected in 1934 and destroyed by the Soviets in 1940. It commemorates 200 Finns who fought in the Estonian War of Independence in 1918.

About 6km north of Valga on the road to Tartu is the Paju Memorial. This commemorates the battle that took place here on January 31 1919 between the Finns and Estonians on one side and the Latvians and Bolsheviks on the other. Although he won the battle, the Estonian commander Julius Kuperjanov died of his wounds two days later. The longest street in Valga is named after him.

The main attraction of **Valka** is the former **seminary** about 3km from the border on the Riga road which carries the name of its founder, Janis Cimze (1814–81). Returning from Germany in 1839 with a thorough university education, he was to spend the rest of his life here, firstly teaching just in German, but then more and more in Latvian and Estonian. As his pupils would be largely training as primary school teachers attached to churches, he concentrated as much on music as on language. The collection portrays his life, shows the variety of texts and songs he used, and some of the tributes sent at the time of his death. Although his pupils were aged 17–25, he felt the need for a detention room, the 'Blue' room as it was called from the colour of its painting. 'Sentences' lasted from six to 24 hours. One room of the building is devoted to the military history of the 1917–20 period, when Latvians in this area were fighting Germans, Estonians, White Russians and Bolsheviks, mostly at the same time.

A smaller, disused barn houses a **farming museum** and depicts former local life around the theme of the four seasons showing how the weather dictated most activity. Outside of work, it shows the production of candles in February, the painting of eggs at Easter, and the preparation of wreaths at Christmas. The long dining table would have belonged to a family rich enough to employ servants. They would eat at the same table and at the same time, but clearly divided. Some of the items displayed, such as the spinning wheel and the baker's oven, are still in regular use. On leaving the building, note Lenin's head, abandoned beside the outside wall.

Visitors driving into Latvia from the large border post outside the town should stop before coming into Valga at the row of five cemeteries restored here in 2003. They show that whilst everybody, whatever their behaviour in life, is entitled to a decent burial, enemies should still be kept apart in death. One cemetery is therefore for the German military, one for the Soviet military, one for the 1918–19 Latvian freedom fighters, one for the local Jewish community and one for everyone else.

Western Estonia and the Islands

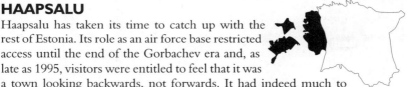

HAAPSALU

Haapsalu has taken its time to catch up with the rest of Estonia. Its role as an air force base restricted access until the end of the Gorbachev era and, as late as 1995, visitors were entitled to feel that it was a town looking backwards, not forwards. It had indeed much to look backwards at, with a turbulent history stretching back to its foundation in 1279. Given its strategic location, every invader over the centuries had to secure the town, no matter at what cost. Most were to rebuild it, but Peter the Great, when he came in 1715, decided simply to destroy it so that the Swedes, with whom he was still fighting, would have little incentive to return. It would never again be seen as a major fortress. By 1715, as a result of war and plague, its population had dropped to around 100 and even a century later it had only risen to 600. Its sudden rise to fame can be ascribed to one man, Dr Carl Abraham Hunnius, and to one product, mud. In 1825 Hunnius opened his first sanatorium and the popularity of the town was quickly established amongst the St Petersburg nobility. Once the royal family showed an interest, as it soon did, the town's continuing status was assured. Tsar Nicholas I himself came in 1852 for the first time, and Alexander II, who succeeded him in 1855, made repeated visits throughout his reign and Haapsalu became a major summer resort with a regular 'season'. Tchaikovsky paid his first visit in 1867 and a wide range of his music was written in Haapsalu, including his 'Songs without Words' and of course the 'Souvenir de Hapsal' written in 1867. He is commemorated by a marble bench on the seafront, the marble coming from Saaremaa Island. The sea is very shallow in the bay, which makes it warmer than elsewhere in Estonia, and the water temperature is often around 21°C in the summer, much higher than elsewhere in the Baltic Sea. The protection of the bay makes the sea less prone to storms, so the town soon became one of the most popular resorts along the Baltic coast.

During the first independence period from 1920 to 1940, the town was so successful that even a Soviet history printed in 1976 had to admit that 'some achievements may be called excellent', a remarkable accolade in view of the normal presentation in such books of 'bourgeois Estonia'. Although Haapsalu was cut off from St Petersburg during this period, visitors from Sweden and Finland, together with those around Estonia, ensured continued prosperity. Most of the buildings around the town date from these years and a stroll along its

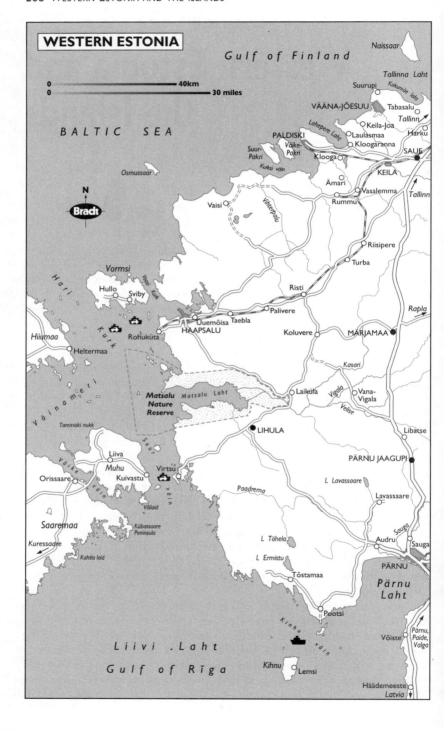

streets reflects the ambience of the town during the first independence period. The town remained a treatment centre during the Soviet period but, as foreigners were banned, it could only receive patients allocated by local trade unions. A small-scale, fish-processing plant was established and a former craft tradition in embroidery was continued. Fortunately the last few years have seen a turnaround and if its prestigious early role does not return in its entirety, Haapsalu will still have a serious role to play in tourism and industry. The major attractions for tourists are the castle, the railway museum and the beach walks, supplemented during the summer by an increasingly sophisticated cultural programme.

Getting there

Buses, both local and long-distance, leave from the railway station forecourt and tickets can be bought in advance from the office inside the station. Ironically, since the closure of the passenger line in 1995, the only tickets the station can sell are those for buses. For many years, the waiting hall was taken over by pigeons and the occasional alcoholic but in 2003 it was repaired and the general public was able to return.

There are hourly services to Tallinn. Express buses take an hour and a half, others about two hours. There are several services a day to Pärnu, Tartu and to Hiiumaa Island. In the summer, buses also operate to Virtsu for Saaremaa Island. Long-distance taxi prices from Haapsalu are good value when several people travel together. 700EEK (£30/US$50) is the normal price to Tallinn and 800EEK (£34/US$60) to Pärnu.

Where to stay

Fra Mare Health Centre/Hotel Ranna 3; tel: 47 24600; fax: 47 24601; email: framare@framare.ee. There is no need to feel guilty being well here. Whilst some people have a genuine complaint, most visitors like to spend some time having a conventional holiday and some time keeping fit and having a check-up. The hotel offers something unique to Haapsalu, with ample space in the building and in the surroundings. Stay up for sunset across the bay and do allow time for a leisurely walk to and from the town. Double 1,000EEK.

Haapsalu Posti 43; tel: 47 33347; fax: 47 33191; email: exotrade@hot.ee; www.haapsaluhotel.ee. This is the main business hotel of the town, located right in the centre on one of the main streets. With only 35 rooms, it is often fully booked both by business travellers and by tourists. Double 1,200EEK.

Kongo Kalda 19; tel: 47 24800; fax: 47 24809; email: kongohotel@hot.ee; www.kongohotel.ee. In taking the name of a former nightclub which was on this site, the Kongo is perhaps bringing some much-needed frivolity to Haapsalu. Colours throughout are light, there is a garden and the kitchenettes attached to five of the rooms will attract families and prove that life need not begin at 50 for holidaymakers in Haapsalu. Double 1,200EEK.

Laine Sadama 9; tel: 47 37191; fax: 47 37193; email: info@laine.ee; www.laine.ee. Rooms are very cheap here, so perhaps one should not complain that it has remained so Soviet, but it is sad to think of the unexploited potential of this lakeside location. There are over 100 rooms, and most visitors come for long-stay health treatment. The

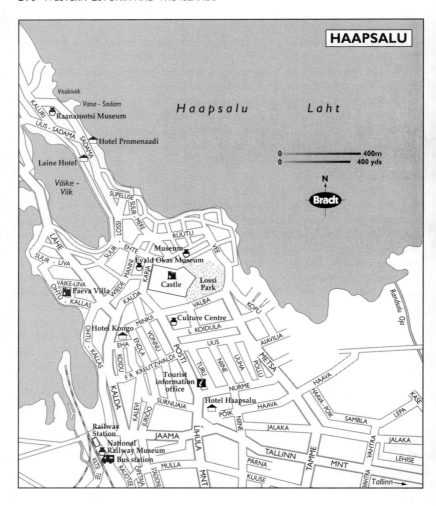

website offers 'Cure and Fun' and whilst the 'Cure' section offers a wide range of diseases that can be treated, under 'Fun' only a café, restaurant, bar and shop are offered. Double 850EEK.

Päeva Villa Lai 7; tel/fax: 47 33672; email: paevavilla@hot.ee; www.paevavilla.ee. This is in fact two newly built villas with 17 rooms between them, situated in a quiet residential area ten minutes' walk from the town centre. Double 800EK.

Promenaadi Sadama 22; tel/fax: 47 37250; email: hotell@promenaadi.ee; www.promenaadi.ee. When the Promenaadi opened in 1999, Haapsalu could perhaps claim to have returned to its former glory. With its exclusive location by the sea, cut off from the 'hoi polloi', and with its luxurious furnishings, what is left of European royalty could happily return here. Part of the hotel, a villa formerly owned by the Ungern-Sternberg family (see page 248), did in fact entertain royalty a hundred years ago. Double 1,000EEK.

What to see

The **castle** has always played the combined role of fortress and cathedral. When built at the end of the 13th century, it had a far more isolated location than it does now as it was right beside the sea and could be more easily defended. The land around it has risen quite considerably in the intervening seven centuries. It has probably had the most turbulent history of any castle in Estonia, with frequent fires adding to the many attempts to conquer it. A convenient legend of the 'Lady in White', whose ghost stalks the supposedly all-male redoubt each August, has given rise to an annual festival centred on the castle with son-et-lumière performances each evening. She was alleged to have had an affair with a priest, disguising herself successfully as a page-boy for two years before being discovered. When this finally happened, her punishment was to be impaled on the castle walls. During full moon in August, her ghost can be 'seen' through the central window of the cathedral. The ruins themselves involve tough climbs, so are not for the frail, but a walk around the outside walls, 800m in length, is not difficult. The church was restored in the 1880s and its acoustics make it an excellent venue for concerts. The church is now part of the **Castle Museum**. It is used as a concert hall and exhibition centre since none of the former furnishings remain. Heating was finally installed in 1991 as previously it could only be used in the summer. Half-hearted restoration had taken place since 1971. Earlier in the Soviet period it had been a granary and there were even plans to convert it into an indoor swimming pool. The interior is a completely bland whitewash over all the walls. The museum has an extensive collection of 15th- and 16th-century weapons and armour. It is spaciously displayed and well labelled in English. Photographers should climb the watchtower for the street and town views that can be enjoyed there.

The **Läänemaa Museum** has taken great trouble to bring to life all of Haapsalu's history. It is also one of very few in Estonia that has set up wheelchair access. There are models of boats used in the harbour as well as Arabic coins to show the extent of early trade links. A wax model of Hans Alver, Haapsalu's most famous pre-war mayor, seated at his desk forms the centre of a display showing the town at that time. Smuggling was very profitable then, with Finland being under prohibition, and displays show how even wooden legs were used to bring spirits into Finland. There are several paintings by Oskar Kallis (1892–1917) who, despite dying so young, had already during his short life become one of Estonia's most famous artists, probably because of his daring use of colour. Before leaving, allow plenty of time to buy postcards. Some are irreverent, some are historic, some are works of art and many combine these three characteristics. All are very cheap.

The statue of the German writer Friedrich Schiller (1759–1805), which stands in front of the museum, is one of several originally commissioned by Baltic Germans in the 19th century soon after his death. Most, including this one, were frequently vandalised during the different military campaigns that afflicted Estonia. This restoration dates from 1957 as Schiller was seen in the Soviet Union as a very progressive writer.

A stay in Haapsalu, particularly out of the main summer season, should always include a visit to the **Haapsalu Kultuurikeskus** (Culture Centre) on the corner of Valba and Posti. The austere exterior is not inviting, but few days or evenings pass without a performance or two taking place here, not to mention the range of paintings always exhibited. It also has a library with many English books and an internet centre.

The **National Railway Museum** is housed in the former station which dates from the building of the railway in 1905. St Petersburg had been linked to Tallinn and Paldiski from 1870 but it took determined lobbying from Haapsalu for the line to be finally extended. Once it was, the royal family made extensive use of it, and the station had to be built accordingly. The passenger service closed in 1995. The platform is covered for a distance of over 200m as there could be no risk of the royal family getting wet, and the museum is now housed in what was the imperial reception room. It displays uniforms, models of the different steam engines used during the 90-year history of the line, some refurbished engines, tickets and snow-clearing equipment. (Items used on Estonia's narrow-gauge railways are at a separate museum in Lavassaare, near Pärnu – see page 220.)

The **Evald Okas Museum**, Karja 24, opened in 2003, commemorating this painter who was born in 1915 and was still active in 2004 when he was approaching 90. It is still to some extent being built, so in 2004 did not have an admission charge. The artistic tradition continues with the next generation, as Okas's three children are respectively a painter, architect and glass designer. His current reputation is tarnished by his very close involvement with the Soviet regime and with his willingness to retreat with them to Jaroslavl during the war. Soviet books refer to his 'significant contribution to Leniniana', given the number of portraits he painted of Soviet leaders. However it is a sign of the times that his work can be displayed in public again.

The **Raanarootsi Museum**, Sadama 31, covers the centuries of links between Estonia and Sweden and the history of the Swedish communities that were settled on the mainland and on the islands until 1944, when they mostly fled ahead of the Russian invasion. Understandably, the labels are only in Estonian and Swedish, but the helpful staff will give a general background in good English.

The **Communications Museum** at Tamme 21a concentrates mainly on telephones and telephone exchanges, though it also covers radio sets, televisions and loudspeakers, plus what probably ought to be called adding-up machines rather than calculators. Considering that the museum dates from Soviet times, a remarkable number of the exhibits come from America and Germany. The sequence from manual through semi-automatic to fully automatic is shown with well-preserved equipment from each era, and space is also given to the many systems that failed. Specialists in this field may want to compare the 200 different forms of cable shown.

PÄRNU

Admitted to the Hanseatic League in 1346, the port for many centuries rivalled Tallinn and Riga, but since the 19th century the town has been better known as a health centre and seaside resort, as well as for its yachting harbour, so competed more with Haapsalu. As a health centre, it was less successful than Haapsalu, but it more than made up for this with its success as a resort. Estonia's most famous man, pre-war President Konstantin Päts, and Estonia's most famous woman, the 19th-century poet Lydia Koidula, both went to school in Pärnu. Lydia Koidula's school is now a museum about her life and a statue in her memory was unveiled in the park in 1929.

The town council granted permission for the building of the first bathing centre in 1837 but support was so poor that in 1857 public bathing on the beach was banned in the hope that this policy would force more people to use it. The council took complete control of the centre in 1889 and in 1904 installed electric lighting; the centre burnt down in 1915 and only in 1927 was a new building opened. Fortunately the council realised at the turn of the century that Pärnu needed to cater for the healthy as well as for the sick. The park was laid out, the yacht club established in 1906, and between the wars it attracted many foreign visitors. By 1938, over half of the 6,500 summer tourists were from abroad. The yacht club closed during the Soviet period but is now thriving again. In other fields, the town council has been active in broadening the economic base of Pärnu. Small and medium-size firms have been established in foodstuffs, textiles and timber, many with foreign backing; companies from 30 different countries now invest here. Yet tourism is likely to remain the backbone of the economy for the next few years, as the number of visitors each year climbs rapidly towards 100,000. Most still come in the summer when music lovers can enjoy a jazz festival, a zither festival and a full range of conventional concerts of classical music. Film shows, art exhibitions and opera, combined with much lower hotel prices, make visits at other times equally worthwhile. Dates of all these events are on the website of the local **tourist board**, www.parnu.ee; pre-booking of hotels during most of them is essential.

Getting there and around

The bus station is beside the Pärnu Hotel and within walking distance of the Bristol and Victoria hotels. There are several departures each day to Tallinn, about two hours away, and to Tartu, around three hours. There are less frequent services to Viljandi, Virtsu (for Saaremaa Island) and also to Riga. Buses to Valga stop at Kilingi-Nomme, from where local connections are available to the Nigula Nature Reserve. Buses to Tõstamaa stop en route at the port of Manilaid which serves Kihnu Island. This bleak port has no proper indoor waiting facilities and no catering so it is fortunate that only a wait of 15 minutes or so is necessary before the departure of the boat. Buses south to Ikla serve Häädemeeste and Kabla. Several of the Eurolines services to Latvia and Lithuania stop in Pärnu. Eurolines have an office in the bus station itself but all other tickets are sold in what was formerly the railway station in Ringli across the road from the bus terminus.

Flights operate from Pärnu to the islands of Kihnu, Ruhnu and Saaremaa but as these services are dependent on fluctuating government subsidies, and often only run once or twice a week, they are unlikely to be of use to foreign visitors. The websites of the local airline, Air Livonia (www.airlivonia.ee) and

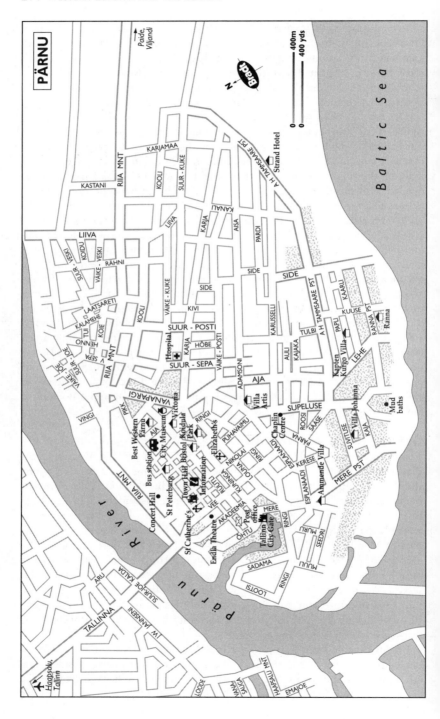

PÄRNU

Baltic Sea

Pärnu River

↑ Paide, Viljandi

0 400m
0 400 yds

Strand Hotel

KARJAMAA
KASTANI
RIIA MNT
KOOLI
SUUR-KUKE
LIIVA
SUUR-VESKI
KOIDU
VÄIKE-VESKI
VÄIKE-RÄHNI
LIIVA
KANALI
KARJA
AISA
PARDI
A H TAMMSAARE PST
SIDE
SIDE
SIDE
VÄIKE-KUKE
KOOLI
LAATSARETI
KALAMEHE
KÖIE
TUI
SIDE
KIVI
VÄIKE-KUKE
KARUSSELLI
A H TAMMSAARE PST
KAARLI
KUUSE PST
RANNA PST
Ranna
HENNO
SEPA
RIIA MNT
VÄIKE-JÕE
SUUR-JÕE
VINGI
SUUR-POSTI
HÖBE
KARJA
Hospital
SUUR-SEPA
VÄIKE-POSTI
ADAMSONI
AULI
KAJAKA
TULBI
PAPLI
Kapten
Kurgo Villa
LEHE
Villa Johanna
Mud
baths
AJA
Villa
Artis
SUPELUSE
ROOSI
SAASE
SUITSUSE
KAJA
MERE PST
Best Western
Pärnu
Bus station
City Museum
VANAPARGI
PKK
Victoria
Koidula
Park
Bristol
RINGI
Elizabeth's
PÜHAVAIMU
Chaplin
Centre
PÄRNA
ESPLANAADI
KERESE
Ammende Villa
Concert Hall
St Peterburg
Town Hall
Information
NIKOLAI
LOUNA
RINGI
KANINGA
RÜÜTLI
St Catherine's
Endla Theatre
VEE
AKADEEMIA
ÖHTU
Post
office
MERE
Tallinn
City Gate
RINGI
MURU
SEEDRI
SADAMA
MUU
LOOTSI
RINGI
RIIA MNT
SUUR-JÕE KALDA
ORU
TALLINNA
JW JANNSENI
HAAPSALU MNT
VANA-SAUGA
LOODE
EMAJÕE
↑ Haapsalu,
Tallinn

of Kuressaare airport (www.eeke.ee) on Saaremaa Island both give current schedules and fares. The 23 bus links the airport with the town, a journey of about 5km. No public catering is available at the airport, but there is a small hotel with prices much lower than those in town. Visitors needing travel arrangements in the Pärnu area and to the islands can book these through Reiser Travel at Adamsoni 1; tel: 44 71480; fax: 44 71482; email: viivika@reiser.ee; www.reiser.ee.

Where to stay

Ammende Villa Mere pst 7; tel: 44 73888; fax: 44 73887; email: sale@ammende.ee; www.ammende.ee. In commissioning this building as a wedding present for his daughter in 1905, local merchant Herman Ammende made sure he would never be forgotten in Pärnu. It is probably the largest private house in the town, and certainly the most eccentric. The bricks are in no less than four different colours – yellow, red, green and white – and the woods vary equally from very dark to totally pale. Polite critics claim it as an example of Jugendstil but visitors just arrived from Riga will hardly find any similarities with what they will have recently seen on Albert iela. The wrought-iron railings around the whole estate and the restrictions on parking in the street to hotel guests reinforce the exclusivity that becomes immediately apparent on entering the building. Only some broken cornices and the occasional chipped stone step will detract from this feeling. Nowhere is space lacking. The library, the sitting room and the restaurant could each absorb all the staff and guests without being crowded. All the bedrooms could host a party. The décor throughout has been deliberately assembled from the early 20th century. Pretend that World War I never took place and leave the modern world firmly beyond the railings. Certainly try to forget that in Soviet times the building was a dental clinic. Double 1,600EEK.

Best Western Pärnu Rüütli 44; tel: 44 78911; fax: 44 78905; email: hotparnu@www.ee; www.pergohotels.ee. When the first foreigners turned up at this hotel in the late 1980s, they were faced with a mammoth but empty entrance hall, spartan rooms and a drab restaurant. The contrast now could not be greater; as the first hotel in the town with email and a website, it clearly aimed to take over the mantle of the Victoria which used to be the obvious first choice for both business and leisure travellers wanting a central location. Its 80 rooms are all regularly modernised and both the bar and restaurant attract considerable local business. There is wheelchair access. Double 1,500EEK.

Bristol Rüütli 45; tel: 44 31450; fax: 44 43415; email: victoria@hot.ee; www.victoriahotel.ee. This central hotel is under the same management as the more famous Victoria, but is very different. The exterior has kept its original red-brick Gothic façade from 1900. The 17 modern rooms, of which about half are singles, have been simply but adequately furnished. There is no restaurant, but the bar serves breakfast and light snacks all day. There are several nearby restaurants. Double 1,200EEK.

Kapten Kurgo Villa Papli 13; tel: 44 25736; fax: 44 25662; email: kapten@kurgovilla.ee; www.kurgovilla.ee. This is an original villa in that it has been totally adapted for family use, consisting of just six suites, each with two bedrooms, a kitchen and a bathroom. It also has a restaurant which is open to non-residents. Double 1,100EEK.

Koidula Park Kuninga 38; tel: 44 77030; fax: 44 77033; email: info@koidulaparkhotell.ee; www.koidulaparkhotell.ee. When the hotel opened in 2003, it certainly offered a contrast to its competitors in the town centre. It was built entirely of wood, in 1904, and if only one room still has the original floorboards, at least the overall design has not changed. It has 39 rooms, all small and with the showers not divided from the rest of the bathroom, but the quiet central location is more than adequate compensation. The hotel closes from October to March. Double 1,100EEK.

Ranna Ranna Pst 5; tel: 44 38950; fax: 44 38318; email: rannahotell@scandichotels.com; www.scandic-hotels.com. This hotel is an architectural monument to Estonian functionalism as well as being the most luxurious hotel in the town. It was built in 1937 by one of Estonia's most famous pre-war architects, Olev Siinmaa, who won a competition organised by the town council to commemorate the 100th anniversary of the town's establishment as a health resort. It is situated on the beach, but whilst this suggests a summer holiday, a stay here in winter is in some ways more dramatic and more enjoyable with fewer guests, a frozen sea and the park completely covered in snow. It is operated by the Scandic Hotel group which was taken over by Hilton Hotels in the summer of 2001. Double 1,700EEK.

St Peterburg Hospidali 6 (but note entrance is in Malmo not Hospidali); tel: 44 30555; fax: 44 30556; email: sanktpeterburg@hot.ee; www.seegimaja.ee. This hotel opened in 2003 in Pärnu's oldest building, an almshouse dating from 1653 but with some wood from the 13th century in the foundations. It is probably the first hotel in Estonia to dare to put up a portrait of Peter the Great in reception. Perhaps the aim is to attract nostalgic Russians as with 53 rooms it is big enough to cater easily for groups. Russians, like the British and Japanese, would enjoy the space in the public areas but would feel short-changed by the lack of pictures in the bedrooms and the absence of baths. Double 1,400EEK.

Strand Tammsaare 27; tel: 44 39333; fax: 44 39211; email: sales@strand.ee; www.strand.ee. This hotel seems to expand in line with the Estonian economy. Fifty rooms in the late 1990s had become nearly 200 by 2004 and there is no reason for stopping there. Each extension brings new facilities, a swimming pool and billiard room being among the more recent ones. Many regulars still however insist on the traditional rooms with a lounge downstairs and a spiral staircase up to the bedroom. It used to matter that there was a 500m walk to the beach. Now the hotel feels very self-contained, given all the spa facilities that it offers. Double 1,500EEK.

Victoria Kuninga 25; tel: 44 43412; fax: 44 43415; email: victoria@hot.ee; www.victoriahotel.ee. For several years after independence this was the only good hotel in central Pärnu and, as it only has 23 rooms, may well appeal to individuals. Building started in 1920 but shortage of funds prevented completion until 1927. In Soviet times it was given the name 'Voit' (Victory). It lost the Best Western franchise in 1998 and it is not hard to see why. Other hotels had by then surpassed it in facilities offered and the level of service provided. Some discreet refurbishment and a more inviting reception area would not go amiss. It could then rightly take on again its pre-war name, 'The Grand'. Double 1,200EEK.

Villa Artis Adamsoni 1; tel: 44 71480; fax: 44 71482; email: reiser@reiser.ee; www.reiser.ee. This guesthouse opened in 2003 and offers the prices of suburbia but the convenience and comfort of a true townhouse. It is situated just far enough from both the beach and the town centre for quiet to be assured and wisely only serves breakfast so it is also spared bar noise. Its novelty is a resident osteopath. Double 900EEK.

Villa Johanna Suvituse 6; tel: 44 38370; fax: 44 38371; email: villa-johanna@villa-johanna.ee; www.villa-johanna.ee. There are many villas converted to small hotels in Pärnu, but this one is probably unique in imposing a total no-smoking policy. It combines the space and views of a villa with the convenience of a central location. Two of the five rooms have balconies. Double 1,000EEK.

What to see
A walking tour
All the traditional sights of interest to tourists are conveniently located within the town centre, which is still partially surrounded by medieval ramparts. However, a walk should include the Chaplin Art Centre and the mud baths. One main shopping street, Rüütli, runs through the town and a walking tour can conveniently start at the **Bristol Hotel**. A wide range of architectural styles will be noted both in this street and in those that run off it. The Bristol Hotel is one of the few brick buildings in Pärnu and dates from the turn of the century. Straight opposite the hotel, on the corner of Hommiku and Rüütli, is a chemist's shop; the exterior is hardly of note, but the interior has been restored to its original 1931 décor. Work on the exterior started in summer 2004. Next door, on the corner of Rüütli and Ringi, is a building that has seen many uses since its construction in 1867. It began as the exclusive 'White Girls School' and more recently was the Soviet military headquarters. It has now rebelled into a casino/nightclub. Many visitors make the mistake of initially turning left into Rüütli and never seeing much of what there is in the other direction. Turn right instead towards the Best Western Hotel through a landscaped garden. This is now **Rüütli Square** but the 40 years of its previous life as Lenin Square needed to be obliterated. The building on the far side of the square, now shared between several banks, was the last in Pärnu to be completed in 1940 before the Soviet invasion. From the end of the war until 1967, the first floor served as a temporary theatre. To the right of the Best Western Hotel, on the corner of Rüütli and Aia, note the model of the former **Endla Theatre** which stood on this site before the war. Built in 1911, it had been the best example of Jugendstil in Pärnu, and could have been restored after bombing but was totally destroyed by the Russians because of its association with the founding of Estonia. Konstantin Päts, later to become president, proclaimed Estonian independence from the balcony of this building on the evening of February 23 1918, the day before a similar proclamation in Tallinn.

Crossing Rüütli on the opposite corner with Aia is the **Pärnu Museum** which is probably the dreariest in the whole of Estonia. Ironically, it is also one of the most expensive charging 30EEK (£1.30/US$2.00) whereas most museums charge only 10EEK. The map at the entrance is still of 'Pärnu Rajoon', *rayon* being the Russian word for county. This term was imposed on Estonia during the Soviet era. Most exhibits look untouched and appropriately unloved. Poor lighting prevents close inspection of what could have been a good history of Pärnu; there is, after all, quite enough to say and plenty to show. Even the recently added two cases covering the 1920–40 period fail to do Pärnu proud. This neglect was particularly surprising in 2001 when Pärnu celebrated its 750th birthday. Initially the website on www.pernau.ee shows promise but then under most entries is the brief turn-off 'Coming soon'. In 2004 there was talk of moving the museum to Aia 3, the warehouse opposite the new concert hall where hopefully it can catch up with the rest of the city.

Continue, perhaps quickly after this depressing experience, along Aia and turn right into **Kuninga**, so named after King Gustav II of Sweden. This street used to link the Riga Gate, now totally destroyed, with the Tallinn Gate (see page 219) at the other end of the Old Town. Many of the neighbouring large buildings date from the late 19th century and have been schools and colleges for most of the time since then.

Equally impressive are the many parks visible from Kuninga; these distinguish Pärnu from other Estonian towns and are the hallmark of Oskar Brachmann (1841–1927), who was mayor from 1871 to 1890. That bordered by Kuninga, Ringi and Louna is named after **Lydia Koidula** (1843–86), Estonia's best-known woman writer. The statue of her done in 1929 was the last work of sculptor Amandus Adamson who died that year. The park has been restored to exactly as it was then, with the import of granite from Finland and bronze from Italy. On the far side of the park is the boys' school attended both by Konstantin Päts and by Paul Keres (1916–75), Estonia's most famous chess player.

Return to Rüütli along Hommiku and cross it keeping the pharmacy on your right. On the left is the 15th-century **Red Tower**, all that now remains of the medieval fortifications. Continue along Rüütli into the Old Town taking the second road on the left, Nikolai, and the baroque façade of **Elizabeth's Church** comes into view. It was built between 1744 and 1747 and is named after the Russian empress. It has two links with Riga: the spire was designed by the architect J H Wulbern, who designed the spire of St Peter's, and the organ, installed in 1929, is the work of Riga's most famous organ-builder of that time, Herbert Kolbe. Returning to Rüütli, and then crossing it, you come to the **Town Hall** which also has a link with Riga. The original classicist design dates from 1797 when it was built as a private house. It then became first the governor's residence and in 1838 the Town Hall. When it returned into private hands again early this century, the Jugendstil north wing was added, having been designed by Wilhelm Bockslaff, Riga's most famous architect in this field. **St Catherine's Church,** opposite the Town Hall, was also named after the empress on the throne at the time. It was built between 1764 and 1768 and provided a model for most subsequent Orthodox churches in Estonia. Opening hours for the church are erratic but, if closed, it is worth returning on another occasion to see the bronze, silver and gold filigree pictures and the portrait of Catherine the Great. On the other side of the road from the church is the 'new' **Endla Theatre** built in 1967 to replace the one destroyed at the end of the war. To the left of the theatre, in the park opposite the post office, is a memorial to the playwright and essayist

August Jakobson (1904–70) who fled to Russia in 1941 with the Red Army and was closely linked to the Soviet regime until his death. He even joined a Soviet censorship committee in August 1940 to control the work of his former colleagues. His work in the 1930s had been respected as he was always keen to expose poor working conditions in factories. Had he been less close to the Soviet regime, he would have had a reputation similar to that of Emile Zola in France. His work was described in the 1960s as 'ideologically militant' so it is not surprising that he is now hardly read in Estonia.

To the right of the theatre, overlooking the river on Aida, is Pärnu's pride and joy, the concert hall which opened in the autumn of 2002. Although famous for the music that is offered year-round, Pärnu has never before had a suitable venue for orchestral music and opera. For the €5.75 million it cost it is a real bargain, and as it's a circular glass building, Estonians can see both by day and by night what activities their taxes are generating. Had the world-famous conductor Neemi Järvi not lobbied and given constant support to the project, it might never have gone ahead. (He now wants Tallinn to have an opera house to rival the one in Sydney no later than 2008.) The main auditorium seats 1,000 and can be easily adapted for choral or theatre performances; it can equally be turned into a private ballroom. The higher floors are a music school. There is also another room for art exhibitions or chamber-music performances. Neemi Järvi's extended family is as musical as the Bachs and many of them participate in the annual David Oistrakh Festival in Pärnu each July. Future programmes at the concert hall can be seen on www.parnu.ee.

The red-brick warehouse at Aida 3, opposite the concert hall, is a centre for temporary exhibitions. Hopefully the museum can move here and, in the process, completely reinvent itself. Retrace your steps along Vee to Rüütli.

Rüütli ends with the house by the functionalist architect, Olev Siinmaa, built for himself in 1933. Many similar houses of his can be seen around the town, although without doubt he kept the best example of his work for his own use. Turning left at the end of Rüütli leads to the **Tallinn Gate**, now a unique example in the Baltics of a 17th-century, town-wall gate. Those in other cities, such as Narva, have been subsequently destroyed. It was originally called Carl Gustav Gate, after the Swedish king, but this was changed after the defeat of the Swedes by the Russians.

Continuing along Mere and then turning left into Esplanaadi, on the corner with Kerese is the **Chaplin Centre**. The official name for the building is the Pärnu Contemporary Art Museum (**Pärnu Uue Kunsti Muuseum**) but this is hardly ever used now. Chaplin would probably have approved of the fact that an institution named after him has taken over the former Communist Party headquarters. He would also have liked the statue now usually placed at the entrance to the building – a Lenin torso with his head replaced by a flashing red light. It is necessary to say 'usually' as where and how the 'remains' of Lenin should be displayed is a major source of dispute between the museum director Mark Soosaar and the town council. Sometimes Lenin is parked in a lorry in front of the building, sometimes he is in the garden at the back. Sometimes another head is added – normally that of Georg Wilhelm

Richmann, an 18th-century, Pärnu-born physicist, who has the macabre distinction of being the first person to be killed by electricity. Mark Soosaar is threatening to add variety by displaying some contemporary heads from time to time but no potential victims have yet been named.

Chaplin's name was used to suggest diversity and hope, although the centre concentrates as much on art as on films. It maintains a permanent collection of modern Estonian art, based entirely on donations, and often has temporary exhibitions as well. Much of the display will appeal only to those totally unaffected by obscenity and blasphemy. For instance, in a portrayal of the Last Supper, the disciples have been replaced by nearly naked women, all of course smoking and drinking to excess. A less provocative picture consists of a toilet roll stuck to a block of wood. More sensitive visitors should limit themselves to the website (www.chaplin.ee) which shows some of the 1,000 pictures donated since the opening in 1992, many from abroad.

Mark Soosaar is a brilliant publicist for the centre, both in the local Estonian press and abroad. It is open seven days a week, 12 hours a day, has no admission charge and 15,000 visitors a year so is the complete opposite to a normal Estonian museum, which is either deserted or closed. The centre will diversify over the next few years; catering has already moved out of doors during the summer and a spice shop has opened next to the internet centre, perhaps to show the contrast with the blandness of what was produced in communist days. Use of the internet facilities is particularly good value at 15EEK (£0.65/US$1.00) for half an hour.

A five-minute walk along Mere pst ends appropriately at the **mud baths** backed by the sandy beach. These mud baths are also by Olev Siinmaa. Following suitable invigoration, a ten-minute walk back into town completes the tour. Enthusiasts for functional architecture on a grand scale will want to continue along the beach to see the **Ranna Hotel**, described above.

Lavassaare

Fifteen kilometres to the northwest of Pärnu is the **Lavassaare Railway Museum**. Out of 630km of narrow-gauge railways that ran across Estonia until the late 1960s, the only 2km left in action are here and the line is of course operated by volunteers as it has no commercial potential. The network had been built up between 1900 and 1940 and was initially maintained under the Soviet regime but, in the early 1970s, tracks were either widened to the standard gauge or closed. The museum brochure refers to this as 'liquidation as the structure of the narrow-gauge railways were a threat to Soviet ideology'. Fortunately the threat cannot have been that great, otherwise the wider range of memorabilia now to be seen in the museum building would not have been kept. It in fact opened in 1987, when the Soviet era still had four years to run. Bus no 44 runs from Pärnu to Lavassaare. The museum is open only in the summer, and on Saturdays the train runs about every hour. Whilst the trains will still operate, there are plans to move the museum to Türi in central Estonia during 2005. For current opening times and an update on future plans check the website www.ee/eesti-mr.

HÄÄDEMEESTE

Visitors who race from Riga to Tallinn, with perhaps just a brief stop in Pärnu, miss a peaceful and elegant section of the Estonian coastline. Häädemeeste and the villages to the south are now able and happy to reveal their international role in the 19th century and their popularity in Estonia as a holiday resort during the first independence period. The construction of the highway a few kilometres inland has spared the coastline the through traffic it used to take, so even in midsummer travel here is congenial. Inevitably in the immediate aftermath of independence, Estonians who could afford to do so travelled abroad but Häädemeeste is now benefiting from an increased interest in taking holidays at home.

Getting there and around

Buses run every 60–90 minutes along the coast from Pärnu to Ikla stopping at all the towns and villages en route. A few continue from Ikla to the main border crossing on the Pärnu–Riga highway where it is possible to connect with local buses on the Latvian side. Otherwise all connections are made at Pärnu.

Where to stay

Lepanina Kabli 86002; tel: 44 65024; fax: 44 37367; email: vabarne@hot.ee. Like several other hotels in Estonia, the Lepanina transformed itself in the late 1990s from barely two-star to clearly four-star. That it needs only a postcode for the address shows its current stature. It is in fact set back from the main road and stretches along the coast so that all 70 rooms have a balcony and a sea-view. The use of brick for all the outside walls is unusual enough; stranger still is its use indoors. Some of the suites have a private staircase to the beach. Furniture, carpets and linen throughout the hotel are of Estonian production. It is encouraging that Estonian hoteliers no longer feel the need to import such goods. The dining room is built as a ship, giving the impression of being surrounded by water and, for visitors only passing through, offers an excellent first or last meal to those combining a tour of Estonia and Latvia. A bonus of an evening visit in low season with the shorter days is to eat seemingly under a starlit sky. A pier was built in 2002 to facilitate boating trips and also to give swimmers direct access to sand, as the beach right beside the hotel is pebbly. Local buses between Häädemeeste and Ikla do not pull into the hotel, but stop along the road nearby. Double 1,000EEK.

Valge Pärnu mnt 18; Häädemeeste 86001; tel/fax: 44 37368. This hotel is centrally situated in the town centre close to the bus station, Lutheran church and the museum. It is under the management of the Lepanina although it is of a much more modest standard. Double 500EEK.

What to see and do

Baltic Germans first mention the village in 1560, but its strategic importance was only realised when the Russians replaced the Swedes as the occupation power around 1700. The gentle beaches that stretch from here well into Latvia made all too easy an invasion from the sea. Although none was ever to be attempted, contemporary visitors can still see the architectural remains of the defences established by the Tsarist and Soviet regimes. Economically, Häädemeeste and two villages further south, Kabli and Treimani, would live from the sea. Their large mansions flaunt the profits that many boatbuilders and captains could draw from this activity. Those who broke the British and French blockades of this Russian coast during the Crimean War became particularly rich. (Salt was the mainstay of this business.) The **Lutheran church** in the town centre at Häädemeeste shows that not all the money made from shipping was consumed personally. It was built with private funds in the 1870s to attempt to draw back the local population from the **Orthodox church**, about a kilometre to the south, which was built like many others in Estonia at the time, to try to keep them loyal to the Tsarist regime. (The Orthodox churches also used the promise of land and education to bring in support.) The architect of the Lutheran church was Johann von Holtz, famous for the number of houses he designed in Riga and for the former Grand Hotel on the Alexanderplatz in Berlin.

The **museum** used to be in the unlikely location of a basement underneath a day centre for the elderly. In 2004 a proper building at Kooli 9 was opened. The collection is one of the most diverse in Estonia and shows the range of activity in an area all too easily written off as a backwater. There are bottles over 100 years old, hunting skis from the early 1950s and, to show the relative affluence of the 1920–40 independence period, cigarette holders, bottle corks, accordions and zithers. The museum was only founded in 1991, so many of the exhibits, in particular the photographs, had been hidden in private houses for the previous 50 years.

The first village south of Häädemeeste is **Jaagupi**, where the sumptuous villas once housed Soviet cosmonauts during their summer holidays. **Kabli** is now best known as a birdwatching centre, which was founded in 1969 and, together with a similar one at Vilsandi National Park on Saaremaa Island, tracks the migrating flocks each May and October. The ringing centre is beside the beach and visitors can climb the watchtowers. Every autumn about 12,000 birds are ringed at this centre. The **Jakob Markson Museum**, 3km south of Kabli, is in the house of this clearly very successful captain who spent most of his long life (1840–1930) here when not at sea. This spanned the most affluent era along the coast, which came to an end firstly with the worldwide economic slump and then with the Soviet occupation after World War II. The museum, opened for the first time in 1968, houses a collection shrewdly and assiduously collected from all over Europe. The dolls, the radios, the Bristol blue glass, his home organ and his Stanfords 1890 Map of the World are likely to be of most interest. Note the two china dolls in the window facing the street; whenever Markson returned home, they would be returned to the mantelpiece. The sitting room has been 'updated' into a Soviet style so shows the furniture most Estonian families would have had in the 1960s. The outhouses are becoming an increasingly important part of the museum and exhibit agricultural machinery from the 19th century. The house has never left the ownership of the family; Jakob Markson's great-granddaughter lives there and is the curator.

Ikla is the village on the Latvian border. Local residents can walk or cycle across but large concrete boulders block motor traffic. It is a pity that others cannot at present cross here, since the Ainazi Naval Museum, formerly the Naval Academy where many Estonians started their seafaring careers, is close to the border and would make a logical conclusion to a visit along this coastline. The grocery store comes straight from the 1950s with every item being individually weighed and wrapped. Many of the customers are Latvian, given the lower prices in Estonia for most basic items.

KIHNU

A visitor to the island of Kihnu immediately becomes a member of the community. A tour will visit the church, the museum and the lighthouse but it could also include delivering the potatoes for the school lunch, stopping at the daily clothes market and having conversations with passers-by. As the population is around 600, the guide will know everyone. He or she will know the exact population too and could probably predict fluctuations at least six months ahead. In early summer 2001, the population was exactly 600. It had been 604 in January but my guide knew the five people who had died and the new-born baby. A drop is unusual since Kihnu families remain large, unlike in the rest of Estonia.

Fishing is again the life-blood of the island. Visitors in the summer will see the nets stretched out across the fields, waiting to be mended. In the spring they are used to catch Baltic herring, and in the autumn perch, pike and eel. The tougher fishermen then turn to rods in midsummer and again in midwinter, having dug a hole in the ice. The nets cannot be used in the summer because of the frequent attacks by seals.

The traditional division of roles between men and women continues on the island. The local brochure writes of the support given by local women to their husbands, and of their knitting, cooking and baking. The women stay at home, bringing up their large families and the men undertake the arduous tasks needed to earn a living either on the barren land or out at sea. Previous generations of men were engaged in ship-building and served in local and foreign merchant navies. The men are proud to have broken the Crimean War blockade in the 1850s to get salt and iron from Gotland. Boatbuilding began here in the following decade when the war was over, with the traffic mainly being in transporting stone to Riga. Nobody made a fortune on the island so there are no grand houses. By 1914 the population had reached 1,200 and there were 68 boats. Boatbuilding obviously came to an end in the Soviet period and has not been revived. The islands take their current social cohesion very seriously and divorce remains rare. As wedding parties last three days, perhaps this is the explanation.

Unlike several other islands such as Ruhnu or Vormsi, the population has always been largely Estonian. The appeal of individual land holdings, offered by the Russian Orthodox Church in the mid-19th century, converted many from their previous Lutheran inclinations. Just before World War II, the population had grown to 1,200 but this could not be sustained and many were unemployed or reluctantly had to leave the island to find work. About 25% fled in 1944.

The island is now serious in promoting tourism. Estonians will come for a long stay at the campsites or in the farmhouses. Finns and Swedes may soon follow suit. Some will want to see the birds, in particular the goldeneyes and the cormorants. All will like the complete lack of commercialism. Other foreigners usually come for the day from Pärnu, taking the morning boat out and the evening boat back, having arranged to hire a car and a guide for the day beforehand. As the island is 7km long and 3km wide, it is just about possible to walk everywhere.

Getting there

During the summer, boats operate at least twice a day from the port at Munalaid, about 40km from Pärnu. Buses from Pärnu to Tõstamaa connect with each sailing. (Munalaid should not be confused with Manilaid, a small island just off the coast to which ferries also operate from here.) In the winter, and sometimes in the summer too, occasional flights operate from Pärnu to Kihnu and when the ice is thick enough it is possible to drive to Kihnu from the mainland. The website of the Pärnu Tourist Board, www.parnu.ee, gives current schedules. Visitors who have not made travel arrangements to Kihnu prior to their arrival in Pärnu, can arrange this through Reiser Travel (Adamsoni 1; tel: 44 71480; email: reiser@reiser.ee). Groups can also charter boats and planes for private journeys from Pärnu.

What to see

The centre of the island brings together the market, the largest shop (there are four others), a café, the church, the museum and the school. The community centre, completed in 2002, is large enough to accommodate the whole population under one roof. The island suffered no damage during the war and no Soviet building was added afterwards so many views are identical to those seen in the 1930s. The Soviets were so unconcerned with Kihnu that they left the airport with a grassy runway and did not tarmac the gravel roads. The **church** was built in 1715 but was extended in 1858 when it became Russian Orthodox. The cemetery has many iron crosses from a hundred years ago and then some recent additions: families who fled in 1944 are bringing back the remains of their dead for reburial in their true home. Perhaps the most famous grave is that of Enn Uuetoa (1848–1913), better known by his nickname Kihnu Jõnn, a reckless seafarer who took to sea after only three days of training. He died on his boat *Rock City*, which is not surprising. What is surprising is that he lived as long as he did.

The **museum**, on the other side of the road, took over the former schoolhouse in 1974. It displays the range of tools and nets used in the fishing industry. Note the family marks on the tools to identify them. It also has some signs from the collective farm that covered the entire island. The pictures are mainly by local sailors, and many were composers too. There are several pictures donated by the family of **Jaan Oad** (1899–1984), who was born in Kihnu but who made his name in Canada. He worked in Kihnu as a carpenter and sailor and continued his woodworking when he fled to Canada in 1944. Painting was always his hobby and under other circumstances he could have become professional. His main theme, shown in the paintings here, is the small boats that were built on the island during his childhood. The current school, situated behind the old building, was completely rebuilt in 1998. Any parent will envy the small class sizes, the impeccable cleanliness and the variety of facilities offered. Eight teachers are provided for about 70 pupils and the prospectus gives the assurance that, in addition to studying the national curriculum, girls will be taught local handicraft skills.

Britain has made its mark at the southern tip of the island, since all the parts of the lighthouse built there in 1864 came from the Tividale Company in Tipton, Staffordshire. It is 29m high and, as the highest natural point on the island is only 8m, it gives the impression of being much taller than it really is.

SAAREMAA

Estonians are often characterised as 'reserved', yet the mention of Saaremaa, the country's largest island, always evokes a passionate response, both from those who now live abroad and from those who have remained in Estonia.

Most families have both tragic and happy memories linked to Saaremaa. In 1944, thousands fled to exile in Sweden rather than face a renewed Soviet occupation of the island. Until 1989, Saaremaa was classified as a frontier zone so travel was severely restricted, even for local people, while visitors from outside the Soviet Union were banned completely. Yet memories of its status in the 1930s as a major health resort, when its fame was such that it warranted guidebooks in English and German, meant that this popularity was instantly restored when travel restrictions were lifted. The 1930s and the 21st century now blend together remarkably well. The island's sole major transport link, an hourly ferry to the mainland, ensures that only discerning and determined tourists make the effort to come. The architecture remains Gothic, classical and baroque. Both horses and windmills maintain their role in local agriculture, and traffic lights and cats-eyes are still unnecessary. The décor in several restaurants is specifically pre-war, while mud baths and concerts are major attractions for long-stay tourists. Between 2002 and 2004 three enormous spa hotels were built in the capital Kuressaare, but elsewhere 'large' hotels have 15 rooms, yet have satellite television, and the reception desk will accept credit cards. Although Kuressaare has a population of only 16,000, there are now two 24-hour shops, three cashpoints, parking meters and an Irish pub.

Getting there

The car and passenger ferry from the mainland port of Virtsu operates hourly to Kuivastu in the summer (June–September) from 06.00 to 21.00 and every two hours during the rest of the year. Icebreakers are used in winter to ensure the maintenance of the service but it is often possible in January and February to drive across the ice to both Saaremaa and Hiiumaa. Exact schedules for the ferry can be checked on the Saaremaa Shipping Company Ltd website, www.laevakompanii.ee. The journey takes about half an hour. It is essential to pre-book car spaces at peak times such as Friday afternoons to the island and Sunday evenings back to the mainland. This can be done by travel agents abroad (see page 58) in conjunction with hotel and car-hire bookings.

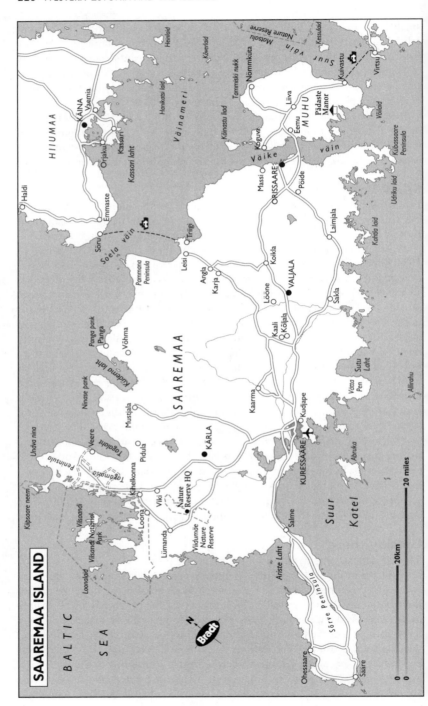

However, it is much more economical to take the bus from Tallinn to Kuressaare and to pre-book car hire on Saaremaa as prices there are much lower than on the mainland. The bus travels on the ferry and its place is guaranteed; the fare from Tallinn to Kuressaare is about £6/US$11 each way and the service operates every two hours, the total journey time being four hours. There are twice-daily services to Pärnu, Haapsalu and Tartu.

A car and passenger ferry service operates three times a day during the summer only from Triigi to Sõru on Hiiumaa Island and local buses connect with these services on both islands. In 2004 discussions began about operating a ferry service from Mõntu in the south of the island to Roja in Latvia. It is hoped that this will start in 2005.

Flights operate twice daily between Kuressaare and Tallinn and, as they are heavily subsidised by the Estonian government, are an attractive way to travel. In 2004 they cost about £15/US$27 one-way and £23/US$40 return. Similar fares apply to Pärnu but these services tend only to operate about twice a week.

History

Estonia's troubled history has always hit Saaremaa particularly hard. Twice the Danes unsuccessfully attacked the island in the early 13th century. However, in January 1227 the Teutonic Knights brought an army of 20,000 across the frozen sea and established German rule, which would last, despite frequent rebellions, until 1559. The next 90 years would see five different conquerors, first the Danes, then the Swedes to be followed by another Danish invasion, then the Russians and finally the Swedes again in 1645, following their victory in the Thirty Years War. The Swedes lost all their Baltic possessions to the Russians in 1710. The British navy under Sir Charles Napier blockaded the island in 1854 to prevent supplies reaching Russia during the Crimean War, and occupied it for one day. As the Russians had already fled to Pärnu and the castle at Kuressaare no longer had any military significance, there was no need to stay. The year 1875 saw the first regular passenger and cargo boats to Riga. The Tsarist Empire came to an end in 1917, but Saaremaa was immediately re-occupied by German troops who only finally left in November 1918.

The devastation of World War II, the deportations to Germany and Russia and the 'boat exodus' to Sweden led to a reduction in the population of more than 30% from 60,000 in 1939 to 40,000 in 1945; it has stayed around this level ever since. The sudden departure of the Soviet military at independence reduced the percentage of Russian speakers from 30% to 3%. A rising birth rate and welcome immigration from the mainland has kept the overall population figure stable. Cemeteries and memorials to all those killed on Saaremaa during the two world wars have now been restored or rebuilt. Estonians, Germans and Russians lie beside each other in equally dignified surroundings, together with members of the Forest Brothers, the guerrilla movement that fought the Soviet occupation in the late 1940s. There were about 40 brothers on the island and their struggle lasted until 1950, when their leader Elmar Ilp was killed.

The late 19th century saw a major growth in the links between Saaremaa, the Russian mainland and other Baltic states. For the first time in its history, the island prospered as its agricultural products reached ever wider markets. Small-scale industries linked with fishing developed, but the lack of minerals prevented the establishment of large factories. As a health resort, Kuressaare developed as rapidly as Pärnu and Haapsalu. Such prosperity returned quickly after World War I, as the health facilities were needed by invalid soldiers. Meticulous statistics were kept at the sanatorium: we know, for instance, that 1,178 visitors stayed in 1924 and that between them they enjoyed 23,371 mud baths.

The local airport reached its heyday in the late 1940s when 10–14 flights a day linked Saaremaa with the mainland. About 2,500 passengers a week used it then, although it would only be in 1958 that electricity would come to the airport, replacing candles, gas lights and radio batteries.

One coherent policy links the Tsarist era, the first independence period, the Soviet occupation and contemporary Estonia – an interest in, and commitment to, the **Vilsandi National Park** (see page 38) which is situated along the west coast of Saaremaa and includes 160 islands. Now, as in the past, human activity has to be compatible with the needs of migrating birds and 500 species of plants. This was not difficult during the Soviet era as the ban on small-scale fishing and the use of pleasure boats in a frontier zone left the reserve totally undisturbed, but pressure on the parks is growing. Inland from the west coast, at Viiudumäe, a second reserve was founded in 1957. Travel agents (see page 58) can book specialist English-speaking guides in both reserves.

Kuressaare

Saaremaa's capital, with a population of around 16,000, was fortunately spared much damage during most of the wars that raged elsewhere on the island. Here, at least, the succession of conquerors left a worthy heritage of baroque, Gothic and classicist architecture and the town is too small to have suffered industrial pollution and urban sprawl in more modern times.

Where to stay
In Kuressaare
Hotels in the town are mainly small, three-star locations, converted from private properties. They are all heavily booked during the tourist season from May to September, with many rooms pre-sold to Estonian in-bound tour operators. It is essential to book well in advance. For visitors who need to make arrangements on arrival or who wish to book additional services such as car hire, boat hire and guides, there is an office of **Arensburg Travel** in the bus station. In the summer, reckon on paying 600–900EEK a night for a twin room and 400–700EEK for a single. In the summer reckon on paying around £40/US$70 for a single room and £50/US$85 for a twin.

Airport Tel: 45 33793; fax: 45 33790; email: eeke@eeke.ee; www.eeke.ee. Perhaps this airport is unique in not requiring double glazing and in being able to offer car parking completely free of charge in front of the terminal. As there are never more than four

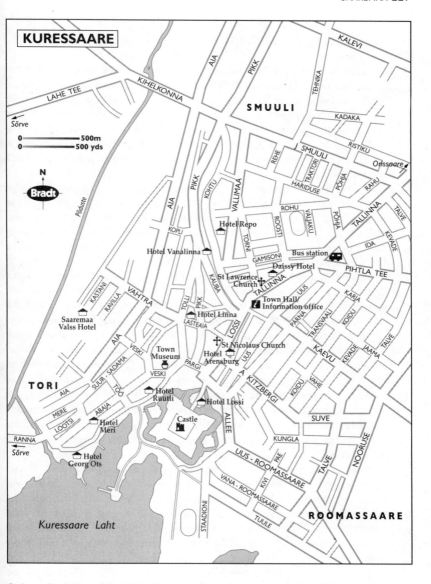

flights a day here, a full night's sleep can always be assured. An hourly bus service provides a link to the town, 3km away, and to the port, a distance of 2km. The low price for the rooms, 250EEK (£10/US$15) for singles and 360EEK (£15/US$26) for twins, well compensates for the location.

Arensburg Lossi 15; tel: 45 24700; fax: 45 24727; email: arensburg@sivainvest.ee; www.sivainvest.ee. When it opened in 2002, the Arensburg immediately appealed to English-speaking visitors. Most of the 30 rooms have a bath, and all have BBC TV. The building dates from the late 18th century and many distinguished local dignitaries lived

TEN YEARS IN SAAREMAA (1934–44)

Linda Reiss

I was born during the first period of Estonian independence 1918–40 in Saaremaa, a large beautiful rural island with many meadows, fields, some lakes as well as birch and juniper trees. On our farm we did not have electricity. Therefore, we had to rely on oil lamps and candles. Water was brought up from the farm's well. There was of course no running water, so we had to use an outside toilet which was cold to use in winter: we had then to be careful so that our bottoms did not get stuck to the toilet seat.

During the harvest time, wheat was collected from the fields. A large threshing machine which separated the wheat from the stems and from the tares would arrive. After the machine had done its work, there was celebration, plenty of food and drink was available. I remember jumping over bodies on the floor, for the men and women had been exhausted by work and play and had fallen into deep sleep.

In 1940 Estonia was invaded by Stalin's armies and things changed dramatically. Large pictures of Lenin and Stalin had to be put on our windows blocking out the valuable outside light. Bicycles, radios and the bible were confiscated and, if found, severe punishment was meted out. Once a Russian armed with a rifle at whose end a bayonet was stuck entered our house in order to check whether we still had any prohibited goods. It was very frightening. Some evil men had denounced my father to the Russians claiming that he had been in contact with German parachute soldiers. He was asked to tell the Russians where they were hiding. Of course, he had no idea. Nonetheless he was arrested, interrogated and only released after a few days. Fortunately he was not tortured, which was the fate of most prisoners who often were killed and thrown into the well of Kuressaare Castle.

Before the outbreak of the war between Germany and Russia Estonian men, including my father, were conscripted by the Russians. An uncle, my mother's older brother, too, had to fight in the Russian army. When the Germans invaded Estonia, his younger brother was conscripted by the Germans. It meant that the two brothers were fighting each other, an appalling fate, but one that was to afflict many Estonian families.

The Germans started to bomb Estonia in 1941 and destroyed quite a few farms in Saaremaa. One day we had a fortunate escape. One aeroplane just missed our farm and crashed in a nearby wood. My father, together with another man, managed to escape from the Russian army. They hid in a farmhouse where the farmer gave them his clothes to wear in exchange for the Russian uniforms which were made of very strong material. The two men hid under mattresses when they heard Russian soldiers come. The Russians ate most of the food and fell asleep.

When the Russians began to reoccupy Estonia in 1944, my parents decided to leave the country. Early one morning my father and my grandfather cycled to Atla village. My grandfather knew that a boat would sail from there to Sweden. They went with a rowing boat to a small island. They intended to spend the night in a small farm or barn. However, in the evening they heard a boat and then the sound of men coming to the house. Assuming that they were Germans, they hid under mattresses. But to their surprise Estonian was spoken. They discovered that the men were Estonians who came from Sweden to pick up clergymen and some important people and bring them to Sweden. But they had lost their way and found themselves in dangerous waters at the bottom of Vilsandi lighthouse between large rocks and close to the German coast guards. A local young man told them that there was another smaller island, Salava island, near by which was surrounded by deep water. With the young man's help they reached that island safely. In the morning the young man cycled to Koimla village and told us to go to Salava island. My uncle, who had escaped from the German army, came with us. Our horse pulled the waggon which was partly filled with hay. I was with my mother and sister as well as with my aunt and her mother. Since my uncle wore his German army uniform, we were prepared to hide him under the hay in case the Gestapo came to ask us where we were going to. If they found us, we intended to say that we were going fishing. Fortunately we reached Salava island without any difficulty. It was a clear night. My uncle burnt his German uniform. We were not able to take anything with us, but I did manage to pick up some family photographs. Unfortunately, there was not enough space on the boat for my aunt, her mother and my uncle to come with us.

I remember being very seasick on the boat, but when we reached Gotland Island in Sweden early in the morning we were escorted to a large room where my father and grandfather, who had gone ahead, met us. There was also hot chocolate and biscuits to greet us, a most wonderful sight that I had not seen for a long time. But soon I felt sad because the other members of the family had had to stay behind. We had our own flat and I went to school there. Understandably my grandfather was very unhappy to be without his wife and daughter and decided to go back to Estonia. However happy he was to be reunited with his wife and daughter, everything else was terrible for him. Because my aunt was not able to tell me the truth since all letters were censored, I discovered it only when I came to Estonia in 1993, for the first time after an absence of 49 years. The Russians did not believe his story but were convinced that he was a spy and imprisoned him for three years. After his release he was so harassed that finally he was unable to bear it any more and hanged himself one night in the attic.

here until 1922 when it became a bank. In Soviet times it was a court, which explains the need for the two double doors at the entrance. A computer is available for guests' use in reception and those less serious can frequent the basement cigar bar, built entirely from local dolomite and the different types of wood available on the island. Double 1,000EEK.

Daissy Tallinna 15; tel: 45 33669; fax: 45 33670; email: daissy.hotell@mail.ee; www.hotel.ee/daissyhotell. For most of the 1990s this was the hotel for business travellers and regular tourists and with 15 rooms was then considered large. Now it has competitors, but its restaurant remains supreme for the variety of its menu and the level of service. Do not judge either the restaurant or the hotel by their equally dismal entrances. Double 900EEK.

Linna Lasteaia 7; tel: 45 31888; fax: 45 33688; email: linnahotell@kontaktid.ee; www.kontaktid.ee. The reception area may be small but where space really matters, in the rooms, it is granted in abundance, and many rooms have balconies too. The location down a side street ensures peace and quiet and the five-minute walk into the town centre is hardly a burden. Double 800EEK.

Lossi Lossi 27; tel: 45 33633; fax: 45 33633; email: lossihotel@tt.ee; www.saaremaa.ee/lossihotell. In the 1920s this was a private house where 'one' had to be seen during the summer season on Saaremaa. In 2000 it was restored to a similar status, but as a hotel. President Meri was one of its first guests so its reputation is assured. The glazier was clearly given an art nouveau brief, although the carpenter seems to have had much less freedom. Several rooms have balconies and views over the castle but indulgence in a suite can certainly be recommended here. There is currently no restaurant, although one is planned for 2005. At present breakfast is of course served and snacks can be provided through the day. Double 1,300EEK.

Piibelehe (Lily of the Valley) Piibelehe 4; tel/fax: 45 36206; email: piibelehe@saaremaa.ee; www.saaremaa.ee/piibelehe. A large suburban house surrounded by gardens and lawns with plenty of parking space makes this guesthouse an attractive option for those not needing the town on the doorstep but not wanting the isolation of the countryside. Double 500EEK.

Repo Vallimaa 1a; tel: 45 33510; fax: 45 33520; email: repo@saaremaa.ee; www.saaremaa.ee/repo. A large family house, tastefully converted into a modern hotel with 14 rooms. It attracts many regular clients, perhaps as much for the flowers outside as for the rooms inside. Double 950EEK.

Saaremaa Valss Kastani 20; tel: 45 27100; fax: 45 27145; email: sanatoorium@saram.ee; www.sanatoorium.ee. Now having 75 rooms, this is where most groups stay. Following independence, it was slow to brighten itself up, but by 2001 it had certainly done so. A nice touch is the national flag of each guest that is displayed at reception. Some may think too brutal the charge of 200EEK (£8/US$12) levied on any smoker lighting up in a bedroom. The same money could provide a bicycle for two days or four meals at the lunch-time and 'happy hour' buffets. The walk into town takes about 15 minutes but many long-stay guests never leave, such is the range of ailments treated in the health centre next door. Not a place for the young, but certainly fine for the young-at-heart. A band plays each evening after dinner in the restaurant; the music chosen will always be sentimental and leisurely. Double 800EEK.

Vanalinna Kauba 8; tel/fax: 45 55309; email: info@vanalinna.ee; www.vanalinna.ee. This was one of the first hotels to open on the island when tourism again became possible after a gap of 50 years. Those early visitors are happy to return here; if its 12 rooms remain simply furnished and are smaller than elsewhere, the family atmosphere is valued highly. No other café can match the cakes served here and no other restaurant manages the variety of sauces for pike-perch. Double 1,000EEK.

Between 2002 and 2004, three enormous spa hotels opened beside the port, the **Meri**, the **Rüütli** (with the same contact numbers as the Saaremaa Valss) and the **Georg Ots** (tel: 45 50000; fax: 45 50001; email: info@gospa.ee; www.gospa.ee). All aim to be health and family centres, with guests not venturing outside the complexes. They are mostly booked for at least a week at a time by regular tourist groups from Scandinavia. The website of the Georg Ots warns that 'clients who have consumed alcohol are withdrawn from the spa for the "sale" of security'. Georg Ots (1920–75) was Estonia's most famous singer, who will always be linked with the country's most famous song 'Saaremaa Waltz'. He did join the Communist Party, but protected many artists who would not and ensured that Estonian songs reached both Finnish and Russian audiences. Those who knew him still treasure his memory and mourn his early death from cancer. The ferry that linked Tallinn and Helsinki in Soviet times was named after him, as is a Saaremaa cheese. Being abstemious, although not in any way teetotal, he made it clear that he did not want any alcoholic drink named after him.

Outside Kuressaare

Loona Vilsandi Nature Reserve (about 30km from Kuressaare); tel: 45 46510; fax: 45 76554; email: loona@loona.ee; www.loona.ee. This hotel was opened in November 1997 and forms part of the reserve's headquarters. It has seven twin rooms and two suites to cater for small birdwatching groups or individuals keen to be based in the reserve. Double 700EEK.

Mannikabi Mandjala (13km from Kuressaare towards the Sõrve Peninsula); tel: 45 44100; fax: 45 44106; email: saarehotell@saaremaa.ee; www.saarehotell.ee. In summer 2001 it was greatly extended and modernised. With 60 rooms, and situated in a pine forest close to the sea, this is an ideal location for visitors with a car wishing to combine sightseeing and relaxation. Double 900EEK.

Nasva Yacht Club Nasva (8km from Kuressaare towards the Sõrve Peninsula); tel: 45 44044; fax: 45 44028; email: nasvahotel@tt.ee; www.saaremaa.ee/nasvahotel. Situated at the end of a promontory, this 18-room hotel was the most luxurious on the island when it was first built in 1995 and it still maintains high standards. Every room has a bath. The sea views are best experienced in brilliant sunlight or during violent storms. Double 800EEK.

Pädaste Manor Muhu Island; tel: 45 48800; fax: 45 48811; email: info@padaste.ee; www.padaste.ee. Many Estonians have talked about converting a country estate into a luxury hotel; by 2001, only one had actually done so and only two others would follow suit between 2002 and 2004. Imre Sooäär, who now styles himself 'Lord Imre', has combined a flair both for architecture and for public relations to ensure that his hotel has received more worldwide publicity than all other hotels in Estonia put together. The hotel refuses to publish a brochure, on the grounds that all potential clients will have access to their website. Two buildings are now complete, one for accommodation and one for a second restaurant. Rooms and the main restaurant are in the former stables, the second restaurant in the former smithy. The actual manor house itself has yet to be restored. Note its modest design compared to those on the mainland. The mixed use of granite and limestone, one light stone alternating with a dark one, is characteristic of Muhu. Visitors coming in the next few years will probably find that a small harbour, a golf course and a heliport have been added. Doubtless the locally mined dolomite stone will continue to be used as much as is practical. The 13 rooms are each on two floors, with an upstairs bedroom and downstairs sitting room/balcony. Double 3,300EEK. The corridor has a permanent exhibition of photographs taken around Estonia in 1913. The private cinema seats 20, in mattress-lined deckchairs. It costs 500EEK (£25/US$35) to hire for an afternoon or evening. The hotel has an extensive, 'classic' video collection or the wide screen can also be used for watching television. Amongst the unexpected dishes in the restaurants are coconut soup, spam in garlic sauce, and baron's feast (pork chop in red wine with herb rice).

Pilguse Manor Tel/fax: 45 45445; email: info@pilguse.ee; www.pilguse.ee. This manor is in the village of Jõgela near Lümanda, about 35km from Kuressaare. It is the birthplace of Fabian von Bellinghausen (1778–1852) who, despite his name, was in fact Russian. He led the first Russian expedition to Antarctica in 1820 – the next one was not until 1946. Accommodation here is simple and geared to families wanting a country base with ample facilities for children. Double 860EEK.

Where to eat

There is now a wide choice of very reasonably priced snack-bars/coffee houses in all directions around the Town Hall Square. Prices are half those in Tallinn so coffee is about £0.30/US$0.55 and most dishes under £1.70/US$3.20. Places listed below are more expensive (prices given are for three courses without wine) but they each have individual, contrasting characteristics and are still very reasonably priced for the quality offered. The Hotel Vanalinna (above) also has a good restaurant.

Amandus Beneath the Town Hall; tel: 45 54688. The best restaurant for a special occasion with its extensive menu and formal service. In winter its fireplace gives it greater intimacy. 160EEK.

Hansacafé Tel: 45 54321. Saaremaa has now finally got a bohemian centre for its artistic community. Do not expect much life before 11.00, do not wear a tie or a dress and do not be in a hurry. Its location opposite the Town Hall, together with a wide menu, make it a convenient port of call at any time of day. They also sell paintings, ceramics and glass. 140EEK.

John Bull Lossipargi 4; tel: 45 39988. This riotous pub has no closing time and brings together anyone under 30 with a passion for both rock music and motorbikes, be they local, Estonian or foreign. 120EEK.

Jurna Turismitalu Kaarma village, 6km from Kuressaare; tel: 45 21919; fax: 45 21920; email: jurna@neti.ee; www.saaremaa.ee/jurna. Vegetarians had better stay away since roasts and grills, both of fish and meat, are the mainstay of meals here. The website has the full current menu. Otherwise, an ideal centre for a long evening, both in summer and winter. Outdoor log fires burn year-round. 200EEK.

Kohvik Classic Lossi 9; tel: 45 54786. Situated almost next door to the Arensburg Hotel, it serves lighter main meals but more lavish teas. 120EEK.

Kuursaal Lossipargi 1; tel: 45 39749. This restaurant has wisely decided to remain in the 1930s so is unlikely to come up against many competitors. The dancing is leisurely, the service calm and the portions ample. It proudly advertises that it has been open since 1888. 140EEK.

Nimeta Tallinna 3; tel: 8 252 39200. This translates into English as the 'Pub with No Name'. It caused a stir when it opened in May 1998 by charging 12EEK for coffee, double or treble the normal Saaremaa prices, but its location, quality and reputation from Tallinn should ensure a full house through the tourist season. 200EEK.

Osilia Kohtu 2a; tel (mobile): 53 478815 (there is no landline on the premises, perhaps a trend that will increase in Estonia). This is undoubtedly the most exciting place to open on Saaremaa in 2004. It is part of an antique shop and the food served is probably the only item there not at least 100 years old. With luck, a meal may be served on whatever porcelain happens to be in stock. The collection is probably more varied than in any of Saaremaa's museums. 160EEK.

Veski Pärna 19; tel: 45 53161. A windmill behind the Town Hall which has perhaps been rather over-restored, but the folk music and local dishes make for a congenial, 1960s- or 1970s-revival experience. 200EEK.

A walk around Kuressaare

Without doubt, a tour of the capital must start at the **castle**, the best-preserved medieval fortress in Estonia, which for many centuries combined the role of episcopal residence, prison and sanctuary. The basic quadrangular structure took 40 years to build between 1340 and 1380 and the massive walls were added in the 15th century. The Germans, Danes, Swedes and Russians all maintained the original structure but the Russians withdrew their garrison in 1836 and from then the castle no longer had any military significance so escaped damage in later wars. Vestments and weaponry from each of these periods survives and is on display. Not even bishops could live flamboyantly on Saaremaa in the Middle Ages. Austerity and simplicity are the impressions that remain. The original heating system still functions. Fortunately an early legal system does not – those sentenced to death in the second-floor Hall of Justice were allegedly thrown down a 20m shaft to be devoured by the animals waiting eagerly below. There is also an extensive exhibition of the history of Saaremaa up to 1940. The later period is of most interest to visitors; a wide range of memorabilia from the first independence period was hidden during the Soviet occupation but is now on view and is described in English. During the summer, there is a full programme of concerts inside the castle; the surrounding park often hosts song festivals and carnivals. The castle stays open till 19.00 every night during the summer. From the photographic point of view, the best shots of it are to be had from the port during early evening.

Kuressaare owes its architectural affluence to Balthasar von Campenhausen, a deputy governor of the Tsarist province of Livonia, who lived there for 15 years from 1783 to 1797. A plague devastated the town in 1710 and by the 1760s less than a hundred buildings, mainly thatched wooden cottages, were occupied. In their places were to come large, stone, classicist houses with red-tiled roofs. Many had courtyards, stone walls and decorative gateposts. Leaving the castle grounds, return towards the town centre along **Lossi** where houses number 12 and 15, almost opposite each other, stand out as examples from this period, despite the imitation Gothic portal added to number 15 in the 19th century. Next on the left is **St Nicolaus Church**, built in 1790. The frieze and the hanging kerchiefs show the dedication to classicism at that time. As we approach the Town Hall Square, houses become appropriately grander. Note numbers 6 and 7 with their stone window frames, pilasters and wide cornices. Number 7 is now the police station. Number 1 has always been the seat of county government so has been well maintained under all political regimes. Opposite the police station is the **monument** to Estonians killed in the 1918 War of Independence against the Germans and the Russians. It was destroyed during the Soviet period after World War II but restored in 1990.

Entering the square, the **Town Hall** is on the right. It dates originally from 1654 but only the 'guardian lions' at the entrance are part of the original structure. Fortunately the classicist and baroque features that were added during frequent restorations blend well. The most recent restoration was in the 1960s. As a typical concession to modern, commercial Estonia, one room in the main building is let out as an art gallery, and the basement has been discreetly converted into a restaurant. The Town Hall also houses the **tourist information office**. Behind it is one of the island's largest windmills, no longer in use as such but restored and converted into a restaurant.

Behind the Town Hall is also the taxi rank and the only public toilets in Kuressaare. In front of the Town Hall, all local buses leave, including the hourly service to the airport and Roomassaare harbour. The south side of the square has a number of useful shops and cafés; the wine merchant has a dual role as an exchange bureau and during the opening hours of the neighbouring Uhisbank, offers good rates. These, however, worsen considerably once the bank has closed, so do not leave this chore until after 16.00 during the week or after 14.00 on Saturdays. The handicraft shop **Käsitööpood** is a convenient one-stop shop having a wide range of souvenirs with all prices clearly labelled. Opposite the Town Hall is a small **market** with tasteful souvenirs, including salad spoons, beer mugs and butter dishes carved from the local juniper wood. The array of woollen goods sold throughout the summer is a reminder of the weather Estonia has to endure for much of the winter. Prices here are much lower than in Tallinn as the goods are all locally produced; this work provides useful employment out of the tourist season.

Coming out of the market back into the square, turn right into **Turu** and then right again into **Kauba**. Here the whole architectural history of Kuressaare is represented, with the first buildings of the 21st century already planned for this street. Numbers 5 and 11 are careful restorations of 17th-century, single-storey, baroque residences whereas numbers 7 and 10 are again classicist buildings with broader windows, cornices and decorative carvings. Number 10 is the café of the **Vanalinna Hotel**. Number 6 was first converted into a discreet Irish pub but in 2002 became a livelier German one. Number 4 is now a casino.

Return to the square and turn left past the market into **Tallinna**. Number 9 is one of the few wooden houses to retain some of its original façade, although the stone columns were restored in the 1980s. It is currently an art shop and café. Number 11, probably Kuressaare's largest private residence until World War II, has retained much of its 18th-century stonework, as has number 19 which has always housed various governmental offices. It is now the customs office. St Lawrence Church, on the corner of Torni and Tallinna, dates from the 1830s, although a church has been on this site since the 17th century. In August 2003 the 13 stained-glass windows, totally paid for by private donations, were unveiled. The artist is Urmo Raus who now lives in Paris. Whilst working here he had to wear a gas mask as protection against the gold vapour. The abstract designs represent St Lawrence who distributed the emperor's treasure amongst the poor.

On the other side of the road, number 20 has maintained the original design of its classicist façade but has had to be frequently restored. It was a theatre in the 1930s and it is hoped that funds can be raised for it to be reopened on this basis. Turn left into Rootsi and then left again into Komandandi. Just before the junction with Torni, on the right-hand side of the road, is the surprisingly modest single-storey house which belonged to Balthasar von Campenhausen during the 15 years that he lived in Kuressaare. It is now a music school.

The walk can end here, but for those interested in late 19th-century buildings, it is worthwhile returning to the castle grounds to visit the **Kuursaal**, now a restaurant. On the other side of the road at 5a Pargi are the county archives and a small **museum** depicting life in the late 19th century. During the Soviet period this building had great significance as it had been the childhood home of the Estonian communist Viktor Kingissepp who was executed in 1922. He lived there until 1906 and returned once more in 1913 but, as he was subsequently involved in clandestine work, the next nine years of his life were spent largely in hiding in Tallinn. To prepare to commemorate the hundredth anniversary of his birth in 1988, the house was turned into an extensive memorial to his life. The museum has now removed most references to him and centres on his conventional father Eduard Kingissepp (1856–1926) although a rocking-horse and some dolls show the link with a family.

In 1955 the name of the town was changed from Kuressaare to Kingissepp but ironically, in 1988, which was still in the Soviet period, it reverted to Kuressaare under the pressures of the burgeoning independence movement. The streets that compulsorily bore Kingissepp's name in every Estonian town were immediately given back their pre-war names. (There is still a town with his name in Russia, between Narva and St Petersburg, but Kingissepp is now completely forgotten in Estonia.)

Take the road beside the museum, called Veski, along to the **sanatorium** (Sanatoorium). Visitors coming in May and June should divert a little en route to enjoy the many gardens of this part of the town. The sanatorium is now back to its pre-war glory. Tourists who returned in 1990 found gloomy corridors, outdated equipment and cafeterias. By 1997, bright lights, dance bands, an excellent restaurant and specialist medical teams had taken over. Finns and Swedes are the main patients for the mud and mineral baths but tourist groups frequently use the **Saaremaa Valss Hotel** as it has 75 rooms and multi-lingual staff.

The Sõrve Peninsula

Before World War II, about 6,000 people lived on the peninsula, mostly engaged in boatbuilding and fishing. Bitter fighting took place here in 1944 between the retreating Germans and the advancing Russians. By 1945 the population was down to about 1,500 following German and Russian deportations and the exodus to Sweden. Most of the area became a military base, although fishing was slowly revived in the 1980s when a daily flight took eel, perch and herring to expensive Moscow restaurants. A visit now is a surreal experience, seeing what was abandoned by the different armies that fought there and speculating on how the area should recover from 50 years of neglect. A day is needed to drive or cycle along this 60-mile itinerary. Whilst it follows a bus route, the service is not sufficiently frequent to allow stops at all the sights mentioned, although a shortened tour could nonetheless be done this way. Take a picnic and, if driving, fill up in Kuressaare as at the time of writing there are no petrol stations on the peninsula.

Kuressaare must be one of the smallest towns in the world with a bypass; the Sõrve road is the southern sector of it. Leave town on Kihelkonna and turn left at the roundabout where it meets the bypass (Ringtee). After 8km, pass the village of **Nasva**, now best known for its yacht club, based at a new hotel built at the end of a pier. For those unable to reach Sõrve, this is the best place to enjoy late sunsets or dramatic storms. After a further 8km note the obelisk on the left, which is the Soviet War Memorial at **Tehumardi**. Local dolomite is blended into the concrete which always dominates such monuments.

Beside the road are the renovated graves of several German soldiers. No German graves or memorials were allowed during the Soviet period but current government policy is to commemorate all fighters during the many wars that raged across Estonia. Tehumardi was the site of one of the worst battles during the German retreat in autumn 1944. About 300 Germans and 200 Russians were killed during the one night of October 9/10. In all, about 10,000 troops on each side would be killed before the Soviet army could conquer the whole island. Fourteen villages were largely destroyed, as was much of the forest. Three kilometres south of Tehumardi is **Läätsa** with a small, smoked-eel processing plant. It produces only two to three tons a year now compared to 200–300 tons before the war, but it is planning to expand. After a further 3km is **Ansekula**. Its lighthouse has been rebuilt but beside it are the foundations of the church destroyed in 1944. Note the cross erected here in 1990 to commemorate the church. After 16km is perhaps the saddest village on the peninsula, **Mõntu**, with a ruined manor house and former fishing village turned into an oil refinery. Remains of its barbed-wire entanglements show its crucial role in the Soviet defence system. However,

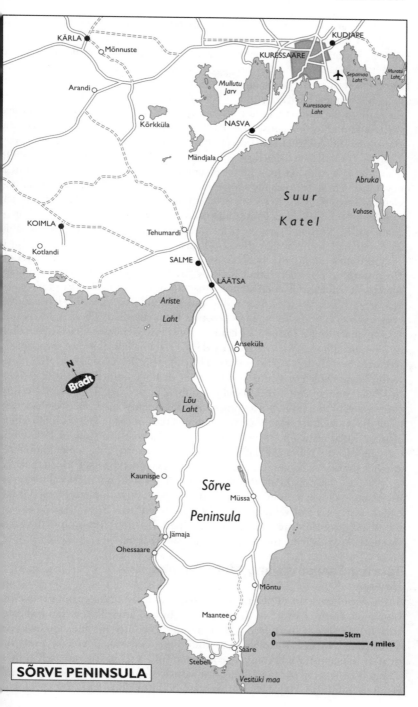

KÄRLA
Mõnnuste
KURESSAARE
KUDJAPE
Arandi
Mullutu Jarv
Sepamaa Laht
Muratsi Laht
Kõrkküla
NASVA
Kuressaare Laht
Mändjala
Abruka
Suur
Katel
Vahase
KOIMLA
Tehumardi
Kotlandi
SALME
LÄÄTSA
Ariste Laht
Anseküla
N
Bradt
Lõu Laht
Kaunispe
Sõrve
Müssa
Peninsula
Jämaja
Ohessaare
Mõntu
Maantee
0   5km
0   4 miles
Sääre
Stebeli
Vesitüki maa

SÕRVE PENINSULA

after the war, it was used for shipping potatoes to Riga. In 2004 plans were discussed for starting a passenger ferry service to Ventspils in Latvia.

Two kilometres further on, turn right to **Maantee**, a completely deserted Soviet rocket station. Poles are left but no wires, rows of empty squares represent former windows, and weeds are slowly beginning to grow again in the soil polluted by leaking oil. There are many other smaller, similar sites throughout the Baltic republics; it is a pity that the Russians chose not to leave with more dignity and consideration. After a further 3km comes the end of the peninsula and **Sääre Lighthouse**, now a meteorological observation post. The current building dates from 1960 although the first one was built in 1770. The Tsarist armies set up a defence station here during World War I, but it never saw action. It is usually possible to climb the lighthouse although ample views towards the Latvian coast can be enjoyed from the ground. On the beach is a shipwreck that dates from Christmas 1995 when 80 Kurds landed, they assumed, in Sweden. They were in due course returned to Latvia but only after they had been fêted by the islanders.

Continuing along the west coast for nearly 2km, turn left to **Stebeli Commando**, a gunnery point built by the Soviets in 1939 under a military agreement imposed on the Estonians that autumn. Like its Tsarist predecessor at Sääre, it was never used. It has four underground storeys, which have not yet been excavated. Soon the scenery becomes Estonian again. There is a windmill at **Ohessaare** and at **Jämaja** is a church that survived the war intact. It was built in 1864 and although the Germans used it for stabling horses it was, surprisingly, reopened as a church by the Soviets. The cemetery has a metal cairn memorial to the *Moero*, which was sunk by the Soviet air force on September 22 1944. It had 3,000 refugees on board, of whom only 650 survived. This tragedy was of course never reported in Soviet times and subsequently has been overshadowed by all the books and films about the sinking of the *Gustloff* in January 1945 which claimed 9,000 lives. The second memorial is to a boat that sunk in 1908 while carrying rails to Tallinn. Keeping along the coast road, after a few kilometres another shipwreck comes into view. This was a Greek oil tanker which capsized in 1980, to the delight of the Soviet border guards and the local Estonian population who, in an unusual display of co-operation, completely looted it and had their first taste of Western consumer goods ten years before anyone else on the island. From **Salme** (where there is a petrol station), return to Kuressaare through Nasva, leaving the horrors of the 1940s behind.

Touring Saaremaa and Muhu islands
Day one

Leave Kuressaare on the Kihelkonna road and after 12km turn left towards Lümanda. In the hamlet of Viidu, turn right and after 3km a sign indicates a right turning which leads after about 200m to the headquarters of **Viidumäe Nature Reserve**. This building was a leper colony until the turn of the century when it was converted into a scientific research centre. The whole reserve is only 16km^2, and consists entirely of forest or swamp; yet it is home to 700 different species of butterflies and 200 species of moths. There is also a unique spring fen that grows here, now called Saaremaa Rattle, which was found for the first time in 1933. Returning to the main road, an observation tower comes into view. Built on the highest point of Saaremaa, which is 60m, the tower adds a further 23m so gives a good view over the reserve and the neighbouring villages. It is an 8km drive to the next town of **Lümanda**. Although not on the coast, it was traditionally a boatbuilding centre and this work is now being revived. Four hundred residents escaped in 1944 on the boats they hurriedly built for this purpose. Turn right towards Kihelkonna and **Vilsandi National Park** is reached after about 5km. Turn left on entering the reserve for the headquarters at the hamlet of **Loona**. The hotel here (see page 233) was built in 1997 and is ideal for specialist visitors. The reserve includes 160 islands and is named Vilsandi after the largest. It is situated halfway between the hibernation areas of central Europe and the breeding grounds in the Arctic for about a million birds, although only a few hundred birds reside permanently on the reserve. No building is allowed within 200m of the sea in order to protect them. With its maritime climate, the reserve is warmer than other parts of Estonia in winter with no more than 60 days of snow a year, half of what is normal on the mainland. As a result, a larger range of plants grows here than is possible elsewhere in the country.

Returning to the main road, **Kihelkonna** is a further 4–5km. The church dates originally from the 13th century when the town had far greater importance as a harbour than it does now. The altarpiece, carved in 1591, has survived remarkably well. The picture of the Last Supper and the didactic texts in Latin and German are characteristic of that period. Belltowers built beside the church rather than as part of it were common in the 17th century but this is now the only one remaining on Saaremaa. The tower was added in 1899 to a height of 60m and it is possible to climb it for a view over the island. It is in fact the highest point in Saaremaa and has therefore also served as a lighthouse. The organ dates from 1805 and is probably the oldest functioning organ in Estonia. There were frequent minor alterations carried out in the middle of the 19th century, but the basic structure has been retained. The stained glass dates from the 1980s, the end of the Soviet period. In either very good or very bad weather a detour can be taken at this point to the leaning lighthouse at Kiipsaare, on the south of the Tagamõisa peninsula. It was built in 1930 and a storm in 1992 washed away the extensive sandy beach that used to surround it. The final 2km are accessible only on foot, but the long summer sunsets visible from here make the walk worthwhile. Otherwise leave Kihelkonna on the Kuressaare road for a short detour and, after a mile, stop at the **Mihkli Farm Museum** which is on the right-hand side of the road in the village of **Viki**. Such museums are common throughout Estonia but this one has particular items to note such as the high stone walls and the long chimney hood which suggest a Latvian model rather than an Estonian one. It also has its own windmill. The tools and furnishings are all from this site; nothing has been brought from elsewhere. Return to Kihelkonna and continue to the **Tagamõisa Peninsula,** an area of wild scenery for walking and relaxing amongst the lakes, cliffs and beaches. Boats from Sweden use the small harbour at **Veere**. There are several routes back to Kuressaare; a leisurely drive will take about 45 minutes.

Day two

Leave Kuressaare on Tallinna, cross the ring road and take the next turn left after 3km. Turn left again after a further 3km and continue for 5km to **Kaarma**, famous for its dolomite mine. This stone was used not only for the castle at Kuressaare but also in buildings as far away as Tallinn and St Petersburg. Some has even been used on the Moscow metro. It is fortunate that stone rather than wood was always the main building material on Saaremaa so more early churches have survived here than on the mainland. St Peter's Church at Kaarma dates originally from 1270 and was probably built by the Germans as proof of their successful conquest of the island. Ironically, the inscription beside the portal giving the final completion date as 1407 is the earliest written in Estonian. Inside, two stone carvings should be noted, the figures of Peter and Paul on the central pillar and the animal carvings on the base of several pillars. The dogs and lions represent good whilst deer, pigs and wolves depict evil. Some of the 16th-century wooden altarpiece remains, but the stone and wooden pulpit is the best-preserved interior piece. The stone reliefs portray scenes from the life of Christ and are modelled on those on the pulpit at Lübeck Cathedral. The village of Kaarma is important to the British Estonian community as it is the birthplace of Oskar Kallas, who was Estonian ambassador in London during the first independence period. A much larger museum is due to open here in 2005.

Twelve kilometres from Kaarma are the **Kaali Craters**, for years the subject of speculation and legend. Lennart Meri, former president of Estonia, joined the debate in 1976 with his book, *Silverwhite*. The truth is in fact straightforward, if dramatic. The craters were formed by a meteorite that fell around 3,000 years ago. The largest lake is over 100m wide and gives the impression of being completely undisturbed since its violent origin. A small geological museum displays the remnants of the meteorite and other archaeological finds from the immediate area.

Take the road north towards Leisi for 18km to reach **Karja**. St Catherine's Church is the smallest on Saaremaa but nonetheless contains rooms for refugees and travellers. Note the symbols that form part of the wall murals, probably of pagan origin. The carvings on the pillars show how international the island had become during the 15th century. Masons trained in Germany, Sweden and probably France all contributed to their diverse themes and designs. Note St Catherine clasping a book as the patron saint of scholars, and St Nicholas, the patron saint of sailors, with a monk kneeling beside him holding a boat. Just to the north of Karja are the five **Angla** windmills, the symbol of Saaremaa. They are almost the only ones remaining on the island; in the mid 19th century, there were about 800 in active use.

Valjala is a 16km drive south from Angla, passing through Parsama and Koikla. St Martin's Church here could equally well be described as a fortress. The original building dated, as did Kaarma and Karja, from the 13th century but following its destruction in 1343 it was rebuilt from massive hewn blocks similar to those used in the castle at Kuressaare. The interior is far simpler than in other churches but the modern stained glass adds welcome colour to it.

Valjala is a 30km drive from the causeway that links Saaremaa with **Muhu Island**. Before leaving Saaremaa, take a short detour to **Maasi** to see the remains of the fortress, and also to enjoy the sea view across to Muhu. The fortress was blown up in 1576 by the Danes in an attempt to forestall the Swedish invasion and nothing was done for the next 300 years. In 2000, serious excavation started and by 2004 electricity had been installed so it is no longer necessary to take a torch to explore the vaults. At the neighbouring port of **Orissaare**, a 16th-century wreck of a cargo boat is now exhibited. It was only brought to the surface in 1987. The nearby café, with its extensive view, is a good place to break for a meal or snack. As Kuivastu, the port for ferries to the mainland, is on Muhu, tourists who bring their own cars can visit Muhu on arrival or departure. Shortly after the end of the causeway, at **Eemu** on the right side of the road, is one of the few working windmills left on either island. Turning left after a mile, the road leads to the **Koguva Village Museum**, a great contrast to the Mihkli Farm Museum on Saaremaa. Here most of the buildings are from the early 20th century and the lifestyle depicted could almost be described as affluent. The author, Juhan Smuul (1922–71), lived in one of the houses. Although he wrote entirely during the Soviet period, his work is still highly regarded in contemporary Estonia. Sadly, the few translations that were published of his books during his lifetime are now out of print. Amongst the equipment displayed is that for home brewing and baking bread. Most coastal areas of Estonia have a history of smuggling and Muhu is no exception. The brandy vats on show were used in the early 19th century for runs to the German port of Memel, now the Lithuanian port of Klaipeda. Drive east for 8km to Piiri and turn left into the woodland. After about a kilometre the clear remains of a Soviet rocket store can be made out. All that is left of the surrounding military base is what could not be dragged or flown back home in 1994.

Right in the centre of Muhu Island, on the main road to Kuivatsu, is the village of **Liiva**, dominated by **Muhu church**. It dates from the late 13th century, so early in the rule of the Teutonic Knights. The base of the altar dates from that time, as does the circular window in the west wall. The mural paintings are probably from a hundred or so years later. They were only rediscovered in 1913, having been concealed under plaster since the Reformation. It is thought that the artist might have come from Gotland since there are similarities with work in churches there. A tombstone for 'Johannes from Gotland' might in fact be that of the artist. Fires destroyed most of the woodwork in 1640 and again in 1710, but the 17th-century pulpit does survive and is similar to the one in Karja church. The thickness of the western wall, with its staircases and in-built rooms, shows how often the church must have been used as a hiding place. The roof was badly damaged in a German bombing raid in 1941 and was only replaced in 1958, after which the building was used as a granary. It was only returned to the church in 1989. With considerable financial support from Sweden, the church was rebuilt after independence and reconsecrated in May 1994.

Return to Saaremaa along the causeway and after 6km turn left. If there is time, stop after a further kilometre at the ruined church at **Pöide**. Before the war it was as splendid as the others already described but its use as a military depot by the Soviet army and the destruction of the tower by lightning in 1940 has ruined the interior. Reconstruction has begun and part of the flooring is of glass to reveal the archaeological discoveries below. The village of **Sakla**, 18km further on, was the location of Estonia's first collective farm, founded in 1947 and called Kingissepp, after the communist leader executed in Tallinn in 1922. Kuressaare is a further 25km drive. Just before the ring road, turn left into **Kudjape Cemetery**. Several of the chapels are in the classicist style noted already in the town. This was the site of a ten-day battle in September 1941, before the Germans defeated the Russians. A year earlier German troops had seized Paris with relative ease; Saaremaa proved much tougher. Their cemetery was turned into a farm after the war but it has now been reconsecrated. Here Saaremaa can finally come to terms with its suffering during the middle of the 20th century. Apart from the main area for the local Estonian population, there are now separate cemeteries for the Jewish community, the German soldiers and the Soviet occupiers. One Briton is buried here, too, a Captain Brown who died in 1917 during the invasion of Riga harbour. In the German cemetery, individual graves are provided for those who died in 1941 as the Germans advanced toward Leningrad. The battles here were the first serious Soviet resistance they faced. For those who died in 1944 during their retreat, only an all-purpose granite memorial can be provided as the Russians made no effort to identify individual German corpses. In the Estonian section, note the memorials for the deportees to Siberia and for the ten local residents who died in the *Estonia* tragedy in 1994. Between them is a memorial to the Kitt family whose suffering during the 20th century is probably paralleled by that of all too many Saaremaa families. One member died en route to Siberia and four others out there. Two drowned trying to escape across the Baltic Sea in 1944. Others who succeeded in escaping died in due course of natural causes in England, Finland and the United States, but none died of natural causes at home on Saaremaa.

ABRUKA

The island of Abruka is situated four miles off the coast of Saaremaa, due south of Kuressaare. A small boat from **Roomassaare Harbour** serves Abruka four times a week, leaving at 08.45 and returning at 14.30. The fare is 20EEK (£0.80/US$1.10) in each direction and the journey takes about 45 minutes so this gives five hours for exploring the island. In 2004 there was no catering available on the island nor any shops, but this is likely to change. This should be checked before departure and, if necessary, a picnic taken from Saaremaa. Small groups may want to consider hiring their own boat to give flexibility to the length of stay. In the winter, it is possible to walk or drive over the ice to Abruka.

The island currently has a population of about 30 year-round residents compared to the 170 or so through much of the Soviet era. A far larger number spend the summer on the island; both Finns and Estonians are now upgrading former farmhouses to serve this purpose.

Much of the land is forested, mainly with elms, mountain ash and oak trees. Orchids grow extensively and a wide variety of moths and butterflies can be seen. The main building is the former **Sibaabaa Centre**. From its design it could only be a collective-farm headquarters and this is indeed the role it served, in the 1950s for fishing and then for the increasing number of sheep and cows brought to graze on the island. There are plans to convert it into a hostel, but a kinder solution would be to remove it. The **cemetery**, as so often in contemporary Estonia, gives a vignette of the struggles fought around it. The Russians and the Lutherans not only required a divided cemetery, but also separate entry gates. Burials in the Soviet period lack any link with religion. The two most famous tombs are those of two cousins whose bodies were returned from Sweden to Abruka for burial. Johannes Aavik (1880–1973) was Estonia's most famous linguist and Joosep Aavik (1899–1989) was equally well known as a conductor, organist and teacher. As in many other communities near the sea, a **memorial** has been built to commemorate the sinking of the *Estonia* on September 28 1994.

RUHNU

Ruhnu has always been an anachronism in Estonian history. It has both benefited and suffered as a result of its isolated location. Events that would be forgotten elsewhere within weeks are still chronicled centuries later. A major event in the 18th century, for instance, was a peasant arriving drunk to church in 1729 and being put in the stocks for four consecutive Sundays. The only civilian murder on the island took place in 1738. A prison with two cells operated throughout the 19th century but it was closed in 1894 through lack of use. The plague however ravaged Ruhnu in 1710 just as much as it did the rest of Estonia as the soldiers of Peter the Great seized it from the Swedes. There would be bitter fighting between the Russians and the Germans in summer 1941 as resistance from Soviet forces slowly began. From 1944 until 1989 Ruhnu was particularly isolated on the pretext of military sensitivity.

In 1919, as the Russian and German empires collapsed, Estonia, Latvia and Sweden all expected Ruhnu to fall into their hands. On January 17 of that year, the provisional government of Estonia proclaimed the island of Ruhnu as part of Estonia but inhabitants only found this out in May when the first boat of the summer was able to get there. Realising that it would be necessary to speak Swedish and to barter (money would only come to Ruhnu about 20 years later), government representatives from Tallinn arrived with flour, spirits, salt, leatherwear and gun cartridges. They accepted 20,000 kilos of seal blubber in return, which in due course went rancid as there were insufficient preservation facilities in Tallinn at the time. The new Estonian government therefore had a political but not an economic victory over its neighbours and Ruhnu has been Estonian ever since. Families received surnames in 1927 and the land that had previously been farmed collectively was divided into private plots in 1930.

In order to escape the return of the Russians, all but two families left for Sweden in 1944, abandoning not only their houses but also 200 cows, 300

ARRIVAL ON RUHNU ISLAND

Arthur Ransome

And then slowly wandering towards us, knocking off the heads of the mushrooms with his stick came man indeed, the Governor-General of the Island, a short, lame elderly man, the keeper of the lighthouse to whom the men of Ruhnu come for a casting vote in all debates. He has no official authority; no laws confer power on him or limit it but he is the Keeper of the Light, the guardian of the one piece of civilisation imposed on Ruhnu by the mainland, the representative of those who do not live on islands and I suppose tradition invests him with a sort of dignity. In the old days he was sent by a Tsar of Russia to keep the light on this little island in a sea surrounded on all sides by Russian territory. The men of Ruhnu are Swedes, and a Tsar of Russia had driven their race from the mainland. Nowadays the sea of which Ruhnu is, as it were, the central pool is no longer Russian. Its coasts are Latvian and Estonian. The Tsar is no more.

'The lighthouse-keeper greeted us. He had heard our fog-horn, and since the people were busy with their harvesting on the other side of the island, he had himself come down to meet us, and to warn us that the wind was changing and that we must soon look to our ship. He knew a few words of English, but more willingly spoke Russian, which he knew well, besides, of course, Estonian and Swedish. He was surprised to see us so late in the year and on learning my nationality, asked with the embarrassing curiosity of foreigners, to whom this bit of our mingled foreign and domestic affairs is always hard to explain 'Well, Mister and how is it with Ireland?' This was the first of several disappointments, for I had hope in voyaging among these remote islands to be quit of politics for once. But I hid my feelings and told him that the Irish were settling their affairs in the Irish way and then got him to talk of his own country.'

Extract from 'Racundra's First Cruise', written in 1922.
Ransome spent much of 1921 and 1922 in the Baltics.

sheep, 150 horses and 300 hens. For at least the previous 600 years, the population had been Swedish speaking and had fluctuated in numbers between 200 and 300. Only around 1710 did it drop to around 100 when the troops of Peter the Great brought the plague with them as they conquered all of Estonia from the Swedes. Peter did however leave the Swedish legal system intact, and the Germans nominally restored it during their three-year rule from 1941 to 1944. Although there were always Soviet military garrisons on the island, the permanent population would never even reach 100 again and it is now around 60, of whom eight serve on the village council.

The Soviets replaced the Swedish population with residents of Saaremaa who were forced to leave what would become military bases. They tried to find oil but after digging down 400m found only hot springs. They set up a collective farm for potatoes in 1949, brought in electricity in 1958 and telephones only in 1988. Yet in 1966, there were 30 motorbikes – one for every seven members of the population. Perhaps because of this quantity of traffic, the lane to the harbour was renamed 'Prospekt Gagarin' after the first man in space. The fish collective, with equal pretentiousness, was called 'Beacon of Communism'. The Soviet commander was the last Russian to leave the island, with his family, on December 23 1994, six months after Soviet troops had left the mainland.

Since the restoration of Estonian independence, logging has begun again and fishing expanded. Tourism has been generated on a small scale, with about 3,000 visitors a year coming to enjoy total peace and quiet. Half of these are Estonian, a quarter are Latvian and most of the rest are Swedes. A church service is held daily, rather than once a year at Christmas which was the Soviet practice.

Within a day tourists can visit the village museum, the two churches and the lighthouse. A minibus meets the plane and drives the couple of kilometres into the village. The museum has a comprehensive collection of artefacts for every occupation. The two churches are side by side but only the modern stone one, which dates from 1912, has services. Over-optimistically, it was built to seat 400. The wooden church, St Magdalena, dates from 1643 and is named after the first girl to be baptised there. It was renovated in 1851. The stained glass is a modern (1990) copy of what was taken to Sweden in 1944. Much of the stone for the later church came from Sweden, as did the crucifix, which was presented by the Swedish navy in 1924. The organ was likewise a gift, in 1991, but over a decade later it still awaited a regular player to make use of it. The font, however, is likely to have been cast in the 14th century so predates even the wooden church.

The lighthouse is about a kilometre's walk from the village. The impressive plaque from '*Force et Chantiers de la Méditerranée*' makes clear its French origin, shared by many Estonian lighthouses. It is 36m high and was built in 1875. It is an easy and worthwhile walk to the top, which offers a view of the whole island.

Individuals can visit Ruhnu during the summer when, at least once a week, a morning flight from Pärnu to Kuressaare on Saaremaa stops there en route, returning in the late afternoon. These flights are heavily subsidised by the Estonian government, so schedules vary year by year according to the level of their generosity and are usually only confirmed in late April. Tour operators can charter boats or planes for groups from both Pärnu and Kuressaare.

HIIUMAA

Popular with Finns, Swedes and the Estonians themselves, Hiiumaa has yet to make itself known in the English-speaking world although it should be the easiest area to visit. Every major site on the island has large, descriptive sign boards in English and the local tourist authority has produced a wide range of guidebooks and leaflets. Their logo is appropriately a lighthouse and it appears on road signs and at sites.

Hiiumaa makes minimal concessions to the early 21st century. Hotels have been modernised, the roads are kept in a reasonable state of repair, and a regular ferry service ensures close links with the mainland. Yet there are few restaurants, little evening entertainment and the former manor houses remain largely unrestored. It is an island for cyclists, birdwatchers and escapists. As on Saaremaa, it is possible to travel around the island by bus. Hiring a car, however, is certainly to be recommended and two full days would be needed to do justice to the island. Take a local guide, not so much to provide a formal background to visits, but to offer an outpouring of legends. Real life on Hiiumaa has been as tough as everywhere else in Estonia, but these stories always have happy endings, appropriate for an island of peace and nature.

One name haunts the island, that of the **Ungern-Sternberg** family who first came to Hiiumaa in the 18th century. Some members had a particularly brutal bent; Otto Reinhold Ludwig von Ungern-Sternberg set up false lighthouses to generate shipwrecks so that he could then loot their contents. Shortly after buying the manor house at Suuremõisa in 1796, he shot one of his sea captains during a meeting there and guides like to point out a stain which they claim is this captain's blood. In 1918, Major-General Baron Roman Fyodorovich von Ungern-Sternberg began a three-year struggle to forestall the establishment of communism in Mongolia. He personally bayoneted, crucified and strangled hundreds of opponents before being shot by a firing squad formed from mutineers in his own army. Not surprisingly he is known in Mongolia as the 'Mad Baron'. Other members of the family remained on Hiiumaa as relatively benevolent landowners, industrialists and shipbuilders. Most of the tourist sites on the island are linked to this family.

The Soviet occupation after World War II was far less harsh than on Saaremaa; the military left in 1961, no building of more than four storeys was allowed and the Russian-speaking population never exceeded a few hundred. The former Communist Party headquarters in Kärdla blend easily into the current surroundings and are now an adult education centre.

Getting there

Visitors will usually arrive from the mainland at the port of Heltermaa, a 90-minute ferry journey from Rohuküla on the mainland. Bus services from Tallinn and Haapsalu are linked to their schedules and they serve most villages on the island. In the summer there is also a twice-daily service from Triigi on Saaremaa to Sõru on Hiiumaa. Details of both ferry services are given on www.laevakompanii.ee. Subsidised flights operate twice a day from Tallinn to Kärdla and as they take about 30 minutes rather than the four hours needed with the bus, the cost of around £15/US$28 one way, or £25/US$45 return, is well worthwhile, at least in one direction. Should the subsidies be withdrawn, these prices will of course increase dramatically. The airport reached its heyday

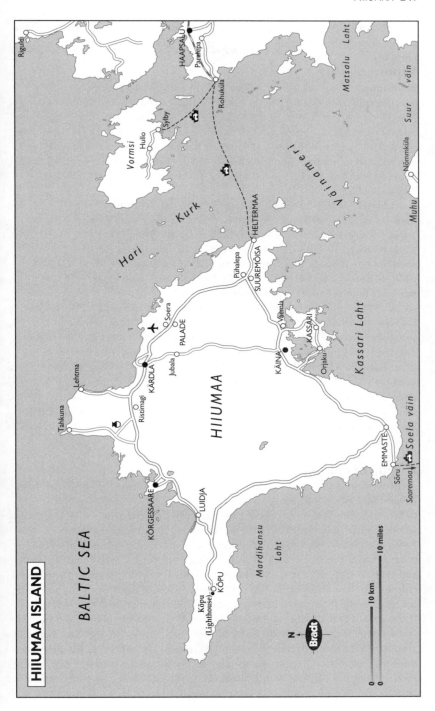

HIIUMAA ISLAND

in 1987 when 34,000 people used it. This dropped to 727 in 1995 but nine years later numbers had risen again to around 5,000.

Where to stay

Heltermaa Heltermaa Harbour; tel/fax: 46 94146; email: info@heltermaahotell.ee; www.heltermaahotell.ee. Opened in 1997, this modern 18-room hotel is part of the harbour complex and is ideal for individuals and groups planning to arrive late or leave early. A two-night stay here with a full day for sightseeing would allow for many of the sights. There are several nearby walks into the juniper forests, enhanced in spring with bluebells and in autumn with mountain ash. Public buses around the island and those to the mainland all stop here so the hotel is a good base for visitors without cars. Double 500EEK.

Katri Motel Tubala; tel/fax: 46 31610; email: katriguesthouse@hot.ee; web: www.hot.eekatriguesthouse.ee. 5km south of Kärdla on the road to Kaina, a cluster of cottages offer in total 12 rooms, all with facilities. Double 590EEK.

Liilia Kaina; tel: 46 36146; fax: 46 36546; email: liiliahotell@hot.ee; www.hot.ee/liiliahotell. This hotel has two features unique on the island, a billiard table and a room adapted for the disabled. The staff speak good English and if any hotel on Hiiumaa joins an international chain, it will be this one. It is situated in the centre of the village and has 13 rooms, each with a separate design. Double 800EEK.

Lookese Kaina; tel: 46 36107; fax: 46 36269; email: looke@hot.ee; web: www.lookese.com. Although a former collective farm on the outskirts of the village, this is in fact a very pleasant place to stay. Being set off the main road, it is quiet, has been modernised and, with 42 rooms, has become the largest hotel on the island. The hotel has a heated outdoor swimming pool. Double 700EEK.

Padu 22 Heltermaa mnt, Kärdla; tel/fax: 46 33037; email: info@paduhotell.ee; www.paduhotell.ee. Although it has only ten rooms, this is the main hotel in Kärdla. It is spacious with an elegant wooden interior. All rooms have a balcony. Guests have the use of the extensive garden. Double 500EEK.

A tour of Hiiumaa

A drive around the coast of the island, with the occasional diversion inland, covers most places of interest.

When Arthur Ransome brought the *Racundra* to Heltermaa in 1921, it could accommodate only three boats, the bedrooms at the inn had only sacks of straw and money was so rare that change was given in loaves of bread. **Heltermaa** is now a modern harbour with an indoor shopping mall, a well-furnished hotel and space for several car ferries. Six kilometres from Heltermaa is the island's oldest church at **Pühalepa**; the basic stone structure dates from the late 13th century but the interior has been frequently abandoned or deliberately damaged. It served as a granary during the Soviet period but with the help of the Finnish government was fortunately restored in 1991. Some of the late baroque sculpture from the 17th century can still be recognised and beside the altar is the tomb of Lawrence Clayton, an admiral in the Swedish navy and one of the earliest Scots to be linked with Estonia. The stairway leading up to the attic was built so that this area could be a refuge whenever the church was attacked.

Members of the Ungern-Sternberg family are buried in the churchyard, with most of the tombstones being inscribed in German. Note the many boulders in the surrounding fields. Inevitably, a legend has arisen about these to the effect that they represent the attempts of the devil to destroy religion by throwing them at the church. A more prosaic explanation is that they were left by retreating glaciers at the end of the Ice Age. The tall, neat pile of boulders about 200m from the church, called the Contract Stones, are thought to be an attempt by the Ungern-Sternberg family to provide a model of the Egyptian pyramids, which several of them had visited.

A couple of kilometres along the road towards Käina is the manor house of **Suuremõisa**. It is easy to imagine what an impressive building it must have been when first constructed in the 18th century and when bought in 1796 by the Ungern-Sternberg family. Equally grandiose was the formal garden, the terracing and the entrance gate. Indoors, only the central oak staircase remains from that time. Since 1924 the building has been used as a school although restoration work is slowly being undertaken, both indoors and outdoors.

Continuing towards Käina, a short stop can be made after 8km at the wool factory in the village of **Vaemla**. Some original 19th-century machines are still in use and the factory produces sweaters, socks and gloves. They do of course have a shop for these goods but there is no hard sell. Turning left off the road to Kärdla and Käina, head to the peninsula of **Kassari**. This is now resuming its role as the summer retreat for Estonian artists and writers. Jaan Kross, the country's best known contemporary writer, has his summer house here, as did Aino Kallas, who was equally famous in the 1930s. Locals like to recall her comment, 'God looked favourably upon me as he gave me Kassari'.

Near the village of Kassari is the Hiiumaa Museum which has an imaginatively presented collection of material covering the political and natural history of the island, both being equally violent. The damage done by storms has been as great as that resulting from warfare. Examples of the different types of wood that grow on the island are shown, as are carvings from them. The most unusual item of furniture is a double rocking-chair. The Soviet era is extensively covered, with green and red being the predominant colours in the early period, switching to blue in the 1970s. Some daring pictures from that time, such as of long queues outside shops, have been brought together here. The museum may well be the only one in Estonia that offers a play area for children.

The surrounding **Käina Bay** has been a bird sanctuary since 1962, although ironically it was before then a well-known area for hunting. Gulls and warblers are the most common species breeding here and it is also the site for many migrating water birds.

In **Käina** it is impossible to ignore the tragic side of Estonian history. The ruins of the church result from a German bombing raid in 1941; the original building had survived from the 16th century. The community centre was once the home of the local Baltic-German landlord, Alexander Hoyningen-Heune, who was the first islander to be sent to Siberia; during World War I, he was accused of spying when a German aircraft made an emergency landing on his estate. The bland exterior of the Lookese Hotel and its location outside the village show that it can only have been a collective farm during the Soviet period. Yet many small wooden houses in the village have survived all political and military turmoil and in May their gardens impress even British visitors.

About a kilometre from the village of Käina is the Rudolf Tobias Museum. The famous composer (1873–1918), shown on the 50EEK note, lived here until he was 12 years old. Later he studied in St Petersburg under Rimsky-Korsakov. The house and much of the furniture were built by his father, who was a joiner. The museum was opened in 1973, on the 100th anniversary of his birth, and since then concerts have taken place regularly. However, much of Tobias's music, including his most famous work *Jonah's Mission*, was not performed during the Soviet period because of its religious overtones. This oratorio had its first performance in Leipzig in 1909 but was 'repremiered' in Tallinn in 1989 when more liberal policies were adopted in the final years of the Soviet Union.

Leaving Käina towards the southwest, another road to Kassari is to the left after 5km passing what is now the small port of **Orjaku**. It is difficult to believe that towards the end of the Tsarist era, shortly before World War I, this was planned as one of the largest ports in Russia, maintaining a fleet of battleships. Some expansion as a yachting and fishing harbour is now envisaged. Boatbuilding was banned in the Soviet period but has recently begun again and provides employment in the villages of Emmaste and Nurste along the western coast.

The bell at **Emmaste church** has now become the most famous one in Estonia. Like all too many others, it stopped ringing in 1943 when the Germans started to seize metal from all possible sources to melt down for arms production. However, despite its weight of 200kg, six brave villagers managed to dismantle it and hide it underground without being discovered. The secret remained throughout the Soviet era and only in the early 1990s did the two survivors from the original team of six start to search for it again. They finally succeeded in December 1994, with the help of a metal detector. It rang again on Christmas Eve, from its original position in the belfry, and in his address to the nation that day, President Meri said: 'Let the restored bell of Emmaste ring out as a symbol of a country whose freedom has also been restored.'

The **Kõpu** lighthouse on the northwestern tip of Hiiumaa has been the island's most significant landmark since it was built on the orders of the Hanseatic League in 1490. Only in 1997 did it lose this role when radar from a smaller lighthouse took over from its beam of light, which could be seen over 40km away. Those fit enough to climb to the top will reach, at 100m, one of the higher spots in Estonia, with views over to Saaremaa as well as across the whole of Hiiumaa. This is best enjoyed around sunset. The interior of the lighthouse was completely renovated in 2002.

Originally, wooden fires provided the light and such enormous quantities of trees were felled to provide for this that, as a result, most of the Kõpu peninsula was deforested. A team of six was on duty every night to guard the fire but it still went out during storms. Oil was used briefly in the late 19th century; the electric light installed in 1900 was exhibited in the Paris Exhibition of that year and its use finally brought to an end both shipwrecks and piracy. Several other lighthouses on Hiiumaa are of French design. Beside the Kõpu lighthouse are the remains of a Soviet border station and a school, converted from a former Russian Orthodox church built in 1910.

The drive along the northern coast of the island from Kõpu to the capital Kärdla is about 40km. On the left-hand side of the road, 2km from Kõpu, a short stairway marks the start of the Hiiumaa **nature trail**. It is an easy walk of about 2km, clearly marked throughout, and for those unwilling to risk the climb up the lighthouse, the view from what is locally described as the 'highpoint'(all of 70m!) provides ample compensation. A varied and constantly increasing number of shrubs, flowers, mosses and trees can be seen on this short walk, and sometimes even elk or deer as well.

Before reaching the small beach resort of **Luidja**, the road becomes narrower, with only a gravel surface and several unnecessarily sharp bends. On the locally produced map, its colour ominously changes from red to white. Luckily this sector is only 5km long and can be driven in all weathers. Inevitably, on Hiiumaa, there is a whole range of stories to explain its original routing and the passion which allows its continuing state of neglect. It will clearly be a further few years before a modernist view prevails and the road is widened and straightened. Luidja is a popular camping site for Estonian families and has the best beach on the island for children.

Ten kilometres further on is the port of **Kõrgessaare** which was the most important settlement on the island in the 16th century when it was the major port for trading with Sweden. The Ungern-Sternberg family hoped to revive it, building a distillery and a fish-processing plant around 1900, but World War I dashed these plans. A local brochure touchingly writes that Kõrgessaare 'is crying out for restoration'; sadly nothing more can be said at present.

About 2km from Kõrgessaare, on the left, is **Reigi church**, isolated in the countryside but once serving a largely Swedish-speaking parish of which now only a few houses remain. This church was built around 1800 to replace an earlier wooden one and little has been altered since then. Many members of the Ungern-Sternberg family are buried in the churchyard and the family coat of arms can be seen over the entrance. To show the contrast between Hiiumaa's international links in the 19th century and its isolation during much of the 20th century, it is worth noting in the churchyard the gravestone of Heinrich Eduard who lived in Reigi but met his Italian wife in Cheltenham, England. The allegedly colourful private lives of early pastors in the village have provided material for a novel by Aino Kallas and an opera by the contemporary composer Eduard Tubin.

After 4km, turn left and continue until the road stops at the **Tahkuna Lighthouse**. Like so many others in Estonia, it is French and was assembled in France before being brought in parts here in 1875. This could be done because it is one of the earliest made of iron instead of from stone. The forest en route has many abandoned military installations from both world wars and also relics of the narrow-gauge railway that used to transport goods on the island until it was abandoned in 1955. Whatever the weather, there are dramatic views across the Baltic from the hamlet around the lighthouse. The lighthouse is also the site of a memorial – a crucifix and bell – to the children who died in the *Estonia* tragedy on September 28 1994. The spot was chosen as the nearest point on land in Estonia to the position where the boat sank. The bell rings when the intensity of the wind parallels that on the fatal night.

On the return journey take the left turning after 6km for Mihkli Farm Museum. This is more interesting than many others in Estonia since it was in use until 1987 so has a livelier feel about it. All the buildings and the tools are original and it was run on co-operative rather than collective principles.

Turn left at the junction with the main road and after 2km note the sign for **Ristimagi**, the Hill of Crosses. This site commemorates the final service held here by around 1,000 Swedes before they were deported to the Ukraine in 1781, a journey which few survived. In the Soviet era, crosses were left on this isolated site as a form of religious defiance and now wedding parties often leave flowers here. First-time visitors to the island are encouraged to make a small cross from twigs and to add it to the site.

A final 5km leads to **Kärdla**, the capital. It is advertised as 'drowning in greenery' since there is no industry, and it has several parks and woods and a population of only 4,200. Because there are no blocks of flats and most houses have a garden, it gives the impression of being bigger than it really is. The local population could afford to live like this because of the success of the factory. Many of the wooden houses dating from the 1880s could only be sold to other workers, not to outsiders. The main square used to be dominated by the textile factory founded by the Ungern-Sternberg family in 1829. By 1845, around 500 workers were employed and Kärdla cloth had become famous around the Baltic. Many of the houses built for the workers are still inhabited. The factory was destroyed by the Russians as they retreated from the Germans in 1941. Only in 2000 was reconstruction completed and the building is now the Long House (Pikk Maja) which is the history museum of the factory and also an art gallery with temporary exhibitions. Behind the gallery is the former Swedish cemetery which was not harmed by any subsequent occupiers. The Lutheran church dates from 1863. The organ, built in 1904, was one of the last in Estonia to be ordered from Germany. Kärdla sensibly makes no concessions to tourists although they double the population to around 8,000 during the summer. Relaxation is the main ingredient of a stay here so those seeking a 'lively' holiday wisely stay away.

Returning to the ferry at Heltermaa, after 7km you will come to **Soera Farm Museum**. The turbulent history of the last 150 years has fortunately passed this farm by and the buildings remain as they were in the mid 19th century. The museum was first opened in 1979 and most of the tools and furnishings are original. The loom and spinning wheel played a major role in day-to-day life, as did the sauna. The museum brews its own beer and most ingredients served at meals come from the island. A 20km drive ends the tour back at Heltermaa.

VORMSI

Whoever nominally controlled the Estonian mainland and its islands from the 12th century onwards, Vormsi would always stay Swedish. No other language was spoken there and no other culture took root. Neither the Baltic Germans, nor the Russians ever attempted to set up estates there. To some extent this explains the poverty prevailing until the 1920s. In the 19th century, four families often shared one large barn as living quarters and, being too poor to buy tools, they would peel potatoes with their hands. That was a very violent period too when most of the wood sent to the mainland was stolen. If there was no money for tools, there certainly was for drink. Thirteen bars served the population of 2,000. Into this bleak environment came in 1873 the Swedish Baptist missionary, **Lars Österblom**, who would stay for the next 15 years and almost single-handedly brought stability and hope back to Vormsi.

The 1920s brought not cars or tractors but horses. Previously the only animal transport had been bulls, but as these were killed for food during World War I, the horses replaced them. Modernisation would follow, but much more slowly than on the other islands. A journey was a memorable visit to the next village; travelling to the mainland was for many out of the question. In 1943, after 700 years, most of the community left in contempt of Nazi Germany and in fear of the Red Army. Twenty people stayed behind, of whom two were still alive in 2001, and the island was repopulated with Estonians from elsewhere. Whilst Saaremaa would have to endure a massive Soviet military presence, Vormsi, like Hiiumaa, was spared this and a collective-farm headquarters is the only architectural legacy of their 45-year occupation. Sweden has however left its place names, and its Lutheranism. Swedish financial support, both government and private, is now helping to restore the earlier links. Descendants of families who fled in 1943 are now returning and building summer houses. It is likely that their land will be returned to them, if they are willing to farm it again.

Getting there

In the summer, Vormsi is reached by a twice-daily boat from Rohuküla, the harbour near Haapsalu which also serves Hiiumaa. Buses go at least hourly from Haapsalu station to Rohuküla. The boat to Vormsi takes cars. In midwinter, several more glamorous ways of travel are available, on skis, by dog-sleigh and, once the ice is more than 30cm thick, driving by car. A local bus meets the ferry and its entire route around the island takes about an hour. The rest of the time can be spent in Hullo before walking back to the ferry or taking the bus again directly to the port.

What to see

Hullo is the main village on the island and is about 2km from the landing stage where the boats arrive. The first sight is that of the ruined **Russian Orthodox church**, nestling incongruously in an equally ruined collective farm. It was probably the most ineffective attempt of all those made around Estonia in the second half of the 19th century to woo the local community into a Russian environment. The congregation was reported in 1886 to be 162; by 1938 it had dropped to seven, with of course services having been abandoned many years previously.

On first arrival, the centre of Hullo looks as though little has changed since the 1930s. However, a big @ sign outside the post office invites customers to the internet and the primary school next door has four on-line computers as well. One of the restaurants, the **Hermann**, has a German name, but uses French wine in its sauces and happily dispenses English gin, Finnish ice-cream and Caribbean bananas. Façades stay in the early 20th century, but the 21st is alive behind them.

About a kilometre north of the village is **St Olav's Church**. A stone at the side of the west door lists the many dates when the church was rebuilt, following either specific attacks or longer-term vandalism. Records refer to an entirely wooden church in the 13th century, with stone being gradually added from the 14th century. The structure seen now dates largely from 1929, although the interior is completely modern. The pre-war pulpit was taken to Sweden where it is now exhibited in the Stockholm Culture Museum. The one now here is an exact copy, paid for like much else in the church by the Swedish-Estonian community. The church was reconsecrated on July 29 1990, St Olav's Day, in front of a congregation of 1,500 who had come especially from Sweden, bringing with them the statue now displayed inside the church. St Olav was the patron saint of craftsmen, which has not been forgotten in the woodwork now on display. Note in this context the 'hanging' boat, a model of a 19th-century sailing ship. The collection of photographs beside the organ shows the church in 1920, 1972 and 1990. The two holes in the wall behind the altar were built to enable lepers to hear the service from outside without infecting the congregation indoors.

The circular crosses in the cemetery number 343, and date from 1724 to 1923. Each one has a family emblem. The large tombstone dating from 1929 which commemorates three freedom fighters who had died in 1919 during the War of Independence is probably unique in Estonia in that it was not removed by the Soviets. The Swedish inscription 'Frihetskämparna' (freedom fighters) probably saved it, as no Russian understood what it meant. Isolated to the east of the church is the tomb of Lars Österblum who, as a Baptist, could not be buried either in the church itself or even in the main cemetery.

Roe deer

Appendix 1

LANGUAGE
Maila Saar

For general information on the Estonian language, see page 43.

Pronunciation

Words in Estonian are pronounced with the stress on the first syllable. Individual letters are pronounced as follows:

Vowels

a as the English **u** in **but**
aa is like **a** in **father**
e as in **bet**
ee as in the English **eh** or French **de**
i as in **pin**
ü as **ee** in **feel**
o as in **off**
oo as **eau** in the French **peau**
u as in **put**
uu as the **oo** in **food**
ä almost as in **cat**, but with a less open mouth
ää is the same as **ä**, but with a more open mouth
ö as **ir** in **girl**, but with rounded lips
öö as the **oeu** in the French **voeu**
õ is peculiar to Estonian and is pronounced with the lips in the position of a short **e** while the tongue is retracted
õõ is the same as **õ**, but longer
ü is produced by pronouncing **i** with a protrusion of the lips and a narrow opening of the mouth
üü is the same as **ü**, but longer and clearer

Consonants

b is voiceless, almost like the **p** in **copy**
d is voiceless as the **t** in **city**
g is voiceless as the **ck** in **ticket**
k, p and **t** are stronger and longer than the voiceless **g, b**, and **d**
h is the same as in English, but less aspirated

257

j like **y** in **you**
l as in **lily**
m is the same as in English, but shorter
n as in English
r is trilled
s is voiceless and weaker than the English s
v as in English
z as the **s** in **was**

Useful words and expressions
Greetings and basic communication

hello	*tere*
goodbye	*nagemiseni*
good morning	*tere hommikust*
good evening	*head õhtust*
goodnight	*head ööd*
yes	*jah*
no	*ei*
please	*palun*
thank you	*tänan*
less	*vähem*
a little (more)	*(natuke) rohkem*
enough	*küllalt*
now (later)	*praegu (hiljem)*
How long?	*Kui kaua?*
How much (is it)?	*Kui palju (see makseb)?*
When?	*Millal?*
Where (is)?	*Kus (on)?*
Excuse me please	*Vabandage palun*
Help me please	*Aidake, palun*
More slowly please	*Aeglasemalt, palun*
Repeat it please	*Korrake, palun*
Write it down please	*Kirjutage see Üles, palun*
I do not understand	*Ma ei saa aru*
I do not want	*Ma ei taha*
It is (too) late	*See on (liiga) hilja*
It is bad	*See on halb*
It is good	*See on hea*
Silence please	*Vaikust palun*
Wait	*Oodake*

Signs

No parking	*Parkimist ei ole*
Speed limit	*Kiiruspiirang*
Entrance	*Sissepääs*
No entry	*Mitte siseneda*

Exit	*Väljapääs*
Emergency exit	*Tagavara väljapääs*
Open	*Avatud*
Closed	*Suletud*
Toilet	*WC*

Travelling

Call a taxi please	*Kutsuge, palun, takso*
Call an ambulance	*Kutsuge kiirabi*
I have lost my way	*Olen eksinud*
My car has broken down	*Mul läks auto katki*
My luggage is missing	*Minu pagas on kadunud*
passport	*pass*
valid visa	*kehtiv viisa*
customs, customs duty	*toll, tollimaks*
baggage room	*pagasiruum*
airport	*lennujaam*
bus stop	*bussipeatus*
coach terminal	*bussijaam*
ferry port	*reisisadam*
railway station	*raudteejaam*
(city) centre	*(kesklinn) keskus*
street, square	*tänav, väljak*
traffic lights	*valgusfoor*
car repair	*autoparandus*
driver's licence	*juhiluba*
traffic accident	*liiklusõnnetus*
traffic police	*liikluspolitseinik*
back	*tagasi*
forward	*edasi*
straight ahead	*otse*
to the east	*ida suunas*
to the left	*vasakule*
to the north	*põhja suunas*
to the right	*paremale*
to the south	*lõuna suunas*
to the west	*lääne suunas*

For additional vocabulary related to bus travel, see page 64.

Money

credit card	*krediitkaart*
currency exchange	*rahavahetus*
exchange rate	*vahetuskurss*
free of charge	*tasuta*
in cash	*sularahas*

Accommodation

vacant room	*vaba tuba*
with bath (shower)	*vanniga (dushiga)*
with private toilet	*oma tualettruumiga*
at the front	*tänava poole*
at the back	*hoovi poole*
on a lower floor	*madalamal korrusel*
reduction for children	*allahindlus lastele*
an extra bed	*lisavoodi*
hot and cold water	*soe ja kulm vesi*
kitchen facilities	*köögi kasutamine*
Is there an elevator?	*Kas teil lift on?*
Please clean this	*Palun see puhastada*
Please wash this	*Palun see pesta*
The voltage is 220	*Elektripinge on 220*

Restaurants and meals

beer	*õlu*
coffee (with milk)	*kohv (piimaga)*
drinking water	*joogivesi*
juice	*mahl*
milk	*piim*
mineral water	*mineraalvesi*
wine (red, white)	*wein (pumane, valge)*
wine list	*veinikaart*
Estonian cuisine	*Eesti köök*
beefsteak	*biifsteik*
boiled/oven-baked potatoes	*keedetud/ahjus kupsetatud kartulid*
brown/white bread	*must/valge leib*
fried fish	*praetud kala*
green salad	*roheline salat*
mutton/lamb	*lambaliha/talleliha*
roast chicken	*kanapraad*
roast pork	*seapraad*
roast turkey	*kalkunipraad*
salt	*sool*
seafood	*mereannid*
sugar	*suhkur*
veal	*loomaliha*
vegetable soup	*köögiviljasupp*
vegetarian dishes	*taimetoidud*

Days

Monday	*esmaspaev*
Tuesday	*teisipaev*
Wednesday	*kolmapaev*

Thursday	*neljapaev*
Friday	*reede*
Saturday	*laupaev*
Sunday	*puhapaev*
today	*täna*
yesterday	*eile*
tomorrow	*homme*

Numbers

1	*üks*
2	*kaks*
3	*kolm*
4	*neli*
5	*viis*
6	*kuus*
7	*seitse*
8	*kaheksa*
9	*üheksa*
10	*kümme*
11	*üksteist*
12	*kaksteist*
20	*kakskummend*
100	*sada*

White stork

Appendix 2

FURTHER INFORMATION
Bookshops

There is no specialist bookseller for new books on the Baltic states in Britain or North America. Websites www.amazon.com and www.amazon.co.uk stock an enormous range and these can be reached by searching under 'Estonia' or 'Baltics'. In Britain, **Stanfords** (29 Corn Street, Bristol BS1 1HT; tel: 0117-929-9966, 12–14 Long Acre, London WC2E 9LP; tel: 020 7836 1321, 39 Spring Gardens, Manchester M2 2BG; tel: 0161 831 0250; website for all three stores www.stanfords.co.uk) stock a wide range of guidebooks, phrasebooks and maps. The leading specialists for secondhand books are:

Harfield Books 81 Replingham Rd, London SW18 5LU; tel/fax: 020 8871 0880; email: info@harfieldbooks.com; www.harfieldbooks.com
Anthony Hall 30 Staines Rd, Twickenham, Middlesex TW2 5AH; tel: 020 8898 2638; fax: 020-8893-8855; email: achallbooks@intonet.co.uk; www.hallbooks.co.uk

There are about seven specialist secondhand bookshops in Tallinn which are listed in *Tallinn in Your Pocket* and one of these, **Juhan Hammer** (Roosikrantsi 6; tel: 6442 633) has a website with the appropriate address of www.oldbooks.ee. The home page apologises for his 'pidgin Englis' but the site gives a full list of his stock and prices. A good source for books published in the late Soviet period and in the early years of independence is **Raamatukoi** (Viru 22; www.raamatukoi.ee – but the website is only in Estonian). Throughout Estonia, most bookshops have a secondhand section. Those in **Rahva Rammat** (Pärnu mnt 10 in Tallinn) and **Ulikooli Raamatupood** (The University Bookshop) (Ulikooli 11 in Tartu) are particularly extensive.

Further reading
History

Only one easily available book in English covers Estonia exclusively. Although titled *Estonia: Return to Independence*, Rein Taagepera's book in fact covers all of Estonia's recorded history. The author was eight years old when he left the country but writes with an accessible warm style unusual in the Diaspora. The first sentence of the book consists only of two dramatic words, 'Estonia exists'; whilst this is now obvious, for 50 years the chances of being able to write such a sentence were very remote. The same author, in conjunction with Romuald Misiunas, has also written *The Baltic States, Years of Dependence 1940-1990*, a more detailed study of the German and Soviet occupations.

The standard book on the pre-war Baltics is *The Baltic States – The Years of Independence* by Georg von Rauch. Covering the entire 20th century is *The Baltic Nations and Europe* by John Hiden and Patrick Salmon. The first edition in 1991 accurately predicted independence and the 1994 edition includes an update to cover it. A much more detailed book on Estonia, going back to prehistoric times, but particularly thorough on the Soviet period, is *Estonia and the Estonians* by Toivo Raun, which was published in 2001. Clare Thomson had the good fortune to travel extensively in the three Baltic states in the run-up to their independence in August 1991 and her *Singing Revolution*, published in early 1992, describes the hopes and still fears of many of the inhabitants at that time.

The standard, and very moving account of the late 1980s and early 1990s is *The Baltic Revolution* by Anatol Lieven, which has sadly not been updated since 1994 but which remains the standard book covering that era in the three Baltic states. *A History of Twentieth-Century Russia* by Robert Service details Tsarist, Soviet and Russian involvement in Estonia. A detailed analysis of the nationality and citizenship issues arising from independence is provided in *The Baltic States, the National Self-Determination of Estonia, Latvia and Lithuania* by Graham Smith. He also co-authored a more recent book on this theme, *Nation-Building in the Post-Soviet Borderlands; the Politics of National Identities*. Graham Smith's premature death in 1999 was a great blow to Baltic studies in Britain.

Baltic Approaches by Peter Unwin has vivid descriptions of contemporary town and country life in Estonia and in its neighbours, together with historical background. It is an excellent introduction for those visiting several countries around the Baltic. A similarly absorbing book is *Fifty Years of Europe: An Album* by Jan Morris which has several vignettes of Estonia and its Baltic neighbours. A fully updated edition of *Racundra's First Cruise* by Arthur Ransome, edited by Brian Hammett, was published in 2003 to coincide with the 80th anniversary of this trip. Arthur Ransome's *Racundra's First Cruise* describes the Estonian coast and islands in the early 1920s. There are detailed descriptions of the Estonian islands he visited, as well as of the mainland ports, together with contemporary photographs alongside those he took then. *War in the Woods,* written by Mart Laar in 1992, shortly before he became prime minister of Estonia, details the guerrilla struggle waged in the late 1940s against the Soviet authorities. *Sentence Siberia, a Story of Survival* by Ann Lehtmets is literally that. She describes her arrest in 1941 and her detention in Siberia until 1957 when she was allowed first to return to Estonia and then to join relatives in Australia. *An Estonian Childhood* by Tania Alexander describes growing up there during the 20 years of independence after World War I.

To readers of French can be recommended *L'Estonie* by Suzanne Champonnois, published by Karthala, which is an excellent general history of the country. In German, a shorter and more general book is *Estland* by Klemens Ludwig.

A number of secondhand books on Estonia are worth seeking out and copies of the following are not too difficult to find. Ronald Seth's *Baltic Corner, Travels in Estonia* published in 1938 describes Tallinn, Saaremaa and Narva, as well as Petseri Monastery which is now under Russian administration. *Man and Boy* by Sir Stephen Tallents covers British military involvement in the Baltics at the end of World War I and his attempts to arbitrate a fair border between Estonia and Latvia. *The New Baltic States* written by Owen Rutter in 1925 is a very detailed travelogue covering the three countries. The Estonian section concentrates on Tallinn and Tartu. *Picturesque Estonia* by Hanno Kompus published originally in 1938 but reprinted and updated in Stockholm in 1950, does not, despite its title, have very many pictures but the text is a moving introduction to Estonia as tourists found it just before World War II. *The Baltic States* published in 1938 by the Oxford University Press for the Royal Institute of International Affairs covers the political and economic development of Estonia from 1918 and includes detailed statistics. *Estonia, a Reference Book* by Villbald Raud and published in 1953 covers similar ground with additional material on the early Soviet period.

Many books published in English during the Soviet period are still sold in Estonia, some at very low prices as booksellers want to get rid of them, others at very high prices as their scarcity value becomes appreciated. Whilst the political commentaries in them will now be seen as offensive in Estonia, the confidence and sometimes arrogance of Soviet writers, even in the late 1980s, contrasts with the constant worries of Estonian ones. Brochures such as *Monuments and Decorative Sculpture of Tallinn* published in 1987 will soon be the only memory of the massive statues of Soviet heroes which used to dominate Tallinn's squares. *The Architecture of Tallinn*, published in the same year, serves as a similar record of the housing estates, sports stadia and government buildings that date from the 1960s and 1970s. Two books from the 1970s simply titled *Haapsalu* and *Viljandi* have enticing text in English from a time when there was no chance whatsoever of English-speaking visitors being allowed into either city. *The History of Tartu University 1632–1982* by Karl Siilivask has much of interest on the 19th century after the university was reopened in 1802. The *History of the Estonian SSR* by Juhan Kahk and Karl Siilivask is useful for the Soviet interpretation of Estonian history from the Middle Ages onwards. Published in 1985, it just misses the subtleties of *perestroika*, except on its final page which quotes a speech from Mikhail Gorbachev in which he looked forward to 'an invigoration of the entire system of political and social institutions'. *Soviet Estonia* by V Druzhnin in 1953 is written with a fervour that would later only be associated with North Korea. After only eight years of Soviet rule his readers are assured that Estonians 'now liberated from slavery, are working with joy and look confidently forward to the future'.

Biography

Harvill Press have published *Winter Sea,* an autobiography by Alan Ross, much of which is set in Tallinn. *Arvo Pärt* by Paul Hillier is a detailed analysis of the music of Estonia's most famous composer.

Fiction

Four books by the contemporary Estonian writer Jaan Kross have been published in English by Harvill Press. They are *The Czar's Madman*, set in the early 19th century, *Professor Martens' Departure*, set in the late 19th century and then *The Conspiracy and Other Stories* and *Treading Air*, both published since independence so able to draw on Kross's grim personal experiences.

The British novelist Denise Neuhaus has set her recent book, *The Christening*, in Estonia under the Soviet occupation. As most books on this reading list are inevitably sombre in tone, it is nice to be able to recommend a very light-hearted read, *Foreign Parts* by Sarah Grazebrook, which is based on an imaginary British theatre group travelling around Estonia.

Estonian publications

Although Estonian publishers now produce many books in English, few of these are available abroad but they can be bought without difficulty on arrival. Prices are much lower than for comparable books in western Europe. *History of Estonia* by Mati Laur and Ago Pajur is comprehensive and well-illustrated both with photographs and maps. The eight-page chronology is helpful for reference but, amazingly, the book has no index or bibliography. *Estonia Free and Independent*, a short paperback by Ignar Fjuk, is in fact a wide-ranging introduction to Estonia shortly after independence and includes unusual photographs of the countryside. Ann Tenno's *Pictures of Estonia* is without doubt the best souvenir to bring home. Many of the pictures are taken from the air and all four seasons are well represented. *Uks Päev Rakveres/One Day in Rakvere* is the result of 13 photographers all descending unannounced on this small town on July 1 1999. On the whole, they were welcomed by those who noticed them, but in some of the pictures, the occasional frown, or the lack of any expression at all, adds great authenticity to the book. Madli Puhvel's *Symbol of Dawn* is a biography of Estonia's most famous poetess, Lydia Koidula, but the book is also an introduction to both town and country life in the late 19th century. Ants Hein's *Ghost Manors of Estonia* charts the sad history of many manor houses abandoned by the Baltic Germans in the 1920s but the book is made hard to use for foreigners by the lack of an index and a map showing the location of the buildings described. In contrast, Ants Hein has also written a book on one of the best-preserved manor houses in Estonia, Palmse in Lahemaa National Park. At present this is only available in German, although it has a short summary in English. *Manor Houses of Estonia* by Ann Tenno and Juhan Maiste covers both restored and unrestored buildings. *Eesti Keskaegsed Linnused* (The Medieval Strongholds of Estonia) by Kalvi Aluve covers the castles and has a summary in English. All the captions to the photographs and plans are also translated into English. *Birds of Estonia* by E Leibak is the definitive work for ornithologists. Similarly definitive is *Lake Peipsi, Flora and Fauna* by Ervin Pihu which also covers birds, fish and reptiles. *Cross and Iron* by Eerik Kouts and Heinz Valk describes burial crosses to be seen in rural cemeteries throughout the country. *Searching for a Dignified Compromise* by Edgar Mattisen outlines the ongoing border- and recognition-disputes between Estonia and Russia. *The Guide to Tallinn 1935 and 1985* by Einar Sanden, which was published abroad, reprints a 1935 text and adds a harrowing commentary on Tallinn in 1985. Prospective tourists are given 17 embarrassing questions on the Soviet occupation with which to taunt their Intourist guides. Arnold Rüütel, elected President in 2001, has published a memoir of the 1985–91 period *Estonia: Future Returned* when he was Head of the Estonian Supreme Soviet.

The Churches on the Island of Saaremaa by Kaur Alttoa will hopefully be a model for other Estonian travel writers to follow. The text is clear, the photographs extensive and the map is up to date. There is surprisingly no serious guidebook to Tallinn but the booklet *Architectural and Art Monuments in Tallinn* by Sulev Maevali has considerable detail on all the main churches in the old town. Most titles available cover just a single building or a single theme. In this later category two recent titles stand out: *20th Century Architecture in Tallinn* by Karin Hallas and *Walking in Old Tallinn* by Tõnu Koger. *Functionalism in Estonia* by Mart Kalm covers this architectural trend of the early 20th century but the book will certainly also interest the general reader as it is well illustrated. Clear maps show the routes to buildings the casual tourist would not otherwise find. The year 2003 saw the Tallinn Tourist Board publish the first of a series for the public called *Curiosity Walks*. The booklets sold at the Adamson-Eric Museum, at Kadriorg Palace, at St Nicholas Church, at Maarjamäe Palace and at the Open Air Museum offer extensive background to their collections. Hopefully, other museums in Tallinn can soon follow suit.

Regular visitors to Estonia find two annual handbooks very helpful for their background on all aspects of business, cultural and government activity. *Life in Estonia* is published every year by Ambassador Collection, and the *International Business Handbook* by Euroinformer. Despite the title of the latter book, it in fact has a number of literary extracts translated into English and in the case of several authors, this is the only place for English readers to find their work.

German-language books

Two books on President Meri appeared before he left office in 2001. He gave a long series of autobiographical interviews to Andreas Oplatka, the Eastern European specialist of *Die Neue Zürcher Zeitung* which have appeared under the title *Lennart Meri, ein Leben für Estland*. *Botschaften und Zukunftsvisionen, Reden des estnischen Präsidenten* is a selection of his public speeches between 1989 and 1996, edited by Henno Rajandi. In 2004 his memoirs were still eagerly awaited, even in Estonian. Conspiracy theorists will enjoy *Die Estonia* by Jutta Rabe, published to coincide with the launch of the film *Baltic Storm*. Both reject the official reports into the sinking of the ship *Estonia* in September 1994, with the loss of 900 lives.

Railway enthusiasts for the area have similarly to read German, as the only, but definitive, book on this topic is *Eisenbahnen im Baltikum* by Herman Hesselink, which covers the complete history from the initial lines built in the Tsarist period to the re-establishment of the three Baltic railway authorities in 1991.

Readers of German are spoilt for choice in all other fields. The Baltic Germans wrote massive works whilst in Estonia and the next generations have continued the tradition from abroad. Since the restoration of independence many German scholars have worked in Estonia so art, architecture and natural history have been extensively covered. Regular catalogues for secondhand books and reprints are produced by Harro v Hirschheydt, Neue Wiesen 6, D 30900 Wedemark-Elze; tel: +49 5130 36758; fax: +49 5130 36799; email: hirschheydt.antiquariat-verlag@t-online.de, and for current books by Mare Balticum, Huhnsgasse 39–41, D 50676 Köln; tel/fax: +49 221 214996. The site www.amazon.de lists all current books on Estonia under 'Estland' and all instructions for ordering can be downloaded in English.

Language

The Lonely Planet phrasebooks for the Baltic languages and for Russian cover most situations the tourist might need. For the dedicated student, the Routledge *Colloquial Estonian* book and cassette course is essential. Available only in Estonia itself is the English–Estonian phrasebook by Mart Aru and Maila Saar which is useful for anyone wanting to make some effort with the Estonian language. *Tere Eestimaa* (Hello Estonia) is a good audio-visual introductory course for those of more serious intent.

Maps and atlases

At the time of writing, there are no good detailed maps of Estonia published abroad. However, Stanfords sell many of those listed below at their British shops. The *Eesti Teede Atlas* (Estonian Road Atlas) published by Regio is updated most years and is essential for tourists planning to hire a car as many smaller roads in the countryside are not signposted. The text, which includes a summary of Estonian driving regulations, is translated into English and it also has town plans. The most recent edition was published in April 2004. Regio also publish regional maps, town plans and reprints of historical town plans from the 19th century and the previous independence period. Their head office is at Riia 24, Tartu 51010; tel: 7 387300; fax: 7 387301; email: regio@regio.ee; www.regio.ee. Their Tallinn office is at Narva 13a; tel: 614 3290; fax: 614 3291; email: pood@regio.ee; www.regio.ee. They started to sell their maps abroad in 2001 or they can be ordered direct. To buy on arrival in Tallinn, the best source is Apollo (Viru 23; www.apollo.ee), which has a dedicated section for maps and guides, including a small selection of maps for Latvia and Lithuania.

The Latvian publisher Jana Seta has a smaller road atlas on Estonia and also produces the standard road atlas covering the three Baltic states. Their individual town plans are useful for visitors concentrating on one or two centres. Like Regio, their publications are frequently updated. Current catalogues are available from their Riga bookshop and orders can easily be sent abroad as they take payment by credit card. Tourists visiting Latvia before coming to Estonia might consider looking in en route for the latest publications as their shop is in central Riga at 83–85 Elizabetes iela, Riga 1050, Latvia; tel: 724 0892; fax: 782 8039; www.kartes.lv.

The *Eesti Linnuatlas* (Estonian Bird Atlas) has detailed maps and lists with a summary of birdwatching possibilities in English.

A historical map of Estonian railways is published and regularly updated by The Quail Map Company, 2 Lincoln Road, Exeter EX4 2DZ, UK; tel/fax: 01392 430277. *Eesti Raudteed (Estonian Railways) 1896–1996* by Mehis Helme, the curator of the Lavassaare Railway Museum, has a number of railway maps which are captioned in English. There is also a short summary of the book in English.

Journals

Two journals are published in English in Estonia: *Museum* and *Estonian Art*. Both review recent exhibitions and have background articles so to some extent cover the lack of publications on specific collections.

The Estonian Institute (PO Box 3469, Tallinn EE0090; tel: 372 6 314355; fax: 372 6 314356; email: einst@einst.ee) produces regular broadsheets on a wide range of topics; recent ones include *Ethnic Issues in Estonia*, *Local Government Reform* and *The Estonian Media*. Estonian embassies stock copies but they can now all be read on the institute's website: www.einst.ee.

Websites

Both the public and the private sector in Estonia have been at the forefront of using websites to provide information and to promote themselves. All the following are English-language sites and are well established. Lapses in updating are now few and far between. The most comprehensive guide to websites in and about Estonia is provided by the Estonian Cultural Centre in Adelaide on their site www.eesti.org.au. Several hundred sites are listed and it is made clear in which language they are and where they are based.

Tourist information

The **Estonian Tourist Board** is at www.visitestonia.com and their site should be the first port of call for any visitor. It has maps, practical information and leads to the websites of all their local tourist offices. Local offices can be reached directly by adding address/name of town to this site address. For instance, the Tõrva Tourist Board site address is www.visitestonia.com/torva. More general information on any particular town can be found by keying in the town name followed by the Estonian two-letter code 'ee'. Most, but not all, of these sites are in English. Therefore to reach Tartu, the address is www.tartu.ee. To cover the county of Tartu, rather than just the town, the address is www.tartumaa.ee. (The suffix 'maa' is the Estonian for 'county'.)

Eurolines **bus schedules** from Estonia to Latvia, Lithuania and Russia are on www.eurolines.ee and **flights** to and from Tallinn Airport are on www.tallinn-airport.ee. Weather reports and details of road repairs can be seen for the three Baltic states on www.balticroads.net.

Hotels

Hotels which had set up websites by the summer of 2004 have had their addresses included in the main text but others may well have followed suit by the time of publication of this guide. Local tourist boards will include them in their lists of accommodation. A local hotel guide *BTG* with site www.btg.ee is updated regularly and is useful for its maps of small towns but it only includes hotels who have paid for an entry so is in no way comprehensive. Visitors spending a long time in Estonia might consider buying *Kontakt*, an annually updated yellow pages just for tourism, which lists all hotels, restaurants, museum shops and other businesses relevant to tourism.

Culture

The most wide-ranging cultural site is that of the **Estonian Institute**, which provides all its fact sheets on www.einst.ee. This site also has the complete contents of the magazines *Estonian Art* and *ELM (Estonian Literature Magazine)*, particularly useful as so few books cover these topics and hard copies of these magazines are hard to find in Estonian shops. The Tallinn concert calendar is at www.concert.ee/eng/index.html. **Tartu University** has a general site on its history at www.ut.ee and details of recent archaeological excavations are on the site of the **Estonian Inspectorate of Antiquities**, www.muinas.ee. The **Tartu Marathon,** not in fact a running race, but a long series of skiing events that take place each February around eastern Estonia, has a site: www.server.ee/tartu marathon.

Shortly before arriving in Estonia, it is worth consulting the crucial sites of both English-language journals in Tallinn, *Tallinn In Your Pocket* at www.inyourpocket.com and the *City Paper* at www.balticsworldwide.com. They list forthcoming events and opening hours for major sites and are always up to date on hotels and restaurants. The *Baltic Times* site is www.baltictimes.com.

Red tape

The **Ministry of Foreign Affairs** is at www.vm.ee/eng and it provides guidance for a range of subsidiary sites. The site www.vm.ee/eng/consularinfo/ikvisa.html is the best source for up-to-date visa information. Addresses of Estonian embassies and consulates abroad are on www.vm.ee/eng/consularinfo/evmreps.html. Most embassies have their own sites. That for the **Washington** embassy is www.estemb.org and for the **London** embassy is www.estonia.gov.uk

Customs regulations are on www.customs.ee

Economy

Background economic information is on the following sites:

Bank of Estonia www.ee.epbe.ee
Estonian Chamber of Commerce www.koda.ee/english.html
Local Government www.munisource.org/municipalities/estonia
Ministry of Finance www.fin.ee
Statistical Office www.stat.ee
Tallinn Stock Exchange www.tse.ee

President Rüütel has his own site, www.president.ee, with a biography, texts of recent speeches and details of his recent activities. Those who prefer to be reminded of the blunter language of his predecessor, Lennart Meri, can turn to www.balticsww.com/quotes/merisms.htm.

Lynx

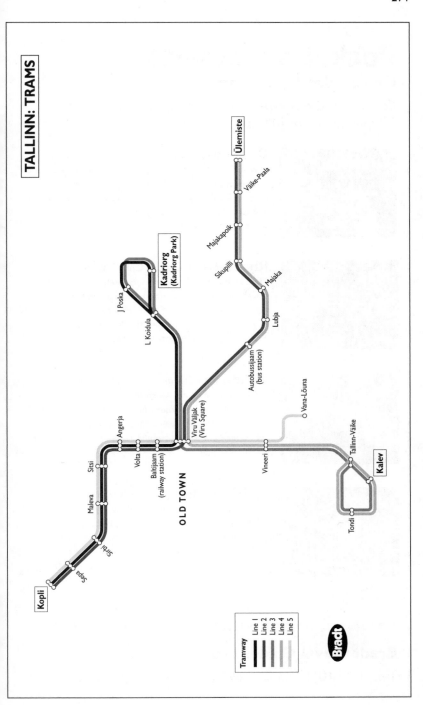

WIN £100 CASH!

READER QUESTIONNAIRE

Send in your completed questionnaire for the chance to win £100 cash in our regular draw

All respondents may order a Bradt guide at half the UK retail price – please complete the order form overleaf.

(Entries may be posted or faxed to us, or scanned and emailed.)

We are interested in getting feedback from our readers to help us plan future Bradt guides. Please complete this quick questionnaire and return it to us to enter into our draw.

Have you used any other Bradt guides? If so, which titles? . . . .
. . . .

What other publishers' travel guides do you use regularly? . . . .
. . . .

Where did you buy this guidebook? . . . .

What was the main purpose of your trip to Estonia (or for what other reason did you read our guide)? eg: holiday/business/charity etc. . . . .
. . . .

What other destinations would you like to see covered by a Bradt guide?
. . . .

Would you like to receive our catalogue/newsletters?

YES / NO (If yes, please complete details on reverse)

If yes – by post or email?. . . . .

Age (circle relevant category) 16–25   26–45   46–60   60+

Male/Female (delete as appropriate)

Home country. . . . .

Please send us any comments about our guide to Estonia or other Bradt Travel Guides. . . . .
. . . .
. . . .
. . . .

Bradt Travel Guides

19 High Street, Chalfont St Peter, Bucks SL9 9QE, UK
Telephone: +44 (0)1753 893444 Fax: +44 (0)1753 892333
Email: info@bradtguides.com
www.bradtguides.com

CLAIM YOUR HALF-PRICE BRADT GUIDE!

Order Form

To order your half-price copy of a Bradt guide, and to enter our prize draw to win £100 (see overleaf), please fill in the order form below, complete the questionnaire overleaf, and send it to Bradt Travel Guides by post, fax or email. Post and packing is free to UK addresses.

Please send me one copy of the following guide at half the UK retail price

Title		*Retail price*	*Half price*
. . .	. . . .	. . . . . .	. . . . . .

Please send the following additional guides at full UK retail price

No	*Title*		*Retail price*	*Total*
. . .	. . . .		. . . . . .	. . . . . .
. . .	. . . .		. . . . . .	. . . . . .
. . .	. . . .		. . . . . .	. . . . . .

Sub total . . . . . .
Post & packing outside UK . . . . . .
(£2 per book Europe; £3 per book rest of world)
Total . . . . . .

Name . . . .

Address . . . .

Tel. . . . . Email . . . .

☐ I enclose a cheque for £ . . . . made payable to Bradt Travel Guides Ltd

☐ I would like to pay by VISA or MasterCard

    Number . . . . Expiry date . . . .

☐ Please add my name to your catalogue mailing list.

Send your order on this form, with the completed questionnaire, to:

Bradt Travel Guides/EST
19 High Street, Chalfont St Peter, Bucks SL9 9QE
Tel: +44 (0)1753 893444 Fax: +44 (0)1753 892333
Email: info@bradtguides.com
www.bradtguides.com

Bradt Travel Guides

Africa by Road	£13.95	Kenya	£14.95
Albania	£13.95	Kiev City Guide	£7.95
Amazon	£14.95	Latvia	£12.95
Antarctica: A Guide to the Wildlife	£14.95	Lille City Guide	£5.95
The Arctic: A Guide to Coastal		Lithuania	£12.95
Wildlife	£14.95	Ljubljana City Guide	£6.95
Armenia with Nagorno Karabagh	£13.95	London: In the Footsteps of	
Azores	£12.95	the Famous	£10.95
Baghdad City Guide	£9.95	Macedonia	£13.95
Baltic Capitals: Tallinn, Riga,		Madagascar	£14.95
Vilnius, Kaliningrad	£11.95	Madagascar Wildlife	£14.95
Bosnia & Herzegovina	£13.95	Malawi	£12.95
Botswana: Okavango Delta,		Maldives	£12.95
Chobe, Northern Kalahari	£14.95	Mali	£13.95
British Isles: Wildlife of Coastal		Mauritius	£12.95
Waters	£14.95	Mongolia	£14.95
Budapest City Guide	£7.95	Montenegro	£12.95
Cambodia	£11.95	Mozambique	£12.95
Cameroon	£13.95	Namibia	£14.95
Canada: North – Yukon, Northwest		Nigeria	£14.95
Territories	£13.95	North Cyprus	£12.95
Canary Islands	£13.95	North Korea	£13.95
Cape Verde Islands	£12.95	Palestine with Jerusalem	£12.95
Cayman Islands	£12.95	Panama	£13.95
Chile	£16.95	Paris, Lille & Brussels: Eurostar Cities	£11.95
Chile & Argentina: Trekking		Peru & Bolivia: Backpacking &	
Guide	£12.95	Trekking	£12.95
China: Yunnan Province	£13.95	Riga City Guide	£6.95
Cork City Guide	£6.95	River Thames: In the	
Croatia	£12.95	Footsteps of the Famous	£10.95
Dubrovnik City Guide	£6.95	Rwanda	£13.95
East & Southern Africa:		St Helena, Ascension,	
Backpacker's Manual	£14.95	Tristan da Cunha	£14.95
Eccentric America	£13.95	Serbia	£13.95
Eccentric Britain	£11.95	Seychelles	£12.95
Eccentric Edinburgh	£5.95	Singapore	£11.95
Eccentric France	£12.95	Slovenia	£13.95
Eccentric London	£12.95	South Africa: Budget Travel Guide	£11.95
Eccentric Oxford	£5.95	Southern African Wildlife	£18.95
Ecuador, Peru & Bolivia:		Sri Lanka	£12.95
Backpacker's Manual	£13.95	Sudan	£13.95
Ecuador: Climbing & Hiking	£13.95	Svalbard	£13.95
Eritrea	£12.95	Switzerland: Rail, Road, Lake	£12.95
Estonia	£12.95	Tallinn City Guide	£6.95
Ethiopia	£13.95	Tanzania	£14.95
Falkland Islands	£13.95	Tasmania	£12.95
Faroe Islands	£13.95	Tibet	£12.95
Gabon, São Tomé & Príncipe	£13.95	Uganda	£13.95
Galápagos Wildlife	£14.95	Ukraine	£14.95
Gambia, The	£12.95	USA by Rail	£12.95
Georgia with Armenia	£13.95	Venezuela	£14.95
Ghana	£13.95	Your Child Abroad: A Travel	
Iran	£12.95	Health Guide	£9.95
Iraq	£14.95	Zambia	£15.95
Kabul Mini Guide	£9.95	Zanzibar	£12.95

Index

Page numbers in bold indicate major entries; those in italics indicate maps